Occupational Crime

Occupational Crime

Second Edition

Gary S. Green
Minot State University

Foreword by Gilbert Geis
University of California, Irvine

Nelson-Hall Publishers/Chicago

Project Editor: Libby Rubenstein
Typesetter: E. T. Lowe
Printer: Capital City Press
Cover Painting: From *Night Series* by Chris Rose

Library of Congress Cataloging-in-Publication Data

Green, Gary S.
Occupational crime / Gary S. Green. — 2nd ed.
p. cm.
Includes bibliographical references and index.
ISBN 0–8304–1421–5
1. Crime—United States. 2. White collar crimes—United States.
3. Corporations—Corrupt practices—United States. 4. Employee crimes—United States. 5. Criminal behavior—United States.
HV6791.G74 1996 96–48076
364.1'68—dc21 CIP

Manufactured in the United States of America

10 9 8 7 6 5 4 3 2 1

The paper used in this book meets the minimum requirements of American National Standard for Information Sciences—Permanence of Paper for Printed Library Materials, ANSI Z39.48-1984.

FOR MY FATHER,
with love.

Contents

7. Individual Occupational Crime 217

8. Sanctioning, Social Control, and Occupational Crime 247

Foreword

The study of occupational crime involves an understanding of a considerable number of different fields of knowledge. Law defines the nature of the kinds of behavior that can result in penalties. Legislative histories, court decisions, statutory interpretations, and the litigation of individual cases are among the range of sources of data that shed light on the occupational crime issue. The informed student of occupational crime has to comprehend such diverse sources as the Sherman Antitrust Act, the regulations of the Securities and Exchange Commission, and the vast array of consumer protection statutes. Distinctions among administrative, civil, and criminal law processes must be appreciated. Such matters as these often necessitate forays into specialized law libraries, familiarity with the way to shephardize (that is, to use special reference books to locate citations to laws and court decisions), and skill in the variety of other information-gathering techniques unique to legal research.

The legal literature includes shelves full of law reviews, with each law school issuing its own publication, usually on a bimonthly or quarterly basis. These reviews often carry material on diverse jurisprudential aspects of occupational crime. Such pieces inevitably are embedded with an armory of citations, given the notoriety of law review writers to support statements with footnotes that often occupy much more of a page than the text above. Today, the *American Criminal Law Review* devotes one entire issue each year to a review of legal developments in the field of occupational crime.

Besides law, occupational crime students have to be familiar with criminology and criminal justice, and with those social sciences that provide a good deal of the underpinning of contemporary criminology—especially sociology. Most work in occupational crime finds its roots in sociological soil; and the theoretical statements are almost exclusively the product of sociologists. Criminal justice, a new and burgeoning discipline since the 1950s, now offers special focus on the police, the court processes, and the punishment system. It also examines the system of lawmaking and law enforcing from a more multidisciplinary perspective than that found in earlier studies.

Contributions from other scholarly arenas also must be scrutinized to obtain satisfactory control over the information necessary for an adequate understanding of occupational crime. Anthropology offers cross-cultural perspectives of how different social structures define and regulate exploitative activities that we categorize as occupational crime. Political science has been especially concerned with the operation of the new regulatory agencies and with questions about the influence exerted over them by pressure groups, within both the regulated businesses and the consumer constituency. History tells us how earlier societies dealt with such phenomena, and psychology offers insights about the manner in which people introject attitudes that underlie the kinds of behaviors that become violations of statutes regulating occupational activity.

Finally, economics (and such adjacent fields as public management, accounting, and business) possesses an impressive body of knowledge that can inform our understanding of occupational crime. Surprisingly, of all the relevant disciplines, these probably have made the least direct contribution to what we know about occupational crime. Economists in particular have a tendency to write off criminal consequences of lawbreaking by businesspeople as nothing but one factor that must be taken into account in cost-benefit analyses. Virtually no article in a major economics journal in the past decade has directly addressed the subject of criminal activity by major businesses or their executives, though popular forums, such as *Fortune,* attend rather often to the subject.

Similarly, business school scholars tend to use more lulling terms, especially "ethics," to camouflage what essentially are considerations of criminal behavior. They may anguish in print over whether company ethical stands are likely to inhibit deviant behavior by employees, but they steadfastly ignore the question of whether tough law enforcement might be a good deal more inhibiting than what sometimes are little more than pious abstract dicta about how things ought to be done.

Given the vital need to encompass so disparate an array of fields of knowledge to comprehend the phenomena of occupational crime adequately, it is particularly gratifying to be able to introduce a book by a scholar who has unique academic qualifications for such a job. Gary Green did his undergraduate work in the Program in Social Ecology at the University of California, Irvine. That program had been formed only a few years before he arrived, and it brought together in an interdisciplinary setting persons with training in criminology and criminal justice, urban studies, and public health, as well as in environmental, social, clinical, and developmental psychology. Several faculty members also possessed law degrees and taught courses in criminal law and criminal procedure.

After leaving Irvine, Professor Green took his master's degree at Rutgers University in its highly regarded criminal justice program. Following this, he did his doctoral work in the prestigious criminology program at the University of Pennsylvania, a program then located in the Department of Sociology, and now established in the Wharton School of Business.

It would be difficult to find a person with educational training more suitable than Professor Green to handle the demanding interdisciplinary rigors required for an understanding of the breadth and nuances of occupational crime. This book provides the student with insights gathered from a uniquely specialized educational background.

Besides the challenge of mastery of parts of a variety of different subject areas, the study of occupational crime offers the student an opportunity to attend to matters that truly bear upon the kind of society we have produced and the kind of society we would like to see. Occupational crime is without a doubt more dangerous, both in physical and in fiscal terms, than street crime. Nuclear control failures, produced by criminal negligence, can wipe out more people in a single day than all the murderers have slain in centuries. Occupational crime can also be regarded as more abominable. It can be argued that muggers, burglars, and drug addicts typically suffer from the slings and arrows of social circumstances that allow them less than a decent share of what the society has to offer. Although being poor may be no excuse for committing a crime, the crimes of poor people should raise concerns about such ills as prejudice and the unequal distribution of wealth. To deal with the offenders and not with the social ailments that give rise to their behavior creates uneasiness in criminologists.

There is much less moral ambivalence associated with the phenomena of occupational crime. People who commit such crimes often need not do so in terms of what most of us would regard as reasonable motives. The doctor who earns $100,000 a year and steals $20,000 more by performing unnecessary surgery, or the congressman who uses his or her office to extort a bribe from a building contractor seems more deplorable to many of us than street offenders, because they have so little excuse for what they do. In this regard, the study of occupational crime highlights philosophical questions of justice, fairness, and equity.

It is only recently—most notably since the Watergate scandals and the unnerving experiences of the Vietnam War—that scholarly and public attention have fixedly focused on occupational crime, its explanation and its control. The present textbook by Professor Green offers an outstanding and interesting inventory and interpretation of these developments.

—Gilbert Geis
University of California, Irvine

Preface

This second edition of *Occupational Crime* contains important changes from the original volume. Users of the previous book will notice that, while the chapter titles have remained the same, the material in all of the chapters has been updated and expanded to a significant degree. There is much greater emphasis on federal case and statutory law, and the work of the United States Sentencing Commission has been integrated throughout. There are also new sections on organizational criminal liability, defrauding government, sexual exploitation by state officials, medical kickbacks, and financial institution fraud. More so than in the first edition, I have tried to integrate general theories of crime into discussions about offending. New pedagogical features include highlighted key terms and suggested readings for each chapter. Sidebars have been added to present additional information, particularly case studies.

Feedback from reviewers has caused me to sharpen some of my earlier criticisms and soften others. After the publication of the first edition, I was delighted to discover that I had been anticipated with respect to the concept of "occupational crime" by Gerald Robin in a journal article he wrote in *Crime and Delinquency* fifteen years earlier. This discovery, along with the adoption of the concept in several recent introductory textbooks, convinces me even more that occupational crime is the most cogent approach to this area of criminology. It is unfortunate that so much time had to elapse before we caught on to Robin's ideas.

Many of my fellow criminologists provided meaningful insights and copies of their work—Bill Laufer, Sally Simpson, Gary Rabe, Travis Hirschi, Daniel Nagin, Diane Vaughan, Richard Hollinger, Madhu Bodapati, and Michael Benson. My supervisors at Minot State University—Eric Shaar, Jim Croonquist, and Dale Elhardt—gave me release time to help complete the project. Debbie Hardin of Darton College was instrumental in obtaining about a hundred articles from interlibrary loan. My chairperson, Dean Champion, generously shared his copies of the *United States Code* and allowed me access to bibliographic tools that were instrumental in my literature searches. Several of my graduate students also brought materials to my attention that I would not otherwise have come across. I thank all of them.

I also extend my appreciation to Stephen Ferrara and Libby Rubenstein at Nelson-Hall. Richard Meade, the managing editor, has been especially patient with me. Their talents are evident in the book's overall production quality.

I have been extremely lucky to have known Gilbert Geis for the past twenty-five years. He is, without doubt, the senior scholar in the area of occupational crime. But that is unimportant to me. What is important is that he has shown me a tremendous amount of love as my mentor, colleague, and friend. And he has done this for many others. Gil pored over every word in this manuscript, and his incisive editing is obvious. For that effort, I owe him yet another debt that will never be able to be repaid.

My wife, Konnie, and my daughter, Jennia, sacrificed valuable time for and with me during the writing of this book. And to my father, to whom this book is dedicated, I say thank you for teaching me to believe in my dreams.

Gary S. Green
Minot, North Dakota

Occupational Crime

Rescue workers help victims outside the Imperial Foods Products plant after the catastrophic fire in 1991. A hydraulic line that ran the conveyor belt used in the processing of chicken parts ruptured and sprayed flammable fluid, which ignited and the subsequent fire incinerated twenty-five employees. Illegally locked doors and the absence of a sprinkler system contributed to the high death count. Imperial owner Emmett Roe, sixty-five, was sentenced to nineteen years, eleven months in jail—the stiffest sentence on record for a worker-safety criminal charge.

1 The Concept of Occupational Crime

Committing a crime by taking advantage of an occupational opportunity is hardly a new phenomenon.

More than three thousand years ago, Horemheb, a pharaoh in the fourteenth century B.C.E., passed what was probably the first law carrying a secular penalty for bribetaking by a judge. Horemheb's edict called for capital punishment for those who committed such a "crime against justice."[1] In ancient Greece, there were the Alcmaenoids, a leading family, who are reported to have contracted to build a solid marble temple, but instead used concrete, veneering it with marble.[2] In ancient Persia, bakers who short-weighted bread or adulterated it with straw were executed in their own ovens.[3] Even Aristotle, in his *Politics,* alluded to embezzlement by road commissioners and other officials.[4] Later, Henry III (1216–1272) outlawed "forestalling," the practice of buying up large amounts of foodstuffs, and thereby controlling prices.[5] In 1575, Franz Schmidt, the notorious executioner of Nuremberg, noted in his diary that a commercial defrauder was one of his victims at the gallows: Wastel Pennas, a butcher, had "sold dog's flesh as mutton."[6] By 1812, England had adopted complex legal regulations regarding labor, and in 1890, the United States Congress passed the Sherman Antitrust Act, which outlawed unfair competition resulting from practices such as price-fixing.

These are a few examples on the long historical road of crime committed in the course of an occupation. Strong indignation against occupational criminals was aroused early in this century by the sensationalized writings of the **muckrakers** (the name given by President Theodore Roosevelt in 1906 to magazine writers who exposed immorality in business and politics).[7] Ida Tarbell's work on the Standard Oil trust, Upton Sinclair's lurid depiction of unsafe practices in the meat industry, and Lincoln Steffens's uncovering of political graft led to tremendous public anger and to business and political reforms. Exploitations by big business were further spotlighted for Americans with the publication in 1934 of Matthew Josephson's history of *The Robber Barons*,[8] demonstrating the ruthlessness with which American capitalists such as Rockefeller, Morgan, Vanderbilt, and Carnegie seized economic power after the Civil War.

During the past three decades, the level of attention to and indignation toward occupational crime has increased dramatically. Since the 1960s, infamous big business and government scandals have created a "confidence gap" or a "legitimacy crisis" in Americans' allegiance and obedience to elites. Stories about political corruption (such as the abuse of power in Watergate, the bribe taking in Abscam) and the callousness of corporations (such as in the purposeful manufacture of unsafe consumer products like the Ford Motor Company's Pinto and the wanton pollution of the environment at Love Canal by Occidental Petroleum) caused a deep sense of citizen mistrust of America's political and economic power structures. These exposures of crime in high places fueled public demands for accountability.

The mass media has encouraged the move toward accountability; every day's news carries stories about occupational crime. The stories may involve consumer fraud, embezzlement, insider trading in the stock market, police corruption, or unsafe working conditions—each episode an example of occupationally related criminal behavior. Particular scandals surrounding the failed savings and loans, the beating of Rodney King by members of the Los Angeles Police Department, Leona Helmsley's and Pete Rose's tax evasion convictions, and the Alaska oil spill by the *Exxon Valdez* are among the more prominent of the recent cases of occupational crime.

The Discovery of Occupational Crime

The concept of "discovery" in science is usually associated with an individual in the "harder" physical or biological sciences who is the first to obtain knowledge of an existing phenomenon. As examples, Marie Curie is credited with the discovery of radioactivity and the geneticists James Watson and Francis Crick with the discovery of the DNA double helix, which helps form the building blocks of life. In the "softer" sciences (such as sociology, political science, and psychology), however, the term *discovery* is not as easily applied, because the phenomena under study are behavioral rather than material. Behavioral scientists actually construct or interpret the realities they observe rather than discover them.

Still, in the historical context of criminology, **Edwin Hardin Sutherland** (1883–1950) is officially credited with the discovery of occupational criminality. The term *discovery* is used here in regard to Sutherland because crime in the course of occupation, though it had been occurring for a long time, had not been systematically identified or analyzed until Sutherland. In his 1939 presidential address to the American Sociological Society (which will be discussed in the next section), Sutherland coined the term "white-collar criminal." This catchy phrase became part of our everyday vocabulary during the half-century since Sutherland's death. The most often cited of Sutherland's various (and sometimes inconsistent) definitions of **white-collar crime** conceptualizes it "approximately as a crime committed by a person of respectability and high social status in the course of his occupation."[9] In particular, Sutherland was concerned with violations of "the laws designed to regulate . . . occupational activities."[10] As we shall see later in this chapter, Sutherland's definition has caused criminologists consternation ever since he introduced white-collar crime in this way.

Although Sutherland is most directly associated with the origin of the concept of occupational crime, his ideas were anticipated by at least three other criminological scholars during the early twentieth century—Charles R. Henderson, Edward Alsworth Ross, and Albert Morris. Henderson probably had the strongest intellectual influence on Sutherland's interest in occupational crime. Using a textbook he had written, Henderson taught a correspondence course at the University of Chicago in which Sutherland was enrolled in 1905. Sutherland was teaching at Sioux Falls College at the time.[11] In that text, Henderson wrote:

> The social classes of the highest culture furnish few convicts, yet there are educated criminals. Advanced culture modifies the form of crime; tends to make it less coarse and violent, but more cunning; restricts it to quasi-legal forms. But education also opens up the way to new and colossal kinds of crime, [such] as debauching of conventions, councils, legislatures, and bribery of the press and public officials. The egoistic impulses are masked and disguised in this way, the devil wearing the livery of heavenly charity for a cloak of wrong. Many of the "Napoleons" of trade are well named, for they are cold-blooded robbers and murderers, utterly indifferent to the inevitable misery which they must know will follow their contrivances and deals. Occasionally eminent legal ability is employed to plan raids upon the

> public in ways which will evade the penalties of the criminal code, and . . . many a representative of financial power grazes the prison walls on his way to "success."[12]

In 1907, Edward A. Ross also anticipated Sutherland by writing about the "criminaloid," referring to those who prosper by engaging in criminal practices in the course of their occupation, yet who have not come under adverse public opinion. As examples of criminaloids, Ross named corporate executives, dishonest bank inspectors, food adulterators, corrupt judges, and labor leaders involved in illegal financial speculation, bribery, and kickback schemes. For Ross, the key to the criminaloid was not evil impulse, but moral insensibility. The criminaloid, Ross wrote, prefers to victimize an anonymous public, and, when accused, he or she willingly makes restitution. The criminaloid is not antisocial by nature, often holding positions of high repute in the local community. Criminaloids have a double standard of morality, demonstrating high virtues in the family and unethical practices in the commercial and civic worlds. And the criminaloid is often piously religious, practicing a "protective mimicry of the good." The criminaloid "counterfeits the good citizen"—on the one hand being patriotic and donating to worthwhile charities, while on the other hand dodging taxes and corrupting government officials. For Ross, the criminaloid would flourish until the "growth of morality overtakes the growth of opportunities to prey."[13]

Third, four years before Sutherland's address, Albert Morris's *Criminology* described "criminals of the upperworld," referring to "that numerous but never clearly identified group of criminals whose social position, intelligence, and criminal technique permit them to move among their fellow citizens virtually immune to recognition and prosecution as criminals."[14] Among the twenty-three examples of criminals of the upperworld offered by Morris were bankers, stockbrokers, manufacturers, politicians, contractors, and law enforcement officials. Morris further states:

> In many instances, the complexity and privacy of their dealings makes a fair identification of [the criminals of the upperworld] difficult. It is not always easy to evaluate their motives and methods. This is especially true if our general ethical notions are befogged or dulled by the near universality of sharp, if not illegal, business practices. Yet it needs to be emphasized that the criminals of the upperworld are genuine, not metaphorical criminals. . . . [Criminals of the upperworld] differ from their upright brethren only in being ethically less sensitive at certain points. . . . It is doubtful that they look upon themselves as criminals. . . . Failure to be caught and brought to account keeps many of them from being jolted out of their com-

> placency. Their conduct becomes apparent in its true light only when a crisis reveals the details of their methods. . . . [T]he criminals of the upperworld are real, numerous, and near at hand.1[15]

This triumvirate—Henderson, Ross, and Morris—shared a pair of common ideas, both of which formed the basis for Sutherland's conception of the problem of occupational crime: (1) the most serious type of such criminality is found among the wealthy and respectable; and (2) these offenders do not see themselves as criminals nor are they perceived to be criminals by society or by the criminal and regulatory justice systems.

Sutherland's Historic Speech

Sutherland's presidential address, "The White-Collar Criminal," was presented at the thirty-fourth annual meeting of the American Sociological Society at Philadelphia on December 27, 1939. Sutherland was fifty-six years old at the time and had been collecting information on occupational criminality since 1928. He had three main objectives in his address. First, Sutherland wanted to emphasize to the field of criminology the idea that "[w]hite-collar criminality is real criminality"[16] because it is in violation of law. The only major difference between white-collar criminality and lower-class criminality is that the former primarily involves a violation of administrative law enforced by regulatory agencies while the latter primarily involves violation of statutory law enforced by the criminal justice system.

Thus, agencies other than criminal courts should be scrutinized in order to identify criminals. Sutherland argued that many occupational offenders are found in administrative rather than criminal courts because their victims are more concerned with restitution than with punishment. In addition, their class has the power to influence the implementation and administration of the law (and criminal courts are class-biased against the poor and powerless). In short, he stated that "[t]he respects in which [white-collar and other] crimes . . . differ are the incidentals rather than the essentials of criminality."[17]

Second, Sutherland wanted to emphasize that poor people are not the only ones who commit crime. Therefore, approaches that equate poverty with crime (that is, virtually all of the theories popular at the time of the speech) are biased with respect to socioeconomic status and "do not even explain the criminality of the lower class, since the [poverty factor is] not related to a general process characteristic of all criminality."[18]

Third, Sutherland wanted to announce that his theory of "differential association," which he had first advanced a little over a decade earlier, constituted an approach that explained a general process characteristic of all criminality[19] (differential association will be discussed in chapter 3). The speech was an iconoclastic strike by Sutherland.

Gilbert Geis and Colin Goff have examined the reviews of Sutherland's historic speech.[20] The *Philadelphia Inquirer* reported that Sutherland's academic contribution was revolutionary, because it would throw "scores of sociological textbooks into a wastebasket."[21] One infers from the *New York Times*[22] coverage, on the other hand, that its reporter believed that Sutherland might be going beyond social scientific inquiry by attempting to use science as a rabble-rousing political tool in his battle against big business.[23] Sutherland rebuffed such allegations, stating that his "[conceptualization] is made for the purpose of developing the theories of criminal behavior, not for the purpose of muckraking or of reforming anything except criminology."[24] This early statement by Sutherland sought to demonstrate to his colleagues that he was following the canons of social science, which require "ethically neutral" and "value-free" social science.[25]

An academic interest and a desire for social decency, coupled with Sutherland's upbringing as the son of a Nebraska Baptist minister, lay behind his ground-breaking presidential address. The monumental importance of Sutherland's contribution to the area of occupational criminality was summed up by Professor Hermann Mannheim twenty-five years after the speech, when he wrote that Sutherland's discovery would have been given a Nobel Prize if one were awarded in the field of criminology.[26] Mannheim's hindsight is probably correct, because Sutherland's 1949 work, *White Collar Crime,*[27] was the third most often nominated book by respected criminologists as their choice of the twenty best works ever published in the field through the first part of the 1970s[28] (see box 1.1). Sutherland's 1945 article, entitled "Is 'White-Collar Crime' Crime?,"[29] tied for fifth among articles nominated.[30]

In the decade that followed Sutherland's address, however, the question of whether his concept of white-collar crime actually dealt with "real crime" would become the subject of heated intellectual debate.

Is White-Collar Crime "Crime"? The Sutherland-Tappan-Burgess Debate

Sutherland's idea of white-collar crime—crime by respected persons in the course of their occupation—was severely questioned by several of his colleagues, particularly **Paul Tappan** (1911–1964), who had earned a doctorate in both sociology and law. In a 1947 piece entitled "Who is the

BOX 1.1

What Sutherland Found

In his monograph *White Collar Crime,*[a] published in 1949 shortly before his death, Sutherland compiled the frequencies and types of certain crimes committed by seventy of the larger American corporations (and their subsidiaries) of his day. He excluded public utilities, transportation and communication companies, financial institutions, and petroleum companies. Sutherland tabulated all officially recorded violations against those organizations from their beginning through the time of his writing. Organizational ages ranged from 18 to 150 years; the average was 45 years.

Sutherland was keenly aware of the shortcomings in his method. He knew that organizations with more violations should not necessarily be viewed as more criminal. He also knew that organizations with more of a given type of violation are not necessarily more likely to commit that type of violation than another kind. At various points throughout the book, Sutherland emphasized the following problems. First, there may have been violations about which he was unaware. Second, opportunities to commit crime vary with organizational size and age. Third, single adverse decisions sometimes involved large numbers of separate violations. And fourth, the kinds of violations committed by organizations are closely related to their location in the economic system. System location affects both direct opportunity to commit crime and profit motivations to commit certain types of crime. For instance, organizations in labor-intensive industries have more opportunity to commit violations of labor laws and derive proportionately more profit from such violations than they would other offenses, and retail industries have more opportunity to violate truth-in-advertising laws and have greater potential to derive profit from that type of violation than organizations in other, nonadvertising industries.

In the original version of *White Collar Crime,* the names of the organizations were deleted, allegedly because, as Sutherland noted in the preface, "First, the identity of criminals is frequently concealed in scientific writings about living offenders. Second, . . . [a] theory of criminal behavior . . . can be better attained without directing attention in an invidious manner to the behavior of particular corporations."[b] However, Donald Cressey, a graduate student of Sutherland's who worked on the later phases of the research for *White Collar Crime,* had a very different story behind the offender anonymity. According to an interview with Cressey more than three decades after *White Collar Crime* first appeared, Sutherland and his publisher were sensitive to libel suits because "in those days, at least, people could sue you if you called them criminals and then could not prove your

(continued next page)

BOX 1.1

Continued

allegation. . . . There was no pressure from the corporations themselves [to delete names]. It was all from the publisher's lawyers."[c] The ever-zealous graduate student Cressey, who would not face liability, suggested to Sutherland that he include the corporate names and then, if Sutherland was sued and won, it would prove that the acts in question were, in fact, crimes. The risks were considerable and Sutherland would have no part of that gamble.[d]

Sutherland was probably correct when he noted that knowledge of the identities of the seventy criminal organizations was not intrinsically important. Nevertheless, thirty-four years after its original distribution, Sutherland's work reappeared in an expanded "uncut" version that finally included the identities of the seventy corporations he had studied.[e]

Fourteen firms had at least twenty violations (restraints of trade; misrepresentations in advertising; patent, trademark, and copyright infringements; unfair labor practices; illegal rebates and other types of violations). Indeed, almost all the companies reviewed were "recidivists" and many were serious repeaters—only two organizations had only one official censure found by Sutherland during their existence. The average number of violations (per firm) was fourteen.

Sutherland found 260 governmental restraint of trade violations (such as price-fixing, rebating, and discriminatory pricing) among sixty of the seventy companies, with a range from 1 to 22. The average was 5.1 per offending organization. Sutherland concluded, "Practically all large corporations engage in illegal restraint of trade, and . . . from half to three-fourths of them engage in such practices so continuously that they may properly be called 'habitual criminals.' "[f] He documented 132 infringements of patents, trademarks, and copyrights among forty-four of the seventy. Sutherland also found 149 decisions against forty-three of the seventy firms by the National Labor Relations Board for unfair labor practices, including interference, discrimination, coercion, illegal union building and union restraint.

Misrepresentations in advertising resulted in a total of eighty-five decisions against twenty-six of the seventy companies for violation of the Federal Trade Commission (FTC) Act. This translates into an organizational offender rate of 37 percent for FTC advertising violations and an average of 3.3 decisions per violator. However, if the twenty-seven "nonadvertising" organizations are excluded, the offender rate jumps to 60 percent.

As noted, inferences about organizational criminality from Sutherland's statistical analysis have limitations. Cressey pointed out that Sutherland's biggest theoretical problem was his tendency in *White Collar Crime* to anthropomorphize organizations into criminal actors rather than to treat individual employees as the criminals.[g] In other words, although Sutherland defined white-collar crime in terms of illegal actions committed by respectable persons in the course of their occupation, he actually studied the crime rates of corporations, not live persons. He frequently treated corporations as persons without specifying how those organizations could take on human qualities. Similarly, Sutherland presumed that an organization can commit crime without acting through its employees. Despite the flaws in *White Collar Crime,* however, Sutherland succeeded convincingly in his main task—to "reform the theory of criminal behavior"[h] through demonstrating that crime is abundant in the upper stratum of society.

Notes

a. Edwin H. Sutherland, *White Collar Crime* (New York: Dryden Press, 1949).

b. Ibid., p. xiii.

c. John Laub, *Criminology in the Making: An Oral History* (Boston: Northeastern University Press, 1983), pp. 137–38.

d. Ibid., p. 138.

e. Edwin H. Sutherland, *White Collar Crime: The Uncut Version* (New Haven, CT: Yale University Press, 1983).

f. Sutherland, *White Collar Crime,* p. 61.

g. Donald R. Cressey, "The Poverty of Theory in Corporate Crime Research," in Willaim Laufer and Freda Adler (eds.), *Advances in Criminological Theory,* vol. 1 (New Brunswick, NJ: Transaction, 1989).

h. Sutherland, *White Collar Crime,* p. v.

Criminal?" in the *American Sociological Review,* Tappan asserted that persons who have not been convicted of criminal charges are not criminals.[31] This completely legalistic idea of Tappan's—that conviction in a criminal court was the only acceptable criterion for criminality—was rejected by Sutherland for two reasons: (1) criminals can be found in any court that adjudicates violations of the law; and (2) persons who commit criminal acts are criminals, independent of whether they have been caught, charged, or convicted.[32]

In his first reason, Sutherland insisted that white-collar "crimes" could involve any violation of statutory or administrative law, and therefore such crimes are not necessarily adjudicated in common criminal courts. Administrative law violations most often result in court-imposed injunctions, consent decrees, desist orders, and fines. An **injunction** can be of two basic types: preventive (which stops defendants from doing particular acts in the future); and mandatory (which commands the defendant to do a positive act such as repair or compensate for previous damage or stop a wrongful act from continuing). A **consent decree** is an agreement by the defendant to stop activities that the government has declared illegal. Upon approval of the decree by the court, the government drops its action against the defendant. The consent decree is not the result of any judicial determination; rather, it is an agreement to be bound by certain stipulated facts. Defendants often agree to pay a fine as part of their consent decree. A **desist order** is a command from an administrative agency stopping a person or business from continuing a particular course of conduct and can be similar to an injunction. Hence, Sutherland argued, because these administrative orders result from violations of law and include government-imposed penalties (including fines, which are also levied against criminals), then such censured acts were equivalent to "crimes."[33]

Sutherland's second reason for disagreeing with Tappan was that offenders punished in any court (criminal or administrative) do not represent the closest possible approximation to those who have in fact violated the law, because there are countless people who commit illegal acts without being caught, charged, or convicted. Sutherland's position is consistent with Thorsten Sellin's dictum that "the value of criminal statistics as a basis for the measurement of criminality . . . decreases as the procedures take us farther away from the offense itself."[34] Thus, Sutherland believed that Tappan's criterion of legal conviction is too far removed from the offense itself because: (1) criminals may operate undetected by various law enforcement and regulatory agencies; (2) if detected, the criminal may not be prosecuted; and (3) if prosecuted, the criminal may not be convicted. These three attrition stages between the offense and conviction render Tappan's conviction criterion too incomplete for determining the number and kinds of offenders. For Sutherland, persons who commit legal violations are criminals, and this is true independent of whether they are officially detected, criminally charged, or criminally convicted for a common crime or a white-collar one.

Tappan opposed the concept of white-collar crime because it was sociological rather than legalistic. Ernest W. Burgess opposed the concept because it was legalistic rather than sociological.[35] Burgess's intellectual development derived from the early traditional sociological school of "symbolic interaction," which focused on individuals' perceptions of reality and how those perceptions become a reality. Burgess asserted that if individuals do not conceive of themselves as criminal or are not considered so by the public, then they should not be treated as such by social scientists. For Burgess, a lack of public outrage, stigma, and official punishment attached to social action indicates that such action is not a violation of society's rules, independent of whether it is legally punishable.

Burgess's conception would eliminate even more persons from the ranks of "criminals" than did Tappan's, because many occupational offenders are otherwise quite respectable and have noncriminal self-images. Unlike Sutherland, Tappan's and Burgess's conceptions of "crime" omit a vast array of behaviors that are in violation of law. However, as broad as Sutherland's conception of crime might seem, it is still limited because it includes only behavior that is illegal.

More recent scholars have gone beyond legal violation in determining a perimeter of study for the type of criminality we are talking about. Jack Douglas and John Johnson[36] conceptualized "official deviance," Richard Quinney[37] and John Clark and Richard Hollinger[38] discuss "occupational deviance," David Simon and Stan Eitzen[39] speak of "elite deviance," and David Ermann and Richard Lundman[40] discuss "corporate and governmental deviance." Others also go beyond the boundaries of the criminal law with their conceptualizations. Ray Michalowski defines "crimes of capital" as "socially injurious acts that arise from the ownership or management of capital or from occupancy of positions of trust in institutions designed to facilitate the accumulation of capital."[41] Hal Pepinsky believes that we should use "exploitation" as the defining concept in our studies.[42] Stephen Brown and Chau-Pu Chiang define "corporate crime" as including organizational acts that inflict "avoidable harm," independent of their legality.[43] These approaches have the benefit of breadth and flexibility, yet, depending upon who is defining the concepts of *harm, deviance, socially injurious,* and *exploitation,* all of these approaches could include a large array of behaviors that are not criminal and could exclude behaviors that are criminal. To give but one example, Brown and Chiang's use of "avoidable harm" as the defining characteristic of corporate crime could conceivably include legal abortions (they are harmful to the unborn) and accepted affirmative action hiring policies (they discriminate against unprotected groups). As James William Coleman notes about going beyond the limits of the criminal law:

> There are . . . a vast number of groups with their own unique norms defining what is and is not deviant. Not only are many of those definitions contradictory, but, because most groups have no direct knowledge of the . . . activities that have come to be labeled as deviant, their definitions are also subject to erratic changes in response to vicissitudes of media coverage and public mood. Because of the absence of clearly formulated public standards for . . . behavior, sociologists using the deviance approach must often rely on their own values and prejudices to define the parameters of their work. In so doing, they not only threaten the integrity of the research process but also undermine the credibility of the entire effort to bring the problem . . . into the arena of public debate.[44]

By including all and only criminal behavior, as legally defined, Sutherland's initial conception still seems to be the most useful and nonvalue-laden approach to the behaviors that constitute "crime." However, his concept of which persons are the "white-collar" ones has caused considerable difficulty for criminologists.

Problems with the Concept of White-Collar Crime

In explaining the *white-collar* portion of his term, Sutherland simply stated that he referred "principally to business managers and executives in the sense in which [the term] was used by a president of General Motors who wrote *An Autobiography of a White-Collar Worker* [sic]."[45] As noted previously, Sutherland generally defined white-collar crime as any violation of law designed to regulate occupational activities by a person of high socioeconomic status or respectability. However, Sutherland's concern with the social position of the white-collar offender went much deeper than the offender's socioeconomic status or respectability. His critical underlying idea was that white-collar crime is "organized crime."[46] He believed that white-collar criminals were formally organized not only by their collusion in their crimes, but also "for the control of legislation, selection of administrators, and restriction of appropriations for the enforcement of laws which may affect themselves."[47] In other words, white-collar criminals purposefully and in concert use their respectability, economic power, and political influences to deflect criminal definitions from their illegal behaviors. These influences that the politically powerful exert on undercutting official censure against them is a major aspect of Sutherland's conceptualization about white-collar crime; it is perhaps *the* major aspect of it. Many recent criminologists have missed this crux and have instead riveted their attention only on whether an offender is "respectable."

By concentrating chiefly upon Sutherland's reference to respectability, students of white-collar crime have undoubtedly become frustrated. On at least one occasion, Sutherland broadened his original connotation of respectability when he stated in a quite literal explanation of what he meant by "white-collar" that "[t]he term is used more generally to refer to the wage-earning class which wears good clothes at work, such as clerks in stores."[48] Hence, rather than limiting the phrase to captains of industry and others with high social status such as politicians and physicians, Sutherland at least at one point was willing to include persons of much lower public prestige such as bank tellers, clerks, and secretaries.

Criminologists have found themselves going well beyond the outer limits of what Sutherland might have entertained as "respectability" in white-collar criminals by including any legitimate occupation.[49] Any occupation that is not illegal in itself would be considered respectable. Even refuse collectors would be respectable white-collar criminals in this sense, although they do not "wear good clothes at work." The notion of respectability in white-collar crime has reached even further for some scholars, who would also include offenders who have the mere appearance of elevated or legitimate status. This connotation would capture persons who fake their position and legitimacy in order to commit their crimes, such as an insurance scam defrauder or check forger.[50] Needless to say, there is no consensus about exactly what constitutes "respectability" in the conceptualization of white-collar crime.

During the past three decades, scholars have courageously tried to improve on Sutherland's original "approximate" working definition of white-collar crime. But in most cases they appear to have created more problems than they have solved. The following are cases in point.

Herbert Edelhertz considered white-collar crime any "illegal act or series of illegal acts committed by nonphysical means and by concealment or guile, to obtain money or property, to avoid the payment or loss of money or property, or to obtain business or personal advantages."[51] Similarly, the *Dictionary of Criminal Justice Data Terminology* defines white-collar crime as "nonviolent crime for financial gain committed by means of deception by persons whose occupational status is entrepreneurial, professional or semi-professional and utilizing their special occupational skills and opportunities; also nonviolent crime for financial gain utilizing deception and committed by anyone having special technical and professional knowledge of business and government, irrespective of the person's occupation."[52] These definitions are of little value in refining Sutherland's concept because they would include a virtually unlimited number of offenses that are not occupationally related.

Other attempts at refining Sutherland's definition include that of Albert Biderman and Albert Reiss, who believe white-collar crime comprises "those violations of law to which penalties are attached and that involve the use of a violator's position of significant power, influence, or trust in the legitimate economic or political institutional order for the purpose of illegal gain, or to commit an illegal act for personal or organizational gain."[53] And James William Coleman defines white-collar crime as "a violation of the law committed by a person or group of persons in the course of their otherwise respected and legitimate occupation or financial activity."[54] The concepts of "respectable" and "significant power, influence or trust" are no less controversial in these definitions than in Sutherland's, because they are terms relative to the definer of "respectable" and "significant." Moreover, Coleman's idea of crime in the course of respected or legitimate "financial activity" could include an essentially unlimited number of offenses that are unrelated to occupation, such as filing a fraudulent insurance claim or knowingly writing a check on an account that has insufficient funds.

There is another fundamental concern with the idea of white-collar crime that goes beyond the difficulties in determining exactly what constitutes respectability, significant influence, and other vertical status concepts. These defining elements cannot be used at the same time as explanatory characteristics, since they are not allowed to vary independent of the definition.[55] In other words, status cannot be an explanatory variable in white-collar crime because, by definition, only higher status persons can commit such offenses.

To combat this problem (and the other problems that are associated with the notions of status, power, and respectability), Susan Shapiro maintains that we should "collar the crime, not the criminal" by concentrating on the way the offense is carried out.[56] Specifically, Shapiro believes that we should determine a white-collar crime by whether it involves any abuse of trust, regardless of the perpetrator's status. Indeed, Sutherland included this view in his initial statement on white-collar crimes when he said that they "consist principally of violation of delegated or implied trust."[57] While Shapiro's approach effectively negates many of the problems that have been discussed thus far in defining white-collar crime, she admits that it is rather limited because it would not include many offenses that are characteristically associated with virtually everyone's idea of white-collar crime, such as restraint of trade, labor violations, unsafe working conditions, unsafe consumer products, and environmental pollution.

Based on our discussion to this point, it is little wonder that Sutherland himself once remarked that "he was not sure" exactly to whom the term *white-collar criminal* referred.[58] It is also little wonder that the area of white-collar crime has variously been referred to by criminologists as a "definitional quagmire,"[59] an "intellectual nightmare,"[60] a "lion's den from which no tracks return,"[61] and simply a "mess."[62] Probably the major reason that scholars have tenaciously clung to the idea of "white-collar crime" is that it has such an appealing rhetorical hook. It is a common term that grabs people's attention.

Regardless of how rhetorically appealing the phrase might be, nobody can agree on what it means. There are those who argue that "white-collar crime" is simply a generic term that cannot and should not have a concrete meaning. As a result, they end up including high school cheating on examinations as an example of white-collar crime.[63] This is but one illustration of how an open definition of white-collar crime has allowed criminologists to speak about vastly different sets of behaviors than are found in Sutherland's original concept. The chaotic state of criminologists' conceptualization of white-collar crime is summed up by what Supreme Court Justice Potter Stewart said about pornography:

> I shall not today attempt further to define the kinds of material I understand to be embraced within that shorthand description; and perhaps I could never succeed in intelligibly doing so. But I know it when I see it.[64]

It must be remembered that Sutherland initially couched his conceptualization in terms of his general explanation for illegal behavior. He was merely pointing out that criminologists should not ignore what he called white-collar crime in their attempts to explain illegalities. More recently, Michael Gottfredson and Travis Hirschi have taken a similar approach, maintaining that white-collar crime should be explained as simply another form of lawbreaking.[65] All forms of lawbreaking, then, share some common characteristics. One of these common characteristics is that crime is dependent on an opportunity to commit it. It follows that persons who hold different occupational positions have different opportunities to commit various kinds of crime. This is the basis for the concept of "occupational crime" in the present book.

The Concept of "Occupational Crime"

Sutherland, and many other scholars to varying degrees, have alluded to this overall link between occupational opportunity and crime. In the late 1960s, Marshall Clinard and Richard Quinney were among the first to focus exclusively on occupational criminal opportunity when they abandoned the concept of white-collar crime and its requirement for respectability.[66] They dichotomized the idea into (1) "corporate crime" (crimes committed for the benefit of an employing organization); and (2) "occupational crime" (all other crimes in the course of occupation that directly benefit the offender).

However, reasoning that corporate crime also occurs during the course of occupation, Gerald Robin argued simply for a *conceptualization* of "occupational crime," which includes neither a specified status for the offender nor a concern about who benefits from the crime. This conceptualization is "all violations that occur during the course of occupational activity and are related to employment."[67] It is Robin's approach that will be used to define the subject of this book. To be more explicit, **occupational crime** is *any act punishable by law that is committed through opportunity created in the course of an occupation that is legal.* The concept of occupational crime seeks only to identify a general type of criminal opportunity that is distributed differently throughout society.

This definition of "occupational crime" includes two major components: (1) an act punishable by law; and (2) one that is committed through opportunity created by an occupational role that is legal. Acts punishable by law are those to which a governmental penalty is attached (e.g., fine, imprisonment, injunction, consent decree, desist order). Opportunity for crime arising in an occupation that is legal, however, is not quite as easily explained.

There have been many approaches to the idea of "occupation" over the years. Closest to the spirit in which *occupation* is used in our definition is what Robert Dubin refers to as "work": "employment, in the production of goods and services, for remuneration."[68] Occupational opportunities for crime come from any role in employment, job, or activity by which a person lawfully earns funds or has the potential to do so. Another way to look at occupational crime is as "role-specific crime."[69]

The criterion of a *legal* occupation is necessary, because without it, occupational crime could conceivably include all crimes (criminals are always "occupied" during the commission of their offenses). A legal occupation is simply one that does not, in itself, violate any laws. Thus, the term would exclude persons with occupations that are illegal to begin with, such as bank robbers, organized crime figures who make money through illegal channels, or the professional "confidence artist."

Offending unrelated to one's legal occupation, in which skills learned from a legal occupation are used, such as an automobile mechanic who "hotwires" a car on the street, should not be considered occupational crime, because opportunities to commit such offenses are not accessed directly through roles in a legal occupation. On the other hand, occupational crime need not take place during working hours or at a given place of employment. A parking lot attendant who duplicates customers' keys for later burglaries or an employee who uses legally possessed keys to burgle the workplace after working hours would not be committing crimes while on the job, but, again, it can be argued that these opportunities for burglary were created through roles in legal occupations.

A question also arises about whether occupational crime encompasses persons who seek or remain in legitimate occupational roles for the primary purpose of committing illegal acts. Examples include a child molester who gains employment at a day-care center in order to have access to children, and the person who takes a job as a bank teller in order to embezzle. In these cases, it might be argued that such offenders actually have illegal occupations, and therefore their offenses would not fall within the spirit of occupational crime. However, from a practical point of view, persons who are in legitimate occupations for purposes of illegal behavior are included within the concept occupational crime, because excluding them based on their intent to use an occupation for criminal activity would involve knowing the point at which legal employment for the purpose of employment changed to legal employment for the purpose of committing occupational crimes (assuming such a point even exists). Of course, such a determination would often be impossible.

Pinpointing exactly what constitutes occupational crime will, at times, become overly technical. Technically, retired persons who cheat on their income taxes by underdeclaring pension payments would not be occupational criminals because their income is not based on a current occupation. The requirement that an occupation must have a potential for income would also exclude other instances that probably should be included, such as the unsalaried lay minister who steals from the offering plate.

Whether certain offenses should be included under the idea of occupational crime may be a matter of opinion. Some critics will demand an exact line between occupational crimes and nonoccupational ones, and perhaps in time finer distinctions can be drawn. In any case, the idea of occupational crime is much less problematic than the idea of white-collar crime.

Critics of the concept of occupational crime undoubtedly will also raise concerns about its failure to spotlight the importance that Sutherland and others have placed on the status of white-collar criminals, particularly as that status shields white-collar criminals from scrutiny for crime and enables them to manipulate the processes of making and enforcing law. But the concept of occupational crime can be equally as useful as "white-collar" in arriving at, as Ray Michalowski states, "a broader understanding of the relationship between law and social order [and] the way[s] in which the law is selective in its criminalization of social injuries."[70]

Four Categories of Occupational Crime

There are criminal opportunities inherent in any occupation. Some offenses are possible in almost all occupations (such as employee theft or income tax evasion), while other offenses are unique to certain occupations (only physicians can perform unnecessary surgery and only politicians can accept bribes in exchange for legislative votes). Some occupational crimes benefit the offender directly (such as embezzlement), while others directly benefit entities other than the offender (such as price-fixing for one's employer). Occupational crime can victimize one person (or organization) or many. Occupational crime can affect the community at large, such as in the case of illegal pollution. Employers, employees, competitors, customers, patients, consumers, governments, political constituencies, and innocent bystanders are all subject to victimization by occupational crime. To cross-categorize all dimensions of occupational crime into an exhaustive typology, however, would be largely an exercise in patience, and not one of much utility.

In the interests of simplicity, the following four categories of occupational crime will be used in this book: (a) crimes for the benefit of an employing organization (organizational occupational crime); (b) crimes by officials through the exercise of their state-based authority (state authority occupational crime); (c) crimes by professionals in their capacity as professionals (professional occupational crime); and (d) crimes by individuals as individuals (individual occupational crime).

Before offering a more detailed discussion of these four types, one point deserves special mention. Crime typologies have a tendency to promote different explanations for each type of crime that is included in the typology. This happens because criminologists generally try to add something "new" to the field. There is no such intention here. These four types of occupational crime are offered only to differentiate individuals' occupational circumstances and to demonstrate how they may lead to different opportunities for criminal behavior.

The first category, **organizational occupational crime,** includes crimes for the benefit of an employing organization in which employers, rather than the offenders themselves, benefit directly. Offenders may benefit indirectly from these crimes through employer organizational systems that allocate rewards (e.g., promotions, bonuses, salary raises), but the major beneficiaries are the owners of the organization for which one works. Price fixing by managers, falsification of product tests by technicians, theft of others' trade secrets by employees, and fraud by salesmen not working on commission are examples. The idea of organizational occupational crime has been used by many scholars, usually under the term *corporate crime*.[71]

The next two categories are occupationally specific. That is, only persons in particular kinds of occupations have the opportunity to commit crimes in these categories. Occupational crimes through the exercise of state-based authority (**state authority occupational crime**), the second category, requires offenders to be legally vested with sovereign governmental powers to make or enforce laws or to command others. This category would exclude criminal acts in the course of a state official's occupation that are unrelated to the exercise of these legal powers (e.g., employee theft, false expense reports, income tax evasion). Police who steal controlled substances confiscated as evidence or who illegally assault a suspect would be embraced under this second type, because opportunities for these activities are accessed through a police officer's legally vested powers. A legislator who takes bribes in exchange for political influence would also be committing crime in his or her capacity to exercise state power. Military personnel who commit crime through their power to command others are also state authority occupational criminals. One may additionally want to include under this category notary publics who falsify documents and jurors who take bribes, for they would accomplish these offenses because of the official power vested in them.

Third, occupational crime by professionals in their professional capacity (**professional occupational crime**) are also occupationally specific, because they arise out of opportunities from legal and professional trusts given only to an elite group of occupations—physicians, lawyers, psychologists, veterinarians, and accountants. Certain professional oaths and trusts call for an ethical commitment to do what is in the best interest of the client or patient. And the legal system trusts professionals to be honest (such as in the signing of death certificates by physicians, auditing by accountants, and guardianships by lawyers). Examples of professional occupational crime include unnecessary treatments and surgeries by physicians and veterinarians, and the use of confidential information for personal gain by lawyers. Professional occupational crime would exclude offenses committed by professionals in the course of their occupation that are unrelated to the trusts given them as professionals (such as income tax evasion and restraint of trade).

Fourth, **individual occupational crime** encompasses all remaining offenses—those in which occupational opportunities are not based on any governmental authority or the profession of the offender, and in which offenders themselves benefit directly. This is simply a miscellaneous category for all occupational crimes that do not fit into any of the other three classes. Just a few of the possible examples of occupational crimes by individuals as individuals are personal income tax evasion, employee theft of goods (cash, office supplies, scrap material, merchandise) and services (personal long distance telephone calls or photocopying), sexual molestation of children by nonprofessionals at day-care centers, fraud by salespeople working on commission, and filing a false expense claim to an employer.

If the owners of an organization (the majority stockholder in a corporation, partners in a medium-sized firm, or the owner of a small mom-and-pop business) were to commit offenses for the benefit of that organization, then they too would be committing crime as individuals (rather than organizational occupational crime), because the potential gains from the offense would accrue directly to them. The same is true for persons who use a nonownership role in an employing organization for personal gain, as did many of the defrauding loan officers in the savings and loan scandals of the late 1980s. As a miscellaneous category, individual occupational crime is virtually limitless.

Just as there will undoubtedly be some disagreement about which offenses belong under the general category of occupational crime, there will be some disagreement about which offenses constitute which of the four types of occupational crime. Are occupational crimes by salaried professionals, such as a physician working for a hospital or a lawyer who is not a law firm partner, committed by professionals or by individuals for the benefit of their employing organization? Are pharmacists "professionals," or are they merely the same as other persons given control over items regulated by the government (such as firearms, liquor, tobacco)? Some occupations, such as the clergy, may encompass all four types of occupational crime, depending on the role and circumstances under which the offense is committed. Ministers can be considered officials (during official acts such as marriage ceremonies), professionals (because of the confidential trusts they are given), individuals working for an employer (because they are supported by a denominational affiliation), or simply individuals. Are employees who own stock in their employer's firm committing crime for the benefit of their employer or for their own benefit? How much stock must be owned before one is considered an "owner" of a firm? Are soldiers who commit war crimes doing so in an official capacity, an individual capacity, or for the benefit of their employer? As with any typology, problems will be encountered when trying to pigeonhole certain peripheral or overlapping cases.

The four categories are not meant to be exclusive; they have been constructed only to help organize the vast array of occupational offenses into manageable topics. In the cases of the first three designations, the categories allow us to examine specific occupational opportunities for crime that do not exist elsewhere.

Public Views about Occupational Crime

Edward A. Ross pointed out more than eighty years ago that a major reason why many forms of harmful occupational behavior were not against the law (or laws against them were not enforced) was a lack of public sentiment directed against such behavior. Many occupational criminals "prosper by flagitious practices which have not yet come under the effective ban of public opinion," Ross wrote.[72] Public sentiment was not sufficiently strong to enact criminal laws prohibiting socially irresponsible business behavior. Nor was it sufficiently strong to lead to enforcement of existing codes, for as Ross also noted: "The law-makers may make their misdeeds crimes, but so long as morality stands stock-still in the old tracks, [occupational criminals] escape both punishment and ignominy."[73] Sutherland too, in his historic 1939 speech, asserted that white-collar occupational criminals are seldom censured because "the community is not organized solidly against the behavior."[74] More recently, a federal commission on crime noted that "the public tends to be indifferent to business crime or even to sympathize with the offenders who have been caught."[75]

According to Francis Cullen and his colleagues, however, "many of the attempts to blame tolerant public attitudes for the [occupational] crime problem have been based on impressionistic rather than on [hard] evidence."[76] They cite several surveys of public attitudes to support this claim. Donald Newman found that 78 percent of his sample believed businessmen violating pure food laws should be given harsher punishments than those usually accorded.[77] Don Gibbons's research showed that 88 percent of the public recommended prison terms for embezzlers, 70 percent for antitrust violators, and 43 percent for false advertisers.[78] A Louis Harris poll showed that the public judged a manufacturer of unsafe automobiles worse than a mugger (68 percent to 22 percent) and a price-fixer worse than a burglar (54 percent to 28 percent).[79] After reviewing several public surveys, John Braithwaite found that "contrary to a widespread misconception, there is considerable evidence to support the view that ordinary people subjectively perceive many types of [occupational] crime as more serious than most traditional crime."[80] Similarly, John Conklin concluded that there is a "greater degree of public condemnation of business violations than is thought to exist by those who claim that the public is apathetic or tolerant of business crime."[81] Studies of public attitudes about occupational crime, then, generally demonstrate that it is sometimes perceived to involve very serious and costly kinds of behavior, and that the apathetic public attitude toward business crime portrayed by Ross, Sutherland, and the federal commission no longer exists, if it ever did.

Perhaps the best way to assess people's perceptions of occupational crime is in relation to their perceptions about other kinds of crime. It is important to note that the "seriousness" of a behavior is a relative phenomenon because no behaviors are inherently harmful. As Donald Black notes:

> What is a "crime" to one person may not be to another, and for a given person, whether an incident is a "crime" may depend upon the conditions under which it occurs. This is because, in commonsense, what is a "crime" is not merely a matter of fact; it is also an evaluation.[82]

How a person perceives the acceptability of an imaginary other's social action varies according to characteristics of the perceiver, such as socioeconomic status, criminal victimization, age, race, education, and geographical region.[83] Each individual invokes his or her own normative standard of seriousness in attaching the label of "bad" to a particular act. For instance, pro-choice advocates consider nonspontaneous abortion a matter of "reproductive autonomy," whereas others view it as murder.

The most extensive effort to survey public opinions about the seriousness of illegal acts was ***The National Survey of Crime Severity*** *(NSCS)*.[84] The *NSCS* was conducted during the last half of 1977 and includes interviews with approximately 60,000 persons eighteen years of age or older. Because each respondent's ratings in the survey were weighted according to his or her representation in the population, the findings of the *NSCS* are expected to be reflective of the entire American adult population. A total of 204 offenses was included in the survey, but each respondent was asked to rate only twenty-five criminal behaviors. Respondents were asked to rate their crimes "compared to a bicycle theft scored as 10," and they could choose any rating between zero and infinity. Box 1.2 presents selected *NSCS* ratings of occupational and nonoccupational criminal behavior. The nonoccupational offenses have been selected here because they are close in magnitude to the occupational crimes.

Some interesting comparisons can be drawn from box 1.2. Fraud by the grocer and a $10 embezzlement are viewed as seriously as an obscene phone call (1.9). A civil rights violation by the realtor is viewed as seriously as a strongarm robbery (5.4). Cheating the government of $10,000 through income tax fraud is seen to be as serious as running a prostitution racket (6.1). Assaulting a person with polluted water is considered to be as serious as assaulting a person with one's fists (6.9). A bribe acceptance by a city politician is perceived to be as serious as a $1,000 armed robbery (9.0). Intentionally causing a person's death through poisoning the public water supply (19.9) is approximately as serious as forcible rape with injury (20.1). And pollution of a water supply from which twenty people become slightly ill (19.7) is perceived to be about as serious as a vehicular homicide (19.5). Both occupational and "common crime" are viewed as serious behaviors. That some crimes are occupationally related does not seem to affect the public's perception of their seriousness.

"Common" street crimes are regarded as the most serious by the national sample, however. Causing the death of a person through knowingly selling tainted cooking oil (17.8) or through knowingly adding poisonous material to the water supply (19.9) was regarded as about half as serious as causing the death of an individual through public bombing (39.1) or by spousal stabbing (39.2). Similarly, causing the death of twenty persons through intentionally poisoning the public water supply received only slightly more than half the seriousness rating (39.1) as causing the same

BOX 1.2

*The National Survey of Crime Severity**

Ratings	*Offense Stimuli*
1.9	**An employee embezzles $10 from his employer.**
1.9	**A store owner knowingly puts "large" eggs into containers marked "extra large."**
1.9	A person makes an obscene phone call.
3.1	A person breaks into a home and steals $100.
3.2	**An employer illegally threatens to fire employees if they join a labor union.**
3.6	A person knowingly passes a bad check.
3.7	**A labor union official illegally threatens to organize a strike if an employer hires nonunion workers.**
5.4	**A real estate agent refuses to sell a house to a person because of that person's race.**
5.4	A person threatens to harm a victim unless the victim gives him money. The victim gives him $10 and is not harmed.
5.7	**A theater owner knowingly shows pornographic movies to a minor.**
6.1	**A person cheats on his Federal income tax return and avoids paying $10,000.**
6.1	A person runs a prostitution racket.
6.2	A person beats a victim with his fists. The victim requires treatment by a doctor but not hospitalization.
6.2	**An employee embezzles $1,000 from his employer.**
6.4	**An employer refuses to hire a qualified person because of that person's race.**
6.5	A person uses heroin.
6.9	**A factory knowingly gets rid of its waste in a way that pollutes the water supply of a city. As a result, one person becomes ill but does not require medical treatment.**
6.9	A person beats a victim with his fists. The victim requires hospitalization.
8.0	A person steals an unlocked car and sells it.
8.2	**Knowing that a shipment of cooking oil is bad, a store owner decides to sell it anyway. Only one bottle is sold and the purchaser is treated by a doctor but not hospitalized.**
8.6	A person performs an illegal abortion.

(continued next page)

BOX 1.2

Continued

Ratings	*Offense Stimuli*
9.0	**A city official takes a bribe from a company for his help in getting a city building contract for the company.**
9.0	A person, armed with a lead pipe, robs a victim of $1,000.
9.2	**Several large companies illegally fix the retail prices of their products.**
9.4	A person robs a victim of $10 at gunpoint. No physical harm occurs.
9.4	**A public official takes $1,000 of public money for his own use.**
9.6	**A police officer knowingly makes a false arrest.**
9.6	A person breaks into a home and steals $1,000.
10.0	**A government official intentionally hinders the investigation of a criminal offense.**
10.9	A person steals property worth $10,000 from outside a building.
11.2	**A company pays a bribe to a legislator to vote for a law favoring the company.**
11.8	A man beats a stranger with his fists. He requires hospitalization.
12.0	**A police officer takes a bribe not to interfere with an illegal gambling operation.**
12.0	A person gives the floor plans of a bank to a bank robber.
13.3	A person, armed with a lead pipe, robs a victim of $10. The victim is injured and requires hospitalization.
13.5	**A doctor cheats on claims he makes to a Federal health insurance plan for patient services. He gains $10,000.**
13.9	**A legislator takes a bribe from a company to vote for a law favoring the company.**
14.6	A person, using force, robs a victim of $10. The victim is hurt and requires hospitalization.
15.5	A person breaks into a bank at night and steals $100,000.
15.7	**A county judge takes a bribe to give a light sentence in a criminal case.**
16.6	A person, using force, robs a victim of $1,000. The victim is hurt and requires treatment by a doctor but not hospitalization.
17.8	**Knowing that a shipment of cooking oil is bad, a store owner decides to sell it anyway. Only one bottle is sold and the purchaser dies.**
19.5	A person kills a victim by recklessly driving an automobile.

Ratings	*Offense Stimuli*
19.7	**A factory knowingly gets rid of its waste in a way that pollutes the water supply of a city. As a result, 20 people become ill but none require medical treatment.**
19.9	**A factory knowingly gets rid of its waste in a way that pollutes the water supply of a city. As a result, one person dies.**
20.1	A man forcibly rapes a woman. Her physical injuries require treatment by a doctor but not hospitalization.
33.8	A person runs a narcotics ring.
39.1	**A factory knowingly gets rid of its waste in a way that pollutes the water supply of a city. As a result, 20 people die.**
39.2	A man stabs his wife. As a result, she dies.
43.9	A person plants a bomb in a public building. The bomb explodes and one person is killed.
72.1	A person plants a bomb in a public building. The bomb explodes and 20 people are killed.

*Occupational crimes are in boldface.

Source: Marvin Wolfgang, Robert Figlio, Paul Tracy, and Simon Singer, *The National Survey of Crime Severity* (Washington, DC: U.S. Government Printing Office, 1985), pp. vi–x.

number of deaths by intentionally detonating a bomb in a public building (72.1). Although the causes of the deaths clearly are attributable to the perpetrators, there nevertheless seems to be a public belief that intentional occupationally related behavior that causes injury or death is sometimes less serious than intentional injury or death inflicted nonoccupationally.

There is no doubt from all of these surveys, however, that the public has little tolerance for occupational crime. Earlier in this chapter we discussed how, over the past three decades, there has been a decline in public perceptions about the trustworthiness of major social institutions such as government and corporations. It is this lack of trust that has spawned the negative public feelings tapped by the *NSCS* and other surveys.

Preview of the Book

Determining the incidence of crime and the distribution of criminals is exceedingly difficult. Establishing this information for occupationally related offenses is especially complicated. Chapter 2 addresses this issue and applies general methods for obtaining information on crimes and criminals to the area of occupational crime. Chapter 3 explores general criminological theories as they relate to occupational crime, including explanations of the creation and application of occupational criminal law, and explanations of the individual behavior of occupational criminals.

The next four chapters detail instances of occupational crime. Chapter 4 will address organizational occupational crime, followed by discussions of state authority crime (chapter 5), professional occupational crime (chapter 6), and individual occupational crime unrelated to official authority or professional status (chapter 7). Additionally, the approaches to counting set out in chapter 2 and the theoretical approaches set out in chapter 3 are applied selectively to the case material in these four chapters. Last, chapter 8 looks at occupational offenses from a criminal justice system perspective, and considers various strategies to reduce occupational crime.

Key Terms

muckraker
Edwin H. Sutherland
white-collar crime
Paul Tappan
injunction
consent decree
desist order
occupational crime
organizational occupational crime
state authority occupational crime
professional occupational crime
individual occupational crime
The National Survey of Crime Severity

Questions for Discussion

1. Identify ten stories about occupational crime found in your local newspaper over the next several weeks. Place each story into one or more of the four categories of occupational crime. Be prepared to explain why each example qualifies as an occupational crime and why you have relegated it to one or more particular categories.
2. It was noted that several scholars "anticipated" Sutherland's seminal work in white-collar crime by writing about the same kinds of offenders that Sutherland did. This is one example of how advances in science are sometimes dependent on previous work in the field (rather than arising independently). What are some other examples from the physical, biological, and social sciences where famous theories were anticipated by earlier thinkers?
3. Sutherland saw his theory of differential association as superior because he believed that it could explain crime in the upper classes as well as in the lower classes, whereas other theories of his day could

not. Should criminologists strive for a single theory to explain different kinds of criminality? Why or why not?

4. According to Paul Tappan, persons cannot be considered criminals unless they have been so defined by a conviction or its equivalent. For Tappan, then, a shoplifter who steals without being caught would not be a criminal. Do you agree? Why or why not?
5. List eight examples from each of the four categories of occupational crime without referring to the examples in this book.
6. Discuss Sutherland's findings in *White Collar Crime* found in box 1.1, and some of the problems associated with his method of counting occupational crimes.
7. Why do people tend to rate occupational crimes with similar harms as less serious than street crimes with the same devastation?

General Readings on Occupational Crime

James William Coleman, *The Criminal Elite* (3d ed.) (New York: St. Martin's Press, 1994).

John E. Conklin, *Illegal but Not Criminal: Business Crime in America* (Englewood Cliffs, NJ: Prentice-Hall, 1977).

M. David Ermann and Richard Lundman (eds.), *Corporate and Governmental Deviance* (4th ed.) (New York: Oxford University Press, 1992).

David O. Friedrichs, *Trusted Criminals* (Belmont, CA: Wadsworth, 1996).

Gilbert Geis and Paul Jesilow (eds.), "White-Collar Crime," *Annals of the American Academy of Political and Social Science* (Volume 525, January 1993).

Gilbert Geis, Robert Meier, and Lawrence Salinger (eds.), *White-Collar Crime: Classic and Contemporary Views* (3d ed.) (New York: Free Press, 1995). This volume contains a comprehensive reference bibliography about occupational crime.

David R. Simon and D. Stanley Eitzen, *Elite Deviance* (Boston: Allyn and Bacon, 1982).

Edwin H. Sutherland, *White Collar Crime: The Uncut Version* (New Haven, CT: Yale University Press, 1983).

David Weisburd, Stanton Wheeler, Elin Waring, and Nancy Bode, *Crimes of the Middle Classes* (New Haven, CT: Yale University Press, 1991).

Marilyn Harrell testifies before a House Subcommittee on Employment and Housing in 1989. Appealing to higher loyalties, the Maryland HUD agent admitted to diverting $5.5 million from funds of the Department of Housing and Urban Development to charitable projects to provide housing for the poor.

2 Counting and Recording Occupational Crimes and Criminals

A necessary first step in the study of occupational crime is to examine the ways in which we determine how much occupational crime exists and the kinds of people who are involved in it. After doing so, we can better understand the level of accuracy of the information we possess about the phenomenon and we can better interpret available data.

Recall Thorsten Sellin's statement, which was quoted in the previous chapter: "[T]he value of criminal statistics as a basis for the measurement of criminality . . . decreases as the procedures take us farther away from the offense itself."[1] In other words, sources should be used that are most adjacent to the crime to obtain the most reliable material on the numbers of crimes and criminals, because such records minimize the disappearance of information. Nonetheless, information gathered from sources close to the crime (that is, from criminals or victims) can be highly inaccurate because of a reluctance or an inability to provide satisfactory data. As we move further away from the crime, we find that data from police, court, and prison records will likely reflect accurately the occupational criminality with which the agencies come into contact. But those sources cannot include information of which they are unaware, which may be a very large proportion of the lawbreaking.

The Importance of the "Criminality Recording Rate"

The two major recorders of crimes and criminals are government agencies and criminology researchers, and these two groups often collaborate to determine how the statistics should be gathered and tabulated. The difference between the actual number of crimes committed (**universe of offenses**) and the number of crimes documented by recorders is known as the **dark figure of crime.** Similarly, the difference between the actual number of criminals (**universe of offenders**) and the number of persons (or organizations) recorded as criminal is known as the **dark figure of criminals.** The universes of crimes and criminals are not necessarily equal for a given offense type since one person can commit several crimes and several persons can commit a single crime. Because these dark figures are not known, there is no way to ascertain the number of crimes and criminals that are not discovered by recorders, though they can attempt to estimate dark figures.

Four general methods are employed to determine the numbers of crimes and criminals, each with its own strengths and weaknesses. All are applicable to the area of occupational crime: (1) agency based records, such as criminal complaints, arrest records, and agency-written violations; (2) victim based records, such as those compiled by asking representative samples of persons whether they have been victimized and requesting details about those victimizations; (3) criminal based records, put together by asking representative samples of persons whether they have committed any crimes and asking for any details about those crimes; and (4) counts of crimes and criminals based on direct observation.

Occasionally, crimes and criminals are counted for a single time period, such as a year. However, such counts are invariably inaccurate indicators of the actual number of crimes or criminals because some amount will not be discovered (that is, there will be a "dark figure"). Therefore, one must always be critical of the accuracy of single time period counts because, except for rare instances, they underrepresent true numbers.

Recorders are most often interested in the study of trends over several time periods because trend analysis will reveal changes in criminality figures. The critical assumption for any crime or criminal recording method used in trend analysis is that the ratio between recorded entities and the universe of entities (the **recording rate**) remains the same over time within the crime category being studied. This allows meaningful comparisons about whether crime is increasing or decreasing and whether proportionate involvement in crime (say, by gender or age) changes. If the ratios between recorded offenses or offenders and their universes do not remain the same over time in a given crime category (that is, if there is a variation in the proportion of the total counted from one time period to the next), then the information is suspect. The degree of variation in recording rates for a given category is the extent to which conclusions are inaccurate; this is true no matter which method is used. Box 2.1 illustrates the importance of constancy in recording rates for both single and multiple time periods.

BOX 2.1

The Importance of Recording Rates in the Counting of Crimes and Criminals

For Single Time Periods

Offenses

Suppose there was a universe of one thousand sexual molestations by physicians in a given year and they were recorded at a rate of 70 percent (seven hundred would be recorded). Suppose also that there was a universe of one thousand criminal unnecessary surgeries by physicians in that same year and they were recorded at a rate of 35 percent (three hundred fifty would be recorded). This would indicate that sexual molestations occur twice as frequently as unnecessary surgeries, which, of course, is an incorrect inference; in fact, both doctor crimes occurred with the same frequency, and the mistake is due entirely to a difference in these offenses' recording rates.

Offenders

The same numbers can be applied to proportionate involvement by criminals in a single time period. Suppose there were one thousand male lawyers and one thousand female lawyers who overbilled clients in a given year. The male offenders were recorded at a rate of .70 and females at .35. The recorded counts would indicate seven hundred male and three hundred fifty female lawyers who defraud, or a 2:1 ratio; in fact, the ratio is 1:1. Again, the discrepancy is due to differences in recording rates.

(continued next page)

BOX 2.1

Continued

For Multiple Time Periods (Trends)

Offenses

Suppose there was a universe of one thousand violations of safe working condition laws in 1996 and the recording rate was .60; the total recorded offenses would be 600. If the universe of offenses was again one thousand in 1997 and the recording rate dropped to .50, then five hundred offenses would have been recorded in the later year, indicating a ten percentage point drop in offenses when in fact the actual number was unchanged.

Suppose there was a universe of fifteen hundred price fixes in 1996, recorded at .50 (750 offenses recorded). In 1997 there was a universe of one thousand offenses, also recorded at .50 (500 offenses recorded). The change in the number of recorded crimes (750:500) proportionately equalled the change in the universe of crimes (1500:1000) because the the recording rate remained constant.

Offenders

Suppose that 40 percent of one thousand male embezzlers and 40 percent of five hundred female embezzlers were recorded in 1996, indicating a true ratio of 2:1 (400:200 recorded; 1,000:500 in the universe). However, in 1997, the rate of recording females increased to 60 percent but the male recording rate remained at 40 percent. Assuming the same universe of offenders as the previous year (one thousand males and five hundred females), recorded male-to-female involvement changes to 400:300 (or, 4:3), when in fact the involvement is the same as the previous year (8:4 or 2:1). If the recording rate is not equal across offender categories over time, then incorrect inferences about relative criminal involvement will be present.

For the four counting methods, there are diverse factors that cause deviations in recording rates over time.

Agency Recordings

Agency records offer information about the numbers of crimes and criminals that are recorded by criminal justice authorities. The best agency crime and criminal data would come from enforcement agencies (police and regulatory agencies), since enforcement agency information is closer to the offense than adjudication (court) agency criminality data. And records from adjudication agencies are closer to the offense than those from penal agencies. However, even if we use enforcement information, which is the optimal agency source because it is closest to the offense, the loss of information can be quite high during the stage between the commission of offenses and the recording of offenses and offenders by the enforcement authorities. Of course, any variation over time in the amount of this loss will cause a variation in the recording rate.

Effects of Disparate Discovery and Recording Practices on Agency Recording Rates

An enforcement agency must first become aware of a crime before a record can be made of it. When an enforcement agency discovers a crime through its own efforts, this is known as **proactive discovery.** Occupational crime enforcement authorities (police and regulatory agencies) do not usually conduct audits of financial records, inspections of products and premises, "stings," or other proactive operations against occupational criminals. Therefore, the proportions of offenses and offenders recorded through proactive discovery will very likely vary over time.

When a crime is brought to the attention of an enforcement authority by an outsider (such as a victim or a bystander), it is known as **reactive discovery.** In many cases of occupational crime, however, people remain unaware that an occupational crime has been perpetrated, unlike street crime in which victims are acutely aware that they have been hurt, robbed, or burgled. Cases such as sexual molestation of unconscious patients by physicians, theft of trade secrets, and exposure to unsafe working conditions or consumer products leave their victims unaware that an offense has occurred. Even if victimization is perceived, not everyone responds in the same manner; some will contact the authorities, others will not. Thus, enforcement agencies will not be informed of many occupational crimes because victims are oblivious to the offense or choose not to contact the agencies even when they are aware of it. Any variation in the proportion of offenses brought to the attention of the enforcement agencies by outsiders will cause a variation in the recording rate.

Only in very rare instances can the assumption be made that there are equal probabilities of an agency discovering a given offense or a particular type of offender. In the area of occupational crime, embezzlement from a national bank may be about as close as one can come to such a condition. Here, legal requirements for periodic audits lead to strong proactive efforts to discover embezzlements. It also seems likely that banks will contact authorities about it (causing reactive discovery), because according to *Orlando v. United States*,[2] failure to report a theft of funds from a national bank constitutes aiding and abetting the offense. Agency records of embezzlement from a national bank, then, consistently reflect very large portions of the universe of such embezzlements, resulting in almost imperceptible variations in the recording rate. Additionally, because a very large portion of the universe of such embezzlements come to the attention of the enforcement authorities, single time period counts are probably also very accurate. However, aside from the extremely few isolated instances such as this, one cannot assume equal discovery over time by the authorities (either proactive or reactive) for occupational and other crimes.

Even if we were to assume that an equal proportion of the universe of offenses becomes known to an enforcement agency over time, disparate definitions of offenses and violations, overlapping jurisdictions, and erroneous or incomplete recording practices may cause recording rates to vary. If an occupational crime becomes known to an enforcement agency, it may not be recorded because it is considered unfounded. If a crime is considered to be founded, the agency may record it incorrectly (e.g., embezzlement mistakenly recorded as larceny or vice versa), or it may be recorded correctly by the agency but never submitted for inclusion in overall statistics, or it simply may be ignored because, among possible reasons, the agency considers it trivial.

Because of differences in offense definitions across jurisdictions, an occupational crime may be recorded as one thing in one jurisdiction (e.g., fraud) and as something else in another jurisdiction (e.g., larceny by trick). Or a single offense episode may be double-counted across two jurisdictions, if, say, it is recorded by both local and federal enforcement agencies. These recording inaccuracies also can be a problem in regard to known criminals—disparate definitions of the crime category to which an apprehended criminal belongs, double-counting of criminals, or failures to record criminals properly once they are discovered. Thus, even if enforcement agencies become aware of offenses and offenders at the same rate over time, which is extremely unlikely, they may still periodically record them at different rates.

Aside from inconsistent recording rates over time, an interpretational problem arises because police agency records do not distinguish between occupational and nonoccupational crimes. The most obvious case in point is the ***Uniform Crime Reports** (UCR)*, published annually by the Federal Bureau of Investigation (FBI) and usually taken to portray America's overall crime total and criminal trends. The data in the *UCR* are based on records kept by thousands of police agencies around the United

States and submitted by them to the FBI. Four theft categories in the *UCR* (larceny, fraud, forgery, embezzlement) are likely to include in their totals some amount of occupationally related stealing, but the *UCR* does not disaggregate its statistics according to that variable. Of the four categories, the *UCR* publishes offense counts for larceny only, which is the one category that is least likely to contain a substantial proportion of occupationally related thefts.

Criminal statistics (arrestees) are published in the *UCR* for fraud, forgery, and embezzlement. However, studies that have analyzed local fraud[3] and forgery[4] arrests generally have concluded that most of them (as high as 98 percent) do not involve occupationally related offenders. Rather, they are mostly concerned with passing bad checks, theft of services, welfare fraud, small confidence games, and credit card fraud. Although many persons arrested for embezzlement have been involved in occupational thefts, the category is still "impure" because it comprises some number of nonoccupational embezzlements, such as failure to return rented merchandise.[5] It is unfortunate that police data in the *Uniform Crime Reports* are essentially useless in their current form for the study of occupational offending, although at times they have been incorrectly used for that purpose.[6]

The enforcement agency statistics that are most likely to contain the *purest* occupational crime and criminal information are produced by state and federal regulatory agencies. The annual reports of these agencies often contain the numbers of criminal, civil, and administrative actions against firms (primarily corporations) and individuals for violation of laws that are occupationally related, such as unsafe working conditions, wage and hour violations, environmental pollution, unsafe consumer products, antitrust violations, and fraudulent advertising. At various points throughout the book, the reader will encounter statistics generated by these regulatory agencies. Marshall Clinard and Peter Yeager used regulatory agency violations as the basis of their comprehensive study on crime committed during the late 1970s by the nation's largest corporations (see box 2.2).

Of course, the tabulations of violations kept by regulatory agencies are subject to all of the previous criticisms shown to affect the constancy of recording rates by the police: multiple counting from overlapping jurisdictions, conflicting definitions of crimes, and failures to record incidents properly. Regulatory enforcement agency records also tend to treat complex organizations (rather than individuals) as offenders, so individual rates of offending are difficult to determine.

Moreover, because discovery of occupational crime by almost all regulatory agencies is due primarily or solely to their erratic proactive ef-

BOX 2.2

An Example of Agency Based Recording of Organizational Occupational Crime: The Clinard and Yeager Study

There have been several attempts to compile regulatory agency statistics on the number of organizational violations. The available counts tabulate the number of regulatory violations recorded against firms in a predefined group. This is known as a "prevalence rate" (the proportion of a group that possesses a particular characteristic; in this case the characteristic is having been recorded as committing a legal violation).

It should be kept in mind that agency-generated information includes only those violations that authorities have uncovered and recorded. Agency records would not include the large numbers of violations not known to authorities, nor those known yet not censured. Criminal violations by organizations and their employees may also be obscured because civil rather than criminal actions were sought by administrative agencies. Moreover, as the discussion in the text has emphasized, administrative agency violations, which constitute the bulk of organizational crime counts, probably reflect selective enforcement policies as much or more than they reflect the occurrence of violations.

Marshall Clinard, Peter Yeager, and their colleagues, in a project funded by the U.S. Department of Justice, studied federal administrative, civil, and criminal actions either initiated or completed during 1975 and 1976 by twenty-five federal agencies against 582 of America's largest corporations.[a] Most of their analysis concerned the 477 largest manufacturing firms; the remainder included 105 of the largest wholesale, retail, and service corporations. Banking, insurance, transportation, communication, and utilities organizations were excluded because, as Clinard and Yeager state, "These types of businesses are subject to special regulations and/or licensing because of the particular nature of their enterprises."[b]

The researchers were aware, as was Sutherland (see box 1.1), of the limitations of federal agency information sources—"official actions taken against corporations are probably only the tip of the iceberg of total violations."[c] They also note, as did Sutherland, that an organization's location in the economic system will affect the kinds of crime it is both eligible and motivated to commit.[d] Unlike Sutherland, the Clinard and Yeager research employed cross-sectional information for the same two-year period (rather than including the varying life spans of the organizations), so that it holds constant the time available in which to commit offenses. It also attempted to keep organizational size constant by differentiating companies according to their annual sales (small: $300 million–$499 million; medium: $500 million–$999 million; large: $1 billion or more).

As many as three-fifths of both groups of corporations studied by Clinard and Yeager had violations charged against them during the two-year period. It is probably even more common because the two-fifths that had no recorded violations may have been adroit at avoiding detection and citation or were not monitored adequately by the regulatory agencies. Of the three-fifths of the manufacturing corporations that had at least one violation, two hundred of them (42 percent of the total and 66 percent of the violators) had more than one violation. Moreover, a small percentage was responsible for a highly disproportionate share of all infractions. Thirty-eight of three hundred violating manufacturing firms (13 percent) accounted for over half (52 percent) of all violations attributable to the three hundred; these corporations averaged 23.5 violations each during the two-year period. In terms of size, small corporations accounted for only one-tenth of all violations, medium-sized firms for one-fifth, while large corporations accounted for almost three-fourths of them (nearly twice their proportionate percentage).

It has been noted that a certain industry may be characterized by differential social organization when many organizations within it commit violations. In particular, Clinard and Yeager found the oil, pharmaceutical, and motor vehicle industries to be the most chronic offenders.

Twenty-two companies in the oil-refining industry accounted for one-fifth of all cases in the sample. Those firms committed almost three-fifths of all serious and moderately serious financial violations, almost half of all environmental violations, almost one in six moderate and serious trade violations, and one in seven administrative violations. Oil-refining firms had 3.2 times their proportionate share of violations.

Eighteen firms in the motor vehicle industry (which includes automobile manufacturers, parts manufacturers, and nonauto motor vehicle manufacturers) were responsible for one of every six violations in the sample, and one-fifth of all serious and moderately serious violations. Those companies were involved with one-third of the manufacturing violations, one-ninth of serious and moderately serious labor violations, and one-eighth of trade infractions. Four of the firms accounted for at least twenty-one violations each. All told, the motor vehicle industry had about four times its proportionate share of violations generally, and five times its share of serious and moderately serious infractions.

The pharmaceutical manufacturing industry accounted for one-tenth of all violations, or 2.5 times its proportionate share. It was responsible for one-eighth of the serious and moderate violations, or 3.2 times its share. All seventeen pharmaceutical companies violated the law at least once during the two-year period, and two of the drug firms had more than twenty violations.

These Clinard and Yeager records indicate clearly that many organizations and many industries are recidivistic in their criminality.

(continued next page)

BOX 2.2

Continued

Notes

a. Marshall Clinard and Peter Yeager, *Corporate Crime* (New York: Basic Books, 1980); Marshall Clinard, Peter Yeager, Jeanne Brissette, David Petrashek, and Elizabeth Harris, *Illegal Corporate Behavior* (Washington, DC: U.S. Government Printing Office, 1979).

b. Clinard and Yeager, *Corporate Crime,* p. 111.

c. Ibid.

d. Ibid., pp. 115–16.

forts at enforcement (which may be affected by politics, budgetary constraints, or decisions of administrative courts), their recorded counts are recurrently a reflection of these varying efforts rather than a reflection of true increases or decreases in the numbers of violations and violators. This factor alone greatly alters the recording rates of offenses and offenders by regulatory agencies over time. Although regulatory enforcement agency data are the purest source for records of occupational crime, those records are nevertheless noncomprehensive and irregular. Like the *UCR,* the majority of the records of regulatory agencies are of virtually no value for ascertaining the number of occupational crimes and criminals in a single time period. And because of the erratic changes in the recording rate from one year to the next, regulatory agency statistics are also of little value for ascertaining changes in the numbers of occupational crimes or criminals over time.

Improving Agency Information

Outlining the requirements of an optimally integrated federal agency crime and criminal recording system, Albert Biderman and Albert Reiss, Jr., note the following requisites, which have been adapted here for occupational crime:

1. That the statistics encompass administrative, civil, and criminal matters.
2. That the changes related to overlapping and concurrent jurisdiction are monitored for their potential impact on the records.

3. That standard definitions and classification procedures for events regarded as occupational crimes be adopted to overcome statutory and administrative variability in defining them.
4. That ways be found to estimate or account for multiple counts of the same event.
5. That there be a clear definition of the totality of occupational crime with decision rules stipulating which occupational crimes are to be counted, whether the total is to be defined by jurisdiction over events, by the territory of jurisdiction, or by special qualifications regarding the population of a jurisdiction.
6. That there be provisions obligating agencies to report information about occupational crime in ways that permit its merging from different sources.
7. That provision be made for central coordination of the processing and reporting of information and for control to ensure uniformity and compliance.
8. That relevant violations of law, regulations, or standards be systematically and regularly reported by each and every agency, whether or not it has a mandate for law enforcement, regulation, or adjudication.
9. That there be explicit criteria for defining referrals and their sources so that referral information can be merged among agencies and their sources of variability investigated.
10. That there be provision for standardization among agencies of data collection, analysis, and reporting.[7]

These suggestions are excellent, though there is some concern about the inclusion of civil and administrative cases in a statistical reporting system about "crime" (see number 1 above). The volume of regulatory violations handled by administrative judges far exceeds that decided by civil or criminal court judges. And the volume of noncompliance matters detected and decided by regulatory agents is often larger than the violations detected by criminal enforcement divisions and adjudicated as criminal matters. Biderman and Reiss,[8] as did Sutherland,[9] argue that civil and administrative cases should be included; to exclude them would force a great many transgressions to lie outside the statistical reporting system. However, the inclusion of civil and administrative cases may contribute to overreporting because the burden of proof required by such proceedings (preponderance of the evidence) is less than that required in a criminal case (beyond a reasonable doubt). Further, it is usually necessary to establish a person's (or organization's) ***mens rea***, or intent, in order to prove that a crime occurred; proving intent is usually not necessary for a judgment in a civil or an administrative law case. These lesser burdens of proof may tend to overincriminate and thereby overcount legal violations, but the alternative of excluding civil and administrative decisions presents the far greater danger of massively undercounting them.

Biderman and Reiss suggest that occupational crime violations can be differentiated in agency data according to whether the case was decided through administrative, civil, or criminal jurisdictions, as long as the system of statistical reporting includes all three. When a regulatory agency convicts an entity on criminal charges and also imposes a civil penalty for the same action, or if there is another overlap (e.g., the same case involving several agencies, several charges in the same case), care must be taken not to double-count the event.

Even if the criteria suggested by Biderman and Reiss are met, however, there still must be an assumption of uniform discovery of a given offense type and its perpetrators before it can be said that agency records are truly representative of crimes that occur and criminals that exist. Currently, enforcement, adjudication, and penal agency records are unrepresentative measures of the universes of occupationally related offenses and offenders. However, as with many things, a little bit is better than nothing, and at least for the moment (that is, until records are integrated in a form something like that suggested by Biderman and Reiss, and an assumption about uniform discovery of offenses and perpetrators can be made), the student of occupational crime must depend on agency records and acknowledge their weaknesses.

Note should also be made of the recent work in this area by Sally Simpson and her colleagues, which offers a change in thinking about agency records of occupational crime.[10] They assert that traditional population incidence measures, such as those suggested by Biderman and Reiss, are too simplistic to capture the essence of organizational crime in particular. Capturing that essence actually requires a measurement that controls both for the differences in opportunities to commit organizational crime and for the distribution of power within organizations.

To construct **opportunity-sensitive rates,** the authors suggest that some measure of "logical units of opportunity" be included in the denominator. Their line of argument is that it makes the most sense to determine the rates of forcible rape and motor vehicle thefts according to the number of logical units of opportunity for those offenses in a population (females and registered motor vehicles, respectively), and the case for organizational crime rates should be no different. Logical units of opportunity for organizational crime would include items such as populations at risk to commit crime within and across organizations, the extent of enforcement, the number and type of business transactions, and the number of laws that potentially can be violated.

To construct **power-sensitive rates,** they suggest a combination of actors' culpability, actors' hierarchical positioning within organizations, and actors' relative share of business transactions. Most of these opportunity-sensitive and power-sensitive rates could be compared within and across organizations. The Simpson et al. essay, then, represents a novel change in thinking about the compilation of organizational crime rates, although the authors admit that coming to grips with how to measure their innovations will be very difficult.

Victimization Surveys

Victimization surveys comprise information about crimes and criminals solicited from the victims themselves. Typically, in these surveys representative samples of persons are asked whether they have been victimized and, if so, are asked to provide details about such victimizations. Victimization for a population as a whole is then estimated from information gathered from the representative samples. Records compiled from victims are intuitively more appealing than agency data as a source of information about crime and criminals because victims are close to the offense; in fact, you cannot get much closer.

Victimization surveys were originally sought to fill in the dark figures associated with agency records. The first major victimization survey was conducted in the United States by Philip Ennis, who was researching for the 1966 President's Commission on Law Enforcement and Administration of Justice.[11] About thirty-three thousand persons in the general population were selected for their representative characteristics and were asked whether they had been victims of a given crime. If they had been victimized, specific questions were then asked about the event.

In addition to information on offenses unknown to agency records, victim information can yield valuable material about the characteristics of criminals (such as their age, gender, and race), the time and location of offenses, the victim-offender relationship (such as relative, stranger, and employee-employer), the effects of the offense on the victim (such as the value of property stolen, extent of injury, time lost from work because of physical injury, and medical expenses associated with injury), the reasons for reporting (or not reporting) the offense to the authorities, and individuals' probabilities of being victimized by a given offense over their lifetimes.

Factors Affecting Recording Rates in Occupational Victimization Surveys

There are three basic kinds of errors associated with all sample survey data: measurement error, sampling error, and response error. The first bias, **measurement error,** involves the inability of a respondent to understand survey questions properly. Measurement error also comprises mistakes in editing, processing, and recording data. Results from an interview can be lost, the wrong key can be punched when the information is entered into a computer, or the wrong figures can be printed when the survey is published. Measurement error in victim surveys can be minimized by carefully worded questions and the avoidance of errors in processing data.

Sampling error in victimization surveys arises when persons in the sample do not accurately represent the population as a whole. If persons in a sample survey of occupational crime victimization over- or underrepresent certain categories of persons in the population (such as in terms of gender, age, race, or size of organization), then the estimates of victimization based on those samples will be inaccurate. The fewer respondents who are asked about victimization, the higher the sampling error is likely to be (asking five thousand people is better than asking five hundred). Moreover, the fewer responses about previous victimization experience, the higher the sampling error for particular information about those relatively few experiences (surveyors who know about one hundred employee thefts can make more reliable estimates than surveyors who know about ten employee thefts). The previous point is especially important to occupational crime victim surveys. As will be shown in the following discussion of response error, victims of occupational crime are generally much less likely than victims of street crime to perceive that they have been victimized, and therefore high sampling error attributable to small groups of victim respondents becomes a particular problem.

Further, as Biderman and Reiss point out, even if respondents are aware that they have been victimized by an occupational crime and are willing to tell an interviewer about it, some occupational crimes occur so seldom or victimize so few persons or organizations that very large samples must be employed in order to include enough victims to obtain reliable statistical results. Therefore, economically feasible occupational crime victimization surveys must be limited to the investigation of offenses that occur commonly. Biderman and Reiss also point out that it may be difficult even to devise adequate sampling techniques that encompass representative proportions of organizations that have been victims (such as according to size, age, and potential for exposure to certain victimizations).[12] When unrepresentative samples are drawn in victim surveys (either of individuals or organizations), then criminality recording rates across victim categories will be unequal.

Response error in victim surveys occurs when persons give inaccurate responses to surveyors. Several response errors have been found to be associated with street crime victim surveys,[13] and there is every reason to believe that those problems exist in surveys of victims of occupational crime. Respondents may exaggerate or fabricate their answers. Or they may inadvertently misinterpret facts to the point of stating a victimization when, in fact, none occurred. A case in point is the first United States victim survey by Ennis, discussed earlier, in which it was found that victimization by consumer fraud had been greatly overreported because of misinterpretations of fact (many respondents claimed fraud when in fact they had simply made a bad purchasing decision).[14]

Because of the nature of occupational crime, there would be more underreporting response error than overreporting error. Victims of occuptional crime, as noted, usually are generally much less likely to be aware of their victimization than victims of street crime. Victims of consumer fraud are not likely to know that they have been duped when, say, a used car salesman turns an odometer back several thousand miles. Patients are not likely to realize that they have been assaulted by a physician through unnecessary surgery. Victims of unsafe consumer products such as pharmaceuticals and automobiles are not likely to be aware of the potential danger of the products. When a miner dies from a lung disease, it is difficult to appreciate that the death occurred because the employer violated mine safety regulations many years earlier. Persons exposed to poisonous living environments (e.g., toxic waste dumping, water and air pollution) may go for many years before the cumulative effects of exposure manifest themselves, and even then the symptoms may not be traced to the exposure. Retailers are often unaware that their inventory "shrinkage" is due to employee theft rather than to shoplifting. Corporations victimized by unfair competition or theft of trade secrets may not learn of the offenses. In political corruption cases, the victim is the public, but because of the covert nature of the offense (the briber and bribee do not want the transaction known), the public often is not cognizant of it. These are only a few examples to demonstrate that nonawareness of victimization contributes tremendous individual and organizational underreporting response errors in victim surveys of occupational crime that are not present in victim surveys of "street" crime.

Occupational crime victim surveys tend to have other underreporting biases. Respondents may have perceived a victimization at the time it occurred but have forgotten it by the time they are questioned. Such "memory decay" tends to increase when the interim between a victimization and the survey interview increases.[15] Further, victims of occupational crime are often too embarrassed to report this to an interviewer. They may not, for instance, want to admit that they were gullible. And victims of occupational crime such as employee theft who may know that they have been victimized may not know other information associated with the offense, such as offender characteristics or the amount of loss per theft.

In sum, the extremely high potential for sampling errors and response errors in victim surveys of occupational crime translate into a high potential for variation in recording rates. While it is possible to identify a few occupational crimes that are sufficiently common (to avoid sampling error) and easily recognizable by the victim (to avoid response error)—such as employee theft—the kinds of material yielded by such studies will at best give us a trivial amount of information on the total incidence of occupational crime.

Criminal Surveys

We now turn to information based on another type of respondent close to the scene of the crime—the criminal. **Criminal surveys** compile information from offenders about their illegal behavior. Because the criminal is at the scene of the crime, criminal based records are extremely close to the offense itself and have the potential to be excellent sources of information. Unlike agency recordings and victimization surveys, which usually attempt to estimate the incidence of criminality for the population as a whole, criminal surveys have typically been used to estimate the prevalence of criminality among a particular group of persons (that is, the proportion of members in a group who have committed a crime within a past time period). Criminal surveys are commonly referred to as "self-reported crime" data, and they can produce high dark figures, especially in the area of occupational criminality.

The first major criminal survey was undertaken by James Wallerstein and Clement Wyle.[16] They asked 1,020 men and 678 women of differing ages and with a wide range of occupations to complete a questionnaire about their past criminal activities. Respondents confessed their involvement in forty-nine different offenses. Because the questionnaires were obtained only from persons who chose to respond to them, the responses are not necessarily representative of the population as a whole. Regarding occupational crime, 57 percent of the males and 40 percent of the females admitted to tax evasion.

Since then, studies of self-reported criminal involvement have become more plentiful, focusing on both juveniles[17] and adults.[18] However, self-report surveys of occupational crime are rare.

Problems with Occupational Criminal Surveys

Sampling error in criminal surveys can be a major problem in obtaining valid information because it is difficult to get individuals to participate in a study in which they must acknowledge their illegal behavior. In a juvenile delinquency self-report study, Michael Hindelang and his colleagues found that only about 50 percent of their sample agreed to participate.[19] There was a strong tendency for persons who had been officially identified as delinquent by the police and the courts to fail to cooperate with researchers. In addition, African-American and female respondents were underrepresented. This sampling error was so great that Delbert Elliott, an eminent researcher in delinquency, commented that "participating subjects can no longer be considered a [representative] sample of . . . youth aged fifteen through eighteen."[20] Failure to cooperate with recorders may be especially high among occupational criminals.

Self-report occupational crime surveys encounter particular problems when organizational occupational criminals are included. It may be difficult to draw adequate samples of organizational employees. Employee function, organization size and diversification, and industrial representation are some of the factors that must be considered when sampling employees of organizations. Further, only employees who commit organizational crimes by themselves or in small groups (in which co-offenders are known in terms of their role in the event) will be able to answer questions about their participation in organizational crime. As Biderman and Reiss point out, "Where offending partners are more diffuse and the behavior involves complex organizational activity, the perpetrator survey seems less appropriate, particularly to estimate frequencies of violation events."[21] Any degree of sampling error will naturally affect the criminality recording rate.

If persons agree to participate as subjects, they may nevertheless give inaccurate answers, which produce **response error in criminal surveys.** Underreporting response error should probably be of greater concern to recorders of criminal based data than overreporting response error, because human nature tells us that criminals are more likely to fail to admit they did commit a crime than to report a crime that they did not commit. Many juveniles admit to no previous delinquency when there is, in fact, an official record of their delinquency.[22] Even if one were to find a concordance between self-reported crime and arrest data, respondents may still be hiding offenses that they know are not verifiable by other records.

Some researchers have claimed 80 percent to 90 percent accuracy in self-reported crime data through cross-checking methods such as peer responses[23] and polygraph questioning,[24] but there remains an understandable concern about self-report data.

There are three sources of response error that are particularly relevant to self-report surveys of occupational crime; each of them can drastically reduce the criminality recording rate. First, as adults who hold a position in the legitimate sphere, occupational offenders might be embarrassed and reticent about their illegal behavior. One would certainly expect a greater extent of embarrassment in such a group than, say, among juveniles who are asked about petty offenses.

Second, some occupational offenders may not see their actions as criminal though, in fact, they are. Politicians who are bribed with gifts and free vacations, employees who pilfer scrap materials, income tax evaders who "interpret" tax laws to their own advantage, or corporate officers who fix prices may not consider (or may not want to consider) their behaviors criminal. Failure to define one's own behavior as criminal when it constitutes a legal offense introduces an important response bias in self-reported occupational crime surveys. Many occupational criminals hold respectable positions and have created a dignified self-image, making them less likely to see the criminal nature of their behavior.

Third, although self-reported criminality studies are supposed to be anonymous, persons may still fear that they have something to lose by admitting criminal behavior. This fear may be much greater if the criminality involves a career or livelihood that has taken years to cultivate than if it involves occupational crime by someone without such an investment. In sum, even if recorders can convince enough people to participate in an occupational crime self-report survey to the extent that a representative sample is drawn, there remain concerns about respondent accuracy. There have been only a few occupational crime self-report surveys undertaken and there has been no attempt to validate them in the same ways as those of self-reported traditional criminal behavior. The figures that are reported in these surveys are probably underestimates.

The few occupational crime self-report surveys have concentrated on tax evasion and employee theft. These are offenses that are relatively common across all occupations and therefore relatively uncomplicated samples can be used.

For tax evasion, based on an extensive sample of more than 1,900 persons from three states, Charles Tittle found that slightly more than 10 percent admitted to purposely cheating the government.[25] Robert Mason and Lyle Calvin sampled 800 households, and found that about one in four admitted to practicing at least one form of tax evasion (5 percent overstated deductions; 14 percent underreported taxable income; and 8 percent failed to file a required return).[26] And, Joachim Vogel estimated a 34 percent willful tax noncompliance rate from self-reports in Sweden.[27]

The extensive study for employee theft, by Richard Hollinger and John Clark, surveyed over 9,000 employees in various sectors (retail, hospital, and manufacturing). They found that about one-third of those returning questionnaires admitted to some sort of stealing from their employer (their response rate was 52 percent). Box 2.3 presents some of their data.

BOX 2.3

An Example of a Self-Report Survey in Occupational Crime: Employee Theft (in percent)

Items:	*Involvement:* Almost Daily	About Once/ Week	4–12 Times/ Year	1–3 Times/ Year	Total
Retail Sector (N=3,567)					
Misuse the discount privilege	0.6	2.4	11.0	14.9	28.9
Take store merchandise	0.2	0.5	1.3	4.6	6.6
Get paid for more hours than were worked	0.2	0.4	1.2	4.0	5.8
Purposely underring a purchase	0.1	0.3	1.1	1.7	3.2
Borrow or take money from employer w/o approval	0.1	0.1	0.5	2.0	2.7
Excessive expense account reimbursement	0.1	0.2	0.5	1.3	2.1
Purposely damage merchandise to buy it on discount	—	0.1	0.2	1.0	2.1
Retail total (percent involved in one or more items)					35.1

(continued next page)

BOX 2.3

Continued

Items:	*Involvement:* Almost Daily	About Once/ Week	4–12 Times/ Year	1–3 Times/ Year	Total
Hospital Sector (N=4,111)					
Take hospital supplies (e.g., linens)	0.2	0.8	8.4	17.9	27.3
Take or use medications intended for patients	0.1	0.3	1.9	5.5	7.8
Get paid for more hours than were worked	0.2	0.5	1.6	3.8	6.1
Take hospital equipment or tools	0.1	0.1	0.4	4.1	4.7
Excessive expense account reimbursement	0.1	—	0.2	0.8	1.1
Hospital total (percent involved in one or more items)					33.3
Manufacturing Sector (N=1,497)					
Take raw materials used in production	0.1	0.5	3.5	10.4	14.3
Get paid for more hours than were worked	0.2	0.4	2.9	5.6	9.2
Take company tools or equipment	—	0.1	1.1	7.5	8.7
Excessive expense account reimbursement	0.1	0.6	1.4	5.6	7.7
Take finished products	—	—	0.4	2.7	3.1
Take precious metals (e.g., platinum and gold)	0.1	0.1	0.5	1.1	1.8
Manufacturing total (percent involved in one or more items)					28.4

Source: Richard Hollinger, "Acts Against the Workplace: Social Bonding and Employee Deviance," *Deviant Behavior* 7 (1986):53–75, p. 60.

Randomized Response Self-Report Models

As noted, a strong obstacle to obtaining truthful responses in self-report studies of occupational crime centers on respondents' belief that what they say will not be held in confidence. If a respondent is embarrassed about past behavior or believes that admitting that behavior will somehow put him or her at risk (with authorities or employers, for instance), there will be a strong tendency to underreport criminal behavior. Recorders need a method to obtain information that allows the respondents to be assured that their answers are anonymous. This is not an easy task. Fortunately, researchers have developed a self-report method that attempts to persuade respondents of the anonymity of their answers—the "randomized response" model. It has been used for the past two decades to increase the truthfulness of responses about sensitive information such as drunk driving,[28] illegal killing of deer,[29] and criminal behavior in general.[30]

According to Paul Tracy and James Fox, **randomized response** is

> a survey technique for reducing response bias arising from respondent concern over revealing sensitive information. The randomized response method utilizes an indeterminate question (i.e., the question answered by the respondent is unknown to the researcher) and thus maintains the anonymity of the responses. In other words, not even the interviewer knows what question the respondent is actually answering; the interviewer merely records the response to a random question. Based on various [statistical] relations between the questions and the observed responses, it is possible to obtain estimates of [criminality] in the aggregate. Because only aggregate estimates are possible, not only are respondents protected, many ethical concerns surrounding the solicitation of sensitive information are nullified.[31]

The most simplified randomized response model presents the respondent with two questions, a nonsensitive one (asking information that is trivial) and a sensitive one (asking sensitive information, such as the number of occupational crimes committed). The question (sensitive or nonsensitive) to be answered by the respondent depends on the outcome of a randomizing device (such as a coin flip, a roll of a die, or a spinner). The recorder needs to know two things before the survey. First, the recorder must know the probability of a "yes" answer to the nonsensitive question. Second, the recorder must know the proportion of respondents to whom the nonsensitive question is posed. With prior knowledge of these two probabilities, the recorder can estimate the number of persons who answered "yes" to the sensitive question.

Here is a very simplified randomized response model for eliciting the prevalence of occupational criminality (in this case, crime by physicians). Let us presume that there is a total (universe) of 500 physicians in a given area. Each is sent the following letter to request participation in the study and to emphasize the anonymity associated with the survey's methodology:

> We are trying to estimate the incidence of occupational crime by physicians. There is no way to trace any given answer to any particular individual, and therefore we ask that you be entirely frank in your responses. Please flip a coin. If the outcome is heads, please answer the following question about your mother's or father's birthdate (choose one randomly by flipping the coin again): "Was he/she born between January 1st and June 30th?" If the outcome of the first coin flip is tails, please answer the following question: "Have you ever submitted a fraudulent claim to a patient's medical insurance company that included services or tests that were never performed?" Please answer only the question designated by the coin flip by checking a "yes" or a "no" on the enclosed stamped postcard. **DO NOT TELL US WHO YOU ARE OR WHICH QUESTION YOU HAVE ANSWERED.** Remember, we cannot trace responses to any individual, nor can we ascertain which question was answered by you. Thank you for your cooperation.

Suppose that all 500 postcards are returned and they contain a total of 150 "yes" answers and 350 "no" answers. The recorder would then estimate that 10 percent of physicians in the survey had submitted at least one fraudulent medical insurance claim. The figure is calculated as 10 percent because the probability of a "yes" answer to the nonsensitive (birthday) question is approximately .5 (about half the population was born during the first six months of the year) and the probability of receiving the nonsensitive question is also about .5 (heads or tails). If half the physicians answered the nonsensitive question and half of that group should have answered "yes" to it, then one expects that 125 "yes" answers are to the nonsensitive question (.5 x .5 = .25; .25 x 500 = 125). The remaining twenty-five "yes" answers (150-125=25), then, should be to the sensitive question. There were about two hundred fifty physicians who were supposed to have answered the sensitive question, and twenty-five is 10 percent of two hundred fifty. Had the physicians who answered the nonsensitive question received the sensitive question instead, then the assumption is that they, too, would have had a 10 percent violation rate.

Of course, the success of the above example is predicated on full cooperation by respondents. The extent to which the subjects fail to follow instructions or fail to send in postcards is the extent to which estimates might be in error. Such a model can also be used to estimate employee theft, tax evasion, price fixing, insider trading, or any other kind of occupationally related offending. Additionally, similar but more sophisticated models can estimate the numbers of offenses individuals commit rather than merely whether an individual has committed at least one offense.[32]

Tracy and Fox, comparing randomized response results with simple self-report results, conclude that this technique yields results that more closely approximate the true number of offenses committed by the sample.[33] They did not include occupational criminality specifically in their survey, but it could be assumed that because randomized response worked better than simple self-report in their study of criminality generally, it will be superior to simple self-report for occupational criminality as well.

Randomized response has limits, however, because there is no way to determine particular characteristics of individuals in the survey. If you wanted to ascertain whether medical fraud is more likely to be committed by male physicians, or specialists, or graduates from less prestigious medical schools, randomized response is of no help unless these groups are sampled separately. And if there are only a few offenders in the sample, known as a low "base rate," then randomized response will not be able to produce a reliable estimate. There is also a question about the extent to which occupational offenders cooperate in a randomized response survey. One could argue that the logical basis of this particular survey method is so tricky that it might arouse even more suspicion about whether answers are anonymous. In any case, there is certainly no compelling reason why sophisticated adult offenders will tell the truth about discreditable behavior, independent of their perceived anonymity.

Criminal based records of occupational criminality, then, are fraught with problems. However, if recorders can identify the biases and confront them methodologically, such as with the development of workable randomized response models, significant reductions in response errors might be realized. Unfortunately, except for a paucity of studies, the occupational criminal based information barrel is currently empty.

Direct Observation of Occupational Crimes and Criminals

The fourth counting method is to observe directly the universes of offenses and offenders or a representative sample of them. Direct observation tends to have very low dark figures relative to the three methods discussed previously. Third-person direct observation is certainly close to the offense itself. Its major drawback, however, is that it is extremely limited in application—only a few offenses lend themselves to direct observation.

Examples of offenses that have been directly observed include cable television-signal theft[34] and traffic violations.[35] In the area of occupational crime, income tax evasion has been estimated through direct observation by an audit of a representative sample of returns.[36] Income tax evasion has also been observed directly by comparing returns with independently determined income and expenses.[37] Bribetaking by elected officials, too, is a directly observable offense, as was shown by the FBI in the ABSCAM cases.[38] John Braithwaite directly observed fraudulent used car dealers who rolled back odometer readings by comparing the mileage of cars on lots with the mileage claimed by the cars' previous owners.[39] And Tracy and Fox directly observed consumer fraud in the auto body repair industry by noting differences in repair estimates as a function of whether repairs were or were not to be paid for by an insurance company.[40]

Another clever attempt to observe occupational crime directly was undertaken by Paul Jesilow in his doctoral dissertation on auto repair fraud.[41] Jesilow sought to determine the proportion of auto repair firms in a given area that engaged in fraud. Members of his research team took "dead" batteries that had been certified to be chargeable by a professional mechanic to a large sample of repair firms and instructed each firm to try to charge the battery. By performing this scenario with a representative sample of firms, Jesilow could count the number of auto repairers who claimed a battery was in need of replacement. Jesilow could not count the prevalence of auto repair defrauders by this method, however. There may have been firms in the sample that engaged in fraud on other occasions but not during the battery incident. These fraudulent firms would be undercounted as criminals. But Jesilow was able to identify a group of occupational criminals that may easily have gone undetected by other methods. Overall, Jesilow found 34 of 313 (or 10.9 percent) of the firms in the study to be dishonest on that occasion, presuming, of course, that they did not make a diagnostic error.[42]

Direct observation does not have response error because responses are not elicited as in victim based and criminal based records. But there is the possibility that mistakes can be made in interpreting observed behavior as criminal or noncriminal. It is this bias that would most affect the criminality recording rate in direct observational studies.[43]

Sampling error in direct observation study would be caused by excluding certain persons or other entities from observation. In the Jesilow study, the relative share of the automotive repair market possessed by new car dealers was about one-third, but because there were so few dealers, all of whom had a high volume, Jesilow could not sample enough of them so that new car dealers represented one-third of his sample.[44] For these reasons, new car dealers were systematically undersampled. Additionally, some firms did not want to bother with such nonlucrative services as battery charging, which could have also resulted in sampling error.

Direct observation of criminal behavior is the preferred method for counting crimes and criminals because it tends to produce the lowest dark figures. It may also allow the recorder to gather data in addition to the number of offenses committed, such as time-location, offender characteristics, victim characteristics, and offense characteristics. However, it is so limited in application that it cannot be depended on for regular use by researchers. When the few opportunities for counting occupational and other crimes through direct observation are realized, they should be fully exploited.

Direct observation may also allow us to learn about causal processes leading to or inhibiting occupational crime. Thus, one may learn much about developing effective programs to control organizational offending simply by studying the interactions within an offending organization.[45] Similarly, studying the socialization of medical students into the role of practicing doctor has yielded significant understanding about why doctors behave the way they do.[46] Analogous observational research can be done during the training of other professionals. Marshall Clinard and Peter Yeager report that a Harvard Business School professor, in his business decision-making course, trained students to misrepresent their positions in negotiations and other business dealings.[47] Students found that hiding certain facts, bluffing, and even outright lying gave them a better position and a better grade. Even if an effort is made to teach ethics to students, the actual occupational experience can negate those endeavors—one law school legal ethics professor found that his students came to him after internships with law firms and reported that their ethical training was of no value because it was ignored by the profession.[48] Careful observations during field research and case studies have the potential to teach more about the dynamics of occupational crime than counting methods that yield raw frequencies and incidences.

Key Terms

universe of offenses
dark figure of crime
universe of offenders
dark figure of criminals
agency recordings
recording rate
proactive discovery
Uniform Crime Reports
reactive discovery
mens rea
opportunity-sensitive rates
power-sensitive rates
victimization surveys
measurement error
sampling error in victimization surveys
response error in victimization surveys
criminal surveys
sampling error in criminal surveys
response error in criminal surveys
randomized response
direct observation
sampling error in direct observation

Questions for Discussion

1. Why is it important to distinguish between the universe of offenses and the universe of offenders?
2. Explain the importance of the recording rate in determining the number of offenses over multiple time periods.
3. Discuss the problems associated with agency records about the following four offenses: insurance fraud by physicians, price-fixing, assault by a law enforcement officer, and unsafe working conditions.
4. Discuss the problems associated with victimization surveys about the following four offenses: unnecessary surgery, unsafe consumer product use, bribery of a public official, and employee theft.
5. Discuss the problems associated with criminal surveys about the following four offenses: sexual molestation of patients by physicians, trade secret theft, insider trading, and tax evasion.
6. How well do you believe the randomized response model example presented in the chapter (study of insurance fraud among physicians) would actually work? What are the strengths and weaknesses of it? How would you improve it?
7. Name three occupational crimes that can be counted by direct observation (bearing in mind people's legal rights to privacy in nonpublic situations).

General Readings on Counting Occupational Crimes

Albert Biderman and Albert J. Reiss, Jr., *Data Sources on White-Collar Law-Breaking* (Washington, DC: U.S. Government Printing Office, 1980).

Thorsten Sellin, "The Significance of Records of Crime," *Law Quarterly Review* 67 (1951):489–504.

Sally S. Simpson, Anthony R. Harris, and Brian A. Mattson, "Measuring Corporate Crime," in Michael Blankenship (ed.), *Understanding Corporate Criminality* (New York: Garland Publishing, 1993).

Paul E. Tracy and James Alan Fox, "The Validity of Randomized Response for Sensitive Measurements," *American Sociological Review* 46 (1981):187–200.

Charles F. Wellford and Barton L. Ingraham, "White-Collar Crime: Prevalence, Trends, and Costs," in Albert R. Roberts (ed.), *Critical Issues in Crime and Justice* (Thousand Oaks, CA: Sage, 1994).

Conflict criminologists have pointed out how the criminal justice system has perpetuated the definition of certain persons as representing the foundation of the "crime problem." Politically powerful occupational offenders often help to contribute to such definitions by undercutting their own censure while at the same time spotlighting others as the "real criminals."

3 *Explanations of Occupational Criminality*

This chapter presents the major explanations that have been offered regarding the causes of crime and applies them to occupational offending. Theoretical approaches in criminology run an intellectual gamut, and each is closely tied to a particular ideology about human behavior. On the far left is the Marxist idea that crime is a byproduct of the government's attempt to harness workers and to help parasitical capitalism survive. At the other end are rightist Lombrosians, who believe that criminality is genetically transmitted. Between these extremes lies a vast array of "theories" that have enjoyed prominence at one time or another during the past sixty years.

The term *theory* is used in this chapter rather loosely, because only a few of the approaches discussed completely meet the minimal requirements for the proper intellectual grounding of a sound criminological theory, including testability.[1] Although occupational crime can be treated as distinctive because it is based on opportunities at the job, there is no single theory that can satisfactorily explain why all occupational crimes occur or why all occupational criminals behave the way they do. Nonetheless, some theories are more robust than others and can explain much larger amounts of occupational crime than can competing perspectives.

Many theories have been developed in criminology. Fortunately, the field can be narrowed a bit when attempting to explain occupational crime. Biologically based approaches to crime causation offer little help. It is difficult to conceive of employee theft, illegal pollution, price-fixing, unnecessary surgery, insider stock trading, or virtually any other occupational offense being caused by criminal genes or an extra Y chromosome. This should not imply that there is no place for biological approaches in the explanation of occupational crime. They may be applicable in isolated instances. For example, a given act of aggression by a police officer may be exacerbated by a body chemical imbalance. However, on the whole, biological explanations add virtually nothing to our understanding of occupational crime.

Other theories are only tangentially related to job crime. For instance, Thorsten Sellin's time-honored ideas about conflict among sets of conduct rules can explain some occupational crime.[2] Sellin believes that crime will occur when the conduct rules of a dominant culture are in conflict with the conduct rules of migrants, colonized peoples, and persons living at border areas between divergent cultures. Suppose that fee-splitting (that is, taking money [kickbacks] for professional referrals) is common among physicians in a particular culture where it is not regarded as criminal. When physicians from this site split fees after moving elsewhere, where the behavior is illegal, then they may be committing a crime because of culture conflict. When there is such conflict among occupational conduct norms and crime results, it can be said that the lawbreaking was "external" to the offender, because he or she was only acting as one would normally in the original culture. But the proportion of occupational crime that can be explained by Sellin's conflict with "external" conduct norms is minuscule.

The explanations addressed in this chapter cover virtually the full spectrum of the remaining approaches in criminology. They will be divided into two major sections. First to be considered are several theories that interpret criminality as a political phenomenon. These "legal conflict analyses" focus on the integral link between the power of some high-status occupations and the making and enforcement of occupational laws. Those who possess money and large amounts of political power can exert influence on legislatures to deflect criminal definitions away from what they are doing. If their behaviors come to be defined as criminal, they use their influence to avoid the law. Sutherland, it will be remembered, viewed powerful offenders' ability to deflect criminal labels as the most important defining characteristic of "white-collar" crime.[3] Conflict analysis theories presume that laws (that is, their establishment and application) are a reflection of the interests of persons with political power. Conflict analysis theorists assert that there are no fundamental differences in the appropriateness of the behaviors of criminals and noncriminals—criminals' behaviors simply have been deemed inappropriate by persons who make and enforce the laws.

On the contrary, the approaches discussed in the second part of this chapter identify factors associated with the individual criminal that are assumed to set him or her apart from noncriminals. They include: (a) differences in responding to perceived threats; (b) differences in learning about conduct rules; (c) differences in access to the legal opportunity to gain wealth; (d) differences in the willingness to neutralize (explain away) criminality; and (e) differences in self-gratification propensities. Unlike theories about the "behavior of law," the presumption in these explanations is that criminals use inappropriate conduct and noncriminals use appropriate conduct.

Explanations of the Behavior of Occupational Criminal Law

Karl Marx

One general group of conflict theorists base their work on the writings of Karl Marx (1818–1883) and Friedrich Engels (1820–1895). The crux of the Marx–Engels theory revolves around the conflict between those who own the means of production (technological equipment and the knowledge of how to use it) on the one hand and the relationships that determine the distribution of goods and profits produced on the other hand. Marx and Engels predicted that capitalist systems will further develop the means of production, but the distribution of profits will continue to favor only those who own the means of production. More property will be concentrated among fewer and fewer people, while at the same time more and more people will become wage earners instead of working for themselves. This will frustrate common workers by alienating or estranging them from the fruits of their labor.

Relatively "big fish" will be gobbled up by even bigger ones because of the "survival of the fittest" basis of capitalism. This, coupled with a decreased need for workers because of mechanization and automation, will result in many more workers than jobs. Because the supply of workers far exceeds the demand, desperate persons will work for extremely low wages. Eventually, then, capitalist societies will polarize into two conflicting groups—the very few rich and the many, many poor. Marx and Engels regarded this tendency toward polarization as the inherent contradiction in capitalism. For them, only a revolutionary restructuring of the ownership of products and profits could restore balance to a society. The inevitable result of such a revolution would be socialism, in which the ownership of products and profits is distributed through the state to all workers collectively. Marxist approaches are considered partisan because they tend to blame virtually all social problems on the inherent evils of capitalism.

Though Marx and Engels did not use the concept of "crime" as a central aspect of their theories, "crime" and "law" are relevant to a Marxist criminology.[4] The establishment or application of both civil and criminal law in Marxist criminology is seen to represent state powers that are used by the rich to take the fruits of poor people's labor away from them. Modern Marxist criminologists view "crime" as an ideological and political category generated by state practices.[5] Marxist analyses posit that laws are very often a reflection of the interests of the "ruling class" or **bourgeoisie** (owners of the means of production), rather than a reflection of **proletariat** (worker class) interests. Early **"instrumentalist"** Marxists saw the state as a political tool easily manipulated by an organized ruling class. However, more recently, **"structuralist"** Marxists maintain that ruling class interests do not necessarily exert direct influence on the making and enforcing of laws. Rather, structuralists see owners' interests as reflected in the law because the economic well-being of a society depends on the overall development of the marketplace.[6]

Structural Marxists view the primary function of the state as ensuring the endurance of the social relations of capitalism, in which the profits from goods produced are returned only to those who own the means of production. This sometimes requires that different interests be served at various times in order to prevent the downfall of the economic system. At some time, there may be interests other than those of the owners of the means of production that have to be served. Even so, the owners may still be described as a "ruling class" because, first, the state will, in the long run, serve more of the owners' interests than the interests of other groups. Second, as instrumentalist Marxism would assert, owners have more political power generally than other groups, and can therefore more effectively pressure the state to serve their immediate and long-term needs.

Marxist criminological analysis has been aimed primarily at explaining common crimes committed by the poor. The initial view that poor people commit crimes of theft and violence because of a frustration with capitalistic conditions of exploitation and domination has been generally abandoned by Marxist analysts. Marxists, however, still hold to the basic belief that behaviors defined as criminal are committed by rational individuals as logical reactions to their alienation from the fruits of their labors. Individuals are said to act and think in ways that are consistent with their economic interests. This view might be applicable to occupational crimes by all strata of society—such as the underpaid employee-thief who steals money to buy food, the middle-class embezzler who steals to have a more affluent lifestyle, and the wealthy corporate decision maker who illegally fixes prices to survive in the capitalist market system.[7]

From the structuralist Marxist viewpoint, actions such as those that promote unfair competition or otherwise adversely affect free enterprise (such as price-fixing, trade secret theft, and insider stock trading) are harmful to the basic competitive foundations of capitalism, so they are outlawed. Price-fixing also is outlawed because it contributes to inflation. In addition to criminalizing behaviors that discourage a healthy marketplace, capitalistic interests tend to criminalize the behaviors associated with a sluggish labor force, such as drug use and vagrancy.

Owners of the means of production may be able to thwart, at least for the moment, the passage of laws that forbid, for example, exposing individuals to dangerous working conditions or unsafe consumer products. If such practices are considered counterproductive to capitalism in the long run, however, laws forbidding such conditions and products eventually will be passed, regardless of their immediate negative effects on owners' interests. A case in point is the Beef Inspection Act of 1906. Although compliance with that law cost meat packers considerable initial financial outlay, in the long run it increased the beef trade because the public no longer feared eating tainted meat.[8]

Some Marxist oriented writers argue that criminologists (and the criminal justice policies they help to create) tend to support ruling class interests in the long run.[9] Criminologists, they maintain, foster a self-perpetuating image of the "crime problem" that emphasizes common crimes committed by the poor and excludes "crimes of the powerful." The image is self-perpetuating because by concentrating on common criminals, the system reinforces such images as the only components of "the crime problem." This emphasis, coupled with middle- and upper-class offenders' alleged benefits from flexible sentencing policies, favorable conditions of court processing, and alternatives to incarceration, underlie Jeffery Reiman's adage that "the rich get richer and the poor get prison."[10]

Marxist analysis may help to explain why some occupational behaviors are legal and some are illegal. It may also aid in discovering individual motivations to commit occupational crimes when such offenses are "rational" responses to the deprivations of the capitalist ethos. The assumption that the legal system, in the long run, is responsive primarily to those who own the means of production constitutes the major point of difference between Marxist analysis and other legal conflict explanations. The other approaches emphasize the relationship between group power on the one hand and law formation and administration on the other, but they do not relate power primarily to capitalistic production. These other theories can be applied to any form of economically or politically organized society.

George Vold

A conflict approach that concentrates on legal power as a generic force, rather than as a force generated by capitalistic interests, is that of George Vold (1896–1967), one of the original modern conflict criminologists:

> [M]an always is a group-involved being whose life is both a part of and a product of his group associations. Implicit also is the view of society as a congeries of groups held together in a shifting but dynamic equilibrium of opposing group interests and efforts. . . . The end result is a more or less continuous struggle to maintain, or to defend, the place of one's own group in the interaction of groups, always with due attention to the possibility of improving its relative status and position. Conflict is viewed, therefore, as one of the principal and essential social processes upon which the continuing on-going of society depends. . . . Groups come into conflict with one another as the interests and purposes they serve tend to overlap, encroach on one another, and become competitive. . . . The logical outcome of group conflict should be, on the one hand, conquest and victory for one side with utter defeat and destruction or subjugation for the other side; or, on the other hand, something less conclusive and decisive, a stalemate of compromise and withdrawal to terminate the conflict with no final settlement of the issues involved. . . . The group that will survive and avoid having to go down in defeat is the one strong enough to force some compromise settlement of the issues in conflict.[11]

According to Vold, then, it is the struggle among **group interests** and the compromise of their positions that constitute the dynamics of the sociopolitical process. Accordingly, the group that controls the greatest number of votes in the legislature will pass laws that promote its interests. Those who hold a legislative majority win control of the police power of the state and can selectively apply criminal definitions.

Vold maintained that some criminality is a symptom of group alliance rather than individual antisocial behavior. For instance, professional labor group leaders sometimes commit crimes during strikes because of their quest for power for their group. Physicians who have a stronger attachment to a medical business group than to the profession may commit insurance fraud or perform unnecessary surgery. Fixing prices in an industry may be caused by alliance to the group that seeks corporate survival. Burglary, bribery, and obstruction of justice were committed in the

Watergate scandal to further the interests of the group to reelect President Nixon—its members believed that the ends justified the means.

Foremost, Vold's group conflict conception, anticipated by Sutherland with his emphasis on formal organization of white-collar crime,[12] explains why many meretricious actions of big business have not been censured by criminalization—big-business groups control the legislative process more effectively than groups that oppose them. On the other hand, actions by big-business groups that have been criminalized by consumer and employee protection laws show that labor and consumer groups have more effectively won in the legislature.

Austin Turk

Austin Turk's[13] conflict analysis is different from those of Marx and Vold in that it does not focus on the dynamics of statutory enactment. Rather, Turk concentrates on what happens between a government and the people it governs after rule has been established and laws have been passed. He concentrates on the enforcement of law by specifying the relative probabilities that authorities will **criminalize**—prosecute and convict particular law violators.

Turk maintains that the extent to which enforcement officials believe in the validity of a law is the most important factor promoting the prosecution and conviction of criminals. He makes a distinction between **lower-level enforcers** (e.g., police and regulatory agency investigators) and **higher-level enforcers** (e.g., prosecutors and judges). If both levels of enforcers consider a law important, then deprivations to its violators (arrest, conviction, punishment) are extremely likely. However, if lower-level enforcers believe legal violations worth citing but higher-level enforcers do not, then arrest rates will be high and conviction and punishment rates will be low. The opposite (low arrest rates and high punishment rates) will occur if judges and prosecutors believe in the validity of the law but the police do not. Turk was anticipated on this point by Sutherland, who stated: "[S]tatutes . . . have little importance in the control of business behavior unless they are supported by an administration which is intent on stopping the illegal behavior."[14]

Turk's emphasis is particularly relevant to occupational criminalization, because much of the occupational behavior criminalized by officials representing government agencies is based solely on their decisions to invoke administrative law in a particular case. This not only means that criminalization is a function of the resources available to such agencies to identify offenders, but also that criminalization is discretionary. In many cases, of course, criminalization of occupational behavior is warranted, such as in the willful violation of environmental pollution or price-fixing laws. In other cases, governmental agencies' discretionary criminalization of occupational behavior is capricious. James Bovard's book, *Lost Rights,* is replete with examples of governmental whim, such as when the United States Postal Service threatened to fine an eleven-year-old Palm Beach, Florida, boy for violating the Service's monopoly on mail delivery when he placed advertisements for his lawn-mowing business in neighbors' mailboxes.[15] In another of Bovard's examples, the Equal Employment Opportunity Commission (EEOC) penalized employers because they terminated workers who had stolen from them or because they refused to hire known felons. The EEOC's reasoning was that because minorities are more likely to commit crimes, barring them from employment because of criminal behavior discriminates against them in particular. Such government criminalization policies were overturned by federal District Court Judge Jose Gonzalez, Jr., who termed them "ludicrous."[16]

Thus, for Turk, the process of criminalization by lower- and higher-level enforcers does not call crimes what they are. Rather, a behavior is not a crime until it is so defined by government.

Two major factors affecting the probability of prosecution in addition to the importance authorities attach to the norm violation are noted by Turk. First, prosecution is more likely if violators have little economic or political power. If violators have sufficient power leverage, they can effectively avoid prosecution because they can influence changes in the law that will assert their position, or at least thwart prosecution in a particular case.

Many industries have considerable economic clout and, therefore, considerable political power. However, less powerful and less sophisticated occupational criminals (such as employee thieves or individual tax evaders) lack the prerequisites to undercut attempts to criminalize them. This means that when the legal norms that these individuals violate are important to authorities, there is virtually no chance of avoiding criminalization.

Second, "realism in the conflict moves" also affects the chances of prosecution—the more realism, the less prosecution. It would be unrealistic for authorities to threaten to increase dramatically the enforcement of, say, worker safety laws, because doing so could provoke the industry into greater violation. Similarly, it would be unrealistic for an industry to ignore openly those safety laws, because such actions could cause authorities to assert their power by increasing enforcement.

Law behavior theories do not view criminality as a reflection of wrong human action; rather, they see criminality as a consequence of the actions by those who have the power to create and enforce the law.

We now turn to the bulk of our discussion in this chapter—individual theories of criminality that assume there are fundamental differences between criminals and noncriminals that are independent of how the law behaves. Nonpurposeful criminal acts (such as those violations of administrative law that do not require an intent to commit the offense), of course, are not explainable by any of these individual theories of criminality because they are based on accidents and mistakes rather than being committed by design.[17]

Explanations of the Behavior of Occupational Criminals

Deterrence

It seems best to open this discussion with the oldest criminological theory, deterrence. Deterrence rests on assumptions about the way individuals react to the threat of sanctions. The first systematic criminological attention to deterrence was by two eighteenth-century writers of the Classical School, Cesare Beccaria[18] and Jeremy Bentham.[19]

Deterrence theory presumes the same things as many economic theories: all humans are hedonistically rational in their behavior, seeking pleasure or profit while concomitantly avoiding pain or loss.

The foundation of deterrence is that lawbreaking (or other rule breaking) is inversely related to an individual's perception of the probability of negative consequences. By consistently rewarding persons for appropriate behavior and withholding rewards for inappropriate behavior, we teach people to expect certain responses. Such understanding derives from personal experience and from watching the fates of others.

In deterrence theory, the difference between criminals and noncriminals lies in the former's lower fear of perceived formal and nonformal consequences. **Formal sanctions,** such as a fine or incarceration, are governmentally imposed after conviction. **Nonformal sanctions** are all other negative consequences that follow being charged with a crime, such as humiliation or loss of a job. Even gunshot wounds or other injuries inflicted by victims defending themselves are seen as nonformal sanctions.[20]

Nonformal sanctions are often more feared than conviction or incarceration. Being caught for stealing company property may involve a minimal formal sanction (a short time in jail or a fine), or perhaps no formal sanction at all. But the nonformal sanctions may be more severe, producing for the thief: (a) loss of the job; (b) failure to receive a recommendation for future employment; (c) removal from the group of co-workers, with whom social activities may have been a source of enjoyment; (d) shame among family and friends; and (e) character defamation through others' gossip. Nonformal sanctions such as disbarment and delicensure by professional associations can be disastrous financially for criminals in the professions.

To illustrate the painful effects of nonformal sanctions, Mary Owen Cameron found that middle-class homemakers apprehended for shoplifting were more worried about others finding out about what they had done than they were about a fine or jail time. They were deeply concerned about the reactions of their husbands, children, friends, and neighbors to their predicament.[21] In another example, a business executive convicted in a major electrical equipment antitrust case said that he and his family had undergone tremendous strains that were unrelated to his formal sanctioning.[22] Nonformal sanctions often exist without formal ones, but the imposition of formal sanctions usually will trigger additional nonformal sanctions. Thus, deterrence theory includes perceived fear of both formal and nonformal sanctions, and, especially in the case of persons who have a respectable public image, nonformal sanctions may be perceived as most severe. Sociologists often refer to nonformal sanctions as "primary" sanctions and to formal sanctions as "secondary."

General deterrence refers to individuals avoiding a particular behavior because they are aware that others have undergone negative formal or nonformal consequences for that behavior. **Specific deterrence** (or "special deterrence") refers to individuals avoiding a particular behavior because they have personally experienced negative formal or nonformal consequences for such behavior, and they fear similar or more severe punishment. General and specific deterrence are separate concepts, but they invariably operate simultaneously—punishing individual *A* may generally deter persons *B* through *Z* while at the same time specifically deterring *A*.

To deter an individual generally and specifically, the probability of receiving negative outcomes need not be realistic; it need only be perceived as realistic. In other words, if a new employee believes there are hidden video cameras in the stock room, when in fact there are none, the person will refrain from stealing based on a perceived probability of apprehension rather than an actual one. The most important variable in deterrence, then, is the potential offender's *perception* about the probability of negative consequences.

There are three aspects of perceptions about the probability of suffering formal and nonformal negative consequences: (a) **certainty** (whether offenders believe they will be caught and receive negative consequences); (b) **celerity** (whether those consequences will occur swiftly); and (c) **severity** (whether those consequences are viewed as serious by the offender). Certainty and severity have historically been seen as more salient than celerity. According to deterrence theory, if potential offenders' perceptions of certain and severe negative consequences are high, they should choose not to commit the offense. Increasing guardianship of targets sought by criminals, of course, will increase potential offenders' perceptions that they will be apprehended if they attempt to obtain those targets.[23]

The more severe sanctions should be reserved for the most undesired behaviors; sanctions should be proportional to the harm inflicted. First, to punish disproportionately to the harm inflicted would be unjust. Second, purely from a deterrence standpoint, the most serious sanctions should be meted out only for the most harmful behaviors; otherwise, hedonistically rational persons may choose to commit the more harmful crimes because they will not perceive more severe outcomes for such behavior.

Many acts, however, are not based on the rational pursuit of pleasure and avoidance of pain. Moral people would not commit outlawed behaviors even in the absence of formal and nonformal consequences. (We shall call these persons **Group 1**.) And persons who commit a crime in the heat of passion or who otherwise have no regard for future personal consequences of such behavior (e.g., terrorists or "psychopathic offenders") would violate the law even if the negative outcome was perceived to be certain, swift, and severe. (We shall call these persons **Group 2**.) Therefore, Groups 1 and 2 are unaffected by deterrence—it is unnecessary to attempt to coerce those in Group 1 (because they would not commit certain offenses in any case) and any amount of fear cannot stop individuals in Group 2 from committing certain crimes.

Deterrence is only workable on those who would or would not commit a behavior depending on their perceived probabilities of the certainty, celerity, and severity of formal and nonformal personal consequences. (We shall call these persons **Group 3.**) We can expect a population to respond to deterrence only to the extent that its members are in Group 3.[24]

Groups 1, 2, and 3 are mutually exclusive. This means that, for a given offense circumstance, one cannot be a member of more than one group at one time. For each offense situation (e.g., murder, employee theft, forcible rape, unnecessary surgery, insider stock trading), and at a given instant, Groups 1, 2, and 3 have different sizes. A person may be in Group 1 for murder (morally opposed to it) but in Group 3 for employee theft (may or may not commit it, depending on perceived probabilities of negative consequences). Group sizes are not constant over time, because, first, people's states of mind can change and, second, the infants of today will in time enter certain groups for certain offenses.

Group 2 (those who commit crime without any regard for negative consequences) is extremely small in terms of those who commit occupational crime. Price-fixing, medical insurance fraud, political bribetaking, and unsafe consumer product distribution are not the result of uncontrollable behavior or compulsiveness. Only a few occupational crimes might be seen as a product of membership in Group 2, such as an employee thief suffering from so-called kleptomania, an alcoholic who drives a bus or subway car while intoxicated, or a child care worker who compulsively molests youngsters.

To determine whether a person belongs to Group 1 or to Group 3 for a given offense, one must ask whether the crime would be committed if there were absolute certainty that no negative formal or nonformal consequence would result. If persons would not commit the crime under such circumstances, they would belong in Group 1—they are opposed to the behavior independent of sanction threat. If they would commit the crime under the condition of zero perceived consequences, then they are in Group 3—the only reason they would not commit the crime is a perceived sanction threat. It is impossible to survey accurately the relative sizes of Group 1 and Group 3 for a given offense situation because many people who do not commit crimes would like to believe that they are in Group 1 when in fact they may be among those deterred in Group 3.

Much of lawful occupational behavior is attributable to the morality of persons in Group 1. Any lawful occupational behavior not traceable to morality must involve persons in Group 3 who have been deterred. Unlawful occupational behavior (except those few instances by persons in Group 2) is committed by persons in Group 3 who have not been deterred.

The size of Group 3 is very likely larger for occupational crimes than for many "common" crimes, because occupational violations (unlike rape, assault, or drug use) are most often the result of calculated risks that seek to increase financial benefits. The vast majority of persons who commit occupational crimes seem to do so after considering the certainty, celerity, and severity of the formal and nonformal consequences. The Ford Company's decision not to install safer gas tanks in Pintos because the litigation costs from burn death lawsuits were calculated to be less expensive in the long run epitomizes this rationality,[25] although most offenders simply have a "gut feeling" about the repercussions from a crime.[26] Because almost all persons who plan to commit an occupational crime are in Group 3, almost all occupational criminals are potentially deterrable. Of course, what sanctions are sufficient to deter them remains an empirical question.

Occupational criminals should perceive a greater severity of punishment for their offenses than do street criminals because occupational offenders usually have more investment in the social order (job, respectability, education, career), and therefore perceive that they have more to lose if caught. If the formal and nonformal punishment systems can create perceptions among potential occupational criminals in Group 3 that their contemplated behavior will bring certain, swift, and severe consequences if committed, then deterrence has remarkable promise to reduce occupational crimes. Moreover, severe consequences for occupational crime not only have the potential to deter persons in Group 3, they also can strengthen the size of Group 1 and the intensity of its moral righteousness, because the very derogation of the behavior deems it morally wrong.[27]

There is absolutely no doubt that deterrence works—imagine how many occupational crimes would be committed if there were perceptions of zero formal and nonformal sanctions. To argue that deterrence does not work by pointing to the number of known criminals is to commit what Frank Zimring and Gordon Hawkins[28] term the "warden's survey fallacy"—it is fallacious because the argument ignores the vast number of persons who *are* deterred.

The question for deterrence, then, is the *extent* to which various threats of formal and nonformal sanctions deter those in Group 3. The three major forms of formal sanctions advocated as the most effective occupational crime deterrents are: (a) monetary penalties; (b) threats of adverse publicity; and (c) incarceration. The strategies are discussed in chapter 8.

Differential Association

As noted in chapter 1, when Edwin Sutherland addressed the American Sociological Society in 1939, he introduced the concept of "white-collar crime" and asserted that, unlike the poverty based theories of the time, his theory of **differential association** could explain why individuals in all strata of society commit crime. Sutherland believed that the best explanations of criminal behavior are those that relate factors "to a general process characteristic of all criminality."[29] Sutherland's theory of differential association attempts to identify that general process among all criminals, rich and poor alike. Differential association and its offshoots[30] have dominated sociological criminology for most of the twentieth century.

Differential association has two levels of explanation, which can be termed "general level" and "individual level." The approach first attempts to explain the criminogenic and anticriminogenic processes that occur on the individual level. Second, Sutherland identifies the broader social conditions under which these individual processes are more or less likely to take place (general-level explanation). Thus, Sutherland uses general-level conditions to predict the likelihood of individual-level processes occurring.

Individual-Level Differential Association

The individual-level basis of differential association is that persons are exposed to others' values, which teach definitions that are favorable or unfavorable toward the violation of law, thereby encouraging or discouraging the commission of certain crimes. Sutherland's individual-level theory, which is deeply rooted in the "symbolic interaction" perspective in sociology, eventually comprised nine points:

1. Criminal behavior is learned.
2. Criminal behavior is learned in interaction with other persons in a process of communication.
3. The principal part of the learning of criminal behavior occurs within intimate personal groups.
4. When criminal behavior is learned, the learning includes (a) techniques of committing the crime, which are sometimes very complicated, sometimes very simple; (b) the specific direction of motives, drives, rationalizations, and attitudes.
5. The specific direction of motives and drives is learned from definitions of the legal codes as favorable or unfavorable.
6. A person becomes delinquent because of an excess of definitions favorable to violation of law over definitions unfavorable to violation of law.
7. Differential associations may vary in frequency, duration, priority, and intensity.
8. The process of learning criminal behavior by association with criminal and anticriminal patterns involves all of the mechanisms that are involved in any other learning.
9. While criminal behavior is an expression of general needs and values, it is not explained by those general needs and values because noncriminal behavior is an expression of the same needs and values.[31]

In short, criminal behavior and noncriminal behavior are the product of learning through individual associations with those who can be termed "significant others," persons who have great influence on one's self-evaluation and who have great impact on one's acceptance or rejection of social norms. In the socialization of a child, for instance, the significant others usually include parents, teachers, and playmates. If a person is exposed to significant others who transmit an excess of values that promote illegal behavior, then he or she will become a criminal. On the other hand, if one is exposed to significant others who transmit an excess of values that do not promote illegal behavior, criminality will not result. These differences in associations constitute for Sutherland the major distinction between criminals and noncriminals. The term *differential association,* then, refers to the difference among significant others with whom one associates. Differential association does not attempt to explain why an individual has the associations he or she has, only the influence of such associations.

Associations with criminal and noncriminal significant others vary in frequency (how often), duration (length of time), priority (how early in life), and intensity (the force of the other to influence). Associations that occur most often, for the greatest length of time, early in life, and with the greatest influence are the ones that have the most important effects in shaping criminal or noncriminal behavior patterns. Simply associating with criminal or noncriminal influences is not the critical factor; rather, close personal associations have the greatest effect. Police and prison personnel who are constantly in the company of criminals are thereby rarely going to become criminals themselves because such associations are not influential on a close and personal level. The same associations may transmit moral influences unfavorable to the commission of some crimes, such as armed robbery and forcible rape, but favorable to the commission of other crimes, such as insider stock trading and tax evasion. Differential association implies that when an excess of definitions favorable to violation of law exists, the offender is less likely to feel remorse or guilt about contemplating or committing such violations.

The learning of criminal behavior includes the specific techniques for crime commission. This point has been attacked by critics who claim that it is not necessary to learn from others how to commit certain crimes—techniques can simply be invented. Stealing office supplies from employers, juggling books for embezzlement, or failing to provide legally safe working conditions need not be learned.

Sutherland used differential association as an explanation for all criminal behavior. For him, the theory would explain, say, why some juveniles commit delinquency and others do not, why some turn to burglary and robbery to gain money and others do not, and why some corporate executives fix prices and others do not. From Sutherland's perspective, delinquents, burglars, robbers, and price-fixers all have had associations that have given them an excess of values favorable to their law violations.

General-Level Differential Association

The general-level social conditions under which differential association results in crime were specified by Sutherland as constituting **social disorganization.** Social disorganization refers to a failure within a social structure to hold common rules of conduct, and it reduces the number of persons who are morally opposed to crime. Sutherland identified two types of conditions that reflect social disorganization: "anomie" and "differential social organization."

Anomie, or "normlessness," refers to a lack of or upheaval of conduct rules in a social structure. Sutherland believed it occurs during the uncommon periods in which the structure moves from one set of rules to a different set. During such transition, there is a breakdown of the former rules, and a failure to define and diffuse the new set throughout the structure. Sutherland specifies the American period of transition from governmental nonintervention *(laissez-faire)* to governmental intervention in the marketplace, which occurred during the period about thirty or forty years after the Civil War, as an example of occupational anomic social disorganization.[32] Before governmental regulation, the business social structure was based on essentially unencumbered competition and free enterprise. During the transition to governmental regulation, "businessmen passed through a period of uncertainty. . . . They were dissatisfied with the system of free competition and free enterprise and had no substitute on which they could reach consensus."[33] Because of an absence of consensus, businessmen were more likely to be exposed to occupational associates who encouraged violation of the new regulatory conduct rules. Eventually, as the business world moved toward more concretely identified regulatory rules, such differential associations were less likely to occur, as was criminal business behavior.

The most common form of social disorganization described by Sutherland—**differential social organization**—applies to a social structure characterized by a conflict in rules for conduct.[34] The conflict is between the prevailing law-abiding rules and the procriminal conduct rules subscribed to by some organized entities within the structure. Most persons will be law-abiding because they are organized around unfavorable attitudes toward violation of the structure's laws. Other people are organized around favorable attitudes toward violation of the structure's laws, promoting criminal conduct. Hence, differential social organization refers to the extent of difference among groups in a social system in terms of their organization around prolegal conduct rules. Juvenile gang culture, in which the commission of crimes is rewarded, is a good example of differential social organization.

An example of occupational differential social organization was found by Gilbert Geis in his classic study of the heavy electrical equipment industry during the 1930s, 1940s, and 1950s.[35] The major manufacturers in that industry specifically encouraged illegal price-fixing among their employees as a normal response to market pressure. Rewards in the forms of promotions and bonuses were given to those who met with their competition to fix prices. Price fixing was an "established way of life,"[36] and new employees entered into it as they would any other aspect of their job. Motives, drives, rationalizations, and attitudes favorable toward violation of antitrust statutes were learned by the offenders. As one of those convicted stated, "We did not fix prices . . . all we did was recover costs."[37] Another conspirator, responding to a U.S. Senate subcommittee, believed his actions were "[i]llegal . . . but not criminal."[38] These executives were not deterred by perceived certainty of formal sanctions (they did not believe they would be caught) or nonformal sanctions (they did not believe they would be ostracized for the behavior; in fact, they were rewarded, at least until they were caught).

By identifying occupational groups organized around conduct norms that are different from prevailing laws (that is, differential social organization)—such as doctors who defraud insurance companies, lawyers who overbill clients, and police officers who take bribes—Sutherland pointed to the probability of learning criminal attitudes from colleagues within those groups. Sutherland referred to business moralities that run counter to the law as the "informal organization" of occupational criminals.[39]

Problems with Differential Association

Differential association is intuitively very appealing as an explanation for criminality, but there are several problems when the theory is applied. First, although researchers such as Geis, in his previously cited analysis of the electrical equipment price-fixing conspiracy, showed that differential association was the root cause of the antitrust violation, others have refuted Sutherland's theoretical approach to occupational crime. Both Cressey[40] in the case of embezzlement, and Clinard[41] in the case of price regulation violations during World War II, found that association with criminal patterns and techniques was not a prerequisite for those offenses.

Second, it is impossible to test empirically any effects of differential association on the commission of criminal behavior. The crux of differential association lies in an excess of certain definitions toward violation of law. To determine which definitions are in excess, one must determine which of an individual's lifelong definitions are favorable and unfavorable toward violation of law, and then tally them. This is an impossible research task.[42]

Third, Sutherland did not come to grips with the crucial role of deterrence in an individual's choice of conduct. A person can be differentially associated away from crime because of exposure to significant others who teach the moral reprehensibility of certain acts. However, for those who have been given an excess of definitions favorable to certain kinds of criminal behavior, some will and some will not actually commit it, based on their perceptions of formal and nonformal sanctions. In other words, even if differential association can account for a person being morally unopposed to committing a crime, a given criminal behavior will depend on the amount of general or specific deterrence operating on the potential offender.[43] Sutherland neglected to address critically important deterrence postulates.

A fourth shortcoming of differential association is that there may be ways to learn about lawbreaking or law-abiding behavior other than from close associations. **Normative validation,** which refers to the moralizing effect of sanction threat, may also be an integral part of learning the rules of proper conduct.[44] Recall that the discussion about deterrence pointed out that punishment for a proscribed behavior not only has the potential to deter those in Group 3 who are deliberating about whether to commit a behavior, it simultaneously strengthens the morality (and perhaps the number) of those in Group 1 against its commission because punishment makes a statement about the unacceptability of the behavior punished.

The concept of normative validation is an important mechanism by which people learn about conduct norms, but it is not a part of Sutherland's emphasis on definitions about the legal code learned from significant others. While a great deal of normative validation is transmitted from significant others (through threatened or actual nonformal sanctioning), normative validation may also be transmitted from nonsignificant others (such as through threatened or actual formal and nonformal sanctioning).

Learning about conduct norms, then, is a combination of differential association with significant others and the extent of normative validation from nonsignificant others. Both strongly affect the learning of conduct norms, thereby influencing whether a person will be morally opposed to crime or be willing to commit it. If the latter is true, perceptions of formal and nonformal sanctions will ultimately dictate whether crime is chosen.

"Strain" Theories

Strain theory concentrates primarily on the financial motivations to commit crime. The major purpose of strain approaches, initially based on the work of Robert Merton,[45] is to explain the higher rates of crime in societies that are dominated by the pursuit of money and wealth.

In these societies social achievement is seen almost exclusively in terms of economic success. Such social systems do not reflect the "sickness of an acquisitive society," but rather the "acquisitiveness of a sick society."[46] The strain approach considers such social systems to be "sick" because they place a stronger emphasis on financial achievement than on conformity. They are characterized by an institutional structure dominated by the economy, and one in which noneconomic functions (e.g., socialization by church, school, and family) and noneconomic roles (e.g., low-paying but worthwhile life pursuits) are devalued.[47] Strain theory, then, sees the degree of domination by economic pursuit as the major explanation for differences in societal crime rates. People are bombarded with monetary status-enhancing definitions favorable to the violation of law.

The individual-level focus of strain theory suggests that people feel a "strain" because they cannot reach their financial goals through legal behavior. They therefore elect to employ illegal means to achieve their financial aims, a resolution more likely in cultures that place a greater emphasis on the ends than on the means. Onlookers are generally ignorant about how one's money was acquired (legally or illegally), and in either case it can be used to purchase the same goods and services.[48]

Financial strain is a very strong motivation, particularly for occupational criminals. Because of the extreme importance of financial success in America and similar societies, there is constant pressure to achieve wealth. The mere veneer of wealth is also important, as evidenced by the leasing of Rolex watches, imitation "belt beepers" and cellular telephone antennae, and expensive homes with particle board furniture. Financial goals need only be relative. Making $25,000 a year is a goal for persons in the lower economic sphere, while making $100,000 is an aim of those in the middle economic sphere, and making millions of dollars is a goal for the very rich and for large corporations. Strain, therefore, can account for the motivations of blue-collar employee thieves, middle-class embezzlers, and corporate crimes by the wealthy.

Lack of legal opportunity to reach corporate financial goals can also be a motivation for occupational crime. Financial success is the major criterion by which profit-seeking organizations are judged. Persons in the business world are in constant competition to make money. Diane Vaughan points out that business managers not only compete for economic ends, but also for the resources that promote achievement of economic ends (e.g., personnel recruitment, product development, land acquisition, advertising space, sales territory).[49] Such resources, she continues,

> may be constrained by the source, nature and abundance of the resource, by the behavior of other organizations in the environment in the roles of

> consumers, suppliers, competitors, and controllers, by individuals in the role of consumers, and by the resources already possessed by the organization and preexisting demands on those resources.[50]

Optimally, a company's managers want to achieve the highest social and economic position in the relevant marketplace. If that is not possible, they will strive to achieve at least a higher status than they have. Minimally, a company manager wants to maintain the firm's existing economic and social position. Even when an economic goal is reached, it is soon replaced with a higher one; there is no necessary limit to profit maximization. A scarcity of resources and an emphasis on constantly enhancing competitive position can create a strain for business managers. Such strain may motivate them to manipulate or secure resources illegally.

One of the long-standing criticisms of Merton's theory is that there are sources of "strain" in people's lives that go beyond the inability to reach socially valued financial aspirations. Robert Agnew has expanded Merton's original conception into a general strain theory that includes four **negative affective states:** (1) *failure to achieve socially valued goals* (this is synonymous with Merton's original source of strain, such as when society's emphasis on personal or organizational financial success cannot be met through legitimate means); (2) *disjunction of expectations and achievements* (such as failing to finish college or gain a promotion); (3) *removal of positively valued stimuli* (such as is caused by divorce, death of a loved one, or loss of a job from which one receives great enjoyment); and (4) *presentation of negative stimuli* (such as spouse abuse, family and peer conflict, unsafe working conditions, and other stressful life events such as environmental pollution and squalid surroundings).[51] All of these can, either individually or in combination, produce intense feelings of anger, disappointment, vengefulness, and depression.

In short, strain approaches generally point to an array of frustrations in people's personal or occupational lives, which supposedly cause them to commit crimes.

Strain theories, unfortunately, do not explain why some frustrated individuals choose to commit crime and others do not. Sutherland's ninth point of differential association succinctly illustrates this shortcoming of strain theories: "While criminal behavior is an expression of general needs and values, it is not explained by those general needs and values, since noncriminal behavior is an expression of the same needs and values."[52] For Sutherland, persons who perceive strain (either within themselves or within their employing organizations) have two options. They can either allow the strain to negatively affect their choices about how to behave (that is, commit crime), or they can fight it and maintain positive conduct patterns (that is, not commit crime). Strain accounts for the impulsion behind the criminal behavior, but not the choice to commit it. Some individuals have abilities to cope with life's frustrations better than others without committing crimes, and these coping mechanisms are very much a product of moral socialization. In short, persons who are morally opposed to a criminal behavior (because of differential association and normative validation) are not going to commit one, regardless of the "strains" they experience. For those who are willing to commit a crime, the effect of deterrence will explain whether they ultimately choose to violate the law.

Neutralization of Criminality

"Neutralization" theory offers another major explanation for occupational crime. **Neutralization** refers to employing a justification or excuse for a wrongful behavior before committing it, in order to alleviate guilt. Whereas differential association implies that law violators do not feel guilt for the immorality of their illegal behavior, neutralization theory assumes that many criminals do feel guilty. For such persons, neutralization of the wrongful behavior is necessary in order to commit the offense. They want to "have their cake and eat it too"—they want to commit a crime and still believe they are not a criminal.

The theory's originators, Gresham Sykes and David Matza, studied juvenile delinquents who seemed uncommitted to criminal values.[53] This seemed odd to them, because most theories of their day (mid-1950s), including differential association, tended to assume that delinquents were committed to an antilegal value system and had little or no remorse about their group-supported actions. Sykes and Matza identified a repertoire of "techniques of neutralization" employed by delinquents to counteract the criminal definition of their behavior and ease their guilt.

Five neutralizations were specified: (a) **denial of injury** (no harm was really done); (b) **denial of victim** (no crime occurred because the entity against whom the act was committed deserved it); (c) **denial of responsibility** (it was not the actor's fault); (d) **condemnation of condemners** (penalizers are hypocrites); and (e) **appeals to higher loyalties** (the act was done because of an allegiance to a more important principle, like loyalty to a group). Carl Klockars later added another neutralization, the **metaphor of the ledger** (there are many more good behaviors than bad ones on an individual's deportment balance sheet).[54] Klockars's metaphor of the ledger differs slightly from the neutralizations of Sykes and Matza because it admits that a behavior is wrong, but it nevertheless is a neutralization in the sense that it is an attempt to mitigate guilt. The concept of neutralization makes an intuitive contribution to the explanation of many kinds of occupational crime, because most occupational criminals are generally law-abiding and do not want to think of themselves as criminals.

The term *neutralization* should not be confused with the term *rationalization,* although the two have been used interchangeably.[55] Strictly speaking, criminal actions are neutralized by perpetrators *before* their commission in order to mitigate criminal perceptions of self. The concept of **rationalization,** on the other hand, is most commonly associated with Sigmund Freud's (1856–1939) ideas about repression. Repression is a defense mechanism by which the perceived wrongfulness of one's action, idea, or impulse is excluded or banished from consciousness *after* it occurs. Repression is a form of "motivated forgetting," that is, automatic and unconscious. Rationalizations, like neutralizations, also take the form of excuses, and are manifestations of repression. If the excuses described by Sykes and Matza and Klockars are invoked before the offense to avoid feelings of guilt, they are neutralizations. If the excuses are used after the offense to repress feelings of guilt, they constitute rationalizations. Of the two concepts, only neutralization is relevant to the causes of occupational crime because it occurs before the offense.

Research shows occupational criminals often justify their offending. When researchers record these justifications, however, it is invariably after the crime is committed. Thus, there is no way to determine whether the subjects used the excuses before their crimes (to neutralize the wrongfulness of the act), or whether the excuses were created after the crimes were committed (as rationalizations to avoid embarrassment). With this caveat in mind, we can examine various justifications for occupational crime.

In particular, occupational criminals seem to employ a "denial of injury." Donald Horning[56] found among employees of a large midwestern electronics assembly plant that well over one-third did not consider the pilferage of company property as theft. One stated: "People have a different attitude toward the company than they do toward each other or you. . . . They wouldn't come into your home and take thirty cents, but they will take from the company. They figure it's got plenty of money and a few cents don't mean nothing [sic] to them." Another said: "They've got plenty . . . they're not losing anything on what I take." In a study by Lawrence Zeitlin there were similar denials of injury expressed by workers discharged for stealing, such as: "It's not really hurting anybody—the store can afford it."[57]

Parallel denials of injury were claimed in Erwin Smigel's investigation of attitudes toward stealing according to a victim's size (small company, large company, or the government).[58] Most disapproved of stealing, regardless of victim size. But more disapproval was found for stealing from a small business than a large business or from the government. In the terms of Thorsten Sellin and Marvin Wolfgang,[59] Smigel's respondents were much less likely to condone **primary victimization** (victimizing discernible individuals or small groups) than either **secondary victimization** (a diffusely large company) or **tertiary victimization** (the community at large).

Smigel's respondents overwhelmingly said they would prefer to steal from larger business and from the government than from a small business. The following reasons were given by some of the respondents who preferred theft from these larger entities: "business can afford it most"; "business is insured against theft"; "business allows for theft by raising prices"; and "government can afford it." Based on these responses documented by Horning, Zeitlin, and Smigel, the inference is that denials of injury are more likely to occur when people perceive of victims as more diffuse.

The same is true for those who commit crime for the benefit of their corporation. Some of these organizational offenders claim that while crimes such as price-fixing may involve millions of dollars in victimization to consumers, the damage is so diffused that individual consumers experience very little loss.[60] Gilbert Geis has pointed out that it is for this reason that organizational crime is less infuriating to victims than is common crime—it hurts less to be victimized a little bit at a time over a long period of time than to be victimized all at once.[61]

"Denial of victim" may be used by occupational criminals when they feel a sense of injustice, such as employees who believe they are underpaid. Two of Zeitlin's employee thieves, for example, felt that their employer-victim deserved to be pilfered for not paying them enough: "The store owed it to me" and "I felt I deserved to get something additional for my work since I wasn't getting paid enough."[62] In his study of stealing among dock workers, Gerald Mars found that thieves defined their behavior as a "morally justified addition to wages." Using a "condemnation of condemners" rationale, workers saw their victims as "exploiters," from whom they were entitled to steal.[63]

Regarding "denial of responsibility," even before Sykes and Matza coined that term, Donald Cressey found that 128 of the 133 embezzlers he studied used variations of the neutralization that they were only "borrowing" the money.[64] Some examples are: "Maybe it was phony reasoning, but I was going to put [the money] back"; ". . . in my way of thinking, it wasn't embezzlement because I was borrowing it"; and "I did not plan to keep the money permanently, though I never thought much about just how I was going to get it back."[65] Michael Benson also observed denials of responsibility among a small sample of tax evaders: "I didn't cheat. I just didn't know how to report it."; and "My records were simply one big mess. . . . If I only had an accountant, this wouldn't have happened."[66] Corporate offenders similarly employ denials of responsibility as a defense to their infractions of obscure regulatory mandates, claiming that such laws are incomprehensible and too complex.[67]

Regarding "appeals to higher loyalties," persons who commit crime for the benefit of their corporation often have tremendous organizational loyalties, and may see their allegiance to the organization as paramount—"I did it for the company" is not an uncommon explanation. Benson documented the use of appeals to higher loyalties as a justification for tax evasion. One violator claimed he was only trying to save his employee-friends money on *their* taxes.[68] Perhaps the most classic (and most literal) appeal to higher loyalties by an occupational criminal is that of Marilyn Harrell, alias "Robin HUD," who admitted diverting to poor people more than $5 million in funds from the Department of Housing and Urban Development. She stated, "I justified my actions inwardly only by reminding myself that I followed a higher law in an attempt to ease suffering."[69] Embezzlers have also been known to use the "metaphor of the ledger" when they view their theft as only a single aberration in an otherwise law-abiding history.[70] And corporate offenders employ "condemnation of condemners" when they claim that regulatory laws constitute unwarranted government interference with a free enterprise system.[71]

Normative validation—the moralizing effect of formal and nonformal sanctioning—plays a significant part in the propensity to neutralize occupational crime. When there is an absence of normative validation, it becomes easier for people to believe that the criminal behaviors are not wrong. On the other hand, if formal or nonformal sanctions are imposed or threatened against occupational criminals, their ability to invoke techniques of neutralization will be diminished because emphasis is placed on the criminal nature of the behavior.

To summarize, neutralizers attempt to make themselves believe that their contemplated illegal behavior is not immoral. Among these neutralizers, some will not be deterred by fear of formal and nonformal sanctions, and it is they who neutralize and then commit the crime. The remaining neutralizers are deterred from committing the crime. This latter group, of course, can appear to themselves and to others as morally noncriminal (even though they are actually morally criminal, but deterred).

It should also be noted that there may be a point at which neutralization becomes differential association. When a person's moral ties with the legal norms are loosened because of a sense of nonresponsibility, then the individual is free to choose among a variety of actions, some illegal, some lawful. Further, as Vold and Bernard point out, after illegal actions are committed, an offender would be "motivated to continue committing them because he has learned the moral [neutralization] necessary to consider himself guiltless, and because he has learned the technical means to carry out the offenses."[72] If neutralizations are learned from significant others and invoked on a regular basis, it could be argued that the individual has been differentially associated into crime. Recall that the fourth proposition of Sutherland's theory of differential association states: "When criminal behavior is learned, the learning includes . . . the specific direction of motives, drives, rationalizations, and attitudes."[73] The reference to rationalizations was to reasons that justify illegal behavior (i.e., neutralizations).

Conspirators in the electrical equipment antitrust case are an illustration in point. They claimed that their actions were "illegal but not criminal," that they were only "recovering costs," that no one was "damaged," that they did not "know that the consumer was injured," and that the actions fell into a "grey area."[74] These excuses are products of internalization (through differential association in a price-fixing environment) of values that promote price-fixing. Rather than having to use neutralizations, the conspirators apparently believed that price-fixing was not inappropriate.[75] When reasons that make criminal conduct appear legitimate are learned from significant others and become internalized, they then reflect Sutherland's differential association—the moral line has been permanently rather than momentarily crossed. When reasons that condone criminal conduct are not internalized, and are used only sporadically to ease moral conflict, they are then neutralizations, and the moral line has not been permanently crossed.

Propensity-Event Theory

Propensity-event theory, the last to be discussed in this chapter, is unlike the others because it explicitly accounts for both morality and deterrence. Like deterrence theory, it assumes that the motivation for crime is part of human nature and that persons naturally would commit crimes at a very high rate if they were not otherwise restrained.[76] Propensity-event theory, conceived by Travis Hirschi and Michael Gottfredson, attempts to identify the factors that refrain individuals from criminal and other uncontrolled behaviors.[77]

Like differential association, propensity-event theory attempts to enunciate a general theory of crime. Propensity-event is allegedly "capable of organizing the facts about [any] crime at the same time it is capable of organizing the facts about all forms of crime."[78] Propensity-event theory has become what is perhaps the most controversial perspective now entertained in criminology.

Propensity-event discards previous emphases on types of criminality (e.g., white-collar vs. common; juvenile vs. adult; female vs. male) and concentrates on characteristics allegedly common to all forms of crime. As Hirschi and Gottfredson state:

> A concept of crime that will reveal attractive properties common to diverse acts presupposes a concept of human nature . . . [that is] motivated by the self-interested pursuit of pleasure and the avoidance of pain. . . . To be maximally pleasurable, events should take place immediately; pleasure is therefore enhanced by the rapidity with which it is obtained. . . . To be maximally pleasurable, events should be *certain* in outcome . . . and require *minimal effort* (emphasis in original).[79]

Propensity

The conception of the commonalities of criminal acts is the basis for Gottfredson and Hirschi's theory about the commonalities of criminals. For them, the tendency to commit crimes is based upon persons' "[propensity] . . . to pursue short-term gratification in the most direct way with little consideration for the long-term consequences of their acts."[80] Hirschi and Gottfredson refer to this personality propensity as **low self-control.** Individuals' self-control varies from very high (or little tendency for short-term gratification) to very low (great tendency for short-term gratification), and all of us fall somewhere within those extremes.[81] "Higher" and "lower" self-control, then, are relative positions on the continuum.

According to the theory, self-control is almost entirely a product of socialization, and self-control tendencies are very stable from early adolescence through adulthood. Parenting is seen as the major source for teaching morality. Morality comprises attachment to the feelings and rights of others and a belief in the legitimacy of society's rules. Its teachings encourage people to delay immediate gratifications. People satisfactorily socialized are more likely to be in Group 1 because they will be more likely to be morally opposed to committing crimes. They would also be more likely to resist impulses for crime caused by personal or organizational strain.

Thus, from adolescence onward, individuals with the lowest self-control commit crimes (and other acts of self-gratification) at the highest rate and individuals with the highest self-control commit them at the lowest rate. According to propensity-event theory, then, there is **stability** in tendencies toward self-control throughout one's life course.

The predictions of propensity-event theory are independent of other offender characteristics. Females commit crimes at a lower rate than males because a greater proportion of females have higher self-control. And, among females, those with lower self-control are more likely to commit crime than those with higher self-control. Further, males and females with the same degree of self-control are predicted to commit crimes at approximately the same rate.

Symptoms associated with low self-control are: risk-taking, or a quest for exciting and dangerous behavior; simplicity, or an avoidance of difficult tasks; low frustration tolerance; physicality, or a preference for physical rather than mental activity; immediate gratification, or impulsiveness (more concern with immediate pleasures than future outcomes); and self-centeredness, or looking out for oneself first and tending to blame oneself last. People who exhibit these symptoms are "relatively unable or unwilling to delay gratification; they are relatively indifferent to punishment and to the interests of others."[82]

Low self-control individuals commit property crimes because they want "money without work."[83] They commit forcible rape because they want "sex without courtship."[84] And they commit acts of violence because they have a low frustration tolerance and want immediate revenge without the delays associated with peaceful conflict resolution.[85]

Criminals are not likely to specialize in their offending, as some criminologists believe. Rather, they exhibit **versatility** in their offending patterns. Under certain circumstances, lower self-control individuals are likely to commit virtually any kind of act that feeds their immediate self-gratification: theft (shoplifting, embezzlement, bad checks, fraud, income tax evasion, or other property crimes), violence (stranger assault, spouse abuse), physically gratifying chemical use (e.g, alcohol, cocaine, marijuana, tobacco), and unsafe sex (with little or no regard for the possibility of unwanted pregnancy or sexually transmitted diseases). Low self-control individuals also are predicted to be more likely to have accidents (they are risk-takers), cheat on examinations (they avoid difficult tasks), gamble (it is exciting because of the risk), have lower employment and educational stability (they avoid difficult tasks, including perseverance), lack significant personal relationships (because they are self-centered), and have a poor credit and money-saving history (they are impulsive spenders). Note that many of these acts of self-gratification can contribute to a financial crisis for an individual, increasing further the motivations to commit property crime. In short, propensity-event theory explains many non-criminal acts of deviance in addition to criminal ones.

Propensity-event also does not attempt to explain those relatively few criminal acts that do not involve immediate gratification. Mercy killing by physicians is a crime, but it is not based on the self-gratification of the offender, so it would be outside the purview of the theory. The same would be true for political and religious protests and acts of political terrorism. Thus, propensity-event is an atypical general theory of crime in that it explains some noncriminal behaviors while at the same time not attempting to explain some criminal behaviors.

Event

The theory's predictions are dependent on two circumstantial factors surrounding a potential criminal event—opportunity and perceived sanction threat. For a crime to occur, the tendency for short-term gratification must be coupled with both physical opportunity to commit crime and a perception on the part of the potential offender that he or she is immune from at least immediate formal and nonformal sanctions. The absence of any one of these three conditions nullifies the theory's prediction that crime is likely to occur.

Perception of criminal opportunity may be based on socialization. For instance, passing unguarded property may be seen as either an opportunity to steal or a chance to make the owner aware of the situation. Making criminal opportunity physically more difficult (such as by installing locks), known as "target hardening," is likely to fend off low self-control offenders because overcoming such barriers may be seen as involving too much effort since such persons are easily frustrated and avoid difficult tasks.

If persons with low self-control are faced with an easy opportunity to commit a crime, their fear of formal and nonformal sanctions becomes the primary determinant of whether they will take advantage of that criminal opportunity. If alarms, video cameras, or other tools that increase the probability of being caught are known to potential offenders, these devices should increase their perceptions of apprehension and punishment. Gottfredson and Hirschi note, however, that persons with extremely low self-control may be concerned only with their immediate gratifications and therefore be rather indifferent to possible punishment. Perceived formal and nonformal sanctions may be the reason why some low self-control individuals engage in certain acts of crime and self-gratification (e.g., alcohol use, tax cheating) but not others (e.g., marijuana use, armed robbery). Deterrence is an integral part of the propensity-event theory.

Propensity-Event Theory and Occupational Crime

Our definition of occupational crime is consistent with that used in propensity-event theory—the offenses are treated as events that take place in an occupational setting rather than as characteristics (such as white-collar) of people employed in those settings. With propensity-event theory, differences in criminality rates (i.e., between occupational criminals and occupational noncriminals, between some occupational criminals and other occupational criminals, and between occupational criminals and nonoccupational criminals) are explained primarily by differences in self-gratification tendencies, assuming that opportunity and perceptions about the immediacy of negative consequences are held constant.

Gottfredson and Hirschi predict that the rate of occupational and other offending by persons toward the high end of the occupational spectrum will be lower than that by persons toward the low end, because selection processes inherent in the high end tend to attract people with relatively higher self-control, such as those with educational persistence and a willingness and ability to defer to the interests of others. In other words, as one goes higher on the occupational ladder, one is more likely to find higher self-control individuals and lower rates of offending. In support of this, studies show that "white-collar" criminals are half as likely as "common" criminals to have a previous arrest history.[86]

As one goes higher in the occupational structure, one is also more likely to find persons who have reached long-term goals because of their greater self-control. These in-hand achievements (such as an education, a career, a nice home, a respectable reputation within and outside of one's family) are held dearly, and such persons therefore are less likely to commit crime because they have more to lose by doing so. They perceive much greater nonformal negative consequences for their criminal behavior, and therefore would be more likely to be deterred from it.

One of the benefits of propensity-event theory is that it can be tested by if-then statements: "If there is less self-control, there will be more crime." It would be a tautological mistake (a circular argument) to treat involvement in crime and other acts of deviance as a measure of self-control because that would be saying that people who have low self-control engage in self-gratification acts; we already know they have low self-control because they engage in these acts. To avoid this, the theory must be tested by using differences in self-control levels (measured by personality traits such as physicality, immediate gratification, or risk-taking) to predict differences in crime rates and rates of involvement in other acts of self-gratification, holding opportunity for crime and perceptions of punishability constant.

Research must also demonstrate that people exhibit versatility and stability in their immediate gratification behaviors (both criminal and noncriminal) that are commensurate with their tendencies toward low self-control. While many studies have shown a versatility in offending patterns, Robert Sampson and John Laub's recent research indicates that the stability in one's tendencies toward low self-control may be reduced by **turning points** in one's life. These events can mitigate tendencies toward low self-control, such as joining Alcoholics Anonymous, getting a good job, or marrying a high self-control person. Sampson and Laub refer to these positive events as acquiring **social capital,** which promotes conventional behavior.[87]

Interrelationships among Theories

Box 3.1 should help the reader to appreciate the commonalities and differences among the various theories in the second part of this chapter (deterrence, differential association, normative validation, strain, neutralization, and propensity-event). Propensity-event states that morality (attachment to the feelings of others) is necessary before one can adhere to conventional values not to violate the law. Attachment also tends to force one to repress self-gratification tendencies. An inability or unwillingness to repress self-gratification tendencies increases the propensity to commit crime.

Perceived negative ramifications of formal and nonformal sanctions act as deterrents against occupational crime and also may act independently as normative validators against occupational crime. Normative validation increases beliefs in conventional values by reemphasizing that occupational crime is unacceptable. Normative validation also increases attachment to the feelings of others by demonstrating the wrongfulness of victimizing. And normative validation helps to counter neutralizations (which increase the propensity to commit crime) because it validates the wrongfulness of the behavior. Similarly, the extent to which one has a belief in conventional values is the extent to which techniques of neutralization are less likely to be invoked, since the techniques will be seen as an attempt to negate the legitimacy of rules.

Differential association states that significant others have the most influence in molding beliefs about conventional (i.e., law-abiding) values. A person is exposed from infancy to a unique variety of significant others who affect his or her beliefs about the legitimacy of rules and levels of attachment to the feelings of others. Thus, a person brings to any given job

BOX 3.1

Interrelationships among Theories about the Behavior of Occupational Criminals

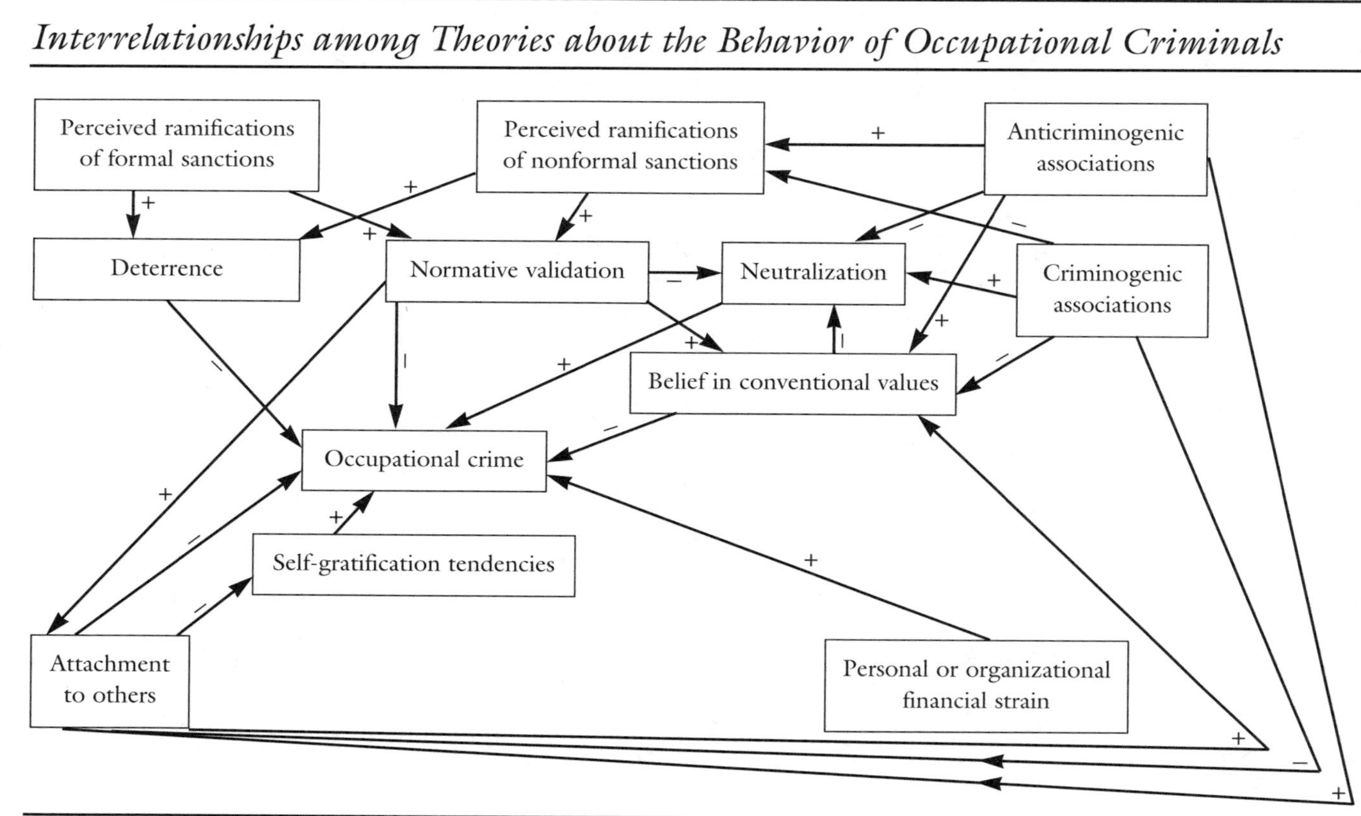

a preexisting set of beliefs that may or may not support certain conventional values to abide by the law and may or may not support feelings of attachment to others. It is only the extent to which postemployment associations alter preemployment value systems (about belief and attachment) that postemployment associations affect propensity toward occupational crime in a given job (such associations need not be job related). Propensity-event theory would argue that because self-gratification tendencies are relatively stable from early adolescence onward, the effects of any later-in-life associations probably have a minimal influence on shaping values.

Any lengthy social interaction, independent of whether it involves significant others, is bound to have at least some effect on an individual. Anticriminogenic associations are likely to relay the message that nonformal sanctions will be meted out for occupational criminal behavior. The opposite is true for criminogenic associations. Anticriminogenic associations also help to negate neutralizations about the wrongfulness of occupational crime, because these associations are not likely to accept the validity of neutralization. On the other hand, criminogenic associations may teach specific neutralization techniques.

Last, perceived personal or organizational frustrations may create impulses to commit occupational crime.

This is not a formal model; it was constructed only to show the various interactions among some of the approaches discussed in this chapter. Testable theoretical specifications have not been given.[88] It would be difficult to test this model because many of the individual components have simultaneous effects on other components; isolating these effects would be difficult. Moreover, all of the relationships in the model are unidirectional; there may be additional unspecified relationships that are reciprocal.[89] For instance, normative validation may increase belief in conventional values and the greater the belief in conventional values, the more likely that person is to be affected by normative validation. Despite its informality, the model should add greater understanding about the unique and interdependent relationships among the various components.

The first three chapters of the book have defined occupational crime, and discussed its measurement and causes. We shall now turn to in-depth discussions of the four types of occupational crime: organizational occupational crime, state authority occupational crime, professional occupational crime, and individual occupational crime.

Key Terms

bourgeoisie
proletariat
instrumental Marxism
structural Marxism
group interests
criminalize
lower-level enforcers
higher-level enforcers
general deterrence
specific deterrence
formal sanctions
nonformal sanctions
certainty of punishment
celerity of punishment
severity of punishment
Groups 1, 2, and 3
differential association
social disorganization
anomie
differential social organization
normative validation
strain theories
negative affective states
neutralization
rationalization
denial of injury
denial of victim
denial of responsibility
condemnation of condemners
appeal to higher loyalty
metaphor of the ledger
primary victimization
secondary victimization
tertiary victimization
propensity-event theory
low self-control
stability
versatility
turning points
social capital

Questions for Discussion

1. What are the differences between theories about the behavior of occupational criminal law and theories about the behavior of occupational criminals? Why is it important to distinguish between the two?
2. How do the legal conflict theorists Marx, Vold, and Turk differ in their approach to the explanation of the behavior of law?
3. What part does deterrence play in the following kinds of theories: differential association, strain, neutralization, and propensity-event?
4. Both deterrence and normative validation arise from the educative effects of punishment. What is the difference between deterrence and normative validation?
5. How might neutralization theory be applied to noncriminal dishonest behavior? Give five examples and the specific neutralization technique(s) associated with them.
6. In the discussion of Gottfredson and Hirschi's propensity-event theory, mercy killing by physicians, protests, and political terrorists were given as examples of crimes that the theory does not purport

to explain. Give five other examples of criminal behavior that is not motivated by immediate gratification.

7. How did Ronald Akers and his colleagues integrate differential association and deterrence?
8. As presented, deterrence Groups 1, 2, and 3 were mutually exclusive and exhaustive. Do you agree or disagree? Why?
9. How is Sutherland's theory of differential association related to Sykes and Matza's techniques of neutralization?
10. To what extent do the theories of Marx, Vold, and Turk account for deterrence?
11. Differential association and propensity-event theories are both general theories of crime. Discuss their major points of similarity and their major points of departure.

General Readings on Criminological Theory

Ronald L. Akers, *Criminological Theory: Introduction and Evaluation* (Los Angeles: Roxbury Press, 1994).

Daniel J. Curran and Claire M. Renzetti, *Theories of Crime* (Boston: Allyn and Bacon, 1994).

Jack P. Gibbs, "The Methodology of Theory Construction in Criminology," in Robert F. Meier (ed.), *Theoretical Methods in Criminology* (Beverly Hills: Sage, 1985).

Michael Gottfredson and Travis Hirschi, *A General Theory of Crime* (Palo Alto, CA: Stanford University Press, 1990).

Joseph Jacoby (ed.), *Classics of Criminology* (2d ed.) (Prospect Heights, IL: Waveland Press, 1994).

Stephen Schafer, *Theories in Criminology* (New York: Random House, 1969).

George B. Vold and Thomas J. Bernard, *Theoretical Criminology* (3d ed.) (New York: Oxford University Press, 1986).

Franklin P. Williams III and Marilyn D. McShane, *Criminological Theory: Selected Classic Readings* (Cincinnati: Anderson Publishing, 1993).

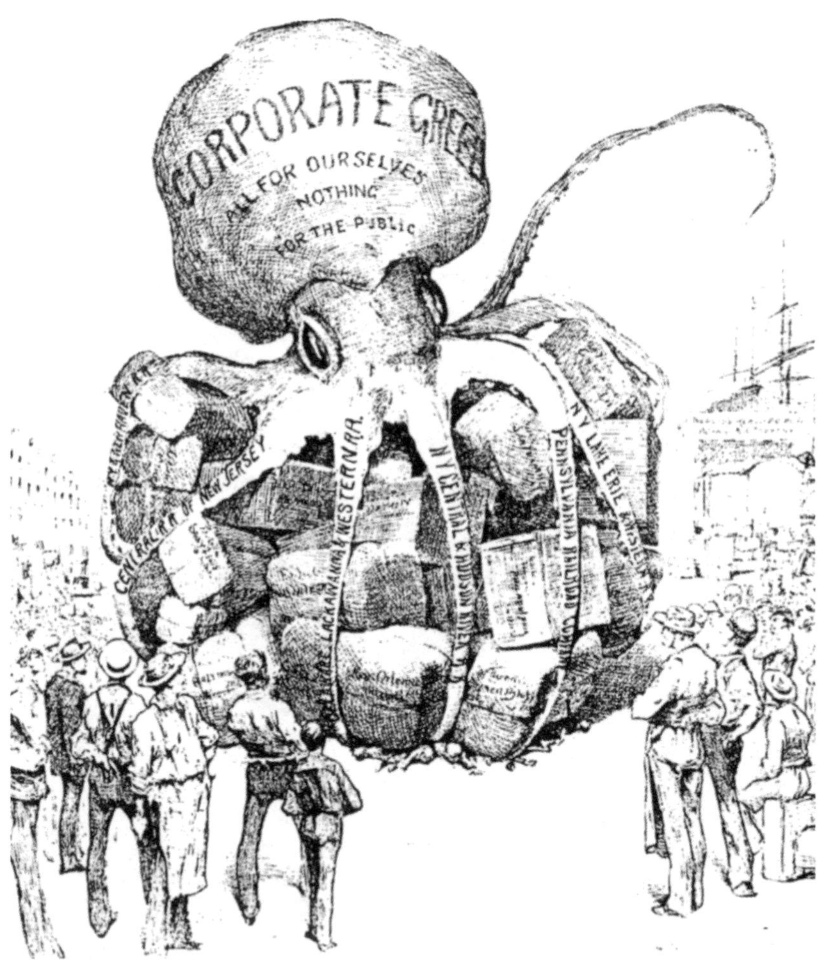

"All for Ourselves and Nothing for the Public" was the modus operandi *among nineteenth-century railroad tycoons, whose ruthless practices milked stockholders and deprived workers of jobs and security. According to group conflict theory, unethical acts by big business have traditionally been uncensured because of a powerful corporate "grip" on the legislative process.*

4 *Organizational Occupational Crime*

Most scholars[1] have used the term *corporate crime* in their study of what this book terms *organizational occupational crime*. Regardless of what they are called, the behaviors at issue are illegal acts intended to further the goals of the organization that are committed by employees of organizations. Most attention has been centered on larger, more complex commercial corporations,[2] but the term ***organization***, as used here, actually refers to anything that has been "established for the explicit purpose of achieving certain goals."[3] Therefore, an organization does not have to be huge or complex for its employees to commit organizational crime. A precise definition for our concept of "organization" is provided in federal law:

> a legal entity, other than a government, established or organized for any purpose, and such term includes a corporation, company, association, firm, partnership, joint stock company, foundation, institution, trust, society, union, or any other association of persons.[4]

Organizational occupational crimes can further the personal goals of the perpetrator-employee indirectly by outcomes such as salary raises, bonuses, and promotions, but its benefits accrue most directly to the owners of the organization. The extent to which a person owns an organization is the extent to which his or her crime for the benefit of that firm is *individual* rather than organizational. The rationale for this differentiation is that if only one or a few persons control the ownership and management of an organization (known as a **close corporation),** they *are* the organization, and crimes that further organizational goals are crimes that directly (rather than indirectly) benefit them.[5]

There can be knotty problems in drawing this line between individual and organizational crime. First, common stockholders, who are technically owners of an organization, rarely play any role in the organization's day-to-day operations, and it is therefore difficult to conceive of them as "individual occupational criminals" when offenses are committed by others for the benefit of the organization. Second, as noted in chapter 1, employees often own stock in their employing firm, and therefore would accrue benefits both indirectly (as employees) and directly (as owners). Third, persons have used their employing organization as a "weapon" to commit offenses that benefit them directly, as was true in many of the savings and loan crimes of the 1980s.[6] The best way to express the concept of "organizational occupational crime" is to regard it as referring to offenses committed by managers and employees *most directly* for the benefit of organizational owners rather than themselves.

Criminal Liability and Organizational Crime

That organizational crime involves both natural persons and organizations gives it a unique dimension that makes the assignment of criminal responsibility more difficult than in the other occupational crimes discussed in this book. There are considerable legal questions[7] about whether individuals or organizations should be held criminally responsible for crimes committed for the benefit of the organization.

Donald Cressey has argued emphatically that organizational crime is in all cases reducible to the actions of human beings.[8] Nicolette Parisi makes a similar point in reminding us of the adage that "guns don't kill people, people kill people."[9] Weapons, like organizations, are subject to the control of human beings. Hence, Parisi continues the analogy, "If [an organization] is like a gun, then there must be someone comparable to a triggerman."[10]

In contrast to this reductionist position, John Braithwaite and Brent Fisse maintain that, at least from a theoretical and a structural perspective, organizations act independently of their employees because: (1) organizations have intentions; (2) organizations have legal and ethical responsibilities; and (3) organizations can be punished for the crimes they commit.[11] In other words, an organization may be seen as a criminal actor in the sense that organizational crime is the outcome of a pattern of activities by interdependent parts that together constitute the form of the organization.

Thus, both Cressey's argument (that individuals commit organizational crime) and Braithwaite and Fisse's argument (that organizations commit it) have their merits.[12] From a legal perspective, however, the question of whether organizations or individuals commit organizational crimes is basically moot, since both are punishable.

Numerous legal statutes outlaw certain "common" criminal acts committed by individuals for the benefit of their employing organization, including criminal homicide, assault, and fraud. Because organizations are treated as "persons" under law, they, along with human actors, fall within statutory and regulatory languages that include phrases such as "any person," "whoever," or "anyone." Among the best known cases involving charges of criminal homicide against organizations are the 1978 Indiana indictment of Ford Motor Company (for marketing unsafe Pintos), the 1983 California indictment of movie director John Landis (for allowing unsafe working conditions), and the 1984 Illinois indictment of Film Recovery Systems Corporation (for allowing unsafe working conditions through arsenic esposure).[13]

Many precedents have affirmed the personage of organizations for the purposes of statutory criminal liability. A notable illustration is the Ford Pinto indictment, in which attorneys for Ford argued that the automaking organization was not a "person" because the statute in question read, "A *person* who recklessly kills *another human being* commits reckless homicide (emphasis added)."[14] Ford's lawyers insisted that "another" means one of the same kind, and therefore "person" refers only to another human being. The court rejected this line of reasoning outright because the general criminal code had explicit provisions for the prosecution of corporations, and had defined *person* to include corporations and other organizations.[15]

In addition to violating statutes that outlaw "common" crimes, both organizations and individuals can violate regulatory administrative criminal statutes. These laws generally forbid organizational acts such as restraints of trade, falsification of product research reports, food and drug adulteration, environmental pollution, unsafe working conditions, and unsafe consumer products. Sometimes, however, organizations are criminalized for nonserious activities, such as using overnight carriers for nonurgent letters, which is a violation of Postal Service law.[16] Such violations result in various consequences along with or in lieu of criminal indictment, including stipulations, injunctions, and cease and desist orders (outcomes discussed in chapter 1).

The rationale (also noted in chapter 1) for including nonindictment violations under the concept of "crime" is that they involve a legal infraction carrying an official punishment. As Sutherland put it: "This is evident both in that they result in some suffering on the part of the [organization or individual] . . . and also in that they are designed by legislators and administrators to produce suffering."[17] Although there are important differences between these sanctions and a criminal indictment (e.g., rules of evidence and proof, assumption of innocence), Sutherland argues that such differences do "not make . . . [them] categorically different from the violations of law by other criminals."[18]

Organizations and individuals civilly and criminally charged with statutory or other violations often plead *nolo contendre* ("I neither admit nor deny the charges"). Although this is essentially equivalent to a guilty plea, *nolo contendre* cannot be used to prove tort liability in civil litigations. Fear of such civil litigation and the financial exposure emanating from it, then, is undoubtedly the major impetus behind entering a plea of *nolo contendre*. In some jurisdictions, organizations and individuals are allowed to enter an ***Alford* plea**,[19] which is a guilty plea without admission of wrongdoing.

Respondeat Superior

An organization can act only through its agents, so organizational criminal liability must be vicarious. An organization has no existence independent from those it has given authority to act for it.[20] Accordingly, organizations are liable for crimes committed by their employees through the modern legal theories of **identification** and **imputation.** These concepts consider the organization responsible for the intent or action of its employees when such intent or action is to further organizational goals.[21] "Identification" presumes direct organizational liability when the criminal actors are the major owners of the organization.

"Imputation," on the other hand, presumes organizational liability when employees who are not major owners commit offenses. The primary doctrine by which organizations have been held legally responsible for their employees' actions is taken from civil tort law and is known as ***respondeat superior*** ("let the superior respond"). The rule originated in England in 1682[22] (although it is traceable to more ancient times[23]), and was meant to deter employers from escaping financial responsibility for the actions of their employees. *Respondeat superior* was first used in England in 1846 to justify a *criminal* indictment; it was first used for that purpose in America in 1852.[24] Since these early cases, organizations have been held criminally liable for the acts of their employees through *respondeat* *superior.* Modern theories based on *respondeat superior* impose both civil and criminal liabilities on organizations, and are very much based on the idea of deterrence.

The critical question becomes whether the acts and intent of the organization's employees can be treated as the acts and intent of the organization.[25] The American Law Institute's Model Penal Code, promulgated in the early 1960s, offered as the primary standard for organizational criminal liability whether the criminal conduct was "authorized, requested, commanded, performed, or recklessly tolerated by the board of directors or by a high managerial agent acting in behalf of the [organization] within the scope of his office or employment."[26] While this standard employs *respondeat superior,* it limits vicarious liability to the conduct of higher ranking employees.

The Model Penal Code's standard has been expanded by the courts to impose organizational criminal liability in situations in which the act and intent of an employee equates with the act and intent of an organization, regardless of the rank of the employee.[27] In other words, whether the person was acting on behalf of the organization is the only relevant criterion. The rationale given by the courts in rejecting the high positional requirement in the Model Penal Code standard is that crimes are not generally officially or formally agreed upon by higher ranking corporate executives, and that the lack of such agreement does not keep the criminal act from being an act committed by the organization.[28] Given the complexity of many organizations, authority to act on their behalf is necessarily accorded to many employees who occupy lower rungs on the organizational ladder. To exclude their behavior from organizational criminal liability (as does the Model Penal Code) would exclude a vast number of criminal actions. The critical legal question is whether the actions, in fact, were committed to benefit the organization in any way or as part of organizational routine, regardless of whether any benefit was actually realized.

Strict Liability

An organizational criminal liability issue closely related to *respondeat superior* is **strict liability.** Both principles allow for the punishment of individuals, including organizations, who may not have intended to commit an illegal act. Most criminal statutes require that the perpetrator have an intention to commit the offense. However, strict liability administrative civil and criminal statutes impose no requirement of intent on organizations or individuals. In essence, strict liability is blameworthiness without fault.

There are two basic purposes for imposing strict liability. First, strict liability supposedly encourages people to find out about the law, however esoteric it may be, and to follow it. In this sense, like *respondeat superior*, strict liability is supposed to act as a deterrent to a claim of nonresponsibility for the offense, and it precludes corporate executives from purposely insulating themselves from knowledge of their employees' activities. The second major justification for strict liability is that it simplifies the prosecution of offenses because intent, which is potentially a very complex issue associated with behavior occurring within organizations, does not have to be proved.

The 1975 U.S. Supreme Court case *U.S. v. Park*[29] essentially cemented the doctrine of strict liability (its precedent is known as the ***Park* doctrine**). John R. Park was the president of Acme Markets and was charged, along with Acme, with violating the Federal Food, Drug, and Cosmetic Act because his employees warehoused food in a place that was rodent-infested. Acme pleaded guilty but Park did not, asserting that although he was generally responsible for the entire operation of the company, he was not personally responsible for the illegal storage because he had delegated storage responsibilities in good faith to persons he believed capable. He was convicted of a misdemeanor and fined a nominal amount. The conviction was overturned by the court of appeals but reinstated by the U.S. Supreme Court. The Supreme Court relied on the precedent[30] that strict liability can be imposed when an offense is committed by a person who has a responsible share in the furtherance of the act that is outlawed. More specifically, the *Park* doctrine holds that a corporate official can be convicted of a crime if the officer's position provided an opportunity to ferret out, locate, and then stop a violation of a public welfare statute. That is, criminal liability exists if the corporate official *should have known* about the violation.

There are disquieting questions about strict liability offenses, however. The dissenters in *Park* (Justices Stewart, Marshall, and Powell) believed that the defendant may have been guilty of civil negligence, but should not have been convicted of a criminal offense since he was not personally culpable. Although the current case was a misdemeanor, it nevertheless set a precedent that strict liability can be imposed in all criminal cases, including felonies. Thus, without the conventional requirement for criminal conduct (one's awareness of some wrongdoing), persons can be sent to prison for long periods of time under the affirmation of strict liability in *Park*. This, dissenters argued, was patently unfair and wholly inappropriate given the meaning of a criminal conviction.

The renowned legal philosopher, H. L. A. Hart, also considers strict liability inappropriate.[31] Hart argues that it will be a deterrent only if potential offenders are aware of the law they are violating, a precondition often absent in strict liability. In response to the second purpose of strict liability—that it simplifies prosecution—Hart argues that criminal justice system convenience cannot be the determinant of whether a person is a criminal. Hart also considers strict liability morally wrong as a basis for criminal conviction, because, as the dissenters in *Park* asserted, a person should be criminally blameworthy only for acts the person intends. Though these oppositions to strict liability may constitute sound arguments, the courts have rejected them because they believe that public welfare supersedes the endangerment of individual rights.

Collective Intent

The notion of **collective intent** is a recent extension of imputation in organizational criminal liability.[32] It has been applied in the relatively few situations in which employees' collective actions constitute a crime but each person's individual actions do not. The concept of "collective intent" is particularly novel because it imputes an intent to an organization that never existed among its human actors. Collective intent may be seen as a unique combination of strict liability and *respondeat superior* in organizational criminal imputation, because, unlike traditional applications of these two concepts, no single action of an employee constitutes a violation.

To illustrate collective intent, in *United States v. Bank of New England*[33], the bank was convicted of failing to file a Currency Transaction Report. Such a report is required by the Bank Secrecy Act when any individual makes a cash transaction involving $10,000 or more at a bank.[34] One individual cashed several checks that did not individually, but did collectively, involve $10,000 in a single transaction. The bank claimed that because no particular employee was aware that the law was violated, the bank itself did not violate a known legal duty. The conviction was affirmed by the court of appeals because a corporation is considered to have acquired the collective knowledge of its employees and is liable for their failure to acquire such knowledge. It could be argued that collective intent crimes, in essence, punish organizations for having faulty communication networks rather than for knowingly committing an illegality.[35]

Some final points should be made about connections between the legal theories discussed here and the criminological theories discussed in chapter 3. As was emphasized in chapter 3, accidental organizational crimes or any other organizational crimes that do not involve human intent (that is, some strict liability and *respondeat superior* offenses and all collective intent crimes) cannot be explained by any theory about the behavior of individuals, because such offenses arise only because of a legal doctrine, and not because of purposeful actions on the part of those charged—the cause is completely independent of the individual. This reality adds credence to the position of Hart, the dissenters in *Park,* and others who assert that it is inappropriate to hold an organization or its employees criminally responsible for illegalities in which they played no part or did not intend to commit.

From the behavior of law perspective in chapter 3, however, the creation and application of statutes and legal doctrines become major foci of attention in the study of organizational occupational crime, because these provisions and ideas come to define which acts and entities are criminal. The establishment of the legal doctrines of *respondeat superior,* strict liability, and collective intent cannot be explained adequately by an instrumental Marxist perspective because the rules are inconsistent with the interests of economically powerful organizations. These legal doctrines are most applicable to the approach of structural Marxist theory—they are necessary to ensure legal compliance in a capitalist marketplace, which in turn ensures the survival of capitalism.

Federal Sentencing Guidelines for Individuals and Organizations

Throughout the 1970s, a great deal of attention was focused on disparities in sentencing—people who committed the same crime rarely received the same sentence. This disparity also produced many cases in which persons received very little punishment for serious crimes. The federal response to sentencing disparity was the Sentencing Reform Act of 1984 (Title II of the Comprehensive Crime Control Act of 1984), which established the U.S. Sentencing Commission. Congress's objective was to enhance the ability of the criminal justice system to combat crime through an effective and fair sentencing system. Most of all, Congress wanted honesty in sentencing, whereby offenders knew what punishments they were likely to receive. Congress also wanted uniformity in sentencing to promote fairness. The U.S. Sentencing Commission was established to review the existing practices of the federal law enforcement system and to create guidelines that were relatively concrete and equitable—the U.S. Sentencing Guidelines.[36]

The **U.S. Sentencing Guidelines for individuals** went into effect in October of 1987. Two factors determine an individual's sentence length: the offense level and the person's criminal history. The offense level is generally based on the harmfulness of the offense and the blame attributable to the offender for the crime in question. The criminal history is generally based on the extent of one's officially documented criminal past. If the individual has a long-standing criminal record, the incarceration length and amount of fine are increased substantially. Such enhancements were justified by the commission on the grounds that repeat offenders are more blameworthy when they commit subsequent offenses and that increased punishments are needed to deter them and to isolate them from society for longer periods.

Most felonies and Class A misdemeanors in the several volumes of the *United States Code* have been assigned an offense level (from 1 to 43) based on relative seriousness. Depending on aggravating factors of the offense (which make it more serious) or mitigating factors (which make it less serious), the level can be increased or decreased, respectively. The monetary value associated with the crime (e.g., amount stolen, pecuniary gain to the offender or pecuniary loss to the victim), the vulnerability of the victim, and the offender's role in the offense are some of the factors that will increase or decrease the base offense level. The extent to which the offense endangered public welfare (national security, public health or safety) would enhance the level of the offense. Whether the offender abused a position of trust or special skill in the commission of the offense is an aggravating factor and would also increase the sentence. Both *nolo contendre* and *Alford* pleas are considered guilty pleas by the U.S. Sentencing Guidelines, and such pleas are not treated as mitigating factors.

Once the offense level is finalized, the offender's criminal history score is calculated. The combination of the offense level and the criminal history level yield an incarceration range of, say, 18–24 months. Offense level and criminal history score also determine monetary penalties for a given offense or set of offenses—fines, the return of all criminal profits (known as **disgorgement**), victim restitution, and prosecution costs. The U.S. district court judge then sentences to any incarceration and monetary penalties within the ranges allowed. Probation for individuals is allowed when the original offense level is low or more serious offense levels have been reduced. Examples of organizational crimes to which individuals can be sentenced under the guidelines include price fixing, fraud against the government, tax evasion, and environmental pollution. There are many nonorganizational occupational crimes committed by individuals that are also federally punishable under the commission's guidelines; they will be discussed at appropriate points later in the book.

The U.S. Sentencing Commission was very careful to base its guidelines on **real offense sentencing**—the general conduct in which the offender engaged. For instance, an individual who files a false tax return for his or her employing organization conceivably could be charged with tax evasion, failure to pay tax, mail fraud, and perjury. Under the U.S. Sentencing Guidelines, the individual would be sentenced only for tax evasion because that was the "real offense" committed. Multiple counts based on separate criminal episodes are sentenced more severely, but not necessarily in a cumulative fashion.

The **U.S. Sentencing Guidelines for organizations** went into effect in November of 1991 and are also based on real offense sentencing. Because an organization cannot be incarcerated, the penalties under the organizational guidelines involve monetary punishments only, including fines, disgorgement, victim restitution, and costs of prosecution.[37] The organizational guidelines are philosophically similar to the guidelines for individuals in that they consider offense harm and organizational culpability, as well as previous organizational criminality, in determining the monetary penalty that is to be paid by the organization. Organizational punishment based on vicarious liability (i.e., *respondeat superior* and collective knowledge) is given in addition to any punishment meted out to persons who committed crimes for the benefit of the organization. Note that when persons in closely held corporations (those with only a few owners) are punished for their offenses, the organization often is not punished. Offense levels for organizations are based essentially on the same criteria as individual offense levels, including the inclusion of aggravating and mitigating factors. Probation is also possible for organizations, especially when necessary to collect a fine or to restructure the organization to prevent future offending.

The commission was very cognizant of the degrees of harm associated with various levels of regulatory violations. It devised four categories of increasing seriousness for regulatory violators. Beginning with the least serious, they are: (1) when an individual purposely fails to follow a regulation without knowledge or intent that substantive harm is likely to follow; (2) when the same failure may be accompanied by a significant likelihood that substantive harm will occur; (3) when the same failure actually results in a substantive harm; and (4) when the offender attempts to conceal the fact that a substantive harm has occurred from a regulatory violation. Unintentional regulatory violations for which organizations and individuals are responsible (e.g., strict liability and collective knowledge) would receive very little punishment under the guidelines. Thus, despite the courts' widening of organizational criminal liability to include *respondeat superior*, strict liability, and collective intent, the federal method for punishing individuals acting in organizations and for organizations themselves essentially uses traditional notions of criminal liability that concentrate on intentional behavior.

The guidelines not only result in more equitable punishments for like offenders, they also punish many individuals and organizations more severely who otherwise would have escaped such sanctioning. This is especially true regarding increased incarceration rates for individuals. The efficacy of these guidelines in reducing organizational misconduct will be discussed in chapter 8.

Criminogenic Organizational Structures and Processes

Edward Gross has asserted that all organizations are inherently criminogenic,[38] but not inevitably criminal.[39] Their inherent criminality is said to arise from the emphases on performance that are both internal and external to the organization—the organizational "strains" discussed in chapter 3.

Perrow sees two types of goals operating within organizations: (1) **official organizational goals,** or "the general purpose of the organization as put forth in the charter, annual reports, public statements and other authoritative pronouncements"; and (2) **operative organizational goals** that "designate the ends sought through the actual operating policies of the organization; they tell us what the organization actually is trying to do regardless of what the official goals say are the aims."[40] When organizations believe they will not be able to attain their operative goals through legal means, they might be motivated to employ illegal practices to reach those goals. The seeking of organizational operative goals has generally been considered the dominant motivation to commit organizational crime. Gross has asserted that "given a situation of uncertainty in attaining goals . . . one can predict that the organization *will,* if it must, engage in criminal behavior to attain those goals (emphasis added)."[41] This statement is a wholesale indictment, undoubtedly unjustified, against the morality of all those who make decisions within organizations. However, it emphasizes operative goal attainment as the primary motivation of those within organizations to violate the law.

Before presenting the following materials on criminogenic organizational structures and processes, it should be understood that spotlighting an inherent proneness to commit a crime when that crime may never occur can be likened to calling someone a "latent homosexual"—it is a meaningless assertion unless the imputed trait manifests itself through an actual behavior.

Criminogenic Organizational Structures

The specialized structure that accompanies departmentalization in larger organizations often creates operative goals for subunits that are different from the overall profitability goals of the organization. As Oliver Williamson has noted, because a subunit's concern with reaching overall organizational goals may be subordinate to its concern with reaching its own goals, lower-level managers may tend to maximize their department's interests rather than those of their organization.[42] This is due in part to organizations being likely to evaluate their subunits based on bottom-line performance. As employees come to realize this, they might perceive a greater inclination to use nonlegal means to achieve their subunit's operative goals.[43]

In addition to promoting an emphasis on departmental rather than organizational goals, specialized organizational structures at times produce what Gordon Tullock called **authority leakage.**[44] This refers to the idea that, as organizations become larger, there is less control over middle-level managers. Anthony Downs formalized this notion into a **law of diminishing control,** which states: "The larger any organization becomes, the weaker is the control over its actions exercised by those at the top."[45] Moreover, specialization isolates subunits from scrutiny by persons both within and outside the organization. Because specialization emphasizes subunit self-interest and diminishes external control and scrutiny, we might expect more crime in organizations that have more departmentalized structures. The fact that departmentalization in complex organizations allows middle managers the autonomy to make decisions independent of those in the highest organizational positions, you will recall, was an important reason behind court expansion of the *respondeat superior* standard found in the Model Penal Code to include the acts of lower-level managers.

This theorizing predicts that those acting in larger organizations (which presumably have more bureaucratic and more departmentalized structures) will commit violations at a higher rate. Testing this prediction, however, involves conceptual problems. Foremost is the question of whether it makes sense to compare large organizations to smaller ones since larger organizations conduct more business transactions and therefore would have greater opportunity to commit violations.[46] Second, it has been argued that the violation recording rate for larger organizations is higher because they are more visible and therefore more likely targets of regulatory enforcement.[47] This argument may be countered, at least in part, by the possibility that larger, more complex organizations may be better able to conceal violations from regulatory agencies. They also have greater resources to fight back, making conviction-conscious regulators less willing to take them on. These problems notwithstanding, Tullock's and Downs's assertions that larger and more complex organizational structures are more criminogenic because of authority leakage have not been strongly supported by research. The finding of one of the most impressive studies ever on organizational crime that the largest (and presumably the most departmentalized) firms, *relative to their size,* do not necessarily commit organizational violations at a higher rate[48] is most devastating to their predictions. Even among much smaller firms,[49] research does not support the idea that their size is directly related to the frequency of their legal violations.[50]

Criminogenic Organizational Processes

Organizational processes also can be criminogenic because they can provide social encouragement for illegal behavior. Sutherland's theory of differential association (discussed in chapter 3), or variants of it, have been used often by scholars to interpret organizational offending.[51] They generally hypothesize that organizational cultures supply the motives, drives, justifications, and attitudes to organizational employees that provide them with definitions favorable to organizational crime.

Before organizational employees can be influenced by their firm's culture, they must first perceive the organization as playing a meaningful part in their lives. Diane Vaughan has considered the several ways in which loyalty to an organization (and accompanying loyalty to the organization's operative goal attainment) is encouraged.[52] First, the organization tends to recruit individuals who are similar to the ones already there; it wants only those who possess the motivations, values, and skills that are consistent with organizational goals. Second, there are formal rewards, such as salary raises, bonuses, and promotions for those who most exhibit the traits of the "company person"—one who gives the organization top priority. There also are perquisites adaptable individuals can earn, such as swankier offices and company automobiles, more assistants, and exclusive parking spaces. Third, long-term commitment to the organization is encouraged by retirement benefits, profit sharing, and other forms of delayed remuneration. In fact, profit sharing allows the employee to have a direct piece of the pie. Fourth, many of the employee's social and recreational activities may be based on organizational membership and involve interaction with other members of the organization. Fifth, isolation from people and ideas outside the organization is achieved by frequent transfers and long working hours. Sixth, employee positions and knowledge may be so tied to the organization that employees are hindered from seeking commensurate jobs elsewhere. In short, the organization creates an environment that is conducive to loyalty by fostering a "dependence . . . that is social, as well as financial."[53] Moreover, one's status in the community is inexorably linked to the status and success of the organization for which he or she works. Thus,

> [o]rganizational processes . . . create an internal moral and intellectual world in which the individual identifies with the organization and the orga-

> nization's goals. The survival of one becomes linked to the survival of the other, and a normative environment evolves that, given difficulty in attaining organizational goals, encourages illegal behavior to obtain those goals."[54]

Christopher Stone described these attitudes as constituting the **corporate culture:**

> A desire for profits, expansion, power; a desire for security (at corporate as well as individual levels); a fear of failure (particularly in connection with shortcomings in corporate innovativeness); group loyalty and identification (particularly in connection with citizenship violations and the various failures to "come forward" with internal information); feelings of [extensive knowledge] (in connection with adequate [product] testing); organizational diffusion of responsibility (in connection with the buffering of public criticism); [and] corporate ethnocentrism (in connection with limits in concern for the public's wants and desires).[55]

The pressure that firms exert on their employees to commit wrongdoing is especially evident in situations of **escalated organizational commitment.** This is when persons in the organization have made a considerable investment to something they find extremely difficult to abandon, even if it may cause physical harm to others.[56] In addition to the time and money associated with the development of an organizational product or program, organizations and their employees also have emotions, egos, and reputations at stake. These are heavy investments that pressure organizational workers to neutralize any potential harm associated with their conduct.

A good example of how escalated commitment can pressure organizational employees into wrongdoing is found in the circumstances surrounding the *Challenger* space shuttle launch disaster in 1986. Diane Vaughan demonstrates that, under internal and external pressures emanating from escalated commitments to the space shuttle program, NASA had already routinely allowed several previous launches with dangerous spaceship structural flaws.[57] Thus, the go-ahead decision for the fatal *Challenger* launch in the face of potential disaster was entirely normal for the space shuttle program at that time. Similarly, Gary Rabe and David Ermann point to escalated commitment as a major pressure in the organizational concealment of tobacco product hazards, and Dennis Gioia points to it in the decision by Ford to market unsafe Pintos.[58]

However, whether organizational pressures ultimately will transform employees into organizational criminals necessarily depends on the moralities of those within the organization. Research consistently has shown that employees perceive business moralities to be dominated by management. Subordinates in organizations very often believe that their superiors pressure them to support illegal viewpoints, sign false documents, overlook superiors' wrongdoing, do business with superiors' friends, or commit other sorts of unethical conduct.[59] The research also has shown that top management, particularly the chief executive officer, is viewed as setting the ethical tone of his or her organization.[60] Although it is sometimes possible for lower level employees to commit organizational crime without the knowledge of their superiors, such instances are probably the exception rather than the rule. Research from the U.S. Sentencing Commission has indicated that in organizational crimes occurring in large, publicly held firms, at least 25 percent of the time it could be proved that top executives knew of their organization's criminal activity and in at least 33 percent of the cases, a manager knew.[61]

Executives concerned with immediate profits for their company may tend to put greater pressure on employees to commit unethical behaviors (including those that are illegal) than persons in top management who are more concerned with long-term benefits to their firm as a whole.[62] Quick-profit executives will feel as though they need to make money in a hurry for a variety of reasons, including making themselves attractive for more lucrative positions. Profit pressure becomes relevant to the explanation of organizational crime only to the extent that it is emphasized by management as a justification to violate the law.

In addition to setting the tone of the moral culture within an organization, executives' motives, drives, justifications, and attitudes, especially their procriminal ones, can permeate entire industries. Using aggregated counts, researchers consistently have found that there are certain industries in which crimes were repeatedly committed by executives.[63] This industrywide propensity to violate the law is an indication of Sutherland's concept of differential social organization discussed in chapter 3. In this case, differential social organization describes the diffusion of definitions favorable to the violation of law among executives throughout a particular business sector.

Sutherland addressed two major causes of such diffusion. The first is through simple differential association—executives' *close* interactions with those in other firms sometimes transmit procriminal values. This would explain why intraindustry differential social organization has been found both universally and regionally. Price-fixing conspiracies, for instance, have been described, literally, as a "way of life" that permeates certain kinds of businesses.[64] Regionally, it has been shown that certain violations are likely to be concentrated in certain locales, even though all organizations in the industry are subject to the same laws.[65] After all, local executives in competing firms often lunch and play golf with one another. And the same firm can provide multiple moral environments—for instance, differences in attitudes toward organizational crime between a home office and less centrally located satellites.[66] The point is that learning procriminal business attitudes through close associations with other executives may be localized as well as universal in an industry.

The second method by which the diffusion of illegal practices in a business sector takes place, Sutherland notes, is through mimicry

> when one firm devises a method for increasing profits, [and] other firms become aware of the method and adopt it, [and this will happen] perhaps a little more quickly and a little more generally if the firms are competitors in the same market than if they are not competitors.[67]

Harold Barnett explains that when nonviolating firms see their competitors gaining advantages through illegal behaviors, the former "may then adopt what they define as an industry standard of honesty, [justifying] their [illegal] action by the need to remain competitive."[68] Sutherland offers the following 1936 case in the automobile manufacturing industry as an example of this mimicry.[69] Studebaker (now defunct) falsely advertised that consumers could purchase cars at the "simple interest rate of six percent"; in fact, the financing plan involved a nonsimple interest rate of more than 11 percent. Shortly afterward, many other automobile manufacturing firms (e.g., Packard, Nash, Hudson, Chrysler, American, General Motors) adopted similar falsely advertised financing strategies. Sutherland cited similar occurrences in the automobile tire and food manufacturing industries.[70] A chemist involved in such fraud summed up contagion rather simply: "Since other firms were making extravagant statements regarding their products, we must make extravagant statements regarding our products."[71]

Both contagion and collusion, then, are often cited as the major reasons behind the concentrations of illegalities in certain industries. In both cases the result is the same—what Sutherland would characterize as industry executives who are "informally organized" around definitions favorable to organizational crime.[72] Such business moralities trickle down to middle management within firms captained by those executives.

The most critical question about ethical behavior within organizations is whether it is based on individual characteristics rather than organizational social processes. The two individual characteristics that have been shown to have a consistent relationship with crime in general are gender and age, and there is no reason to believe that this would not hold true for organizational crime as well. This perspective would be most consistent with the Gottfredson and Hirschi theory of propensity-event discussed in the last chapter. Specifically, males and younger persons would be predicted to commit organizational crime at a higher rate because males and younger persons are hypothesized to have a greater propensity than their counterparts (at the same place on the organizational ladder) to satisfy immediate gratifications, and this would be independent of occupational enculturation. Based on surveys of both business students and organizational employees, researchers have found that these predictions are supported very strongly.[73] The relative dominance of individual propensities over organizational culture is undoubtedly the most important research issue in the explanation of organizational crime.

To recapitulate, contrary to what many scholars believe, the fact that organizational structures and processes—and the attitudes they produce—can be criminogenic does not necessarily mean that crime is virtually inevitable within organizations. First, the extent to which a person's preemployment morality rejects the breaking of rules or the harming of others is the extent to which that employee will be immune to criminogenic organizational arrangements. Second, after entering an organization, persons will be bombarded with a variety of normative cultures generated by their immediate work groups, other professional associates, their organizations, and their general business sector. Organizational workers often are exposed to conflicting norms about the commission of organizational crime. When environments emphasize legal behaviors, socialization away from organizational crime is most likely to occur. In both the first and second instances, people are more likely to be morally opposed to organizational offending.

Third, if individuals are not morally opposed to committing organizational crime, they will weigh the personal benefits and detriments of such action. It is possible that, after consideration, their route to goal attainment may be directed away from illegal alternatives because of a fear of the consequences (both formal and nonformal) associated with the discovery of those behaviors. In other words, they may be deterred from the illegalities.

Fourth, organizational pressures to commit violations are not constant because they vary over time for each firm and each subunit within an organization. Fifth, because organizations function within interorganizational settings, organizational crime may be reduced by the multiple organizations that can contribute to its control. In particular, the actions of regulatory agencies, other organizations within the same industry, and consumer and labor advocate groups can promote normative validation and general deterrence, thereby discouraging organizational crime.

Thus, it is individuals' moralities, their choices, and the contextual variations in which those choices occur that affect the extent to which organizational structures and processes will ultimately be criminogenic. Crime in organizations can also occur independent of human choices to commit it, such as in the cases of strict criminal liability arising from occurrences that are unintended, including unavoidable accidents.[74]

False and Misleading Advertising

False and misleading advertising practices are harmful to both consumers and competitors. They victimize consumers by duping them into purchasing goods under false pretenses. They are harmful to truthful competitors because such practices cause consumers to buy others' products based on lies and deceptive assertions. Fraudulent advertising can run a gamut from college athletic violations (fans are sold tickets under the false impression that the team is playing fairly under the National Collegiate Athletic Association rules[75]) to unadulterated fraud (such as in the mislabeling of gasoline pump octane ratings, costing motorists as much as $600 million each year[76]).

In the late 1940s, Sutherland labeled the following well-known American products found in and around homes as having been illegally advertised in one form or another: Quaker Oats, Wheaties, Cream of Wheat, Fleischmann's Yeast, Knox Gelatin, Carnation Milk, Morton Salt, Welch's Grape Juice, Ivory Soap, Scott's Tissue, Schick Dry Shaver, Bayers' Aspirin, Phillips Milk of Magnesia, Absorbine Jr., Murine Eye Wash, Elizabeth Arden cosmetics, Hart Schaffner & Marx men's suits, Life Savers candy, Wurlitzer pianos, radios (Philco, Zenith, Magnavox), Hoover Sweepers, *Encyclopedia Britannica,* Buick automobiles, Goodyear tires, and Quaker State motor oil.[76]

Consumers are constantly bombarded with advertising. There are usually several brands of a product from which to choose, and manufacturers must convince consumers that they need *their* product and that their product does the best job for the price. False advertising involves claims that are simply not true (e.g., claims about the presence of an ingredient or the effectiveness of a product). Misleading advertisements, on the other hand, contain true statements that are considered to lead the prospective user to believe erroneously that the product will result in or contain something desirable.

Falsities and misrepresentations in advertising affecting interstate commerce come under the jurisdiction of the Federal Trade Commission Act of 1914 (Title 15 *United States Code (USC)*, chapter 2). Under this act, whether a firm's advertising represents "unfair or deceptive acts or practices" (Section 45 (a){1}) is usually determined by the Federal Trade Commission and subsequent court interpretations of the commission's actions. The Federal Food, Drug, and Cosmetic Act of 1938 (Title 21 *USC*, Sections 301–392) also has jurisdiction over false advertising.

It is acceptable to claim that your product is the "best" or the "finest," because this would be a matter of opinion. It is not acceptable, however, to assert falsely that your product "works better" than other products, because such claims are not a matter of fact. Some cases involve blatant falsities and are easily judged. For instance, milk producers were not permitted to assert that "Every*body* needs milk," because this is not true; they later changed their slogan to the more acceptable "Milk has something for every*body*." It is doubtful that the illegal slogan hurt consumers by tricking them into drinking milk when they otherwise would not have, but the false statement certainly hurt other beverage manufacturers, who were the major instigators behind the complaint. Some blatant falsities in advertising clearly do inflict harm on consumers, such as General Motors's 1950s' claim that there was safety glass in their automobile side windows when only the front windshields were safety-plated.[78]

The decision about whether a particular item constitutes **unfair or deceptive advertising** is the result of a subjective determination by the federal government. That determination is based on what the average person would understand from an advertisement, not what the government believes. According to the courts, "a statement acknowledged to be literally true and grammatically correct [may] nevertheless [have] a tendency to mislead, confuse, or deceive."[79] The psychology of implication in advertising is very tricky. To illustrate, the claim by the maker of Anacin pain reliever that the product reduced "inflammation that comes with most pain" was judged to be true but misleading, because one could infer that the product offers greater general pain relief than others.[80] Large manufacturers make extraordinary efforts to prove to courts that their advertising does not mislead (or that their competitor's advertising does mislead), usually by conducting tests and surveys that measure the reactions of groups of consumers.

Visual effect is important to advertisers of major products, and they often "mock up" their products for presentation by substituting other materials for the real thing. Photographing ice cream under warm lights is a problem, for instance, so other materials are substituted. Mock-ups become unacceptable only when they do not portray the product truthfully. An instance that has come to epitomize unethical mock-ups involved the Campbell Soup Company.[81] Campbell put marbles in the bottom of a soup bowl before filling it with soup so their advertising would suggest that the soup was so filled with solid ingredients that they are visible on the surface when the soup is placed in an ordinary bowl. Fortunately, there are private consumer-interest watchdogs to identify product advertising deceptions, such as the National Advertising Division of the Council of Better Business Bureaus, in addition to the government's Federal Trade Commission (FTC).

The following instances of illegal advertising appeared in recent newspaper stories:

> A Wendy's fast food restaurant in Philadelphia was fined $100 in 1994 for each of 960 hamburger patties it falsely advertised as weighing "a quarter pound"; in fact they were one-quarter ounce overweighed. The irony is that one of Wendy's recent advertising campaigns emphasized the slogan, "Where's the beef?"[82]

> Wal-Mart stores in Michigan falsely advertised lower price comparisons with competitors through in-store displays during 1993. For instance, Wal-Mart stated that one of their coffee products sold for $1.45 less than their competitors', but failed to tell customers that the Wal-Mart coffee contained 5½ ounces less coffee. In another example, Wal-Mart advertised a hand-held vacuum for $15 less than their competitor, but failed to tell customers that the Wal-Mart vacuum did not have attachments. The retailer promised to correct the problems.[83]

> Several manufacturers falsely advertised their products' environmental safety (e.g., "ozone-safe," "recyclable," "compostable"): Keyes Fiber Co. (Chinette Paper Plates), $100,000 fine in 1993; Proctor and Gamble (Luvs and Pampers disposable diapers), $50,000 fine in 1991; Bristol-Myers Squibb (hair spray, household cleaners, suntan lotions), $75,000 fine in 1991; Tetra Pak/Combibloc (juice boxes), $75,000 fine in 1991; and Mobil Corp. (Hefty plastic bags), $150,000 fine in 1991.[84]

> Three companies were forced in 1991 to change their product descriptions from "fresh" to "made from concentrate" under pressure from the Food and Drug Administration: Proctor and Gamble (Citrus Hill Fresh Choice Orange Juice); Citrus World, Inc. (Fresh 'N' Natural Orange Juice); and Ragu Foods Co. (Ragu Fresh Italian pasta sauce).[85]

> Mattress Discounters of Atlanta was fined $100,000 in 1990 by the state of Georgia for running 13 fraudulent ads over a two-year period. The ads included ambiguous sale percentages and unsubstantiated sale claims. In particular, the firm's claim that one could buy a "$1 box spring" with the purchase of a mattress was found to be fraudulent because the mattress price was inflated to compensate for the low cost of the box spring.[86]

> Prudential Securities was assessed more than $370 million in fines in 1994 based upon the firm's fraudulent involvement in the sale of its limited part-

nerships, in which Prudential misled investors about the safety and liquidity of the risky partnerships.[87]

Defrauding the Government

Organizations can not only defraud individual consumers, they can defraud all of us by overcharging for the goods and services they provide to the government and by tax evasion (underdeclaring income or overstating deductions).

The criminal penalties for defrauding the federal government by overcharging are covered by Title 18 *USC*, Section 287 (false claims) and Section 1001 (false statements). Each violation of either statute can be punishable by a five-year prison term and a large fine. Past episodes of overcharging the government for goods and services, particularly by defense contractors, have goaded Congress into passing additional legislation to curb such abuses and to help the government recover monetarily. The Truth in Negotiations Act (Title 10 *USC*, Sections 2304–2311) and the False Claims Act (Title 31 *USC*, Sections 3729–3711) were amended during the 1980s to widen and quicken government recovery. The Truth in Negotiations Act is a recodified and amended version of the Armed Services Procurement Act of 1962. The original civil False Claims Act was passed in 1863 in response to the fraudulent use of government funds during the Civil War. Recent amendments to the False Claims Act eased the burden of proof by the government, protected whistleblowers (see box 4.1), and authorized private parties to institute suits on behalf of the government. Congress also passed the Program Fraud Civil Remedies Act (Title 31 *USC*, Sections 3801–3810) in 1986, which created a process for the adjudication of smaller program fraud cases up to $150,000; both false statements and false claims are included.[88] According to U.S. Sentencing Guidelines, the minimum punishment for a false claim involving less than $2,000 in victimization is probation or up to six months of incarceration; the minimum fine is $500. As the false claim dollar loss increases, so do the incarceration and fine. A $10,000 false claim, for instance, requires at least four months in prison and a $1,000 fine.

Without doubt the most exceptional piece of antifraud legislation passed by the federal government is the Major Fraud Act of 1988, codified as Title 18 *USC*, Section 1031. It provides for up to a ten-year prison term and a $1 million fine for those who are convicted under it. To be within the scope of the act, persons must intend to defraud the government (including by means of false pretenses, representations, and promises) in contract work that totals at least $1 million. Both contractors and subcontractors are liable under the statute, and only the total value of the contract need meet the $1 million threshold. Moreover, the fine can be increased to $5 million if the gross loss to the government (or the gross gain to the defendant) is $500,000 or more. The $5 million fine can also be levied if the offense involves a conscious or reckless risk of personal injury, such as the use of unsafe products or the falsification of research data on products related to safety. The fine cannot exceed a total of $10 million for multiple counts of violations of this act, but it can exceed that figure when fines are levied under other statutes. For instance, the $10 million can be added to an additional fine totaling twice the amount of government loss or defendant gain. The statute of limitations for the Major Fraud Act is seven years after the commission of the offense, plus any other delays that are allowed by law.

The Major Fraud Act also protects **whistleblowers** (see box 4.1). *Whistleblower* is a metaphorical reference to a person who tells the government about an employer's illegal acts; whistleblowers are akin to street-level informants. To be protected under the Major Fraud Act, persons not involved in a fraud must first bring to the attention of their employer the allegedly illegal behavior. If the employer fails to make reparations to the government, the whistleblower can bring the crime to the attention of the authorities. After doing so, the informant cannot be fired, demoted, harassed, or discriminated against in any way. The act allows informants to seek relief through a federal court, including reinstatement at the same level, twice the amount of back pay (with interest), and litigation costs associated with the lawsuit, such as attorney fees. In special circumstances, the U.S. attorney general can make payments to informants up to $250,000, and can ask the court to pass this expense on to the defrauder as an additional fine. Law enforcement officers and other governmental employees are not eligible for this award if they discover the fraud in the course of their official duties. Informants who fail to inform their employer first about the alleged fraud are also ineligible, unless they can prove that doing so would have subjected them to extreme adverse consequences. The award cannot be given if the fraud was detected from public or governmental records, and any decision by the attorney general to refuse or limit payment cannot be disputed by the whistleblower. In one of the first big cases under the Major Fraud Act, VSI Corporation pleaded guilty in 1990 to falsifying inspections of aerospace fasteners, and was ordered to pay $18 million in fines and other settlements. Whistleblowers in that case received more than $2 million.[89]

Legislation such as the Major Fraud Act has grown out of the public's concern over defense contractors' inflated billings. The Department of Defense inspector general and the Defense Contract Audit Agency found that, on the average, almost half (47%) of the bills by ninety-five

BOX 4.1

Whistleblowing

In 1979, Karen Silkwood was killed when the car she was driving, shown here, left a road near Oklahoma City and crashed. The state highway patrol said she probably fell asleep, but the union at Kerr-McGee Corporation, a plutonium plant where Silkwood had raised the issue of unsafe working conditions, stated they had evidence she was pushed off the road. There are many incidents in which "whistleblowers" have met with death or physical injury as a result of exposing company crimes.

Whistleblower is the term given to a person who informs the authorities about the wrongdoings of an employer. In their book, *The Whistleblowers,* Myron and Penina Glazer describe these individuals as "ethical resisters."[a] The Glazers emphasize individuals' personal belief systems as the major impetus behind their decision to blow the whistle. Those who blow the whistle generally are not "malcontents, misfits, neurotics, nor radicals."[b] Those who fail to act when they observe crime or other unethical behavior in their organization (either by confronting the employer or informing the authorities) have allowed their indignation to become subordinate to the operative goals of the organization. (Recall our earlier discussion about how organizations strive to foster supreme loyalty among their employees.)

Robert Jackall, in *Moral Mazes,* lists excuses people use when they choose not to blow the whistle, including: your job is not to report something that your boss does not want reported, but rather to cover it up; operating on the basis of

(continued next page)

BOX 4.1

Continued

a moral code is inappropriate because it makes people uncomfortable, thereby eroding the fundamental trust and understanding that make cooperative work possible; one always can disclaim responsibility or resign rather than notify the authorities; and all organizations commit some crime.[c] Ignoring organizational wrongdoing seems to be rather pervasive, as evidenced in a survey done at the University of Wisconsin at Madison, which found that about half of 725 respondents did not report fraud, waste, and mismanagement that they observed, including that which victimized the company itself or other entities outside the company.[d]

The rationales for blowing the whistle have been promulgated by Norman Bowie: (1) the basis of the action is to prevent harm to others (economic, physical, or emotional harm); (2) authorities should be contacted only after all internal mechanisms for rectifying the problem behavior have been satisfied; and (3) there is reasonable documentation of the illegal behavior.[e] Based on these criteria, the Glazers interviewed sixty-four whistleblowers: professionals (thirty-six), government workers (fifteen), and white-collar and blue-collar workers (thirteen). Eighteen of their subjects were women, some of whom had blown the whistle in very important cases involving risks of physical harm. At the time the whistle was blown, two-thirds of the resisters were in their thirties or forties, eleven were in their fifties, and only a few were at the extreme ends of their careers (just beginning or almost retiring).

The Glazers' whistleblowers brought to light many kinds of deplorable organizational behavior, including unsafe conditions at nuclear power plants, medical research that was harmful to subjects, marketing of carcinogenic pharmaceuticals, bid-rigging and other fraud against the government, political bribery, inadequate pollution control by the Environmental Protection Agency, and dangerous medical service delivery.

Most of the whistleblowers suffered severe adverse consequences as a result of their decision to inform the public about their organization's wrongdoing. Retaliation against them by employers and others adversely affected by the whistleblower's allegations included: transfer to less sensitive occupational positions within the same firm, personal and sexual exploitation, dismissal from employment, and having a career ruined by "blacklisting" (being kept from finding a new job based on collusion among employers in an industry). These kinds of retaliatory actions, of course, often adversely affect the whistleblower's emotional stability and general quality of life.

Of greatest concern is the threat to a whistleblower's physical safety. The mysterious 1974 car crash death of Karen Silkwood, a nuclear plant worker who exposed unsafe handling of plutonium by Kerr-McGee Corporation, embodies the reality of potential physical harm to whistleblowers. In a recent case, two wom who worked at the Rocky Flats weapons plant in Colorado told the Federal Bureau of Investigation about safety problems there. They subsequently experienced purposeful nuclear contamination, sabotage of a personal vehicle, and the riddling of one of their homes by bullets. One of the women, after being contaminated with radioactive ash, was told by a co-worker, "That's what you get for making waves." And a plant manager was quoted as stating to employees of Rocky Flats, "Whistleblowers will be dealt with severely and completely."[f]

Federal laws have encouraged whistleblowers to expose wrongdoing by protecting them financially and threatening penalties against those who harass them, particularly employers. In addition to the Major Fraud Act, whistleblower protection provisions include the following: Toxic Substance Control Act, Comprehensive Environmental Response Compensation and Liability Act (Superfund), Water Pollution Control Act, Solid Waste Disposal Act, Clean Air Act, Energy Reorganization Act, Safe Drinking Water Act, Federal Mine Health and Safety Act, Fair Labor Standards Act, Occupational Safety and Health Act, National Labor Relations Act, Surface Transportation Act, and Longshoreman's and the Harbor Worker's Compensation Act.[g]

a. Myron Glazer and Penina Glazer, *The Whistleblowers* (New York: Basic Books, 1989).

b. James Bowman, "Whistle-Blowing in the Public Service: An Overview of the Issues," *Review of Public Personnel Administration* 1 (1980):17.

c. Robert Jackall, *Moral Mazes* (New York: Oxford University Press, 1988), pp. 109–110; Glazer and Glazer, *The Whistleblowers,* p. 111.

d. Tom Walker, "Whistle-Blowing Just Not Popular," *Atlanta Journal and Constitution,* May 10, 1990:D–2.

e. Norman Bowie, *Business Ethics* (Englewood Cliffs, NJ: Prentice-Hall, 1982). For a discussion of how the Glazers' subjects fit these criteria, see Glazer and Glazer, *The Whistleblowers,* p. 4.

f. Associated Press, "'Whistleblowers' Harassed, Quit Job," *Albany Herald* (October 9, 1991):14C.

g. For bibliographies related to legal remedies for whistleblowers, see: Glazer and Glazer, *The Whistleblowers,* p. 259 (n. 11); Steven Kohn and Michael Kohn, "An Overview of Federal and State Whistleblower Protections," *Antioch Law Journal* 4 (1986):99–152.

---

defense contractors involved overpricing.[90] Even the most respected organizations may have tried to defraud Uncle Sam. The state of Ohio, for instance, was sued under the civil False Claims Act in 1990 by the Justice Department for overcharging the army's National Guard more than $2 million in 229 instances related to the costs of labor, utilities, and materials at Camp Perry.[91]

Educational institutions apparently cannot resist unwarranted dips into the government's pocket either. In a 1991 scandal involving at least twelve universities, $14 million in overbilling for "research" costs was uncovered, including an antique toilet and a seventy-two-foot yacht illegally purchased by Stanford University with government funds. One school even charged the government for its president's wife's trips to Grand Cayman Island and Florida. Half of the Ivy League schools also were found to have overcharged, repaying $500,000 (Harvard), $720,000 (Yale), $940,00 (University of Pennsylvania), and $1 million (Dartmouth). The greatest disallowances were against Rutgers University ($4.8 million) and the University of Southern California ($3.1 million). The schools excused their gross overbillings by invoking a "denial of responsibility" justification—they generally claimed that the cheating was merely a product of errors and misjudgments.[92]

Criminal penalties for defrauding the government by tax evasion are covered in the Internal Revenue Service Code (Title 26 *USC*), Sections 7201 (tax evasion) and 7202 (failure to pay tax), each of which carries a maximum penalty of five years in prison and fines and costs of prosecution. Filing a fraudulent tax form is also cumulatively punishable under the false statements statute mentioned above (18 *USC*, Section 1001) and, if the mails or wires are used, mail fraud and wire fraud (18 *USC* 1341 and 1343, respectively). However, in practice, the U.S. Sentencing Guidelines punish tax offenders for tax evasion only. The amount of tax loss (excluding interests and penalties) determines the offense level. Incarceration of at least one month begins with a tax loss of more than $1700 and escalates from there. Tax losses of $50,000 carry at least a year in prison, losses of more than $325,000 carry at least two years, and so on up to losses of more than $80 million in taxes, which carry at least five years and three months in prison. Fines are additional, and those for organizations are more hefty than for individuals. Professional tax return preparers who commit or abet tax fraud are more punishable than others. If the offense involves both personal and organizational tax returns, the combined tax loss is to be used. Organizational employees who aid their organization in tax fraud are more or less punishable based on the extent to which they played an active role in the offense. When establishing these tax evasion sentencing guidelines, the U.S. Sentencing Commission believed that there would be many more tax evaders who would be incarcerated than during the preguideline period.

The commission also believed that the deterrent value of these greater punishments is warranted by the amount of unpaid taxes each year. It has been estimated that the forty-five thousand foreign corporations with American subsidiaries fail to pay as much as $50 billion in taxes each year.[93] Two-thirds of American corporations are believed to fail to report at least some of their income, resulting in a tax avoidance of almost

$30 billion yearly. The gap between the amount that American corporations owe the government and what they voluntarily pay nearly tripled between the late 1980s and the early 1990s.[94] An example of how American corporations cheat on their taxes is Georgia-Pacific, who pleaded guilty to criminal tax evasion in 1991 for attempting to fashion a $2 million land donation into a $24 million deduction; it was fined $21 million in criminal and civil penalties, back taxes, and interest.[95] In another case, the American Association of Retired Persons (AARP), a nonprofit organization, was forced to pay the Internal Revenue Service $135 million in 1994 based on a dispute over assessments on AARP's for-profit royalty enterprises.[96]

Antitrust Crimes

Antitrust offenses generally involve collusive unfair trade practices, including price-fixing, bid-rigging, discriminatory pricing, rebating, establishing trusts, and related agreements that threaten fair competition in interstate and foreign commerce. These crimes may harm only competitors, such as in the case of discriminatory pricing (charging less money for the same product to some vendors than to others similarly situated). With discriminatory pricing, consumers can actually benefit because the price break may be passed on to them, but they are driven away from purchasing the products of other vendors in the same market. Collusive unfair trade practices may also harm only consumers, such as in a retail price-fixing conspiracy by all firms in a highly concentrated industry. Price-fixing may also lead to inflation and discourage industrial innovation. Antitrust laws seek to redistribute economic market power when transgressions have been discovered. Research indicates that antitrust litigation has produced these intended effects, especially the approximately 90 percent of antitrust litigation that is instigated by competitors rather than the government.[97]

Collusive unfair trade practices are illegal primarily under Title 15 *USC,* Chapter 1 (Sections 1–50). This provision includes the Sherman Antitrust Act of 1890 (restraint of trade and monopolies[98]), the Wilson Act of 1894 (restraint of import trade), the Clayton Act of 1914 (different pricing to similarly situated buyers, stock acquisitions in restraint of trade, agreement not to use goods of competitors, and interlocking directorates), the Robinson-Patman Act of 1936 (discriminatory pricing to large buyers), and the Celler-Kefauver Act of 1950 (amended the Clayton Act to outlaw stock and asset acquisitions that "may" be anticompetitive). Additionally, the Federal Trade Commission (FTC) Act of 1914 also has provisions against unfair competitive practices, and its 1970 Magnuson-

Moss Warranties Act amendment increased FTC jurisdiction to additional matters concerning consumer protection. Finally, under the Hart-Scott-Rodino Antitrust Improvements Act of 1976, the Antitrust Division of the U.S. Attorney General's Office reviews premerger papers to decide whether a proposed amalgamation will affect fair market competition.

Federal antitrust prosecution is handled by the Antitrust Division of the Department of Justice. Individual states also have laws against unfair competition affecting intrastate commerce. The major federal antitrust law is the Sherman Act, which forbids any business behavior or conspiracy that is "in restraint of trade or commerce among the several States or with foreign nations" (Title 15, Section 1). Currently under the Sherman Act, based on increased penalties passed by Congress in 1990,[99] corporations are punishable by a fine of $10 million and divestiture; individuals face fines of as much as $350,000 and three years' imprisonment. Violators are also subject to civil liabilities for damages, including treble (triple) damages. It has been argued that increases in penalties have affected enforcement dramatically by (1) causing more defendants to plead not guilty and creating greater difficulty in obtaining convictions;[100] and (2) increasing penalties for convicted offenders who actually are not subject to the new higher statutory penalties.[101]

The provisions of the Sherman Act and similar legislation are vague and ambiguous, and therefore both businesspeople and the government at times report difficulty deciding whether a particular act constitutes a restraint of trade. However, more than a century of Sherman Act case law interpretation has rather strictly defined key terms, and objections about vagueness were rejected by the Supreme Court as early as 1913.[102] Although antitrust enforcement is discretionary, the Department of Justice claims that it seeks indictments only when there is a clear intent to price-fix, monopolize, or knowingly engage in other illegal predatory market practices.[103]

The first sixty-nine years of the Sherman Act saw only four individuals incarcerated for pure antitrust charges.[104] Twenty-two others were also incarcerated during that period, but were charged with other offenses in addition to antitrust.[105] Incarceration sentences for antitrust offenders have increased dramatically since then. The number of antitrust offenders incarcerated almost quadrupled during the first full year of the U.S. Sentencing Guidelines—from eleven in 1987 to forty-three in 1988.[106] The minimum sentence is six months in prison, and this is applicable only if the value of the commerce affected was less than $400,000. Offense severity and incarceration increase as the value of commerce affected increases. The fine is calculated for individuals at 1 percent to 5 percent of the value of commerce affected, but at least $20,000. For organizations, it is 20 percent of the value of commerce affected or the amount of pecuniary gain, whichever is greater, up to $10 million.[107] Recently, however, the use of incarceration for antitrust offenders seems to be declining. In fiscal year 1994, only six of eighty persons convicted of antitrust offenses were sent to prison, and their sentences averaged only three and a half months.[108]

Price-fixing in particular can inflict very serious financial damage. As an example, after a pharmaceutical manufacturers' price-fixing conspiracy on the antibiotic tetracycline was exposed in the early 1970s (involving Pfizer, Cyanamid, Bristol, Squibb, and Upjohn), the price per hundred (250 mg) tablets dropped by about 90 percent, from as high as $30.60 in 1955 to as low as $2.47 in 1974.[109] Civil damages awarded in the tetracycline cases exceeded $250 million.[110] Another price-fixing conspiracy in Seattle during 1955–1964, involving a few pennies on each loaf of bread, resulted in overcharges to consumers of approximately $35 million for the decade. If that conspiracy were to have operated nationwide during the period, Americans would have paid in excess of $2 billion more for bread.[111]

Scholars have analyzed general economic conditions over long periods of time to ascertain which circumstances contribute most to antitrust crimes. Most studies have found that while organizational financial performance is at best marginally related to antitrust behavior, changes in the general economy and industrywide financial problems have a much stronger relationship to antitrust.[112] In particular, high unemployment and general dips in stock prices are most associated with increases in antitrust offenses.[113] However, because the only antitrust crimes that come to light are those associated with enforcement actions, any conclusions about when they are most likely to occur are speculative.

Some recent violations (and alleged violations) of federal collusive unfair trade practice laws include:

> Baby formula manufacturers (including Gerber, Carnation, Mead-Johnson, Abbott Laboratories, and Wyeth-Ayerst Laboratories) were investigated in 1990 by the Federal Trade Commission because prices had uniformly risen during the 1980s. The U.S. market is worth about $1.3 billion each year, a third of which represents purchases by the federal government for more than 4 million low-income families under the Special Supplemental Food Program for Women, Infants and Children.[114]

> Cox Enterprises, a media giant, settled in 1991 with the Justice Department for $1.75 million in fines from charges that it violated the Hart-Scott-Rodino Act by not reporting its plans to acquire $101 million of Knight-Ridder, Inc. stock.[115]

The Justice Department began a probe of the U.S. automobile manufacturing industry in late 1994 because of alleged price-fixing on cars and trucks, particularly in the setting of costs for no-haggle "value priced" vehicles.[116]

In 1994, six airlines agreed to rules that prohibited price-fixing. While the Justice Department did not file criminal charges, it estimated that price-fixing had cost air travelers up to $1.9 billion from 1988 through 1992. During the previous year, nine airlines agreed to distribute more than $450 million to air travelers (in the form of coupons) to settle private antitrust damage suits.[117]

In 1991, U.S. West paid a $10 million fine for violating the 1982 consent decree that broke up the American Telephone & Telegraph monopoly. U.S. West, one of seven regional holding companies created by the breakup, admitted to four violations involving, among other things, discriminatory pricing and the offering of unauthorized services.[118]

Nintendo, a Japanese-based home video game manufacturer, paid $5 million in fines to New York and Maryland in 1991 because it had coerced retailers into not cutting the price of its game system.[119]

Borden, Inc. (and its subsidiary Meadow Gold Dairies) pleaded guilty in 1993 to rigging prices on milk sales to schools and military bases in Mississippi, Alabama, and Georgia. The Justice Department's probe culminated in Borden's agreeing to pay $5.2 million in federal fines.[120]

Six defense contractors pleaded guilty from 1989 through 1991 to a variety of criminal charges based upon their illegal efforts to obtain confidential bid information submitted to the Pentagon by competitors. One of those convicted, Unisys Corp., was assessed $190 million in fines, penalties, civil damages, and forfeitures stemming from illegal bid-rigging practices and other crimes.[121]

The American Institute of Architects agreed to a consent decree with the Justice Department in 1990 in a restraint of trade lawsuit charging that AIA attempted to prevent its 54,000 members from engaging in competitive bidding, giving discounts, and providing free services.[122]

In June of 1994, Premdor Corp., one of America's largest manufacturers of residential doors, agreed to pay a $6 million fine for price-fixing. The case arose from Premdor's attempts to collaborate with other manufacturers of residential flush doors.[123]

Unsafe Consumer Products

The federal government's first major effort to regulate consumer product safety was the passage in 1906 of both the Pure Food and Drug Act and the Beef Inspection Act. Muckraking reformers at the turn of the century provided the impetus behind the passage of these laws. Novelist Upton Sinclair was probably the most influential of these reformers.

Sinclair's *The Jungle*,[124] which was dedicated to the "workingmen of America," educated the public about the horrors of the meat-packing industry in Chicago. "For seven weeks Sinclair lived with the underprivileged, wretched aliens of the Chicago stockyards, and then returned to his home in New Jersey to write about what he had seen, heard, and smelled."[125] Sinclair's work vividly depicted the unhealthy labor and sanitation conditions of slaughter houses in "Packingtown" (as Sinclair called the stockyards) through the eyes of a young Lithuanian immigrant, Jurgis Rudkus. The gruesome details included ground poisoned rats used in meat products, hogs dead of cholera used for lard, the sale of steer carcasses condemned as tubercular, and, most dramatic of all, humans who occasionally fell into boiling vats and became part of "beef" products sold to the public.

Although only a dozen of the more than three hundred pages in Sinclair's novel were devoted to the horrors of the meat-packing industry, the book had a profound effect on public opinion. A familiar rhyme was parodied in the press after the publication of *The Jungle*: "Mary had a little lamb, and when she saw it sicken, she shipped it off to Packingtown, and now it's labeled chicken!"[126]

Sinclair, a socialist, tried to use *The Jungle* to publicize the undesirable effects of unchecked capitalism. Besides unsafe labor conditions and consumer products, the novel depicted prejudice, graft, and price-gouging. Fellow socialist and novelist Jack London wrote, "What *Uncle Tom's Cabin* did for the black slaves, *The Jungle* has a large chance to do for the white slaves of today."[127] The novel did more to inform the public about unsafe consumer products than rally the public against the oppressions of places like Packingtown. Sinclair later wrote, "I aimed at the public's heart and by accident I hit it in the stomach."[128] *The Jungle* was one of the major forces behind movements to rectify the consumer hazards of big industry through federal legislation. President Theodore Roosevelt, moved by *The Jungle*, ordered federal investigations of the meat-packing industry. Although ninety years have passed since that presidential order, many unsafe meat products still appear on grocery store shelves (see box 4.2).

BOX 4.2

The Jungle *Revisited*

Upton Sinclair in 1934.

Infamous cases over the past several years of unsafe meat products conjure up the sort of material Americans read in Upton Sinclair's *The Jungle*[a] ninety years ago. In May 1991, inspectors for the U.S. Department of Agriculture informed Americans that they have consumed "chickens leaking yellow pus, stained by green feces, contaminated by harmful bacteria, or marred by lung and heart infections, cancerous tumors or skin conditions."[b] Of eighty-four U.S.D.A. poultry inspectors interviewed by the *Atlanta Constitution,* sixty stated that they are so concerned about contamination that they do not themselves eat chicken; seventy-five stated that thousands of birds that are diseased, contaminated, or stained with feces are shipped every day; forty-seven stated that maggots, especially in summer months, infest cutting and processing machinery; and seventy stated that thousands of chickens are salvaged by cutting away visibly diseased meat and selling the rest (much of which is also diseased) as chicken parts.[c]

According to the Centers for Disease Control, millions of people become ill annually after eating food contaminated with salmonella or campylobacter, two bacteria that infect poultry. Several thousand die from these sources of food poisoning each year, especially the elderly, the very young, and those with weakened immune systems. Since 1970, the number of reported cases of food poisoning caused by salmonella has more than doubled, and as many as half of the cases are caused by tainted chicken. The public's increasing desire for low-cost, low-cholesterol poultry has given rise to high-speed slaughtering machines whose designs spread bacteria. Poultry industry executives admit that at least one-third of their processed chicken is contaminated. According to one U.S.D.A. inspector, the U.S.D.A. seal on chicken is "meaningless."[d]

In 1993, hundreds of children were sickened and one died after eating hamburgers contaminated with a strain of E. coli bacteria known as 0157:H7. The burgers were sold by Jack-in-the-Box restaurants.[e] In February of 1994, the CBS television show "48 Hours" ran an undercover videotape taken at the Federal Beef Processors, Inc. plant at Rapid City, South Dakota, which showed "a worker sharpening his knife on the floor" and "pus spurting from an abscess onto a boning table, which [was] then hosed down next to piles of meat."[f]

a. Upton Sinclair, *The Jungle* (New York: Vanguard Press, 1906).

b. Associated Press, "Make Sure Birds Cooked Properly," *Albany Sunday Herald* (May 26, 1991):9A.

c. Ibid.

d. Ibid.

e. Associated Press, "Espy Pledges to Upgrade Inspections," *Albany Herald* (February 6, 1993):6A.

f. Associated Press, "Meatpacker Fired after Helping CBS Film Plant," *Albany Herald* (February 20, 1994):7A.

James William Coleman[129] has traced the first identifiable consumer movement in America back to the publication of Stuart Chase and F. J. Schlink's *Your Money's Worth* in 1927. The book attacked deceptive advertising and dubious sales techniques, and called for scientific testing of consumer goods. In 1929, Schlink established Consumer Research, Inc., which began publishing *Consumer's Bulletin* to disseminate research on consumer products. A few years later, Schlink teamed with Arthur Kallett to produce *100,000,000 Guinea Pigs*,[130] which detailed the pharmaceutical industry's failure to test drugs. However, it was not until 1938, after more than one hundred people died from an untested sore throat remedy called Elixir Sulfanilamide (contaminated with di-ethylene glycol, which is usually used in antifreeze), that government regulation of the drug industry was strengthened.[131] Federal legislation then allowed the Food and Drug Administration (FDA) to ensure that products were safe *prior* to marketing.

Congress passed another Pure Food and Drug Act over a half century after Sinclair's muckraking novel. The 1962 law allowed the FDA to determine the *effectiveness* of drugs (rather than only their safety) before marketing. In 1966, Congress enacted the Motor Vehicle Safety Act, which, among other things, established the National Highway Traffic Safety Commission, which is charged with setting standards for the automobile industry and ordering recalls of defective vehicles. Ralph Nader, whose book *Unsafe at Any Speed: The Designed-in Dangers of the American Automobiles*[132] had just been published, was a major influence in promoting this automobile safety legislation.

The most important piece of recent consumer health legislation is the Consumer Product Safety Act, which was signed into law by President Nixon in 1972. The act established the **Consumer Product Safety Commission** (CPSC). Before the creation of this commission, there was no federal agency that could remove unsafe products from the market (other than products regulated by the FDA and the National Highway Traffic Safety Commission). The CPSC seeks to reduce the estimated 20 million injuries caused each year by 10,000 consumer products,[133] a quarter of which may have been preventable by better product design.[134] This commission is charged with setting safety standards on products marketed in the United States (except autos, tires, food, and the few other products regulated by other agencies), recalling or banning products it deems harmful, and prosecuting those who do not heed its orders. Penalties inflicted on individuals for violations can be hefty—as much as a year in jail, a $50,000 fine, and up to $1,250,000 in civil penalties (this amount was raised from $500,000 in 1990). Corporate monetary penalties are the same as for individuals and also include seizure of corporate assets. Activities regulated by the CPSC are found in Title 15 *USC,* Chapter 47.

According to Section 2064 of Title 15, it is incumbent upon manufacturers to notify the commission when they "obtain information which reasonably supports the conclusion that [one of their products] . . . creates a substantial risk of injury to the public." If a company becomes aware of injuries caused by their product and does not notify the commission, they can be assessed a civil penalty. The following are a few examples from the early 1990s of manufacturers who, according to the CPSC, failed to contact the commission even though they were aware of their products' danger: Wagner Spray Tech Corporation, $120,000 (facial injuries caused by the ejection of canister lids on power paint rollers); Graco Children's Products, Inc., $100,000 (babies' fingers were crushed or amputated in "stroll-a-bed" recline mechanism latches); Century Products Company, $50,000 (choking hazards in the horn of Roadster baby walkers); Amerex Corporation, $30,000 (inoperable dry chemical fire extinguishers); Russ Berrie and Company, $30,000 (child choking hazards on toy "Baby Bibi" bears); and Black and Decker (U.S.) Inc., $125,000 (dangerous electric weed trimmers). As one might expect, these manufacturers denied that their products were dangerous and claimed that a report to the CPSC was not necessary, yet they agreed to pay the civil penalties.[135]

There have been many egregious cases involving the willful distribution of highly unsafe consumer products that have received widespread public attention in recent years, including the sedative drug Thalidomide (which caused thousands of prenatal deaths and birth defects; see box 4.3);[136] the Dalkon Shield intrauterine device (which caused thousands of spontaneous abortions and other health hazards; see box 4.3);[137] Beech Aircraft planes (with allegedly known crash-causing defective fuel systems);[138] the cholesterol reduction drug MER/29 manufactured by Richardson-Merrell (whose executives pleaded "no contest" to charges of fraudulently hiding debilitating side effects such as cataracts and sterility);[139] and Ford Motor Company's Pinto automobile (known to be susceptible to rear end fiery crashes; see box 4.3).[140]

The following stories highlight some of the more recent cases involving the marketing of unsafe consumer products:

> In response to a 60-count federal indictment in 1991, Eastern Airlines, now defunct, acknowledged in court that it conspired with top managers to thwart federal investigators looking into allegations that employees falsified maintenance and safety records at New York and Atlanta airports. Eastern pleaded guilty to conspiracy and was fined $3.5 million.[141] That same year, Delta Airlines was charged with failing to inspect aircraft in a timely manner and waiting too long to replace critical components, such as engine blades on an L-1011.[142]

> In 1990, the Justice Department and the Consumer Product Safety Commission sued seven major toy distributors (including Toys 'R' Us, Child World, Illco Toy, and Lionel Leisure) for selling imported toys that were unsafe either because of their lead paint content or because their small parts could choke children.[143] In a similar case, the CPSC criminally indicted on eight counts Luv N' Care brand pacifiers and rattles, because they could choke babies that suck on them.[144]

> After pleading guilty to six felonies, a military contractor was ordered to pay $2 million in fines and settlements in 1993 for submitting falsified test results on battlefield radio equipment to the U.S. Army. The organization was convicted under the False Claims Act discussed earlier. Some of the radios sold by Aydin Corp. failed to work properly during the Gulf War, putting American soldiers at unnecessary risk while in combat (fortunately, the army was able to use back-up communications equipment).[145]

BOX 4.3

Corporate Violence against Consumers

A 1979 Ford Pinto burns during consumer testing following the Indiana indictment against Ford for marketing vehicles the company knew were unsafe. According to the Clinard and Yeager study, the motor vehicle industry is one of the three most chronic violators of laws pertaining to organizations.

The following provide details about three of the most infamous cases in which corporations knowingly marketed consumer products that were highly injurious, and sometimes fatal, to users.

Thalidomide. Thalidomide was first manufactured in the 1950s by the German company Chemie Grunenthal. It was prescribed primarily as a sedative. John Braithwaite estimates that ingestion of the drug by pregnant women resulted in eight thousand deformed babies (born with no appendages or blind) in forty-six countries and as many as 16,000 deaths at birth.[a] Thalidomide was never approved for marketing in the United States. FDA scientist Dr. Frances Kelsey refused to pass the drug, an action for which she was honored by President Kennedy. However, 2.5 million tablets were distributed to 1,267 doctors in the United States by Richardson-Merrell (of MER/29 infamy). The doctors gave the drug to twenty thousand patients, to whom at least ten "Thalidomide children" were born.

Grunenthal, which had ignored complaints about the drug and had lied for several years about the extent of its adverse effects, was charged with intent to-commit bodily harm in September 1965 by prosecutors in Aachen, Germany. After a six-year court battle, Grunenthal bargained with prosecutors to drop the criminal charges in exchange for $31 million in compensation to German Thalidomide children. Many other settlements were also reached, including a $550,000 jury award against Richardson-Merrell.[b] The lack of international communication about the problems of Thalidomide and the name variations under which the drug was marketed prolonged its period of infliction on unsuspecting patients.

Dalkon Shield. The "Dalkon Shield" was an intrauterine birth control device (IUD) sold by the A.H. Robins Company beginning in January 1971. The shield was touted as safe and effective. Seriously injured victims of the Dalkon Shield worldwide numbered in the tens of thousands.[c] Nearly all suffered infections known as pelvic inflammatory disease (PID), which killed at least eighteen women in the United States. Most of those who suffered the infection lost the ability to bear children.

The shield was also ineffective, causing a pregnancy rate of 5 percent (almost five times the rate claimed by promotional advertising). An estimated 60 percent of women in the United States who conceived with a Dalkon lost their unborn children, or about ten thousand more than would have done so had they been using other IUDs. Some women elected to have abortions, some suffered spontaneous abortions, and others suffered septic spontaneous abortions. According to the Food and Drug Administration, 248 women in the United States endured this latter form of abortion, 15 of whom died from them. In addition, hundreds of women who conceived while the shield was in place gave birth prematurely during the third trimester to babies with severe birth defects, including cerebral palsy, mental retardation, and blindness.

Robins distributed almost 4.5 million Shields worldwide, 2.2 million of which were implanted into women in the United States and 800,000 outside the country. Although the Dalkon Shield was officially taken off the market in the United States in June of 1974, it was used as late as 1980 in parts of Latin America (where there are fewer resources to treat medical complications related to the device). Many PID victims of the shield continue to suffer chronic pain and illness, often requiring prolonged hospitalization. By 1983, almost a decade after Dalkon was removed from the market, estimates of the number of women who still used the device ranged from a few hundred to a half million. After a recall program by Robins, in which Robins bore the expense for the removal of the Dalkons, almost five thousand women filed claims. In 1985, the A.H. Robins Company asked for reorganization under Chapter 11 of the Bankruptcy Code.[d] In 1989, a federal court approved the bankruptcy reorganization, and set aside $2.5 billion for distribution to Dalkon victims.[e]

Ford Pinto. The Ford Pinto is a particularly noteworthy example of an unsafe consumer product. The car model was involved in one of the few cases in which an

(continued next page)

BOX 4.3

Continued

organization was criminally indicted for homicide. According to Mark Dowie, in "Pinto Madness,"[f] by 1977 Pinto crashes had caused at least five hundred burn deaths to people who would not have been seriously injured if their cars had not burst into flames.

Before putting the Pinto on the market, Ford allegedly knew that a crash into the rear end of the vehicle would easily rupture the fuel system. But assembly line machinery was already tooled when this defect was found. To avoid the increased production costs associated with retooling, top Ford officials decided to manufacture the car with the planned gas tank, even though Ford owned a patent on a safer tank.[g] Ford's infamous memorandum about the benefits associated with a refusal to redesign the Pinto's fuel system projected a net savings of about $90 million—$11-improvement costs per vehicle for 12.5 million vehicles ($137 million) versus $49.5 million in damage suits involving 180 deaths, 180 serious burn injuries, and 2100 burned vehicles.[h]

This cold calculation demonstrated Ford's lack of concern for anything but profit. In 1978 one civil jury award to a Pinto crash victim was more than $125 million. Most of this award, which was reduced to $6.6 million in 1981, was based on punitive damages equal to the savings Ford would have accumulated for its decision to market the unsafe vehicle.[i] In the criminal trial, Ford Motor Company was indicted in 1978 by a grand jury in Elkhart County, Indiana, on three counts of reckless homicide. The victims—Judy Ulrich (age eighteen), Lyn Ulrich (age sixteen), and Donna Ulrich (age sixteen)—died in a fiery rear end collision a month before the indictment. Although Dowie's "Pinto Madness" unleashed a national consumer crusade against the large automaker, Ford was acquitted on March 13, 1980, of the three criminal charges after a ten-week trial and twenty-five hours of jury deliberation.[j]

a. John Braithwaite, *Corporate Crime in the Pharmaceutical Industry* (London: Routledge and Kegan Paul, 1984), p. 65.

b. Ibid., pp. 71–74.

c. Morton Mintz, "At Any Cost: Corporate Greed, Women, and the Dalkon Shield," in Stuart L. Hills (ed.), *Corporate Violence: Injury and Death for Profit* (Totowa, NJ: Rowman and Littlefield, 1988).

d. Ibid.

e. Associated Press, "Shield Victims Awarded Cash," *Albany Herald* (June 17, 1989):4B.

f. Mark Dowie, "Pinto Madness," *Mother Jones* (September/October, 1977):18–22.

g. Mark Dowie, "Pinto Madness," in Stuart L. Hills (ed.), *Corporate Violence: Injury and Death for Profit* (Totowa, NJ: Rowman and Littlefield, 1988), p. 14.

h. Ibid., p. 21; Francis Cullen, William Maakestad, and Gray Cavender, *Corporate Crime under Attack* (Cincinnati, OH: Anderson, 1987), p. 162.

i. Ibid., 164.

j. Ibid., 189–308.

Four officials of Bolar Pharmaceuticals were indicted on charges of lying to federal regulators on their applications for generic drugs, including those for heart conditions and high blood pressure. The company was fined $10 million for selling adulterated and mislabeled generic drugs. At the time (1991) this was the largest fine ever imposed by the Food and Drug Administration.[146]

In 1994, Food Lion grocery stores allegedly routinely sold outdated baby formula in eight Southeast states. Government inspectors removed 3,549 expired cans from 212 Food Lion stores. One can that was sold to a consumer group was 563 days overdue.[147]

Organizational Crimes against Workers

Unfair Labor Practices

The United States Department of Labor is the major enforcer of unfair labor laws, including those involving minimum and prevailing wages and overtime, worker discrimination, labor-management disputes, child labor, and migrant or immigrant workers. Criminal and civil charges are usually brought through the Labor Department's Office of the Solicitor for the alleged violation of various federal labor laws (e.g., Fair Labor Standards Act, Labor-Management Reporting and Disclosure Act, Vietnam Era Veterans' Readjustment Assistance Act, Urban Mass Transit Act, Immigration Reform and Control Act, and the Comprehensive Employment and Training Act). These laws, in the vast majority of cases, are designed to protect Americans at their workplaces.

A 1993 U.S. Department of Labor (DOL) report indicates that DOL forced employers to pay more than $160 million in back pay (76.5 percent of the amount considered by the DOL to be due) for wage and hour violations during that fiscal year.[148] Child-labor laws pertaining to the working hours for fourteen- and fifteen-year-olds have been a major DOL problem. Under the Fair Labor Standards Act, these children are allowed to work only three hours on school days (a maximum of eighteen hours in a school week) and eight hours on a nonschool day (with a maximum of forty hours in a nonschool week), and they cannot work before 7 A.M. or past 7 P.M. during the school year. Some industries are exempted from these time-of-day restrictions (such as newspaper delivery workers, farmworkers in certain states, and batboys and batgirls for professional baseball teams[149]). Many believe that restricting the hours in which teenagers can work is unfair to them and to their families, who may need the money. In 1990, Burger King Corporation, the fast-food hamburger chain, was charged with allowing fourteen- and fifteen-year-olds to work longer and later than legally permitted at nearly all of its eight hundred company-owned restaurants; it was fined $500,000.[150] During recent years, grocery store chains were major offenders against child labor hour-laws—in 1993, the DOL announced the settlement of several child labor violations against A&P markets, Publix, and Food Lion.[151] In addition, Food Lion, in the largest DOL wage settlement ever, was ordered to pay $13.2 million in back wages and overtime to its employees (in addition to $3 million in fines). Adults are also cheated out of their wages and overtime, such as the 713 garment workers who in 1994 were awarded $438,000 in back wages from 66 employers.[152]

BOX 4.4

Eavesdropping by Organizations

Persons in organizations are increasingly invading individual privacy by eavesdropping on customers and employees through the use of listening devices. Many of these actions may constitute the federal crime of wiretapping. Title 18 of the *United States Code* (Section 2511) prohibits any interception or disclosure of any wire or oral communication. These communications include any oral utterances by a person who believes that such communication is not being intercepted by others. This law, of course, excludes legal wiretaps by law enforcement. The maximum federal penalty for eavesdropping is five years imprisonment and a $10,000 fine.

Dunkin' Donuts franchises had routinely installed hidden audio taping machines "for security purposes" at almost three hundred stores in the Northeast (the microphones were removed in 1994). One Florida company has put in place at least one thousand hidden microphones in retail stores, including dime-sized microphones on clothing racks to eavesdrop on potential shoplifters.[a] Eavesdropping on others' voice or computer mail could also constitute invasion of privacy. In one case, McDonald's was sued for $1 million when a supervisor tapped into a worker's voice mail, recorded messages from his mistress, and played them back to the worker's wife.[b]

Expectation of privacy is one of our most important individual freedoms. The International Labor Organization of the United Nations has estimated that as many as twenty million Americans, or a sixth of the work force, are subject to electronic monitoring (excluding the telephone), and that number quadruples in the telecommunications, insurance, and banking industries.[c] Employers have the right to monitor the quality of their workers, and this can cause a waiver of privacy rights as a condition of employment. At the minimum, customers and employees must be informed that their conversations are being monitored in order to dispel any false expectations of privacy, and employees must be guaranteed access to all information gathered and must have been informed before employment regarding how the information derived from eavesdropping is to be used.

a. Associated Press, "Dunkin' Donuts Workers Had 'Fun' While it Lasted," *Albany Herald* (May 29, 1994):10C.

b. Associated Press, "Eavesdropping Employer Sued for Monitoring Mail," *Albany Herald* (January 24, 1995):7A.

c. Associated Press, "More Employers Snoop on Workers, Report Says," *Albany Herald* (August 2, 1994):5A.

The Office of Federal Contract Compliance Programs (OFCCP), administered by the Employment Standards Administration of the DOL, monitors violations of federal contractors' adherence to affirmative action requirements. This body regulates the hiring practices of the approximately 400,000 corporations and companies that do business with the United States, either directly through contracting or indirectly through subcontracting, and who employ 42 percent of the country's workforce. During fiscal year 1993, the OFCCP conducted 979 investigations into complaints against federal contractors, which yielded financial agreements totaling $34 million, including back wages of $14 million for 3,800 workers.[153] The OFCCP protects workers, but its policies also may have created unintended negative effects. It has been alleged, for instance, that the government's emphasis on its contractors' hiring of minorities has often eliminated the need for a high school diploma as a precondition of employment, thereby not rewarding those who finish high school, including minorities. This policy, of course, encourages the hiring of less educated persons.[154]

Unsafe Working Conditions

The other major area of organizational crime against workers involves unsafe working conditions, which, like unsafe consumer products and pollution, cause physical harm or have the potential to do so. Many industries are known to be inherently dangerous—conditions at some coal,[155] asbestos,[156] and textile[157] plants have been found to cause lung disease (pneumoconiosis, silicosis, and byssinosis) from dust inhalation. Mines explode[158] and steel mills cause injuries and death.[159]

The Department of Labor's **Occupational Safety and Health Administration** (OSHA) is the primary federal agency responsible for job sites. OSHA began in 1970 under President Nixon and estimates it covers 90 million workers at 6 million workplaces, which includes its cooperative efforts with half of the states.[160] While these figures may at first glance appear impressive, in 1989 the United States had six times as many fish and game inspectors (approximately 12,000) as it did job safety inspectors (approximately 2,000).[161]

In fiscal year 1993 OSHA conducted more than 39,500 federal enforcement inspections and the states conducted another 62,000 inspections of the nation's 6 million worksites. Although the number of federal inspections has declined since 1989, the intensity of the inspections has increased, yielding a higher proportion of citations for serious violations.[162] During the five-year period 1989–1993, OSHA referred 49 cases to the Department of Justice for criminal prosecution, more than double the total number referred during the previous five years.[163] OSHA also completed close to 2900 investigations of discrimination complaints filed by whistleblowers.[164]

The 1977 Federal Mine Safety and Health Act (Public Law 95-164) established the **Mine Safety and Health Administration** (MSHA), which currently is responsible for safety at approximately 14,500 mines in the United States. The Mine Safety and Health Act mandates four annual inspections of each underground mine and two annual inspections of each surface mine. During the past several years, MSHA has managed to complete more than 95 percent of its statutorily mandated mine inspections, including more than 99 percent of them in fiscal years 1992 and 1993.[165] Nonetheless, the annual mining fatalities in the United States have remained relatively constant over the past several years—about a hundred. The rate of fatalities in coal mines is twice that of metal mines, and smaller coal mines (fewer than fifty employees) have more than twice the number of fatalities as in the overall mining industry average.[166] Besides dying in accidents, coal miners often develop the potentially fatal condition called pneumoconiosis ("brown lung") from inhaling coal dust, and MSHA operates an X-ray health program that monitors miners for the development of that disease.

During fiscal year 1993, 43 individuals and 15 companies were convicted of mine related criminal offenses. Sixteen individuals and four companies were convicted for violation of mandatory safety standards, and 27 individuals and 11 companies for fraudulently submitting dust samples in the monitoring of brown lung disease potential. MSHA has recently helped develop a tamper-proof dust sample kit to help reduce fraud in the submission of these dust samples.[167]

Annually, a little more than 6,000 Americans suffer a workplace fatality, and more than 90 percent of them are men (men constitute about 55% of the workforce).[168] Automobile crashes (20%) and homicides (17%)

(primarily robbery-homicides) are currently the leading causes of workplace fatality. Women are proportionately more than twice as likely as men to be killed in a workplace homicide.[169] Thus, more than a third of on-the-job deaths are unrelated to worksite safety conditions.

Some research has concluded that women "tend to be less well-protected than men from the effects of workplace hazards."[170] It cites carpal tunnel syndrome (a cumulative trauma disorder often associated with typing on a word processor), exposure to video display terminals (which allegedly causes reproductive anomalies such as miscarriages, stillbirths, and birth defects in pregnant women),[171] and female textile workers who develop byssinosis, a form of "brown lung" disease.[172] Nonetheless, men are less protected in the workplace than women because men generally have the most dangerous jobs. The major reason for this, it has been argued, is that because men are generally expected to be the major family income-earners, they accept the more dangerous jobs because those occupations pay more.[173] The more hazardous the job, the greater the proportion of workers who are men, and the greater the injury and death rate.[174] Working environments for both men and women, of course, should be as safe as possible, but the relative paucity of state and federal inspectors and the tendency of organizations to pursue profits undercut this goal.

The fatal fire at North Carolina's Imperial Food Products chicken-processing plant on September 3, 1991, has come to epitomize the current lack of worker safety enforcement in America. The fire started when motor oil heating a large fryer spurted into flames. It spread rapidly, killing twenty-five employees and injuring another fifty-five; those dead and injured made up almost 90 percent of the employees in the plant at the time of the blaze. Emmet Roe, the owner of the plant, had illegally ordered doors locked to reduce employee thefts of chicken parts. The lack of exit routes, coupled with the absence of a sprinkler system, was the major cause of the high fatality and injury rate.

In its eleven-year history, the plant never had been inspected by North Carolina's OSHA. North Carolina (25% of whose workforce is in manufacturing) had only sixteen inspectors to cover the entire state's worker safety program; this represented the lowest ranking among all states. After the fire, Roe was sentenced to two to nineteen years in prison after pleading guilty to twenty-five counts of involuntary manslaughter, the plant was bankrupted after being assessed more than $800,000 in fines, and the state of North Carolina hired twenty-seven new inspectors and enacted a dozen workplace safety bills.[175] Scholars have pointed out that although the media tended to blame the lack of regulatory enforcement for the fire, legal noncompliance by Imperial was the true cause of the tragedy.[176]

The Occupational Health and Safety Act contains provisions for criminal penalties, but they have rarely been used. Fines have been relatively mild, given the harm or potential harm involved. Generally, it is only in regard to a worker's death that OSHA invokes incarceration penalties. During the first twenty years of OSHA, not a single instance of imprisonment had occurred.[177] Even the groundbreaking 1985 homicide conviction in the Film Recovery Systems case, in which three Illinois workers died after exposure to cyanide, was overturned on a technical point in 1990.

Currently, organizations and individuals are liable under most federal law (OSHA excluded) for incarceration when they "knowingly endanger" employees if the activity is in relation to hazards that violate provisions of environmental laws. The Resource Conservation and Recovery Act (RCRA), for instance, carries a maximum individual penalty of $250,000 in fines and fifteen years of incarceration, and a maximum organizational fine of $1 million.[178] Only when OSHA includes a "knowing endangerment" provision punishable by incarceration can we expect deterrent impact (recall that organizational managers may be held criminally responsible under the strict liability provisions of the previously discussed *Park* doctrine).[179]

Organizational Crimes against the Environment

Ralph Nader captured the essence of environmental pollution when he stated that it amounts to "a compulsory consumption of violence."[180] The truth of Nader's assertion is buttressed by the results of the *National Survey of Crime Severity* (box 1.2). Results showed that a single instance of mild illness from air pollution was viewed by Americans to be as serious as an aggravated assault requiring victim hospitalization, and twenty instances of mild illness from water pollution were seen to be as serious as a reckless vehicular homicide. As many as 140,000 deaths each year in the United States (about 9% of all deaths) have been blamed on air pollution alone.[181] Box 4.5 details some of the worst of recent environmental disasters.

The Rivers and Harbors Act of 1899,[182] now known as the Refuse Act,[183] represents the federal government's first attempt to criminalize pollution.[184] The act provides for a misdemeanor maximum penalty of a year in prison and a fine of $2500 for anyone who discharges refuse matter into the navigable waters of the United States (including any tributary of those navigable waters). The Refuse Act punishes on the basis of strict liability. In the earliest days of the act's enforcement, penalties were imposed only when the discharged refuse blocked navigation. As Robert Milne has pointed out, this limitation reflected both the public's failure to

BOX 4.5

Environmental Disasters

Clean-up of the Exxon Valdez *oil spill begins.*

Hooker Chemical and Plastics Corporation is perhaps the best known rogue in the gallery of notorious polluters, having dumped extremely toxic substances into our air, water, and ground. Hooker was responsible for the Love Canal toxic waste dump (near Niagara, New York), which came to light during the late 1970s. This catastrophe led to the Superfund legislation discussed in the text, since it vividly demonstrated the lack of governmental response to environmental pollution.

Love Canal was named for the civil engineer William Love, who in the 1880s sought to build a canal around Niagara Falls. Love's plan never materialized, and the site was sold to Hooker in the late 1930s. It was used by Hooker to dump more than forty million pounds of chemicals and their waste for about fifteen years.[a] In 1953, Love Canal was turned over to the local school board, which sold it to a private developer. Hundreds of houses were built directly above or near the dump site. Persons who lived at Love Canal developed high rates of miscarriage, birth defects, and other health problems. More than two hundred families were forced to flee these homes.[b] Hooker Chemical became a subsidiary of Occidental Petroleum in 1968.

(continued next page)

BOX 4.5

Continued

In 1994, almost a half century after the scandalous acts began, federal court judge John Curtin criticized Occidental for not warning residents about the pollution, but ruled that Occidental Petroleum did not have to pay the state of New York punitive damages of $250 million because the company had not demonstrated a "reckless disregard for the safety of others."[c] However, Occidental was found liable for at least $350 million in cleanup costs, and additionally had to pay many millions of dollars to defend itself in liability lawsuits, to reimage itself, and to pay off former Love Canal residents who sued the company.[d]

Matt Tallmer describes Hooker as illegally dumping chemicals "as a corporate way of life," and recounts other dumping violations by Hooker that affected residents and employees: Bloody Run Creek, New York (where chemicals were dumped after Love Canal was closed); Taft, Louisiana (where smoke discharges polluted the surrounding farmers' crops); Syosset and Bethpage, New York (where Hooker unloaded hundreds of tons of vinyl chlorides and other highly toxic chemicals from its processing plant in nearby Hicksville); and White Lake, Michigan (where water was found to contain dangerous levels of Mirex, dioxin, and Kepone—three deadly chemicals that Hooker had buried on vacant plant property).[e]

Allied Chemical, identified by Sutherland in *White Collar Crime* as an organizational criminal recidivist almost fifty years before,[f] also was involved in an illegal toxic-dumping scandal similar to that of Hooker. Allied was found guilty of illegal disposal of Kepone related toxins (Kepone is a DDT-like insecticide) at its Hopewell, Virginia, plant. The sloppy handling of the poison caused workers to experience liver and brain damage, chest pains, personality changes, diminished ability to walk and stand, and sterility. Forty nonemployee nearby residents showed traces of Kepone in their blood. An examination of frozen seafood caught from the James River revealed Kepone in oysters and fish. Allied dumped Kepone into the Gravely Run, a tributary of the James, during the years 1966–1974.[g] Both Allied Chemical and Hooker Chemical knew the dangers of their deeds when they committed them and attempted to hide the illegal dumping from authorities.[h]

The world's worst industrial pollution disaster occurred December 3, 1984, when a cloud of deadly methyl isocyandate gas escaped from a Union Carbide pesticide plant in Bhopal, India. The human damage was tremendous: more than 3,300 people died within a short period; more than 20,000 were injured; and, since 1989, there has been a continuing death toll. Warren Anderson, the former Union Carbide chairman, was charged with culpable homicide in the disaster, and more than 500,000 people filed a joint civil suit against Union Carbide for $3 billion. Fifty months after the disaster, the Supreme Court of India, in a form of "plea bargain," dropped the criminal charges against Anderson and ordered Union Carbide to pay $470 million in damages as "full and final settlement of all claims."[i]

Perhaps the greatest damage to the American environment to date was caused by the Exxon tanker *Valdez* when it spilled oil in March of 1989—eleven million gallons of oil smeared across Prince William Sound off the coast of Alaska, killing countless birds, mammals, and fish. *Valdez* captain Joseph Hazelwood, who allegedly was intoxicated at the time of the spill, was acquitted of operating a ship under the influence of alcohol (and other charges), but was convicted for negligently discharging oil. He was sentenced to one thousand hours of cleanup duty and $50,000 in restitution. Exxon currently has paid or has been ordered to pay at least $8 billion for its involvement in the calamity—$5 billion in punitive damages to individuals in the Alaska fish industry and $3 billion to settle cleanup charges and state and federal lawsuits.[j]

a. Associated Press, "Company Won't Be Punished for Love Canal" *Albany Herald* (March 18, 1994):5A.

b. Matt Tallmer, "Chemical Dumping as a Corporate Way of Life," in Stuart L. Hills (ed.), *Corporate Violence: Injury and Death for Profit* (Totowa, NJ: Rowman and Littlefield, 1988), p. 113.

c. Associated Press, "Company Won't Be Punished for Love Canal."

d. Associated Press, "Occidental Tries to Exorcise Past," *Albany Herald* (April 3, 1994):6D.

e. Tallmer, "Chemical Dumping as a Corporate Way of Life."

f. Edwin H. Sutherland, *White Collar Crime: The Uncut Version* (New Haven, CT: Yale University Press, 1983), pp. 64, 78.

g. Christopher Stone, "A Slap on the Wrist for the Kepone Mob," in Stuart L. Hills (ed.), *Corporate Violence: Injury and Death for Profit* (Totowa, NJ: Rowman and Littlefield, 1988).

h. Ibid., pp. 121, 124; Tallmer, "Chemical Dumping as a Corporate Way of Life," pp. 115, 188.

i. Associated Press, "Union Carbide to Pay $470 Million," *Albany Herald* (February 14, 1989):1A.

j. Associated Press, "Exxon to Take Up Myriad of Lawsuits," *Albany Herald* (March 20, 1990):6B; Associated Press, "Exxon Agrees to Pay Fine," *Albany Herald* (March 13, 1991):6B; Associated Press, "Judge Accepts $1 Billion Exxon Settlement," *Albany Herald* (October 9, 1991):11C; Associated Press, "Fishermen Get $286.8 Million for Exxon Spill Damages," *Albany Herald* (August 12, 1994):7A; Associated Press, "Exxon Ordered to Pay $5 Billion for Spill," *Albany Herald* (September 17, 1994):1A.

perceive pollution as a significant environmental problem and a lack of knowledge about the dangers of pollution.[185] During the late 1960s and early 1970s, the Refuse Act was strengthened when the Supreme Court expanded its strict liability to include any act of discharging any foreign substance into American waterways.

The next federal effort to control pollution, passage of the Water Pollution Control Act of 1948, did not occur until almost a half century after the Rivers and Harbors Act. This law represented a conciliatory rather than a punitive approach by Congress in its attempt to abate pollution. The Water Pollution Control Act did not dictate incarceration for its violation. Rather, the surgeon general was granted authority to notify violators (and the states in which they operated) about alleged violations. Only after the company ignored a second notice could the surgeon general request that a lawsuit be filed by the Department of Justice.[186] This procedure is rather unwieldy, and it was not until 1965 that the first lawsuit was initiated.

Also in 1965, Congress passed the Water Quality Act, which established procedures for states to determine pollution levels for their waterways. The Water Quality Act also sought to make prosecution easier under the Water Pollution Control Act. The Water Quality Act was also difficult to enforce, however, because it proved to be virtually impossible to demonstrate that an instance of pollution or a single polluter was responsible for the total contamination of a given body of water.[187] It was not until the early 1970s, when pollution gained high priority as a national problem that Congress tried to "get tough" by passing environmental laws with stiff monetary and incarceration penalties.

In 1970, President Nixon established the **Environmental Protection Agency** (EPA). In addition to those already discussed, major laws enforced by the EPA include the Resource Conservation and Recovery Act of 1976 (42 *USC,* Sections 6901–6991), the Emergency Planning and Community Right to Know Act (42 *USC,* Section 11045), the Hazardous Materials Transportation Act (49 *USC,* Sections 1801–1813), the Clean Air Act (42 *USC,* Sections 7401–7642), the Clean Water Act (33 *USC,* Sections 1251–1376), the Toxic Substances Control Act (15 *USC,* Sections 2601–2654), and the Federal Insecticide, Fungicide, and Rodenticide Act (7 *USC,* Sections 135–136). Because of these laws, many American chemical manufacturers market their poisonous products in Third World countries to avoid costly safety regulations.[188]

In 1981, the Office of Criminal Enforcement was created within EPA. However, as with any government regulatory agency, enforcement is primarily a function of resources. Although great importance had been placed upon the protection of the environment, the EPA Office of Criminal Enforcement had a staff of only thirty-five investigators during its first four years.[189] Despite these limitations, the EPA enforcement effort has been very impressive. For fiscal years 1983 through 1986, EPA returned 252 indictments (more than 80% against corporate officers in their official capacities), to which 211 individuals and organizations pleaded guilty, resulting in more than ten accumulated years of actually served jail time.[190] During fiscal year 1987, 58 defendants pleaded guilty to environmental crimes and were fined a total of $3.6 million and given a total of eighty-four years in prison.[191] And during fiscal year 1992, EPA boasted 191 criminal indictments and more than $160 million in fines.[192] Under the U.S. Sentencing Guidelines, individual and organizational punishments for environmental violations can be as low as probation, but such cases must involve a first-time offender, a one-time offense, and no bodily harm. For environmental crimes involving willful public endangerment, such as the purposeful mishandling of toxic substances, the minimum punishment is fifty-one months in prison. If serious bodily injury or death results, then the punishment can be increased significantly.

In 1980, Congress passed the Comprehensive Environmental Response Compensation and Liability Act (42 *USC,* Sections 9601–9675), or CERCLA, which established a **Superfund** to pay for the cleanup of more than 1200 hazardous national waste sites identified on a "National Priority List" created by the EPA. It has been estimated that it takes a decade and $30 million to clean up the average site on this list.[193] Cleanup of the hazardous areas is financed by a combination of revenues raised through a tax on petrochemical industry corporations and enforcement-induced cleanup expenditures from many of these same corporations.[194] Under Superfund, which is based on strict liability, private corporate cleanup responsibility can be mandated for 40 percent to 50 percent of the toxic sites. When there is a question about organizational proportionate responsibility for a mess, the cleanup costs are shared equally by all corporations who contributed to it. If a corporation refuses to pay its share, the EPA can pay for the cleanup and then sue the recalcitrant organization for quadruple the costs (costs plus treble damages). As one might expect, the polluters believe that the costs of the cleanup should be paid by the taxpayers, arguing that Americans have benefited from the chemical industry and therefore they should bear the expenses, much like Americans did in the savings and loan bailouts of the early 1990s.[195]

Superfund has been criticized in particular instances of enforcement against small business. James Bovard has cited many reasons to call Superfund "robbery with an environmental badge."[196] The EPA requires virtually no evidence to enforce Superfund; as Waste Programs Enforcement Director Bruce Diamond noted: "All you have is an aging truck driver who says, 'I took yellow liquid and think it was from them.' "[197] In one case, the twenty-year-old memories of scrapyard employees were used by the EPA to assess cleanup responsibilities.[198] In another case, a small business was notified by the EPA that it must share in a Superfund site's cleanup costs because it had paid someone $14 several years earlier to haul trash there.[199] In New York, a judge ruled that a butcher shop owner was liable for a share of a cleanup because the glue on the boxes he threw into his dumpster contained hazardous materials (the boxes later appeared at a Superfund landfill site).[200]

The EPA's enforced cleanup ignores the federal government's contributions to pollution at Superfund sites, such as the Rocky Mountain Arsenal in Colorado, where Shell Oil Company was charged with the entire cleanup even though the U.S. Army also used the site for several years for chemical warfare tests.[201] The unfairness of the EPA's use of Superfund's legal powers is epitomized by its attempt to place a Texas waste site on a national priorities list because the site posed a possible threat of airborne arsenic contamination at temperatures greater than 1000 degrees Fahrenheit.[202]

Large corporations fight the EPA primarily by suing third parties that they allege are coresponsible. Defendants in these suits are often local governments. By 1993, major corporations had brought responsibility-sharing litigation against fifty local governments in New Jersey, twenty-four in Connecticut, and twelve in Massachusetts. In Los Angeles, sixty-four corporations sued twenty-nine suburbs for a cleanup that is estimated to cost between $650 million and $800 million. The costs of private cleanup have spilled over into the insurance industry, which covers the EPA's liabilities, and into financial institutions that loan money to purchase polluted property.[203] Barnett argues that the current Superfund tax is passed on to consumers because of rising prices due to corporate cleanup costs and special Superfund taxes, and is passed backwards to taxpayers through income tax deductions of cleanup costs paid by corporations.[204]

Many actions by the EPA and other governmental regulators constitute what Joseph Dimento has called "lawmaking irrationalities."[205] These irrationalities can be based on gaps between scientific consensus and government regulation.[206] They may also grow out of attempts by regulatory agencies to gain public prestige and legal power. Lawmaking irrationalities foster perceptions among organizational actors that regulators lack legitimacy, which in turn foster organizational attitudes supporting noncompliance.[207]

Political Bribegiving

Political bribegiving is the final general category of organizational occupational crime that will be addressed in this chapter. **Political bribegiving** encompasses outright bribes and gratuities to public officials or agents and illegal political campaign contributions, both domestic and foreign, for the purpose of influencing government actions. Political bribe*taking* is covered in chapter 5. The penalties for bribegiving are generally the same as for bribetaking, and are also discussed in chapter 5.

The systemic forces that create an environment that encourages political bribegiving include the facts that: "(1) The fruits of governmental action are often extremely valuable (or, in the case of penalties and sanctions, extremely costly), with demand for benefits frequently exceeding supply; (2) These benefits and sanctions often can be gotten or avoided only by dealing with the government; and (3) The routine process through which benefits and sanctions are conferred is time consuming, expensive and uncertain in its outcome."[208] A lobbyist for the Associated Milk Producers, which illegally contributed $100,000 to President Nixon's 1972 campaign, explained that organization's rationale for the contributions: "One way a small group makes itself heard is to help politicians get into office and give him [sic] some physical help and they won't forget your favor when they do get into government."[209] Shortly after Nixon's reelection campaign received the contribution, the White House announced increases in dairy price supports. Political bribegiving, then, is a cost-effective and time-effective way of gaining advantages. When Sutherland referred to white-collar crime as "formally organized crime," he highlighted the efficacy of bribegiving by implying how it and similar behaviors can help to accomplish "the control of legislation, selection of administrators, and restriction of appropriations for the enforcement of laws which may affect [organizations]."[210]

To provide an idea of the scope of these activities, the Securities and Exchange Commission's disclosure drive on illegal or questionable domestic and foreign payments revealed that by 1978 at least $1 billion had been paid by more than three hundred of the five hundred *Fortune* leading industrial corporations.[211] Research during the 1970s by Irwin Ross indicates that several of America's leading firms have attempted to bribe public officials and agents.[212] In the late 1970s, for instance, executives of six alcoholic beverage manufacturers pleaded guilty to bribery offenses—American Brands (Jim Beam Bourbon), Heublein, Liggett Group (Paddington Corp.), National Distillers, Rapid-American (Schenley), and Joseph E. Seagram (Seagram Distillers and three other subsidiaries). Seagram was again charged in 1979 with bribery of members of a state liquor control board; it pleaded guilty and was fined $1.5 million. In 1972, Northern Natural Gas was charged with mail fraud related to bribery of local officials to obtain right-of-way permits for pipeline construction. In 1977, Gulf Oil Company and two employees were charged with giving illegal gifts to an Internal Revenue Service agent—Gulf pleaded guilty, one executive pleaded *nolo contendre*, and the other was convicted after trial. And in 1978, Tenneco Corporation pleaded guilty to mail fraud in connection with the bribery of a local government official.

Illegal domestic campaign contributions are probably the most common method of political bribegiving. Since the 1907 passage of the Tillman Act, corporations have been forbidden from making contributions to candidates for federal office. The Federal Corrupt Practices Act, passed in 1925, organized and revised the Tillman legislation and other federal laws, but did not make substantive changes. For almost a half century, the Federal Corrupt Practices Act to a large extent was powerless because it was fraught with loopholes. Federal campaign law was completely renovated in 1971 by the Federal Election Campaign Act and its various amendments. These put a limit on a candidate's expenditures on advertising, self-contributions, and total campaign expenditures. The election act also required a detailed itemization of contributions exceeding $100. Some of these provisions were later ruled unconstitutional by the Supreme Court, but the Court left intact the limitations on campaign spending and independent and personal contributions. As it stands now, individual candidates can receive a maximum of $1,000 from other individuals and $5,000 from political action committees. The net effect of the Federal Election Campaign Act is to some extent negligible, because a single individual or organization can contribute to several different political action committees, each committee having the same purpose.[213]

To avoid prosecution for illegal contributions, organizations must resort to subterfuge, particularly by "magical" bookkeeping practices (e.g., false entries, mislabeled accounts, inventions of phony subsidiaries). To avoid direct payments that can be traced, organizations make "third-party" contributions by secretly supplying employees with funds to give to particular candidates. Employees have been secretly compensated for their contributions through higher salaries, "bonuses," or "reimbursements" on overstated expense accounts.

Oil corporations were one of the most visible sources of illegal contributions to Nixon's reelection campaign. Five Rockefeller brothers, who owned 1 percent of Exxon stock, together made payments to Nixon's campaign of $5 million. Other secret Nixon contributions from the petroleum industry included Gulf Oil ($1.3 million), Getty Oil ($77,000),

Standard Oil of California ($102,000), Sun Oil ($60,000), Phillips Petroleum ($100,000), Exxon ($100,000), and Ashland Oil ($100,000).[214] Several other large companies made illegal domestic political contributions, including American Airlines, Braniff International, Carnation, Diamond International, Firestone, GTE, General Dynamics, General Tire and Rubber, Goodyear, Greyhound, 3M, Northrop, Occidental Petroleum, and Singer.[215]

Political bribery of foreign officials also has been common. Although bribegiving to foreign officials can be seen as an accepted way to protect American business interests abroad, it promotes unfair trade practices and it can have damaging political fallout by creating negative images of America among other nations.[216] To discourage this behavior, Congress passed the Foreign Corrupt Practices Act in 1977. It provides stiff penalties for both organizations and individuals—fines as high as $1 million for organizations, while executives face as much as five years imprisonment and a $10,000 fine.

The major impetus behind the passage of the Foreign Corrupt Practices Act was a scandal involving aircraft manufacturers who commonly made payments to foreign governments in order to secure sales. The bribers included Northrop Corporation ($30 million), Lockheed ($25 million), and McDonnell Douglas ($15.6 million). Other organizations caught during the 1970s for bribing foreign officials and executives include Exxon, ITT, Xerox, and United Brands.[217] At least one corporation, Lockheed, apparently did not learn its lesson from earlier chastisement, for early in 1995 the giant defense contractor pleaded guilty to conspiring to bribe a foreign legislator, this time to promote the 1989 sale of three C-130 Hercules cargo planes. The $1 million bribetaker was Egyptian Assemblywoman Leila Takla. After admitting that high-ranking executives made "mistakes in judgement," Lockheed agreed to pay a $24 million fine for the offense.[218]

Conclusion: Five Myths about Organizational Occupational Crime

This chapter has set out information about organizational occupational crime. There are at least five commonly held, but generally unproven, assumptions about organizational occupational crime that emerge from the many discussions. These "myths" about organizational offending are a fitting recapitulative close to the present chapter.

Myth 1: Organizations commit crime. (No organization can act independently of its employees or agents.)

Myth 2: Organizations commit crime on purpose. (Many of the acts committed by organizations are unintentional, such as some *respondeat superior* and strict liability crimes, and all collective intent offenses.)

Myth 3: The more complex an organization, the more criminogenic its environment. (Higher violation counts among larger organizations are caused by their involvement in greater numbers of business transactions rather than their greater complexity.)

Myth 4: Organizations that are financially strained are more likely to commit illegal acts. (Financial performance, is, for the most part, empirically unrelated to violation counts.)

Myth 5: Government-imposed censure against organizations is always based on organizational wrongdoing. (Although organizational censure by the government is often well deserved, it also can be based on idiosyncratic legal interpretations, power-seeking by regulatory agencies, and unfairness toward organizations.)

Key Terms

organization
close corporation
identification
nolo contendre
Alford plea
imputation
respondeat superior
strict liability
Park doctrine
collective intent
U.S. Sentencing Guidelines for individuals
disgorgement
real-offense sentencing
U.S. Sentencing Guidelines for organizations
official organizational goals
operative organizational goals
authority leakage
law of diminishing control
corporate culture
escalated organizational commitment
unfair/deceptive advertising
whistleblower
collusive unfair trade practices
Consumer Product Safety Commission
Occupational Safety and Health Administration
Mining Safety and Health Administration
Environmental Protection Agency
Superfund
political bribegiving

Questions for Discussion

1. Aside from collective intent offenses, can organizations commit crimes independent of the actions of their employees or agents? If yes, give examples. If not, why not?
2. Describe the criminal liability of organizations.

3. Is it fair to hold individuals criminally responsible for acts they did not intend, such as under the legal doctrines of *respondeat superior*, strict liability, and collective intent? If yes, then you must argue your position to include long terms of incarceration for those you are holding criminally responsible for unintentional acts. If no, how do you propose to deter managers in large organizations from ignoring acts of their subordinates that clearly are illegal?
4. Describe the purposes behind the U.S. Sentencing Guidelines for organizations. How are the guidelines applied to both individuals and organizations?
5. When analyzing organizational occupational crime, why is it necessary to differentiate between "official" and "operative" goals of organizations?
6. Which structures and processes associated with organizations are criminogenic? How would you suggest that these be improved?
7. How does "strain" theory apply to crimes committed within organizations? Be sure to include strains both internal and external to the organization.
8. How does differential social organization increase organizational crime? Can you give any additional examples not found in this chapter?
9. Do you believe that crimes committed by persons within organizations are a result of their own levels of self-control or a result of organizational processes? Why?
10. This chapter discussed several organizational crimes against property. What are some additional cases of misrepresentation in advertising? Price-fixing? Illegal labor practices?
11. This chapter discussed several organizational crimes against persons. What are some additional cases of unsafe consumer product distribution? Unsafe working conditions? Environmental pollution?
12. Can you identify instances where "commitment escalation" has pressured the government to continue wrong and potentially harmful courses of action? The Vietnam War? The War on Drugs? Cover-ups?
13. Suppose that your salary at your current job is much higher than you can expect to earn elsewhere with your skills. Suppose also that you are aware that your employer is cheating on federal tax. Would you blow the whistle on your employer if it meant that you might lose your job? Apply this situation to your current employment and try to be realistic.
14. Five myths about corporate crime are presented at the end of this chapter. A myth is defined as an accepted but unproved assumption.

For each of the five, use chapter materials to support the idea that the statement is a myth.

General Readings on Organizational Occupational Crime

Michael Blankenship (ed.), *Understanding Corporate Criminality* (New York: Garland, 1993).

John Braithwaite and Brent Fisse, "On the Plausibility of Corporate Crime Theory," in William Laufer and Freda Adler (eds.), *Advances in Criminological Theory (Volume 2)* (New Brunswick, NJ: Transaction Books, 1990).

Marshall Clinard, *Corporate Ethics and Crime: The Role of the Middle Manager* (Beverly Hills, CA: Sage, 1983).

Marshall Clinard and Peter Yeager, *Corporate Crime* (New York: Free Press, 1980).

Ronald C. Kramer, "Corporate Criminality: The Development of an Idea," in Ellen Hochstedler (ed.), *Corporations as Criminals* (Beverly Hills, CA: Sage, 1984).

William S. Laufer, "Corporate Bodies and Guilty Minds," *Emory Law Journal* 43 (1994):647–730.

Willaim S. Lofquist, Mark A. Cohen, and Gary A. Rabe (eds.), *Debating Corporate Crime* (Cincinnati: Anderson Publishing, 1997).

Laura Schrager and James Short, "Toward a Sociology of Organizational Crime," *Social Problems 25* (1977):407–19.

Christopher Stone, *Where the Law Ends: The Social Control of Corporate Behavior* (New York: Harper & Row, 1975).

Diane Vaughan, "Toward an Understanding of Unlawful Organizational Behavior," *Michigan Law Review* 80 (1982):1377–1402.

Central figures in the 1991 beating case of Rodney King (bottom right) were, clockwise from upper left: LAPD officers Timothy Hind; Stacy Koon (far right with lawyer); and Laurence Powell (bottom left) and Theodore Briseno. This case of police brutality left a wake of more violence when, in 1992, a three-day riot broke out in Los Angeles after the acquittal of the four officers in a state trial.

5 *State Authority Occupational Crime*

This chapter describes **state authority** crimes. A state is any independent government entity, such as a city, county, state, province, or country. "State authority" refers to powers lawfully vested in persons by a state with which those persons can make or enforce laws or command others. State authority is usually acquired by taking a public oath. State-based legal authority carries unique opportunities to commit occupational offenses that do not exist elsewhere.

In one sense, of course, all government employees work "for" the state or "on behalf" of it. However, "state authority" does not refer merely to public authority to make everyday decisions such as hiring and purchasing. It has to do specifically with the legally vested power to represent the force of state law in doing certain things. Ethical violations by elected and appointed officials are not always criminal violations, and if they are criminal, they still may not involve the use of the official's vested powers.

Crimes related to the making and enforcing of laws can be committed in various ways. For instance, legislators have the authority to pass laws in the name of the state, as do presidents, governors, and mayors. Public executives also have the legal power to make official appointments to public offices. Legislators make legal judgments on public officeholders when they confirm or deny appointments and vote in impeachment proceedings. Judicial officers represent state law in their decisions about bail, guilt or innocence, sentencing, search and arrest warrants, and civil judgments. Judges also produce constitutional and other case law for the state. And criminal justice system personnel such as police officers, prosecutors, prison guards, parole officers, and regulatory inspectors make direct decisions about enforcing laws.

Persons with valid military rank (or its equivalent) have the state authority to command others to do certain things, even when doing so may result in the commission of a crime. A classic example is that of Captain William Calley, who was convicted in 1968 for ordering the killing of innocent women and children during the Vietnam War. Commanding military subordinates to torture or murder, as some Nazis did during World War II, or to perform other illegal acts, would constitute the use of state authority for criminal activity. This would be true for all war crimes.

Many occupational crimes by public officials would not be included under the concept of state authority. Although a senator who embezzles government funds commits a crime against the public, powers that carry the force of state law may not have been used to steal those funds. On the other hand, if a senator accepts a bribe in exchange for his or her vote, the criminal act falls squarely within the concept of state authority. It may seem dubious to distinguish between a senator who embezzles and a senator who takes bribes, because both offenses victimize the community at large. However, the embezzling senator needs only a trusted economic position, while the bribetaking senator needs a vested state authority to vote on legislation.

Crimes associated with the prestige of a government position should not be confused with crimes committed through the authority of a government position. In the Watergate scandal, the obstruction of justice allegations against Richard Nixon by the House Judiciary Committee did not involve the use of state authority. The charges stemmed from attempts to bribe witnesses with "hush" money and favors; influencing through bribegiving was the crime, not bribetaking for influence. Other crimes associated with the Watergate affair also had nothing to do with the exercise of state authority, such as the burglaries of Democratic headquarters and the forgery of discrediting evidence against Senator Muskie.

Nixon was guilty of state authority crime to the extent that he used his powers as president of the United States to commit offenses. Nixon may have offered the presiding judge in the Ellsberg burglary case the directorship of the FBI in exchange for the judge's influence. There were similar allegations that presidential political appointments, such as ambassadorships, were offered in exchange for campaign contributions.[1] These would be crimes facilitated through the exercise of a president's authority to make certain nominations.

Falsification of evidence or public record often constitutes a state authority offense. A postal worker who files a false employee expense reimbursement form would be committing fraud by an individual, but the postal workers who falsified postmarks to coincide with a Super Bowl contest deadline committed their crimes through a legal enforcement authority vested by the state.[2] Many government employees directly represent the enforcement of state law when they give sworn court testimony on behalf of the state. If they commit perjury in that process, their actions can be seen as state authority crime.

There will be some disagreement about whether an action by a state official actually falls under the construct of "state authority crime." However, there are many clear examples of this type of offending, some of which will be presented under five general categories: government brutality, civil rights violations, sex crimes, theft, and bribetaking. These topics help to organize the discussion and are not meant to be exhaustive.

Government Brutality

Government brutality can range from systematic and coordinated genocide and torture by the highest officials to individual acts of assault and murder by persons at the lower levels of government. Our focus will be on individual acts of brutality by lower government agents, which are criminal primarily under assault, battery, and homicide statutes. (See box 5.1 for a discussion of the systematic government brutalities of torture and genocide.)

The term *brutality* conjures up situations in which police and prison officers commit acts of violence against innocent and defenseless people. Albert Reiss has identified behaviors most likely to be viewed by the public as police brutality: (1) the use of profane and abusive language; (2) commands to move on or get home; (3) stopping and questioning people on the street or searching them and their automobiles; (4) threats to use force if not obeyed; (5) prodding with a nightstick or approaching with a pistol; and (6) actual use of physical force or violence.[3]

Prisoners, too, often are threatened and physically abused by prison officials. Prisoners may also consider authorities to be inflicting vicarious brutality when the institutional staff denies them adequate protection from other inmates. Additionally, prison authorities may inflict sensory deprivation, physical exhaustion, and deprivation of adequate nutrition, though these conditions also may be the result of an inability to provide adequate care. Psychological pain inflicted on prisoners may be difficult to

BOX 5.1

Genocide and Torture

Lt. William Calley, (right) charged with murder in connection with the shooting deaths of 102 South Vietnamese children, leaves a closed-door preliminary court martial hearing in 1970.

The text discusses specific instances of government brutality; however, such brutality also can take the form of systematic infliction of genocide and torture. A clause in the 1948 *United Nations Universal Declaration of Human Rights* specifically prohibits torture by public officials: "No one shall be subjected to torture or to cruel, inhuman, or degrading treatment or punishment." As a specific response to the atrocities during World War II, the United Nations, also in 1948, outlawed genocide. That document defines genocide as:

> any of the following acts commi tted with the intent to destroy, in whole or part, a national, ethical, racial, or religious group, as such: (a) Killing members of the group; (b) Causing serious bodily or mental harm to members of the group; (c) Deliberately inflicting on the group conditions of life calculated to bring about its physical destruction in whole or in part; (d) Imposing measures intended to prevent births within the group; (e) Forcibly transferring the children of the group to another group.

Forty years after the United Nations drafted this treaty, America finally ratified it in 1987 as the "Genocide Convention Implementation Act" (also known as the "Proxmire Act"), joining more than ninety other countries. The United States' version of the law is codified under Title 18 *United States Code*, Section 1091. This statute punishes any *intent* to commit any of the acts outlined above. An individual is liable under Section 1091 if the act occurred in any location governed by the United States or if the offender is a national of the United States. The maximum punishment under this law is twenty years imprisonment and a $1 million fine; if death results from an intention to commit genocide, the offender is subject to the fine and capital punishment, and there is no statute of limitations.

In the first case to come before the United Nations World Court on the genocide issue, Yugoslavia was unanimously ordered in 1993 by a fourteen-judge panel to stop acts of genocide against Bosnians. The Bosnian government accused the Serbs of "ethnic cleansing," conducted by pushing out Muslims so that Bosnian land could be annexed to Greater Serbia.[a]

We can point to a few historical instances from the twentieth century that would qualify by most definitions of torture and genocide: the Stalinist purges of the 1930s (involving forty million victims), the campaign by the Nazis to extirpate the Jewish people and other racial and religious groups, the systematic extermination of opponents to Idi Amin in Uganda in the 1970s, and the massacres of five hundred thousand Tutsis by the Hutus (and similar retaliatory acts by the Tutsis against the Hutus) in Rwanda in the 1990s.

An explanation of torture and genocide would have to include logistical, social structural, and individual psychological items. Logistically, to carry out torture and genocide, state authorities must possess the manpower and technology to dominate victims. They must have loyal military or civilian police and needed weaponry, and they must be in a position to control the flow of information about their actions. History suggests that even the modern conventional war machines of the most powerful countries may not be able to dominate a citizenry that has its own armed power, as the American experience in Vietnam and the Soviet experience in Afghanistan demonstrate.

On the social structural plane, genocide and torture probably are least likely to occur in societies in which most persons share several statuses in common. Under such conditions, there is less chance of singling out a group that has a unique status. Genocide and torture are likely to be most common when status differentials, particularly those of a political nature, are more pronounced.[b]

Psychological studies provide some answers regarding the willingness of one person to inflict injury and death on another. Unthinking obedience may be behind an individual's infliction of torture and genocide. Classic studies by Stanley

(continued next page)

BOX 5.1

Continued

Milgram[c] demonstrated that almost all of us are willing to inflict some degree of pain on another person if commanded to do so by the proper authority. Such obedience appears particularly likely in a well-disciplined police or military force—subordinates will seldom question orders, even if they are morally opposed to them.

Criminal prosecution of high-level political torturers and murderers is difficult unless the offending regime is ultimately overthrown. Prosecuting them from outside the country is almost impossible unless nations organize to invoke international sanctions, such as in the prosecution of Nazi war criminals at Nuremburg. Laws forbidding relations with governments who violate human rights—for example, the United States Foreign Assistance Act of 1976—are of little use unless joined by the community of nations. Even if a few powerful countries abide by such laws, offending regimes may meet their economic and military needs from states not participating in the sanctions.

a. Associated Press, "Court Orders Halt to Genocide," *Albany Herald* (April 9, 1993):12A.

b. Paul Eisenhauer, "Genocide," in Marvin Wolfgang and Neil Weiner (eds.), *Surveying Violence across Nations* (Philadelphia: University of Pennsylvania Center for Studies in Criminology and Criminal Law, 1981) (Unpublished manuscript).

c. See, e.g., Stanley Milgrim, "Behavioral Study of Obedience," *Journal of Abnormal and Social Psychology* 67 (1963):371–78; Stanley Milgrim, "Some Conditions on Obedience and Disobedience to Authority," *Human Relations* 18 (1965):54–74.

---

determine because the causes of such pain can range from semi-isolation for security purposes to the more obvious purposeful production of chronic anxiety through the threat of physical violence or the denial of early release.

Brutality is certainly not inexorably tied to injury. A police or prison officer who maliciously overtightens a set of handcuffs is inflicting brutality, but no injury (other than pain) might result.[4] That which constitutes brutality or unnecessary force in a given situation often boils down to judgment by an agency review board or a trial jury, though there are situations in which "excess" is easily identified. These include, in the case of arrest:

- If a policeman physically assaulted a citizen and then failed to make an arrest.

- If the citizen being arrested did not, by word or deed, resist the policeman; force should be used only if it is necessary to make the arrest.
- If the policeman, even though there was resistance to the arrest, could easily have restrained the citizen in other ways.
- If a large number of policemen were present and could have assisted in subduing the citizen in the station, lockup, and the interrogation rooms.
- If an offender was handcuffed and made no attempt to flee or offer violent resistance.
- If the citizen resisted arrest, but the use of force continued even after the citizen was subdued.[5]

The 1991 beating of Rodney King, an African American, by at least four white members of the Los Angeles Police Department, captured on videotape by citizen-witness George Holliday, is the most vivid depiction of police brutality in recent memory. After the four officers were acquitted in a state trial in 1992, a three-day riot broke out in Los Angeles, resulting in fifty-two deaths and tens of millions of dollars in property damage. Two of the four officers, Stacy Koon and Laurence Powell, were found guilty of criminal violations of King's federal civil rights in 1993, and were sentenced to thirty months in prison.[6] In 1994, King was awarded $3.8 million in damages from the City of Los Angeles in addition to his legal expenses.[7] Another police brutality case that received national attention around the same time involved the fatal bludgeoning with heavy metal flashlights of another African American, Malice Green, by two white Detroit police officers, Larry Nevers and Walter Budzyn. The officers were convicted of second-degree murder and sentenced to hefty prison terms (twelve to twenty-five years and eight to eighteen years, respectively).[8]

In *Tennessee v. Garner*[9], the U.S. Supreme Court found that protection against the use of deadly force falls under the Fourth Amendment to the Constitution regarding search and seizure, because it involves the seizure of a person. The Court ruled that the use of deadly force is legal only if it is necessary to prevent the escape of an individual who can reasonably be assumed to pose a danger of serious bodily harm or death to innocent persons. Any use of deadly force that does not conform to the Court's prerequisite, then, is deemed unnecessary, and can be prosecuted criminally as assault or homicide.

Unnecessary fatal and nonfatal violence perpetrated by police against citizens sometimes has been attributed to stress-inducing job factors, most notably life-threats, social isolation, peer pressures, departmental policies (or lack of them), discretionary decision-making pressures, physiological stress, and anticipatory fear in responding to calls.[10] These conditions contribute to what Jerome Skolnick has termed the **policeman's working personality.**[11] This personality is said to be nurtured on the job and has been said to include the elements of authoritarianism, suspicion, racism, insecurity, hostility, and cynicism.[12] Police are expected to establish authority immediately in a tense situation. They sometimes resort to physical force to achieve that authority. Police are constantly exposed to danger, so they are likely to become suspicious about those who are not part of the police fraternity. Suspicion and authority, coupled with hostility and insecurity, can easily promote the use of unnecessary force.[13] Role socialization may also partly explain brutality by prison authorities, for it has been demonstrated that even ordinary citizens will develop authoritarian personalities while temporarily in the role of human custodians.[14]

Police and prison personnel often become cynical about the social value of many citizens with whom they come in contact, thereby promoting a "denial of victim" neutralization for brutality (the person had it coming). And, because the court system is often seen as impotent, an "appeal to higher (justice) loyalties" may be used to help render brutal police behavior acceptable. Moreover, some police and prison personnel believe that bending or breaking the law is acceptable in order to get their job done, and this would include the protection of fellow officers from brutality accusations. Carl Klockars has termed these tendencies among police the **Dirty Harry Problem** (after the Clint Eastwood movie character); officers believe that it is acceptable to use "dirty" means to achieve "good ends" (that is, justice), and only "dirty means will work" in attaining those ends.[15] These attitudes are often transmitted to new officers and assimilated into a shared departmental value system.

In terms of Edwin Sutherland's differential association theory discussed in chapter 3, there may exist an excess of definitions favorable to the justification for criminal brutality that have been learned by officers who employ it. Such schooling may encompass various ways of inflicting brutality. Standard police and prison guard training entails the learning of "compliance techniques" to be applied to suspects who resist their authority; these techniques can be used outside of legal control situations to brutalize citizens and prisoners. The techniques include the use of body pressure points for inflicting pain, against-the-grain hair pulling, and other methods of wreaking anguish. Police may also learn from other officers how to assault suspects with objects that will not leave visible cuts or bruises. Police also have been known to carry "throw-down" weapons (knives, unregistered guns) that are placed in the hands of assaulted suspects in order to justify the use of police force as "self-defense." This practice, too, is undoubtedly learned from other officers.

Sutherland would assert that some groups of police officers may be "differentially socially organized" around occupational conduct norms that encourage excessive force. A survey of police officers found that only 12 percent believed their fellow officers would report cases of police brutality "every time," while 42 percent would report it "sometimes," 37 percent would report it "rarely," and one in ten (9 percent) would "never" report it.[16] The Rodney King case is a good example of an almost complete tolerance of brutality. There were fifteen nonparticipating officers aware of the beating, but they did virtually nothing to report the misconduct or to stop it.[17]

Group socialization, coupled with job stress, then, have generally been seen as the major explanations behind police brutality. There also may be nonoccupational factors associated with individuals' personalities that provide an equally plausible explanation. The Gottfredson-Hirschi propensity-event theory, discussed in chapter 3, would conceptualize brutality as an attempt by police to gain "revenge without court delays."[18] They would argue that brutality contains many elements of low self-control behavior—it provides excitement, thrills, and risks; there are few long-term benefits associated with it; it takes little skill; it results from a low frustration tolerance; and it demonstrates a lack of attachment to the feelings of others. Propensity-event would also see police work having a natural tendency to recruit a high proportion (relative to other occupations) of lower self-control individuals because of the risk, physicality, excitement, and comparatively low educational requirements[19] that are associated with law enforcement as an occupation. The theory would also emphasize that situations in which brutality occurs invariably are perceived to have low visibility, thereby decreasing offenders' perceptions of being punished. For propensity-event to be supported as an explanation of brutality over occupational differential association, it would have to be demonstrated that *preemployment* levels of self-control are lower among officers who ultimately are more likely to use excessive force. This finding would support the theory's notion of stability. Demonstrating that brutalizers also are involved in other police deviance would support the theory's notion of versatility.

Poor training and unclear departmental policies about the use of deadly and nondeadly force further escalate the possibility of brutality by police. Most importantly, a low belief regarding the likelihood of formal sanctions (e.g., criminal conviction and incarceration) and nonformal sanctions (e.g., dismissal from employment) meted out to those who resort to brutality undercuts deterrence and leads to an absence of normative validation against excessive use of force. Perhaps the control of this state authority offense can come only through stiff incarceration and monetary penalties, such as those imposed in the Rodney King case. To reduce the Dirty Harry Problem, Klockars notes:

> [We must] apply the same retributive principles of punishment to the [brutalizer's] acts that he is quite willing to apply to others'. It is, in fact, only when his wrongful acts are punished that he will come to see them as wrongful and will appreciate the genuine moral—rather than technical or occupational—choice he makes in resorting to them. . . . [There is a] likelihood that juries in civil suits will find dirty means dirtier than police do. . . . Finally, severe financial losses to police agencies as well as to their officers eventually communicate to both that vigorously policing themselves is cheaper and more pleasing than having to pay so heavily if they do not.[20]

Civil Rights Violations

Persons who intentionally commit brutality or other civil rights violations against inhabitants of the United States while acting in any state authority capacity are considered to be acting under **color of law**, and can be charged with a federal crime under **Title 18 *USC* (Section 242)**, which states:

Deprivation of Rights under Color of Law

> Whoever, under color of any law, statute, ordinance, regulation, or custom, willfully subjects any inhabitant of any State, Territory, or District to the deprivation of any rights, privileges, or immunities secured or protected by the Constitution or laws of the United States, or to different punishments, pains, or penalties, on account of such inhabitant being an alien, or by reason of his color, or race, than are prescribed for the punishment of citizens, shall be fined under [Title 18] or imprisoned not more than one year, or both; and if bodily injury results from the acts committed in violation of this section or if such acts include the use, attempted use, or threatened use of a dangerous weapon, explosives, or fire, shall be fined under [Title 18] or imprisoned not more than ten years, or both; and if death results from the acts committed in violation of this section or if such acts include kidnapping or an attempt to kidnap, aggravated sexual abuse, or an attempt to commit aggravated sexual abuse, or an attempt to kill, shall be fined under [Title 18], or imprisoned for any term of years or for life, or both, or may be sentenced to death.

Additionally, Title 18 *USC* (Section 241) considers *any* conspiracy between two or more persons to violate civil rights a federal crime, independent of whether it occurs under color of law. The punishments under

Section 241 are similar to those under Section 242, including the death penalty. Conspiracy requires some overt act that clearly implies the beginning of an attempt to violate another's rights, such as driving around looking for a victim.

Title 42 *USC* (Section 1983) allows individuals to recover monetary damages from persons who, under color of *nonfederal* law, purposely deprive (or conspire to deprive) an individual of a civil right. Through *respondeat superior,* plaintiffs under Section 1983 are also entitled to recover from nonfederal governments. However, because monetary damages from federal agents for their civil rights violations are not included under Section 1983, the federal courts have extended Section 1983 to cover federal encroachment of rights by allowing a ***Bivens* claim,** based on the case of *Bivens v. Six Unknown Federal Narcotics Agents.*[21] A *Bivens* claim essentially gives an individual the rights one would have under Section 1983 for claims against individuals (but not the federal government) acting under color of federal law. Persons must use the Federal Tort Claims Act (Title 28 *USC,* Chapter 171) to recover monetary damages from the United States in a civil rights violation case. It should be noted that a criminal conviction under Sections 241 or 242 (Title 18 *USC*) does not necessarily entitle one to recover monetarily under Title 42 (Section 1983), a *Bivens* claim, or the Federal Tort Claims Act.

The most egregious violation of Section 242 occurred during World War II—involving the internment of about one hundred twenty thousand persons on American soil who were of Japanese descent, about three-quarters of whom were citizens of the United States. The Japanese were thought to constitute a "yellow peril" because they were racially tied to a country at war with America. They were "relocated" (that is, incarcerated) in eleven concentration camps in Arizona, Arkansas, California, Colorado, Utah, and Wyoming. This action, authorized by President Franklin Roosevelt seventy-four days after the bombing of Pearl Harbor, clearly constituted a violation of the Fourth Amendment (unreasonable seizure of a person) and the Fifth Amendment (deprivation of liberty without due process of law). Almost fifty years later, the United States government offered a formal apology and $20,000 to each of those interned or their heirs.[22]

Many government officials, particularly those in law enforcement, have been charged with violation of Sections 241 and 242. While any use of brutality may seem like an obvious civil rights infringement, for a conviction it must first be proven that an officer *intended* to breach civil rights. In a flagrant case, Steve Phillips was convicted in 1992 of violating the civil rights of homeless people. While working for the Gastonia, North Carolina, police department, Phillips doused them with oil, coffee, and urine.[23] Failure to act is also included under Section 242, as in the Georgia case in which a sheriff and his deputy were guilty of civil rights violation because they did not stop members of the Ku Klux Klan from beating victims.[24] A police officer who arrests[25] or searches[26] an individual, knowing that there is no legal basis, is also guilty of this offense. Klockars's conceptualization of the "Dirty Harry Problem" explains the willful violation of civil rights—the police find it acceptable to do "dirty things" to achieve "good ends."

Federal police agencies have been implicated in several searches. The Federal Bureau of Investigation illegally opened private mail for over twenty years in at least eight major cities—as many as 42 million pieces of mail from 1959 through 1966 in New York City alone.[27] Several criminal civil rights violations by the Bureau of Alcohol, Tobacco, and Firearms (BATF) are alleged to have occurred before the first raid on the Branch Davidians' complex at Waco, Texas, in February of 1993, including intentionally lying in an affidavit to secure a search warrant, illegal searching of mail and other private packages, and illegal wiretapping.[28] It has also been alleged that the BATF conspired to oppress the Branch Dividians because of their unusual religious beliefs, a violation of their First Amendment rights.[29]

Willful violation of the Eighth Amendment (which forbids cruel and unusual punishment) by prison or jail officials also constitutes a federal crime under Title 18 *USC* Section 242. The Arkansas prison official who willfully beat a prisoner as summary punishment was judged to possess an intent to deprive the inmate of his Eighth Amendment constitutional rights.[30] In West Virginia, a deputy sheriff's failure to protect persons detained by him from group violence or to arrest members of a mob that assaulted the prisoners was also judged a violation of his common law duty to preserve the peace.[31] In a similar case a county police officer in Michigan was held liable for allowing a prisoner to be beaten by other inmates.[32]

Police and prison officers are not the only persons in the criminal justice system to have been prosecuted under Section 242. Prosecutors acting within the scope of their state authority to initiate and prosecute a case who willfully deprive an accused person of rights are subject to criminal punishment under this statute.[33] A public defender's action was also found to fall within Section 242 when he attempted to exact money from those he represented and from their friends by telling them that an adequate defense could not be mounted otherwise.[34]

One need only be acting under official authority to be criminally liable under Section 242. Railroad police in Illinois who assaulted a group of vagrants were liable because, by state law, they possessed the same authority as city police.[35] Similarly, a private detective, who was sworn as a peace officer, was found liable for beating a confession out of a suspect, because, at the time of the beating, he was acting as a peace officer.[36] Professional process servers who falsely claimed on affidavits that defendants had been contacted about their civil court cases were also liable under Section 242 because their actions ultimately deprived the defendants of property without due process of law.[37]

Further, "color of law" within the spirit of Section 242 goes beyond the justice system. If voting authorities enforce election laws maliciously, then they are subject to liability under the statute. If an official makes it difficult for individuals to register to vote, or purposely fails to count votes, such acts can also fall under Section 242. Even private individuals are subject to violation of Section 242 if they participate in a rights infringement with state officials who are acting under color of law.

Currently under the U.S. Sentencing Guidelines, if injury or death does not result from a color of law rights violation, the recommended punishment is six to twelve months in prison and a fine of $2,000 to $20,000. If bodily injury results, the minimum punishment is forty-six months in prison and a $10,000 to $100,000 fine.

Sex Crimes

Receiving sexual favors in exchange for influencing state authority can be felonious under several laws. If the sexual favor is suggested by an official, the crime is extortion, regardless of whether the sexual activity occurs. State extortion statutes cover a public official's attempt to obtain "property" (which embraces "services") by means of threatening state action or inaction. Second, regardless of who suggested the exchange or whether the exchange actually took place, one or both parties would be guilty of bribery since the solicitation (or receipt) was for the benefit of actions done for or on behalf of a government. Third, if the official is influenced to exercise state authority in exchange for a sexual favor, regardless of who suggested the transaction, the act can constitute criminal malfeasance for an intentional "violation of the oath of office." Fourth, because citizens enjoy an inherent right to be free from the misuse of state power, coercive sexual exploitation by state authorities may also fall under the violation of civil rights encompassed by Sections 241 and 242. In one case *(U.S. v. Lanier,* 33 F.3d 639, 1994) a judge in Tennessee was convicted under Section 242 after he used his state authority to extort oral sex from a woman. His violation of Section 242 was found to involve bodily harm by the Sixth Circuit Court of Appeals—and therefore a substantially enhanced sentence—because the woman suffered discomfort during the act.

Most instances of criminal state authority sexual exploitation involve agents of the justice system. One example from the judiciary implicated former state legislator and Family Court Judge Sam Mendenhall, who was sentenced to eighteen months in prison for awarding a woman child support and custody of her child in a trade for sexual intercourse.[38] Correctional personnel have obtained sexual favors from female inmates in exchange for protection from discipline. Serious and widespread allegations of this sort were raised at the Georgia Women's Correctional Institution throughout the late 1980s and early 1990s.[39] Fifteen staff members were criminally charged after 160 female inmates complained of homosexual and heterosexual harassment.[40] From 1989 to 1991, Georgia was billed for almost $15,000 in nonspontaneous abortion costs for 28 inmates. Some women claimed that they were coerced to seek an abortion by prison officials.[41] Police officers, too, have at times been involved in sex-for-leniency scandals. Lloyd Shoemaker, who, while a Los Angeles County deputy sheriff, allegedly stopped female motorists for trumped-up charges on at least three different occasions, ordered them to remote locations, and then tried to coerce them to have intercourse under the threat of otherwise going to jail.[42]

Professor Allen Sapp has been collecting information about criminal sexual misconduct by police in their role as law enforcement officers since 1981. The following are some illustrations[43]:

> You bet I get [sex] once in a while by some broad who I arrest. Lots of times you can just hint that if you are taken care of, you could forget about what they did. One of the department stores here doesn't like to prosecute, but they always call us when they catch a shoplifter. Usually, we just talk to them and warn them and let them go. If it's a decent looking woman, sometimes I'll offer to take her home and make my pitch. Some of the snooty, high-class broads turn on real quick if they think that their friends and the old man doesn't have to find out about their shoplifting. I never mess around with any of the kids, but I know a couple of guys who made out with a couple of high school girls they caught on a [burglary]. (Detective, theft squad, large municipal department.)

> Over in a county west of here, they tell me that a sheriff will sometimes grab a hooker working one of the truck stops or the rest areas on the [highway] over there and keep her in jail over the weekend. He works out some kinda deal where he turns them loose without any charges or anything and they put out for the sheriff and the deputies that might be interested. (Patrolman, working as jailer at a medium municipal jail)

> I've been offered sexual services from barmaids, gamblers, narcotic addicts and dealers, and damn near every other kind of case you run into. Most of

> those cases are just between you and the suspect and they will do almost anything to avoid the arrest. Guys that would never even consider taking money will take [oral sex or intercourse] from a good-looking woman. (Vice squad sergeant, large municipal department.)

Several common themes emerge from these scenarios. The behaviors appear to be similar; almost all of the officers referred to others engaging in the same kinds of actions. Second, the officers exploited individuals' fears of the consequences that would arise from the decision to take legal action, including nonformal sanctions such as embarrassment in front of family members. Third, one infers that the tactic of this criminal sexual exploitation is learned from other officers. In Sutherland's terms there is an excess of occupational definitions favorable to these crimes involving the specific learning of justifications for and techniques of the behavior.

A rival causal explanation is propensity-event theory. A propensity-event perspective would view the behaviors outlined above as attempts by the police to procure "sex without courtship."[44] The scenarios from Professor Sapp represent behaviors that propensity-event posits as being common among those with low self-control—they feed immediate self-gratification and the desire for thrills without concern for the feelings of others. Whether police deviance, sexual or otherwise, is caused by personality traits or occupational differential association is a research issue. Propensity-event would be supported only to the extent that officers who exploit situations in sexual terms have lower self-control than those who do not do so, and this trait differential is present before employment on a police force.

Theft

Persons often are presented with opportunities for theft or access to theft sites through the exercise of their state authority (e.g., theft from fire or burglary scenes, theft of suspects' and prisoners' confiscated property and evidence). Four recent cases from Georgia serve as examples:

> Giri Peterson, an Albany fire inspector, was charged with two counts of theft for pilfering $150 from a church secretary's purse while he was conducting fire inspections. The secretary suspected Peterson of a $50 theft during one inspection and notified the police. They set up a video camera for a subsequent inspection, during which Peterson was recorded stealing two $50 bills from the secretary's purse. He was arrested, and found in possession of the planted bills.[45]

> Former Camden County deputy Wade English was found guilty of stealing $33,000 of the $316,000 he and two other deputies seized from suspected drug couriers along Interstate 95. English was also found guilty of falsifying a department report to hide the theft of $50,000 during a traffic stop. Floyd Basil, English's partner, pleaded guilty to theft and other charges stemming from these incidents.[46]

> Steve Roe, a Sylvester police officer, was charged with four counts of stealing and selling items retained as evidence in criminal cases, including $248 in cash.[47]

> Former Chatham County drug agent Johnny Ray Moore was convicted on federal charges of possessing five ounces of cocaine that he stole during a drug raid. Moore tried to sell the drugs to his partner, who later turned him in.[48]

Evidence pilfering can be very sophisticated. A former federal Drug Enforcement Administration (DEA) agent, Darnell Garcia, was convicted of stealing cash and narcotics worth more than $3 million. His partners, Anthony Jackson and Wayne Countryman, testified after pleading guilty as accomplices that Garcia prepared the cocaine and heroin for street sales while at his DEA desk. The agents tried to launder their proceeds through bank accounts in Luxembourg, Switzerland, and the Cayman Islands. Garcia claimed that he earned his money smuggling gold jewelry for an Italian firm, Oro Aurora. Pietro Saltarelli, the owner of Oro Aurora, said he had paid Garcia $200,000 in bribes to use his federal identification to sneak the gold past U.S. Customs agents. Garcia was willing to admit to smuggling gold because such an offense is not grounds for extradition from his hiding place in Luxembourg, but drug charges are.[49]

In a ghoulish example of opportunistic theft accessed through state authority, New York City police admitted to taking money from corpses in their charge. They also admitted to stealing house keys from corpses that were later used to burgle the deceaseds' homes.[50] Opportunistic theft by police can also take the form of looting. The following two accounts demonstrate how New York City officers took advantage of their official access to burglary scenes:

> Me and my partner went in the back of the building [where] a door was open. There was about six or seven radio cars out front. A lot of cops was inside. Everybody was stuffing clothes down their pants, in their shirt, up their sleeves. Everybody looking fat because they were stuffing so much clothes in their pants. And my partner was telling me that the owners usually take it out on their income tax. Usually declare—say—more was stolen than was actually taken. Or, they would take it out on their insurance.[51]

> [M]en in police uniforms emerge[d] from the [meat] packing company carrying large, paper-wrapped packages which they loaded into the [patrol] car. In the next few hours, four other police cars . . . half of the precinct . . . responded to the site. Police officers . . . were seen putting packages from the company into their cars. . . . [P]ackages [were transferred] into two private automobiles . . . which were registered to . . . patrolmen.[52]

James Inciardi has documented several other incidents of opportunistic thefts by public safety employees in various cities[53]:

> While searching a purse snatching suspect, a police officer found seventy-two diamond rings. The officer turned in only seventy of them.
>
> While dusting a burglary scene for fingerprints, one officer removed a man's gold watch that the burglar had overlooked. He then stated that the victims had theft insurance.
>
> Contraband was seized after raiding the premises of a local receiver of stolen goods. Several televisions, radios, and musical instruments were put in a private automobile. Officers later divided the booty.
>
> Police divided $18,000 in cash that they discovered while searching the premises of a dead man.

In addition to opportunistic theft, public safety employees steal through planned theft. Here they have access to information or to property by virtue of their official authority. The police are trusted with the locations of empty stores and homes, and often know where valuable or unattended property can be found. Police have also been known to seek out drug dealers and then rob them of money and drugs.[54]

Guards at the Mississippi State Penitentiary used their official status to smuggle low-denomination Postal Service money orders into the prison, where the orders were altered by inmates to a higher amount. The money orders were then sent to unsuspecting "pen pals," primarily widows and elderly women. The pals were persuaded to cash them and forward the proceeds to friends and relatives of the inmates or to guards at the prison. The Postal Service lost in excess of $2 million from the caper. Approximately a third of the forty persons convicted in the scheme were guards.[55]

Another case of planned theft through the use of state authority involved the falsification of odometer readings by Laurel County, Kentucky, clerk C. A. Williams. Williams and his brother pleaded guilty to charges of conspiracy in a multistate auto title-laundering and odometer-tampering scheme. Investigations by the Kentucky State Police and the FBI revealed that as many as 1,400 car titles with false odometer readings passed through the Laurel County clerk's office during a five-month period.[56]

Neutralization techniques sometimes are employed by public safety officers who steal from suspects or from crime and fire scenes. Thefts in two of the above scenarios were neutralized by the offenders on the ground that the victims had insurance or could deduct the loss from income taxes (denials of injury). As in the case of neutralizations for brutality and for sexual exploitation, the acceptability of theft may be learned from colleagues and eventually become a regular part of an officer's conduct norms through occupational differential association. Or state-authority theft may simply be explained as an attempt by low self-control individuals to obtain "money without work."[57]

Political Bribetaking

The state authority occupational crimes discussed thus far have for the most part inflicted physical or monetary harm on discernible victims or groups of victims. Bribetaking for influence, however, is a state authority offense that diffuses its harm throughout the populace. It is perhaps the quintessential violation of public trust. The practice is by no means only a modern phenomenon; John Noonan's encyclopedic *Bribes* documents its occurrence over the past four millennia.[58]

At the beginning of the seventeenth century, only judges and witnesses could be criminally charged for taking money for their influence in court. By the eighteenth century, legislators were criminally chargeable for bribetaking. By the middle of the twentieth century, virtually all government officials and employees were potential criminal bribetakers, either explicitly by statute or implicitly by court precedent. Currently, virtually any public employee who peddles authority or influence over state matters for a price can be convicted for bribetaking.

Laws against bribetaking involve more than payments of cash. Many statutes also include in the crime of bribery the taking of "favors" by officials, though there is some difficulty in interpreting what constitutes a favor. For instance, if Congressman Smith agrees to vote yes on Congresswoman Jones's bill in exchange for Congresswoman Jones's yes vote on Congressman Smith's bill, the agreement technically might fall under the umbrella of the payment of favors for state influence, but in practice it clearly would not.[59]

Intent to be influenced is not a necessary element of bribetaking under many statutes; bribetaking often requires only the acceptance of something "for" or "because of" an official's act. Even a policeman's acceptance of a free cup of coffee from a restaurant in exchange for "official" presence at the establishment might be considered criminal bribetaking under a strict statutory interpretation. Modern bribetaking laws, which include the payment of nonpecuniary rewards, then, may technically permeate even the customary behavior of state employees who use their authority in good faith.

Bribery involving federal employees is covered primarily under **Title 18 *USC,* Section 201,** including attempts to bribe. The statute also encompasses jurors in federal courts and some future and former federal officials. A bribe consists of "anything of value" "for or because of any official act" involving persons who are acting "for or on behalf of the United States." If the bribe is offered or accepted "corruptly" (i.e., solicitation of an official act in exchange for anything of value or vice versa), it carries a maximum prison term of fifteen years and a fine equal to $20,000 or to triple the amount of the bribe, whichever is greater. Otherwise, the maximum punishment is two years imprisonment and a $10,000 fine. A noncorrupt bribe is generally considered to be a **gratuity,** which is given or taken for an official act that was not originally conceived because of the payment.

Official acts for or on behalf of the United States certainly include acts that exercise "state authority," such as those by police and prison officers, judges, and elected and appointed officials. The Section 201 designation of "public official" also includes persons who are making decisions on behalf of the United States that do not involve the exercise of state authority, such as purchasing and hiring by employees in their normal administrative roles. The statute also punishes bribegivers—persons who, acting either individually or on behalf of an organization, bribe or attempt to bribe any of these government agents.

In nonfederal cases, if the circumstances involve "influencing" the enforcement of a law or a legislative action, there can be criminal violations in addition to bribery. Nonfederal obstruction of justice statutes typically punish state officials who offer false statements about an official action. The federal obstruction of justice statutes, found under Title 18 *USC* Chapter 73, outlaw giving bribes to persons influential or material to a federal trial, hearing, or investigation, such as witnesses, jurors, prosecutors, and judges.

Both federal and nonfederal public agents who take bribes can also be charged with the following federal offenses, depending on the circumstances: extortion, interstate travel to commit a crime, mail and wire fraud, tax evasion, and racketeering.

The **Hobbs Act** (Title 18 *USC,* Section 1951) was passed by Congress in 1946 to combat robbery and extortion that interfere with interstate commerce. Bribery has been considered synonymous with extortion under Hobbs, although it is not mentioned explicitly. Subsection (b)(2) of the Hobbs law defines extortion as those acts that obtain the property of another with the other's consent, when such consent was induced by "wrongful use of actual or threatened force, violence, or fear, or *under color of official right*" (emphasis added). Extortion under color of official right is considered to be the wrongful taking by a public officer of money or property not due him or his office, independent of whether such taking was accomplished by force, threats, or use of fear. Even if the bribetaker did not have the official authority to do the deed requested by the briber, the taker is still guilty, because the briber believed that the official had such a power and the taker accepted the bribe under the auspices of having the official power.

Interpreters of the Hobbs Act see no difference between accepting bribery and kickbacks (or conspiring or attempting to secure them) for state influence on the one hand and extortion under color of official right on the other hand. Violation of Hobbs carries a penalty of as much as twenty years in prison in addition to a fine. This federal statute has jurisdiction over all bribetaking officials because misuse of any public position will always have a threatened or probable, if not an actual, effect on interstate commerce. The nexus between the bribetaking official and interstate commerce can be established, for instance, simply by claiming that the government employer of the bribetaker transacts business with firms that deal in interstate commerce. This minimal connection between state authority actors in a bribe and interstate commerce effectively puts all acts of political bribery under Hobbs.

The **Travel Act** of 1961 (Title 18 *USC,* Section 1952) makes it illegal to travel or to promote travel from one state to another (including foreign travel) in order to carry out any one of several federal and state criminal offenses, explicitly including bribery (subsection (b)(2)). If a bribetaker or bribegiver causes (or attempts to cause) another person to cross state lines or the federal border, or uses the federal mails or interstate wires to complete a bribe, he or she is guilty under the Travel Act, and is subject to as much as five years in prison and a fine. Parties also are punishable if they travel interstate for matters related to the bribe. Bribery of persons in both public and private roles is punishable under the Travel Act.

In addition to violating the Travel Act, any political bribetaking that uses the mails or interstate wires in the process of proposal, payment, distribution, or carrying out the agreement is a violation of federal mail fraud (Title 18 *USC,* Section 1341) and federal wire fraud (Title 18 *USC,* Section 1343) statutes. Included under mail and wire fraud is "a scheme or artifice to deprive another of the intangible right to honest services."[60] Thus, political bribetaking or bribegiving is punishable if the mails or wires were used in any way to effect it, because citizens have the right to expect elected and appointed state authorities to act honestly.[61] In addition, bribetaking officials can be prosecuted for evading federal and state income tax if they do not report payments (cash, goods, services) from bribes as income.

The **Racketeer Influenced and Corrupt Organizations Act** (Title 18 *USC*, Chapter 96), or RICO, was passed by Congress in 1970 to battle "organized" crime. RICO Section 1962 outlaws using a pattern of racketeering activities to invest in or gain control of an enterprise that engages in or affects interstate commerce. Section 1962 also prohibits persons from using a pattern of racketeering activities while in association with any enterprise that engages in or affects interstate commerce. Conspiracy to commit these acts is also punishable under RICO. "Racketeering activity" specifically includes bribery (public and private bribetaking and bribegiving) chargeable as a felony under state and federal law. In addition, racketeering activity comprises many other felonies (e.g., murder, kidnapping, extortion, arson, robbery, gambling). RICO penalties provide for as much as twenty years in prison, a fine, forfeiture of any gains from or interests in racketeering enterprises, and triple damages to be paid to any person harmed by a RICO offense.

To be guilty under RICO, one must practice a "pattern of racketeering" to the extent that it affects an "enterprise." A pattern must comprise at least two racketeering events within a ten-year period, excluding the time the perpetrator was incarcerated (Section 1961.5). Racketeering acts must be connected with each other by some common scheme, plan, or motive so as to constitute a set of related events. A public agent who takes bribes from two different entities within a ten-year period or from the same entity on two different occasions during that time period is guilty of a RICO offense. Even the acceptance of two installment payments on a single bribe within the specified period constitutes a pattern of racketeering under RICO. And there is ample precedent to indicate that governments are enterprises that are affected by bribetaking and that affect interstate commerce. Moreover, acquittal of bribery, obstruction of justice, or other charges does not preclude one from being charged under RICO. Indeed, RICO gives the federal government power to ferret out virtually all political bribers and bribetakers in the United States. Many states also have RICO laws.

Technically, a bribetaker can be charged cumulatively with all of the above federal violations—Section 201, the Hobbs Act, the Travel Act, mail fraud, wire fraud, and RICO—given that the elements of each exist.

However, under U.S. Sentencing Guidelines, the Department of Justice will charge bribery offenders with the most serious offense only; it does not consider multiple payments of a single bribe a violation of RICO. Sentencing for a typical bribe-take or bribe-give prosecuted under Section 201 begins at six months for a lower-level state authority bribee and escalates to a minimum of twenty-seven months for a higher-level bribee, including the following at the local, state, and federal levels: prosecuting attorneys, judges, agency administrators, supervisory law enforcement officers, and other appointed and elected officials with similar or greater responsibility. If the bribe involves more than $2,000, the sentence increases accordingly—a $10,000 bribe would carry an additional ten months and a $50,000 bribe would carry an additional seventeen months. The fine is levied according to whichever of the following is greatest: (1) the value of the bribe; (2) the value of the benefit to be received through the bribe; or (3) the damages that result from the bribe. The punishment and fines can be slightly less if the bribe was a noncorrupt gratuity.

Operation Greylord, initiated by the Federal Bureau of Investigation in 1978 against Illinois' Cook County court system in Chicago, resulted in what has become the most infamous case of judicial misconduct and bribery in American history. The three-and-a-half-year "sting" resulted in the conviction of nine judges, thirty-seven attorneys, and nineteen other court personnel between 1983 and 1985. Although some have argued that the tactics used by the federal government were immoral—wiretaps, lies, and the bugging of judges' chambers and other conversations—they may have been the only possible means by which to gather concrete evidence in a wide-ranging corruption scandal.[62]

Boxes 5.2 and 5.3 detail two additional infamous cases of state bribery (police corruption in New York City and the ABSCAM scandal involving members of the United States Congress), and the following depict recent state authority corruption cases:

> In 1991, federal District Judge Robert F. Collins was convicted of scheming with a New Orleans businessman to split a drug smuggler's $100,000 payoff. Collins was sentenced to six years in prison.[63]

> In November of 1994, Pat Nolen went from California State Assemblyman to convict when he resigned his office and six hours later pleaded guilty to bribery related offenses. Nolen is said to have been "conducting his Assembly office as a racketeering enterprise to solicit bribes." He had attempted to extort $12,500 from an undercover FBI agent who posed as a businessman seeking legislation to help a fictitious shrimping business. Nolen was sentenced to 33 months in prison, three years probation, and a fine of $10,000.[64]

BOX 5.2

The Twenty-Year Curse

Witness "X" wears a hood obscuring his identity while testifying in 1993 before the Mollen Commission hearings on alleged corruption in the New York City Police Department. Police corruption has ratings between 9 and 12 on the National Survey of Crime Severity. Frank Serpico (right) testifies before the Knapp Commission investigating police corruption in New York City.

Every twenty years over the past century, the New York City Police Department has been rocked by a bribery scandal. In 1892, the Reverend Charles Parkhurst sermonized that the New York City Police Department was "a lying, perjured, rum-soaked and libidinous lot."[a] State investigation discovered that officers were systematically extorting money from prostitutes and gamblers. Attempts at reform were carried out under the department's new Police Commissioner, Theodore Roosevelt. Similar scandals struck New York's finest in 1911, 1932, and 1951, each episode followed by changes to discourage corruption.[b]

The twenty-year clock struck again in 1972 when the findings of New York's *Knapp Commission Report on Police Corruption* became public.[c] This report is the most comprehensive collection of cases involving bribetaking by police officers. The investigation was the result of information about police corruption brought to light in 1967 by former New York City detective Frank Serpico. The

(continued next page)

BOX 5.2

Continued

Knapp Commission, chaired by Whitman Knapp, was in operation from 1967 through the end of 1972. It found pervasive corruption throughout virtually all lower ranks (through lieutenant) of the New York City Police Department, as well as among some higher officials. Not all police officers in the lower ranks were involved in blatant corruption, but most at least accepted gratis meals and services, and did not take steps to prevent what they knew or suspected as corrupt police activities.

The commission differentiated two major forms of bribetakers: "meat eaters" and "grass eaters." *Grass eaters*, the most common form, refer to those passively accepting bribes when "appropriate" situations present themselves. *Meat eaters*, on the other hand, are the police officers who aggressively seek out situations they can exploit for financial gain. These include gambling, drugs, and other offenses that can yield bribes totaling thousands of dollars. One highly placed police official told the commission that $5,000 to $50,000 payoffs to meat eaters were common; one narcotics bribe amounted to $250,000.

There are two types of bribes taken by the police: "pads" and "scores." The *pad* refers to regularly scheduled (e.g., weekly, monthly) bribes in exchange for nonenforcement of the law. Illegal gambling operations are probably the largest source of pad payments. Some detectives had collected monthly or every-other-week pads amounting to as much as $3,500 from each gambling establishment in their jurisdiction. The monthly share (or "nut") per officer ranged from $300 or $400 in midtown Manhattan to $800 in the Bronx, $1,200 in Brooklyn, and $1,500 in Harlem. Supervisors' nuts often were a share-and-a-half. Newly assigned plainclothes officers were not given a share until after a few months in order to ascertain whether they were informants.

A *score* is a one-time bribe that an officer solicits from (or is offered by) a citizen for not enforcing the law. A police officer can "score" from a motorist for not writing a traffic citation or from a narcotics peddler for not making an arrest. Many officers were implicated in the solicitation of payoffs for nebulous court testimony that would result in the dropping of charges. Additionally, narcotics officers took bribes in exchange for information about an impending arrest, for the results of telephone wiretaps or other confidential police information, and for influencing the justice process for known dealers or addicts.

Gratuities (variants of the pad) refer to free meals, free goods and services, and cash "tips" received by officers. Gratuities were by far the most widespread form of misconduct the commission found.[d] Several thousand free meals were consumed by the New York officers each day. The sheer numbers of gratis meals posed problems for some establishments. Tips were often given at Christmas and for the performance of normal duties. The Knapp Commission concluded that an intense sense of organizational loyalty and a disdain for outside scrutiny were the major reasons why corruption flourished.

Again like clockwork, twenty years after the Knapp Commission a new anticorruption commission was appointed to investigate the New York City Police Department. The Mollen Commission—named for its head, Milton Mollen, a former deputy mayor and appellate judge—began its hearings in September of 1993. Evidence uncovered by the Mollen Commission included many of the same things found by its predecessor—extortion, pads, and scores. Additionally, some officers were implicated as drug dealers themselves. A major offender, Michael Dowd, admitted to running a drug-protection racket netting $4,000 each week, some of which he spent on a personal cocaine habit. Although the corruption uncovered by the Mollen Commission was more isolated than that found by Knapp, organized corruption was discovered within various pockets of the city. The 75th Precinct, for instance, would customarily set daily extortion goals and periodically plan robberies of drug dealers.[e] The department's Internal Affairs Division was said to bear much of the blame for the new generation of corrupt officers. It had failed to investigate allegations of wrongdoing, such as that of Dowd, about whom it had been receiving reports for more than four years. The Mollen Commission's solution to continual corruption was the appointment of a full-time external watchdog.[f]

The Knapp and Mollen Commissions' materials demonstrate that scoring, padding, and other forms of bribery were *learned* through differential association with other officers.[g] There are also indications from both commissions that participation in police corruption is individualized. Because bribetaking involves obtaining "money without work,"[h] propensity-event theory may be a more robust explanation, but this is true only to the extent that bribetakers can be shown to have lower levels of self-control in other aspects of their lives than police officers who refuse to participate in corruption.

a. Associated Press, "NYC Police Again Tainted by Scandal," *The Albany Herald* (September 27, 1993), i. 3A.

b. Ibid.

c. Whitman Knapp, *The Knapp Commission Report on Police Corruption* (New York): George Brazziler.

d. Ibid., p. 170.

e. Associated Press, "Officer Says Police Code Led Him Astray," *The Albany Herald,* (September 28, 1993): 7A.

f. "NYC Police Again Tainted by Scandal."

g. See, for example, *Knapp Commission,* pp. 100, 102; "Officer Says Police Code Led Him Astray."

h. Michael Gottfredson and Travis Hirschi, *A General Theory of Crime* (Palo Alto, CA: Stanford University Press, 1990), p. 89.

BOX 5.3

Legislator Corruption: "ABSCAM"

The first statute punishing bribetaking by a member of Congress appeared in 1852, but no convictions were obtained before the twentieth century. As of 1970, ten members of Congress had been convicted of crimes involving bribery; most of them received relatively mild censure. Two received presidential pardons, some returned to their practice of law, one was sentenced to a day in jail, and another was put on probation. During the 1970s, several more members of Congress were prosecuted for bribetaking or variants of it, but sentences continued to be light (e.g., fine only, probation, three months in jail).[a] Lackadaisical efforts to prosecute bribetakers in Congress ended in 1978 with ABSCAM.

Abdul Enterprises was a fictitious company (thus ABSCAM) set up with money provided by the Federal Bureau of Investigation. The firm allegedly represented two rich Arabs, Kambir Abdul Rahman and Yassir Habib, who wanted to invest large sums of money in the United States and did not particularly care about violating official rules while doing so. The credibility of the firm was predicated on the general beliefs that, first, Arabs had money to invest, and second, foreigners were generally not likely to be concerned with American laws.

The FBI paid an experienced confidence man, Melvin Weinberg, to play a major role for Abdul Enterprises during the sting. John Noonan described Weinberg's role in ABSCAM as follows: "A swindler formerly outside the law, he now swindled swindlers who had prospered in American society. A criminal, he turned lawmakers into lawbreakers like himself."[b] The allegedly oil-rich Abdul Enterprises first lured thieves trying to sell stolen art, securities, and other items. One of the forgers with whom the "firm" was dealing proposed that the Arabs build a casino in Atlantic City. He assured Abdul Enterprises that a New Jersey casino gaming license could be arranged without trouble through Angelo Errichetti, the mayor of Camden. Thus, the first politician who took the bait in ABSCAM was not specifically targeted by the authorities.

Through Errichetti, other government officials were introduced into ABSCAM. Ultimately, the trap ensnared a member of the New Jersey Casino Commission; members of the Philadelphia City Council; public agents for sewer contracts in Connecticut, New York, and New Jersey; several middlemen; and several members of the United States Congress.

Errichetti brought to Abdul Enterprises U.S. Representatives Michael Myers (D–NJ), Frank Thompson (D–NJ), and Raymond Lederer (D–PA), all of whom accepted bribes in exchange for introducing a private immigration bill to allow the fake Rahman and Habib to remain in the United States. Thompson brought in Congressman John Murphy (D–NY), who also pledged support for such a bill in exchange for cash. Errichetti also recruited U.S. Senator Harrison Williams (D–NJ), a twenty-three-year veteran of Congress. Williams agreed to influence the U.S. government to contract with a nonexistent titanium venture allegedly financed by the fake Arabs in exchange for a large lump of stock in the titanium company. Other middlemen unwittingly netted U.S. Representatives John Jenrette (D–SC) and Richard Kelly (R–FL). Kelly later tried to argue in court (quite unsuccessfully) that he had actually planned to turn the bribegivers over to the FBI at a later date, and that he had spent some of the bribe money only to convince the bribers that he was earnestly involved with them.

The crimes committed by these public officials and their middlemen were captured graphically on video and audiotape by the FBI. Never before had Americans seen public corruption so vividly. Bribes in ABSCAM were as high as $100,000.

All told, Jenrette, Kelly, Lederer, Myers, Thompson, and Williams were convicted of bribery, and Murphy was convicted of the lesser offense of taking money to perform an official action. Kelly, Lederer, Myers, and Williams were also convicted of violating the Travel Act, and Thompson and Williams of criminal conflict of interest. Kelly received eighteen months in jail, Jenrette two years, and the remainder three years. Jenrette, Lederer, Murphy, Myers, Thompson, and Williams were fined, ranging from $20,000 (Murphy) to $50,000 (Williams). Jenrette, Kelly, Murphy, and Thompson failed to be reelected, Lederer resigned, Myers was the first person expelled from the House of Representatives for bribetaking, and Williams finally resigned from the Senate under intense pressure.[c]

The legal and moral message sent by the ABSCAM scandal to wielders of public power was that persons entrusted with state authority are expected to keep themselves beyond temptation. This expectation is not unrealistic, as South Dakota's Senator Larry Pressler demonstrated during ABSCAM. Pressler was offered a campaign contribution by Abdul Enterprises in exchange for a promise to help the Arabs with a private bill. Pressler, recorded on tape, refused to promise anything. ABSCAM may well have also sent another message to those in public office: the next person who offers you a bribe may be a federal undercover agent.

In the ABSCAM cases, the evidence supporting differential association would be somewhat inferential. Bribetaking did not appear to be an accepted practice in Congress or other specific government positions; rather it seemed to flourish in particular locales. New Jersey, according to Lincoln Steffens, had always been corrupt.[d] The roles played by Errichetti, Myers, Thompson, Williams, and others in ABSCAM did little to dispel that state's criminal image. Errichetti easily

(continued next page)

BOX 5.3

Continued

produced for the FBI other officials he knew would be willing to take a bribe, many of whom were from his geographic area. Various techniques of bribery designed to camouflage offenses and offenders were commonly used by the players (e.g., a middleman or "bagman," the avoidance of literal references to cash). Because of the close collusion between many of those involved, especially Errichetti, it seems likely that these protective techniques were learned rather than invented independently by each of the ABSCAM participants. In short, differential association may be a very relevant explanation for the ABSCAM scandal.

a. John Noonan *Bribes* (New York: Macmillan, 1984), pp. 601–19.
b. Ibid., p. 606.
c. Ibid., pp. 604–19.
d. Ibid.

Former Telfair County [GA] Sheriff Ronnie Walker pleaded guilty in 1993 to federal charges that he provided protection from police to marijuana growers, cocaine dealers, and gamblers in return for profits from their crimes. Walker and 24 others were indicted as a result of a three-year federal investigation dubbed "Riversweep."[65]

Former Tift County [GA] Deputy Sheriff Wilbert Roberson was sentenced to two years in prison in 1990 for taking $150 in bribes in exchange for information about law enforcement activity against drug trafficking.[66]

In 1991, Dade County [FL] Circuit Judge Roy Gelber pleaded guilty to federal corruption charges stemming from his acceptance of bribes in exchange for judicial favors in criminal cases. Investigators created fictitious cases and defendants, then had a well known lawyer approach Gelber and three other judges to offer bribes related to bond reductions, suppression of evidence, and disclosure of confidential police information.[67]

Five South Carolina legislators were charged in 1990 with selling their votes on a parimutuel betting bill. Like "ABSCAM" [see box 5.3], the FBI videotaped or electronically recorded the legislators accepting money at various locations; "installments" on the bribes ranged as high as $7500.[68]

Walter Tucker, U.S. Congressman from California, was indicted in 1994 for taking $30,000 in bribes while he was mayor of Compton [CA]. The bribe came from a company that wanted to build a waste-to-energy plant. Tucker was said to have been dissatisfied with the $30,000 and demanded an additional $250,000.[69]

Differential association as a cause for bribetaking was discussed in regard to police (in box 5.2) and politicians' wrongdoing (in box 5.3). Propensity-event would treat bribetaking as merely one of the many low self-control behaviors committed by those who engage in it—simply another way to gain "money without work."[70] While there may be "work" involved in arranging and completing certain bribes and, in some cases, fulfilling the task for which the bribe was intended, such work would be much less than would be required to accumulate the same amount of money legally. Propensity-event would hypothesize that state authority positions that require a higher level of self-control to attain, such as elected and appointed offices, would have fewer bribetakers than other state authority positions. Thus, proportionately, there should be fewer bribetakers in politics than in police work, assuming perceptions of punishability and opportunity for bribetaking are constant in both groups.

Key Terms

state authority
policeman's working personality
Dirty Harry Problem
Title 18 *USC* (Section 242)
color of law
Bivens claim
Title 18 *USC* (Section 201)
gratuity
Hobbs Act
Travel Act
Racketeer Influenced and Corrupt Organizations (RICO)

Questions for Discussion

1. State authority crimes are sometimes committed by persons who have the power to define their actions as noncriminal. Give examples. Which factors affect the exercise of such self-definitions?
2. Because of the danger and authority involved in their everyday work, the police tend to isolate themselves from other citizens. Should the attitudes associated with police work (e.g., suspicion, authoritarianism) be discouraged, or are they necessary for law enforcement officer safety?
3. What formal and informal mechanisms would you implement to control police use of excessive force? One must be careful here to limit but not *deny* the use of force.
4. The chapter suggested that many activities associated with police and police work reflect the correlates of low self-control propensi-

ties. This implies that police and criminals are very much alike because they both demonstrate low self-control propensities. Do you agree? Why or why not?

5. Discuss problems in enforcing criminal civil rights violations under Title 18, *USC,* Section 242.
6. Private companies often subject their workers to periodic polygraph examinations to discover dishonest employees. Should police officers be given regular polygraph examinations regarding theft or bribetaking on the job? What about physiological tests for the use of illicit drugs? What positive and negative ramifications might such testing produce for members of a police department specifically?
7. Is it permissible for police officers to accept certain noncash gratuities, such as free or discounted meals and services? What are the undesirable outcomes of a policy that allows police to accept free meals?
8. Describe the several crimes associated with the trading of sexual acts for official favors. Be specific regarding who initiates the act and whether the act actually takes place.
9. What reforms would you suggest to reduce bribetaking by police?
10. How "fair" were the actions the government took to incriminate those implicated in Greylord and ABSCAM? Should the government continue such stings against other, nonelected, government employees? Why or why not?

General Readings on State Authority Occupational Crime

Thomas Barker and David L. Carter (eds.), *Police Deviance* (2d ed.) (Cincinnati: Anderson, 1991).

David Ermann and Richard Lundman, *Corporate and Governmental Deviance* (4th ed.) (New York: Oxford University Press, 1992).

David M. Jones, "Organization or Individual Corruption? An Examination of Operation Greylord," *Justice Professional* 7 (1992): 35–52.

Victor E. Kappeler, Richard D. Sluder, and Geoffrey P. Alpert, *Forces of Deviance: Understanding the Dark Side of Policing* (Prospect Heights, IL: Waveland Press, 1994).

Carl Klockars, "The Dirty Harry Problem," *Annals of the American Academy of Political and Social Science* 452 (November 1980):33–47.

Whitman Knapp, *The Knapp Commission Report on Police Corruption* (New York: George Brazziler, 1973).

Julian Roebuck and Stanley C. Weeber, *Political Crime in the United States:Analyzing Crime by and against the Government* (New York: Praeger, 1978).

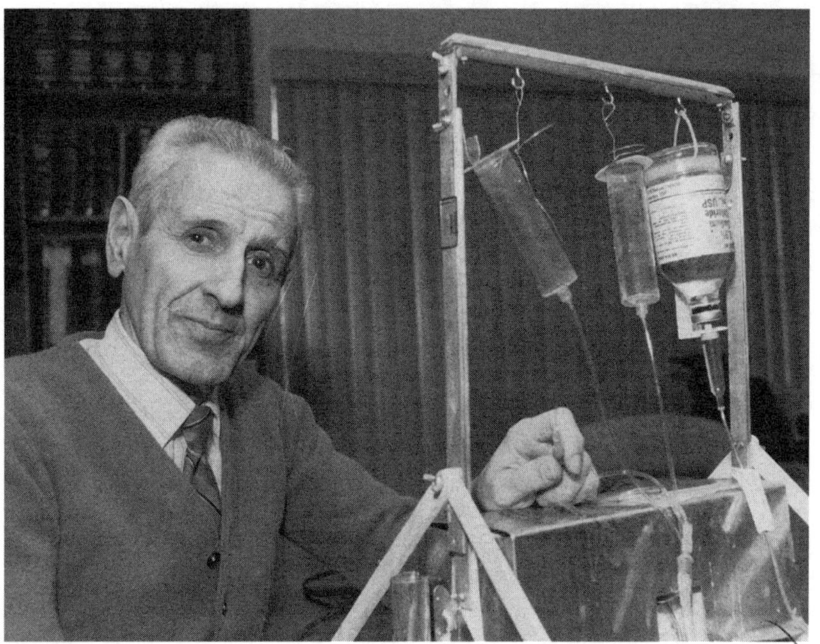

Dr. Jack Kevorkian and his "suicide machine" in 1991. The murder charges judicially disallowed against Kevorkian for helping severely ill patients kill themselves illustrate the reluctance of courts to equate euthanasia with homicide.

6 *Professional Occupational Crime*

The *Oxford American Dictionary* defines the word *profession* as: "an occupation, especially one that involves knowledge and training in a branch of advanced learning."[1] Self-regulation is a distinct element of the professions. As Freidson notes, the right to control their own work and the right to deem "outside evaluations illegitimate"[2] have been accorded to professions. Although there may be "professionals" in all occupational areas, the traditional conception of professional is limited to careers such as human and veterinary medicine, psychology, law, pharmacy, and accountancy. This chapter will focus on doctors and lawyers.

Crime in the professions is conceptually distinct from other occupational offending because the professions invariably require some sort of oath or ethical commitment that bestows on practitioners a special trust on which the persons they serve believe they can rely. For example, the Hippocratic Oath for physicians states, "I will adopt the regimen which in my best judgment is beneficial to my patients, and not for their injury or for any wrongful purpose." The American Psychoanalytic Association's *Principles of Ethics for Psychoanalysts,* Section 6, states, "Except as required by law, a psychoanalyst may not reveal the confidences entrusted to him." These kinds of special trusts set the professions apart from other occupations.

Clients typically share their innermost physical, mental, and financial problems with professionals, who are often perfect strangers. Generally, a client's trust in a professional involves a belief that the professional will do what is in the best interests of the client rather than what is in the professional's best interests. Because crime by professionals in their professional capacity often involves a violation of this special trust, it may be seen as particularly deceitful. The state also entrusts professionals with certain legal responsibilities, such as the signing of death certificates, the dispensing of prescriptions, and various fiduciary duties.

The existing data on crimes in the professions are poor, largely because they are primarily based on proactive enforcement by investigators. Available figures more accurately reflect enforcement agency policies and budgetary constraints than they do the totality of professionally related offenses and offenders. As one Medicare fraud enforcement official put it, "To go after these guys we need an army and all we've got is a battalion, if that."[3] Usually, it is only through an audit or by chance occurrence that improprieties by doctors and lawyers are brought to light. In the case of medical insurance fraud,

> [O]ne investigator compared the prevalence of lawbreaking doctors to a grossly overstocked fishpond, where the merest attempt easily nets prey. But the way the system actually works, he pointed out, is that "the only ones we get are the fish that jump into the boat." Only the blatantly indiscreet, seemingly totally disorganized, or astonishingly thoughtless physicians are snared. . . .[4]

There is some evidence that legal authorities are more lenient with at least some professionals than they are with other kinds of offenders. One federal agent noted:

> U.S. attorneys are extraordinarily kind to doctors, because even if they are crooks, theoretically they're still providing some useful services for the community. There's a double standard for doctors because there aren't many other categories of [occupational] criminals that are looked upon as a community of people who save lives.[5]

Even when offenders in the professions are found out and an attempt is made to prosecute them, there is often tremendous difficulty in establishing criminal intent to commit the crimes of which they are accused, especially given the "beyond a reasonable doubt" burden of proof in criminal cases. There often is a fine line between intentional criminality on the one hand and a "difference of professional opinion" on the other. Because of mutual respect and an interest in keeping the integrity and public image of the profession intact, only the grossest abuses will arouse intraprofessional pronouncements of criminal violation. While some crimes by professionals come to the attention of the authorities through victim complaints (such as double-billing medical patients, embezzlement from clients by lawyers, sexual assaults on patients), many victims remain unaware of their victimization (as in the cases of unnecessary surgery and adulterated prescriptions).

Medical and Mental Health Professions

Doctors who treat human beings—physicians, osteopaths, chiropractors, podiatrists, dentists, psychologists, psychiatrists—commit many occupational criminal acts. Fee splitting, prescription drug violations, fraudulent medical insurance claims, aggravated assault (unnecessary surgery or other needless painful treatment), and sexual assault are the "common crimes" among medical professionals. Doctors have also committed criminal homicide within their occupation in the forms of illegal abortion and euthanasia. Other professionally related criminal violations include fraudulent reports and testimony in criminal and civil court cases (including the falsification of death certificates and other official documents) and failure to report certain treatments to authorities (e.g., for gunshot wounds, child abuse). Veterinarians who inflict unnecessary surgery or treatment on animals are guilty of at least two offenses: cruelty to animals and fraud. The professions can facilitate individual crimes as well, such as price-fixing (e.g., fees and laboratory tests) and kickbacks (e.g., prescribing medical treatments to be performed at facilities owned by the prescribing physician).

Criminal Unnecessary Medical Procedures

From the standpoint of the criminal law, willfully committing unnecessary surgery (or other unnecessary medical treatments) is fraud because it results in money being obtained under the false pretense that the medical procedure is necessary. It is also a crime against the person because, depending on the extent of the intrusion, the unnecessary surgery or treatment would involve battery, mayhem, or criminal homicide. The victim's consent cannot be used as a defense by the offender because consent was obtained under false pretenses. Francis Cullen and his colleagues report some public concern with the criminality associated with this type of physician behavior—among those they surveyed, about two persons in five (42 percent) favored a prison term for a doctor who performs a needless operation.[6] The following case epitomizes criminal unnecessary medical treatment:

> [A] California ophthalmologist was convicted [in 1984] for subjecting poor patients to unneeded cataract surgery in order to collect Medicaid fees. In

> one instance, he totally blinded a 57-year-old woman when he operated needlessly on her one sighted eye.[7] [He] was convicted of performing unnecessary eye operations that left 14 patients with impaired vision.[8]

There has been concern about unnecessary medical procedures in America for more than two centuries. In his classic 1775 work, *Plain Concise Practical Remedies on the Treatment of Wounds and Fractures,* the first surgical textbook written by a U.S. physician, John Jones wrote:

> As every operation is necessarily attended with a certain degree of bodily pain, as well as terrible apprehension to the patient's mind, a good surgeon will be in the first place, well assured of the necessity of an operation, before he proceeds to perform it; and secondly he ought to consider whether the patient will in all probability be the better for it, or whether he may not be the worse.[9]

In calling for reforms to combat unnecessary medical procedures, Jones also wrote in that treatise:

> Among the variety of public errors and abuses to be met with in human affairs, there is not one perhaps which more loudly calls for a speedy and effectual reformation than the misapplied benevolence of hospitals for the sick and wounded.[10]

However, standards regulating American physicians' decisions to perform surgeries and treatments were not forthcoming for at least a century and a quarter after Jones's plea for reform. It was not until the first decade of the twentieth century that Ernest Amory Codman proposed to assess the competency of hospitals and physicians through his "end-result plan," which tracked hospital patients after medical procedures. Codman was appointed chairperson of the Clinical Congress of Surgeons' (the forerunner to the American College of Surgeons) Committee on Hospital Standardization, a role in which he crusaded for a national standardization in hospital medical care.[11] In 1920, John G. Bowman, the first director of the American College of Surgeons, advocated "minimum standardization" to identify ". . . if any unnecessary surgical operations are performed in [a] hospital . . . or if lax, lazy, or incomplete diagnoses are made."[12]

Defining exactly what is "unnecessary" surgery or treatment can be problematic, however. Whether a medical procedure is ineffective or inappropriate for a given medical circumstance is the crux of what is meant by unnecessary. Yet any operation or treatment that fails to produce its desired result can be judged *post factum* as ineffective and inappropriate, though there initially was a presumed potential to help the patient. Perhaps the best way to define **a criminal unnecessary medical procedure** is when a doctor knowingly lies by telling a patient that his or her condition *requires* a particular surgery or treatment. This approach includes nearly all connotations of intentional fraud in the delivery of medical procedures by legally practicing physicians. It would include the delivery of procedures known by the physician to be ineffective. It would also encompass delivering procedures without advising the patient about other methods known to the physician that would have the same outcome and be less expensive or less intrusive.

Unintentional unnecessary medical procedures should not be confused with the intentional ones in our definition; the former are civil wrongs (torts) and result from incompetence while the latter are crimes that result from the intent to defraud. An unintentional unnecessary medical procedure may be so negligent as to constitute criminal negligence, but this crime would fall under a strict liability legal doctrine—such as those associated with regulatory law, discussed in chapter 4—rather than necessarily within the present context of intentional behavior. Of the many billions of dollars paid each year for unnecessary physician procedures, a portion is spent because of incompetence and the rest is the product of doctors' willful attempts to defraud and to maim. Box 6.1 details some of this incompetence.

Research on the delivery of unnecessary medical treatment has concentrated on surgery. Four methods have been used to estimate its extent: (1) geographic surgical rate variations; (2) second surgical opinion studies; (3) comparison of surgical rates between prepaid health maintenance organizations and fee-for-service practitioners; and (4) experts' examinations of preset criteria for surgery decision making.

Regarding the first method, students of public health have for decades analyzed the differences in surgery rates according to geographic location.[13] For tonsillectomies, elevenfold (in Vermont[14]) and fourfold (in Massachusetts[15]) variations have been documented. A sixfold variation in hemorrhoidectomies was found in Maine[16], and as much as an eightfold variation for other common operations was found in Wisconsin.[17] Other American studies have shown: (1) an 80 percent higher hysterectomy rate south of the Mason-Dixon Line; (2) Des Moines residents' 100 percent higher open-heart surgery rate than that of Iowa City residents; (3) San Diegans' two-thirds higher open-heart surgery rate than that of their fellow Californians in Palo Alto; (4) a 400 percent difference in elective surgery rates across Kansas; and (5) a 400 percent difference in hernia operation rates and a 1,000 percent difference in pacemaker operation rates across Massachusetts.[18] Internationally, surgical rates for selected opera-

BOX 6.1

Criminally Incompetent Medicine

As noted in the text, some doctors are so incompetent that their practice of medicine is criminally negligent. Criminal negligence means that the offender does not premeditate a harmful act, but the failure to exercise the legally required degree of care was so egregious that it constitutes a crime.

Many doctors cannot prescribe medicine correctly. One study found an average of 2.5 errors a day in written prescriptions at the 640-bed Albany (New York) Medical Center Hospital. Of the 289,000 prescriptions written in 1987, 905 mistakes occurred, including 182 (or a fifth) that could have caused severe harm or death. Mistakes ranged from prescribing too strong a tranquilizer for the size or age of the patient to prescribing drugs to which patients were highly allergic. Statewide in New York hospitals in 1984, 4,700 patients were unintentionally injured or killed from prescription medicine.[a]

Some physicians do not even know their left from their right. For instance, within a month at one Tampa (Florida) hospital doctors amputated the wrong foot of a diabetic and operated on the wrong knee of another patient[b], and at Emory University Hospital the former head of ophthalmology performed a cornea transplant on the wrong eye of a seventy-eight-year-old man.[c] As a result of such incompetence, hospitals are beginning to mark the limb or organ that is not to be operated upon with a big NO in black marker.[d] These cases from the media are not isolated instances. A 1991 Harvard University study concluded that nearly one in every twenty-five patients in New York state hospitals was injured by doctors or staff, while hospitals in California have been found to injure one in twenty patients.[e] It has also been estimated that hospital-caused blood infections cost $5 billion annually and cause almost as many deaths as suicide.[f]

Whether a doctor is charged with criminal negligence is at the discretion of the prosecutor. Incompetent physicians are most often punished civilly through exorbitant malpractice settlements and awards. However, this was not the case for Gerald Einaugler, a New York City physician who mistook a patient's dialysis catheter for a feeding tube and made the fatal order to pump food into her stomach. Prosecutors stated that they pursued criminal charges of reckless endangerment and willful violation of health laws against Einaugler primarily because he attempted to hide his misdeed without any regard for the maimed patient's welfare: he left her in her nursing home for ten hours after the mishap, even though he was advised by two colleagues to hospitalize her immediately. Although the judge in the case sentenced Einaugler to fifty-two weekends in jail, his fellow doctors felt he was entirely justified in his actions. He was not disciplined by the State of New York Board for Professional Medical Conduct and his appeals were supported by the American Medical Association and the Medical Society of the State of New York.[g] This tendency toward self-protection among physicians is pervasive. Experts believe that as many as a tenth of physicians are incompetent or impaired, but less than 1 percent are disciplined and even fewer are delicensed.[h]

a. Associated Press, "Medication Errors Told," *Albany Herald* (May 2, 1990):12C.

b. Associated Press, "Are Hospital Horror Stories the Trend?" *Albany Herald* (March 18, 1995):7A.

c. Associated Press, "Settlement Reached in Lawsuit," *Albany Herald* (May 3, 1990):7A.

d. "Are Hospital Horror Stories the Trend?"

e. Ibid.

f. Richard P. Wenzel, "The Mortality of Hospital Acquired Bloodstream Infections: Need for a New Vital Statistic?" *International Journal of Epidemiology* 17 (1988):225–27.

g. Associated Press, "Doctor Jailed after Patient's Death," *Albany Herald* (March 17, 1995):8A.

h. "Are Hospital Horror Stories the Trend?"

---

tions during the mid-1970s in the United States were 43 percent greater than those in Canada and 125 percent greater than in England and Wales.[19]

Critics of the medical profession have asserted that doctors practicing in the regions with higher rates of surgery commit unnecessary surgery.[20] The reverse is equally plausible, however; regions with lower rates of operations may underutilize surgical procedures. Alternatively, different rates of surgery across regions may be explained by variations in the rates of disease, the supplies of beds and physicians, the demographic characteristics of patients (e.g., age and gender), and the patients' abilities to pay. Although research results conflict on the extent to which these factors explain differences in regional surgical rates[21], clearly the discrepancies in the rates often are not entirely attributable to unnecessary operations. Gross discrepancies (such as a tenfold difference) are at least partially attributable to a criminal overutilization of surgical procedures, but wide conclusions about purposeful unnecessary surgery from geographic studies are at best inferential. Perhaps the most instructive geographic research supporting intentional unnecessary surgery is the finding that when a group of physicians was admonished that their surgery rates were higher than those of their colleagues, the chastised doctors reduced their number of operations significantly (e.g., decreasing hysterectomies by as much as 50 percent and tonsillectomies by as much as 90 percent).[22]

The second method for detecting unnecessary surgery is assessing the concordance between first and second surgical opinions that is required under some insurance plans. The logic of this approach is that if the second doctor does not agree upon the need for surgery, then the surgery would have been unnecessary had the patient relied only upon the physician who recommended the operation. Rates of second opinion nonconfirmation in these studies vary from 7 percent to 19 percent.[23] As compelling as these kinds of figures might be, however, the studies fail to measure unnecessary surgery because they do not tell us the proportion of surgery recommendations that were *incorrect.* In other words, simply pointing to a disagreement between a first and a second opinion tells us nothing about the accuracy of either opinion. Even if the second surgical opinion studies could identify the number of incorrectly recommended surgeries, there is no way to learn whether these errors were based on incompetence or an intent to defraud.

Third, researchers have suggested that, because of the profit motive, fee-for-service (FFS) health providers will knowingly involve themselves in more unnecessary operations than prepaid health maintenance organization (HMO) providers because there is no financial incentive for the latter to do surgery. One study of federal employees showed a 120 percent higher surgical rate for patients enrolled in FFS Blue Shield programs compared to those in HMOs. The discrepancy between the two types of providers was greatest for controversial operations such as tonsillectomies.[24] The evidence is not unequivocal, however; virtually no difference in surgical rates has been found by other researchers between the two types of providers, including for controversial operations.[25] Similarly, a third study[26] using Seattle data found that both FFS and HMO providers generally did operations considered justified by independent criteria. But FFS providers were judged considerably more unjustified in two controversial operations—tonsillectomies and hysterectomies. In toto, there is a definite indication that FFS providers perform controversial operations unnecessarily more often than do HMO providers, but the evidence is mixed, and the assertion that FFS providers are clearly driven to profit by a criminal excessive use of surgery is not established by these comparisons.

The fourth method used to identify unnecessary surgeries is expert reevaluation of surgery decisions according to preset criteria. If the preset criteria are medically sound and the reviewers are experts, this method has the greatest potential to identify unnecessary surgeries, but, as noted, it cannot identify a criminal intent to perform unneeded operations. In one well-known study, upon reexamining 1,356 patients recommended for major surgery, researchers at Cornell Medical School found that one in four of the operations was not needed.[27] Researchers in other criteria studies found that 20 percent of pacemaker operations[28] and 14 percent of coronary artery bypass surgeries were judged to be unnecessary.[29] In the latter study, an additional 30 percent of the bypass surgeries were controversial—that is, experts disagreed about the appropriateness of the operations. For tonsillectomies, one expert review judged more than four-fifths (86 percent) to be unneeded.[30] Thirteen to 32 percent of carotid endarterectomies (cleaning plaque from the carotid artery) were considered done for inappropriate indications in several studies by the RAND Corporation in the late 1980s.[31]

The four methods of studying unnecessary surgery have presented information of varying strength to support the idea that many operations need not happen, particularly those that are controversial and based on uncertain outcome. Nevertheless, none of these data allow us to infer the extent of doctors' criminal intent to perform unneeded operations.

Because the line between criminal intent and the permissible exercise of professional judgment is so vague, the best source of reliable information on the incidence of intentional unnecessary treatment may be self-reports by the offenders themselves. They are the ones who should know whether their actions were needless. The example given for a randomized response approach in chapter 2 might be used by researchers to attempt to estimate the number of unnecessary surgeries and treatments (and other crimes committed by professionals), because it guarantees anonymity and thereby alleviates respondents' fears of reprisal for admitting abuses. However, such a self-report method would not be feasible unless physicians were to view their behavior objectively. Here they would have to perceive honestly their unwarranted treatment as fraudulent.

Another method for estimating the amount of unnecessary surgery and treatment may be found in direct observational study. Methodologies analogous to Jesilow's "sick" car battery study (see chapter 2) have been suggested. Contrived illnesses would be described to doctors to detect whether they would render unnecessary treatments. This is much like the tactics of the U.S. Senate fraud investigators who frequented some of New York City's suspect medical clinics with feigned ailments, usually described as a cold to the physicians. The investigators found themselves subjected by eighty-five different doctors they visited to eighteen electrocardiograms, eight tuberculosis tests, four allergy tests, hearing and glaucoma tests, and three electroencephalograms.[32]

There are two major problems with such an approach, however. First, subjecting a research team to the risks of unnecessary treatments and surgeries would be unethical. Second, just as the courts have had difficulty proving intent because of the ambiguity of professional judgment, so too would the researcher.

Knowing the extent of unnecessary medical treatment is not required to understand the factors leading to such behavior. As noted in chapter 2, counting need not precede theoretical explanation of wrongdoing; the aim should be to explain the processes leading to illegal behavior. There have been several hypotheses related to the practice of medicine that try to explain erroneous decisions to deliver medical treatment, including training (doctors practice the way they were taught in medical school), insufficient knowledge to make competent diagnoses (doctors often do not pay attention to all of the relevant symptoms or keep abreast of medical developments), individual physician characteristics (age, experience, personality, and medical specialty), and "defensive medicine" (doctors overprescribe medical procedures as a defense against possible medical malpractice lawsuits). None of these ideas purporting to explain the incorrect practice of medicine assume intentional fraud by the doctor.

When the unnecessary medical procedures *are* based on an intention to defraud, we can utilize the criminological theories discussed in chapter 3. Because making money is the impetus behind duping patients into believing that their condition requires a particular medical procedure, greed would be the relevant motivation for criminal unnecessary surgery. Keisling describes the insidious processes leading to a physician's desire for affluence, which may necessitate unneeded treatments to support such a lifestyle:

> Fee for service medicine subtly corrupts its own practitioners. Motives for medicine are many and complex but the strongest is the desire to be a healer. . . . Unfortunately, the feelings of dominance that inevitably accompany the healer's role frequently overpower whatever native idealism a doctor might have brought to his profession. . . . As he gets older, he also begins believing that the same power and respect he commands in the office or operating room should extend into the community, where the badges of success and status, instead of centering on the value of one's work, center on material possessions and social standing. And as the fee for service system combines with the doctor's revered status to make these things so accessible, what increasingly becomes important are not the satisfactions of medicine itself but the benefits that result from practicing it. For these doctors, stories of million-dollar incomes do not provoke outrage, but envy.[33]

Such desires for affluence, along with high practitioner expenses, exorbitant malpractice insurance costs, and a defensive practice of medicine, may place financial pressure on doctors to render unnecessary treatments. Physicians also may believe they are insulated from prosecution because of their "social position and the inadequacies of program policing."[34]

Medical school training would not overtly encourage unnecessary medical procedures, but interaction with local colleagues may produce, through differential association, socialization favorable to their use. The term *surgical signature* has been coined in reference to variations in surgical decision rates across geographic regions.[35] A "professional dominance"[36] often prevails in the minds of physicians, which

> supports informal professional norms which encourage some doctors to exploit [patients]. The behavior which enables a doctor to engage in fraud probably is at least partially learned from others in the profession in most instances, and professional values may effectively neutralize the doctors' conflicts of conscience.[37]

There undoubtedly are cases in which the professional values that neutralize the wrongfulness of unnecessary surgery or treatment are not internalized, and the physician needs to avoid feelings of guilt for such behavior. Physicians who practice defensive medicine may involve "condemnation of condemners" or "appeals to higher loyalties" if they believe that ordering unnecessary tests is acceptable because it insulates them from potential malpractice claims that would allege that they did not consider every possible avenue for diagnosis during treatment. To illustrate, a medical fraud investigator claimed that medical review boards are sensitive to self-defense against malpractice: "[Medical review boards will] say, 'Oh well, you know, it's malpractice time and I can understand why he might have ordered unnecessary tests'."[38] As noted in chapter 3, the extent to which these and other neutralizations are learned and then internalized as acceptable behavior is the extent to which differential association is the explanation rather than neutralization theory.

Propensity-event theory would see the collection of fees for unnecessary surgeries and medical treatments as "money without work."[39] Although the procedures certainly involve some effort, there is a great financial return for the effort expended; in other words, the services produce easy money. For propensity-event to explain occupational crime by doctors, research would have to show that violating physicians are more likely to exhibit symptoms of lower self-control than physicians who do not violate. It would also have to be shown that those who perform unneeded operations and provide unnecessary treatment would be more likely to sexually abuse patients, violate prescription laws, submit fraudulent insurance claims, and commit other crimes both within and outside the profession.

Patient Sexual Abuse

At times doctors also commit willful sexual assault against their patients. Taking sexual advantage of patients, especially when patients are unaware of the assault because of anesthesia or are otherwise incapable of giving informed consent, is a particularly heinous form of violation of that special trust between professional and client. In addition to issues of occupational criminality by professionals, sexual assault on patients by doctors also raises issues of sexual harassment, exploitation, and domination (almost invariably by men over women) in the workplace.

By means of an anonymous self-report questionnaire, Kardener, Fuller, and Mensh investigated the prevalence of nonmedical patient sexual contact by male physicians in their practice.[40] Among their 460 respondents (1,000 questionnaires were distributed), 59 acknowledged having sexual contact with patients. These were the results by speciality: obstetrics/gynecology, 18 percent; general practitioners, 13 percent; internists, 12 percent; and psychiatrists and surgeons, each 10 percent. Another survey, published in the *American Journal of Psychiatry* in 1986, reported that among 1,314 psychiatrist-respondents, 7 percent of males and 3 percent of females acknowledged sexual contact with patients. Two-thirds of the respondents stated that they had treated at least one patient who had a sexual encounter with a previous therapist (only 8 percent of them reported the case to the authorities).[41] For the period between 1986 and 1993, Ralph Nader's Public Citizen's Health Research Group reported 173 formal administrative cases against physicians practicing in the United States involving either sexual abuse of patients or sexual misconduct with them; at least a third were allowed to continue practicing medicine without interruption.[42]

The chicanery used by doctors to fool patients into submitting to sexual molestation is illustrated in the following vignettes:

> A psychotherapist told the mother of one of his adolescent patients that hyperactivity can be transmitted to a child through breast milk, and was then given permission by the mother to "examine" her breasts.[43]
>
> A psychiatrist who had sex with his patients told them that the sexual acts were therapy for their psychological discomfort.[44]
>
> An Iowa optometrist told women they needed to strip to the waist to have their eyes examined.[45]
>
> A psychiatrist hooked a female patient on prescription drugs and, monthly for seven years, continued to supply the controlled substances in exchange for oral sex.[46]

Because sexual exploitation of clients is clearly a strong violation of medical ethics, professionals who violate this norm need to neutralize their behavior so that it is not seen as unprofessional. Kardener et al. indicated that respondents who committed sexual violations defended what they had done by stating that it: "demonstrates doctor's effectiveness to his patient," "supports and reinforces a patient's sexual appeal," and "stimulating the clitoris helps a patient relax."[47]

The compulsive behavior involved in patient sexual abuse would be explained by propensity-event theory's emphasis on self-gratification and the theory's assertion that low self-control individuals seek "sex without courtship."[48] Several instances involving sexual misconduct by physicians demonstrate the theory's postulate that this low self-control behavior is "stable" over the long-term.

Perhaps the best-known case of long-term medical sexual abuse was documented by author Jack Olsen in *Doc: The Rape of the Town of Lovell.*[49] The physician in that Wyoming community, Dr. John Story, was found to have molested his patients over a twenty-five year period during so-called gynecological examinations. Estimates of the numbers of victims ranged from one hundred fifty to more than a thousand[50] and included a gamut of ages, from teenagers to the elderly. In large part, his patients allowed Story to continue offending because they were reticent about sexuality and sexual matters.

The discovery of a doctor's sexual misbehavior does not necessarily stop the physician from moving elsewhere and continuing those practices. Dennis Kleinman was convicted of sexually assaulting a patient in New Jersey, and was then issued a medical license to practice in New York, although regulators there were aware of his past. Dr. Kleinman was then rearrested within four months of the New Jersey conviction for fondling another patient.[51] A similar case involved Julian Sellek, who, after being put on probation by the medical board in Maryland for sexual misconduct with patients, was charged with sexual misconduct again in Georgia. Sellek was sentenced on charges stemming from sexual misconduct with at least nineteen women.[52] The cases of Kleinman and Sellek spotlight problems in the licensing of medical practitioners.

In another well-publicized case of long-term sexual exploitation, described in the *American Journal of Psychiatry,* a gynecologist used his physical examinations to masturbate at least sixteen patients for an average of twenty to thirty minutes.[53] Although eight of the ten women who described sexual arousal had orgasms, none reported any subjective pleasure associated with their physiological response. Most were humiliated but uncertain about how to deal with such an assault, knowing, but not absolutely positive, that what was happening to them was not part of the regular examination. Ten of the women described feelings of physical discomfort and pain during the internal examination.

Only three of the victims tried to end the examination, either by asking the physician to stop or by physically changing position. Eight patients allowed the doctor to continue until he was finished. Although unaware of their exploitation during the assault, afterwards some said that they felt degraded and upset with themselves. Many believed they should have pressed charges against the doctor, but there was a perception about their credibility compared with the doctor's ("What good would it do—my word against his" and "doctors are so well protected").

Most of the patient-victims immediately changed physicians, though others returned for several more visits. Those who continued to see the doctor after he assaulted them did so because of necessity (serious medical need or because they could not find another doctor to take them in the late stages of pregnancy). Other gynecologists in the area tended to ignore their colleague's behavior ("I've heard lots of complaints but I have no facts"; "[You are] not the only one [to complain about his methods]").

Criminal Homicide

Because of their professional knowledge, doctors and nurses can sometimes kill with impunity for their own benefit by making their victim's death appear to be natural. Cesare Lombroso, the father of modern criminology and a physician himself, noted almost a century ago that "[h]omicide with the aim of getting the benefit of life insurance, is an example of a new form of crime committed by some physicians, and favored . . . by new advances in scientific knowledge."[54] When offenses such as these occur outside regular medical practice, they should be considered professionally facilitated rather than as occurring within the occupation.

Nonspontaneous Abortions

Before the Supreme Court's 1973 decision in *Roe v. Wade*[55], nonspontaneous abortions were illegal in the United States, except in states that allowed abortion if conception occurred in rape and incest and those that permitted it if it was believed to be medically necessary to save the mother's life. The pre-*Roe* **California Therapeutic Abortion Act** also allowed a legal abortion for the mental well-being of the mother.[56] Here, because of the exercise of professional opinion, we see another instance in which the application of criminal definitions is controlled intraprofessionally. According to the *Roe* decision, any nonspontaneous abortion involving a viable fetus (i.e., one performed during the third trimester) that is unrelated to maternal physical health would be a criminal homicide. Such homicides have undoubtedly occurred since *Roe*, but are purposely obscured. Physicians can intentionally underestimate the age of the fetus.

There is no information available about the number of physicians who have performed illegal abortions. However, a self-report study of 388 obstetricians before *Roe* found that about one in ten admitted that he or she illegally referred patients to abortionists. Respondents guessed that about one in seven of their colleagues did so also.[57] Illegally performing an abortion or illegally referring someone to an abortionist may be caused by "ideological and humanitarian impulses of physicians pushing them into law-breaking."[58] Thus, an appeal to higher loyalties (i.e., the procedure is necessary for the mental or social well-being of the pregnant woman) may serve as a justification that allows doctors to view their illegal abortions of fetuses as professionally acceptable behavior.

Euthanasia

Euthanasia, or mercy killing (which could conceivably include some nonspontaneous abortions), may also be the result of humanitarian impulses, because it is usually said to be for the benefit of the patient. Euthanasia typically has been legally treated as criminal homicide in the United States.

While it is common for physicians to withdraw treatment and allow death to take its natural course, it is illegal for physicians to hasten death. There are only a few cases of medical professionals convicted for having killed to end the suffering of a patient or for withdrawing or omitting therapy. Juries tend to be sympathetic toward euthanasia committed by the victim's relatives.[59] To illustrate the reluctance of courts to equate euthanasia with homicide, on at least five separate occasions murder charges were judicially disallowed against Dr. Jack Kevorkian for helping severely ill patients kill themselves, although Kevorkian was convicted for violating Michigan's assisted suicide law, which was passed in response to his high-profile actions.[60]

Most cases of assisted euthanasia are not as blatant as those associated with Kevorkian. Doctors often can hasten their patients' deaths, say, by overprescribing morphine. Euthanasia in such cases is another example of those offenses in which intent is difficult to determine because violations of the law are interpreted in terms of professional opinions. Unless the medical community asserts that a given instance of euthanasia was not within the realm of acceptable medical practice, the doctor who has done it is not guilty of homicide or other crimes. While there is no dispute that purposeful mercy killing decisions of physicians are the immediate causes of death, there can be a considerable legal question about whether such sions are the true (or "proximate") causes of death. The medical community clearly disagrees about euthanasia ethics. Diana Crane has found through surveys of about 3,000 physicians that doctors are increasingly invoking a social interpretation of death (the potential for the patient and family's quality of life) rather than a clinical one (brain death).[61]

The decision to practice euthanasia revolves around three major types of cases: (1) the conscious terminal patient; (2) the irreversibly comatose patient; and (3) the brain-damaged or severely debilitated patient whose chances of long-term survival in his or her present state are good.[62] The following are the polarized positions on mercy killing:

> *For:* [T]he life of the dying patient becomes steadily less complicated and rich, and, as a result, less worth living or preserving. The pain and suffering involved in maintaining what is left are inexorably mounting, while the benefits enjoyed by the patient himself, or that he can in any way confer on those around him, are just as inexorably declining.[63]

> *Against:* It is ethically wrong for a doctor to make an arbitrary judgment at a certain point in his patient's illness to stop supportive measures. The patient entrusts his life to his doctor, and it is the doctor's duty to sustain it as long as possible. There should be no suggestion that it is possible for a doctor to do otherwise, even if he were to decide that the patient [was] better off dead.[64]

The official medical policy about treating patients is clear: treatment should be continued as long as life, defined in physiological terms, can be preserved.[65] Crane's research suggests that an informal system of counternorms to this official policy has developed. Justifications such as "appeals to higher loyalties" (minimization of suffering for patients and their families) or "denials of injury and responsibility" (the patient will die anyway) may encourage the practice of mercy killing by some doctors. The fact that doctors increasingly are invoking criteria other than physiological death for prolonging life points to an internalization of such ethics, which, if learned through socialization in medical school or from colleagues, would point to differential association. Because the motivation for euthanasia is to end another's suffering rather than to enhance self-gratification, propensity-event theory would consider euthanasia to be outside the behaviors it tries to explain.

Turk's theory of criminalization, discussed in chapter 3, is applicable to the explanation of the absence of prosecution against doctors who may criminally be practicing euthanasia. Recall that a congruence between laws and authorities' perceptions about the correctness of those laws is probably the greatest variable related to the prosecution of crimes. Apparently, authorities do not hold the legal norms against mercy killing to be very important; otherwise, more open conflict between criminal justice authorities and physicians would have resulted over euthanasia laws, and there would also have been more criminal prosecutions of physicians.

According to Turk, norm violators' power compared with that of authorities influences the probability that norm violators' behavior will be criminalized. Doctors wield considerable power in our society. Their very high status is well recognized, as is the collective power embodied in the American Medical Association. Physicians favoring euthanasia also have displayed "sophistication" and "realism in conflict moves" with authorities by promoting their position through respectable lobbying organizations such as the Euthanasia Society and the Foundation for Thanatology. Such organizations have made legal inroads toward redefining mercy killing as ethical medical practice. For instance, living wills have been allowed, which instruct doctors about the wishes for a dignified death in the event the patient cannot give consent to disconnect life-support systems. The reduction of the criminality associated with euthanasia, then, will continue as long as the offenders possess enough power to control the definition of the offense. When physicians become "unrealistic in their conflict moves" with authorities, such as clearly flouting laws against euthanasia, authorities are more likely to respond with greater criminalization, such as in the cases related to Dr. Kevorkian's open defiance of euthanasia ethics.

Sutherland would argue that criminal euthanasia most likely would occur under the two conditions of social disorganization. First, there may be a differential social organization promoting euthanasia within the ranks of physicians. Second, an anomic lack of rules about its appropriateness, part of the present normative transition from clinical to social criteria of death, would encourage euthanasia. Criminal euthanasia may become a common practice unless standards are established inhibiting its use; otherwise physicians will employ loose legal interpretations of the situations in which it is considered appropriate.

There may be an inverse and self-regulating relationship between the extent of euthanasia and the medical resources available. Henry Pontell has described such a "system capacity" hypothesis in criminal justice, in which the incarceration rate decreases as prison overcrowding increases and vice versa—incarceration is merely a function of available prison space.[66] In this way, the criminal justice system self-regulates its capacity to be equal to the demands upon it. Similarly, if available medical resources (physicians, equipment, hospital space) are scarce, doctors may opt to expend the resources they have on patients who have the greatest chance for a high quality of life. A medical system capacity hypothesis would predict a greater amount of extended treatment for those with poor social prognoses when there are sufficient available medical resources than when such resources are in short supply. If, on the other hand, there is an abundance of doctors and hospital space, there may be a tendency to expend these resources on patients, even if the prognosis for a decent quality of life is bleak. This latter tendency would be similar to the behaviors predicted by Parkinson's law (named after C. Northcote Parkinson), which states that "work expands so as to fill the time available for its completion."

On an individual patient basis, the practice of euthanasia may be inversely related to financial capacity. If a patient, or their relatives, can afford prolonged treatment or there is adequate insurance to cover its costs, withdrawal of treatment may be less likely than in situations in which the patient cannot pay. Here, the decision for mercy killing is based on a hospital's or a physician's profit/loss considerations rather than on humanitarian concerns.

Medical Kickbacks

Doctors are in a position to receive illegal kickbacks in exchange for their medical judgment. Like any kickback scheme, such payments can restrict competition and artificially inflate costs. They also can lead to unnecessary surgeries, treatments, and drug therapies, many of which cause pain and some of which kill.

Any payment of cash, property, or other tangible valuable is considered to be a **medical kickback** if it is used to influence medical judgment. The best known form of medical kickback is **fee splitting,** which is a crime in almost all states, and grounds for the revocation or suspension of a physician's license to practice. The kickback usually goes to a general practitioner who refers patients to a surgeon or specialist. The referral can be for necessary or unnecessary patient care. Sutherland mentioned this illegal practice almost fifty years ago in *White Collar Crime:* "The physician who participates in fee splitting tends to send his patients to the surgeon who will split the largest fee rather than to the surgeon who will do the best work."[67] Split-fee cases would naturally gravitate to the highest bidders and to the worst doctors. An example of a fee-splitting statutory prohibition is Section 650 of California's *Business and Professions Code:*

> [T]he . . . receipt or acceptance, by any [physician] of any rebate, refund, commission . . . or other consideration, whether in the form of money or otherwise, as compensation or inducement for referring patients . . . to any person . . . is unlawful.

The most punitive felonious prohibition against fee splitting is found in the federal Medicare/Medicaid fraud and abuse statute, passed in 1982 (Title 42 *USC,* Section 1395). It mandates up to five years' imprisonment and a $25,000 fine for anyone who gives or receives any remuneration (cash, property, or favors) for referring a patient to a person (or hospital or clinic) for any item or service that can be reimbursed by Medicare or Medicaid. U.S. Sentencing Guidelines begin with a two-month sentence, and escalate according to the amount of the kickback.[68] The purpose of this law is to discourage doctors from providing more care than is necessary. Interestingly, a 1986 federal law[69] also makes it illegal to induce physicians to provide *less* care than is necessary to Medicare and Medicaid patients. The U.S. Sentencing Commission punishes this offense under the same guidelines as Medicare kickbacks.[70]

A more subtle medical kickback akin to fee splitting is **self-referral**—the prescription for a medical test, drug, or other treatment that is administered at a site (other than the physician's normal place of practice) in which the doctor has a financial interest. It has been estimated that about one in ten physicians have a financial interest in a health care facility to which they can refer patients—diagnostic laboratories, centers that perform computerized axial tomography (CAT-scans) and magnetic resonance imaging (MRIs), dialysis clinics, physical therapy centers, ambulatory surgery centers, hospitals, and other medical facilities.[71] The investing physician depends on high-volume patient referral for profit maximization. The tendency, of course, is to overprescribe patients to self-owned facilities—a routine MRI or CAT-scan can cost more than $1,000. One study found that almost 75 percent of Florida's CAT-scan and MRI laboratories are owned at least in part by physicians.[72] Another federal investigation revealed that doctors prescribe 40 percent more laboratory work when they have ownership interest in the facility.[73] A third study by Hillman et al. concluded that doctors with financial interest in diagnostic imaging facilities referred patients at a *400 percent higher rate* than noninvesting physicians.[74]

Self-referral is such a widespread and deleterious practice that there have been numerous laws to prohibit it. In many states self-referrals are permissible only after physicians disclose any financial interests in the facility to which they send a patient for treatment, a position that is consistent with the American Medical Association's (AMA) ethical rules on disclosure put forth in 1984:

> [A] physician may own or have a financial interest in a for-profit hospital, nursing home or other health facility, such as a free-standing surgical center or emergency clinic. However, the physician has an affirmative obligation to

> disclose his ownership of a health facility to his patient, prior to admission or utilization.[75]

Not only is it professionally unethical to fail to disclose a self-referral, some states' medical governing boards consider nondisclosure grounds for disciplinary action.

By 1992, the practice of self-referral was perceived to present such a great conflict of interest that the Council on Ethical and Judicial Affairs of the AMA felt compelled to strengthen its position: "In general, physicians *should not* refer patients to a health care facility outside their office practice at which they do not directly provide care or services when they have an investment interest in the facility" (emphasis added).[76] However, because certain communities are in dire need of local health facilities, physicians are allowed by the AMA to invest in them only if alternative financing is not available. In such cases, all community physicians must be allowed to invest equally in the facility, especially if they are not in a practice that can refer patients to it. Financial return on the facility cannot be based on the number of referrals, referring physicians should not receive any favors from the facility, and an internal utilization review board should be established to determine if a physician is abusing self-referrals. If a physician's financial interests are so obviously at odds with the patient's interests as to be incompatible, the physician should withdraw from caring for the patient. Last, the physician's financial interest must be disclosed to the patient and, if requested, to insurance providers.[77] Physicians who have previously invested in health facilities and who cannot comply with the 1992 guidelines within three years have been asked by the AMA to divest their financial interests in those facilities.[78]

Another common form of kickbacking, a form of bribery, involves pharmaceutical companies, which expend great effort and much money to influence doctors' medical opinions. One estimate puts pharmaceutical company spending at more than $5,000 per physician, or $2 billion yearly, all of it seeking to convince doctors to prescribe one brand over another.[79] The bribes are given to doctors in the forms of noncash gifts (equipment, supplies, and samples), entertainment (invitations to parties, dinners, resorts, and sporting events), and "consulting fees." One company offered a round-trip airfare to a physician in exchange for that doctor writing fifty prescriptions for their heart medicine.[80] Some companies have paid doctors for recruiting patients as subjects in research studies necessary for government approval of a new pharmaceutical product, including medications with controversial or unknown side effects.[81]

The fact that self-referrals and the acceptance of perquisites from pharmaceutical companies is extremely common points to occupationally shared norms that are learned through differential association. Thus, only the physicians who have the highest self-control in the exercise of professional ethics would not succumb to the financial benefits of kickbacking. Those who take kickbacks may have convinced themselves that their judgments are completely immune to corruption by financial incentives. As one resident of internal medicine observed:

> Most doctors I know feel they are above being influenced by drug-company propaganda and laugh at the notion that the care of their patients might in any way be affected. But I'm willing to bet that [these companies] wouldn't be paying a huge sales force millions of dollars a year unless their strategies were working.[82]

Alternatively, through neutralization techniques such as an appeal to higher loyalties, physicians reason that the patient is helped regardless of, say, where a CAT-scan is performed or which of several similar drugs is prescribed. The use of denial of responsibility may enter into the decision to make a needless self-referral when the physician claims that malpractice lawyers force the defensive practice of medicine. Regardless of doctors' psychological justifications for kickback-influenced medical advice, the truth is that the behavior is corrupt, and without regard for the sacred trust of patients.

Fraudulent Medical Insurance Claims

The unnecessary procedures we have discussed thus far are often charged to an insurance company, and therefore are integrally related to the submission of false insurance claims. **Pingponging** refers to the needless referral of a patient to another physician for additional treatment. Physicians also needlessly prolong treatments and **family gang** (needlessly request to see members of a patient's family).[83] Doctors, especially surgeons, also use the practice of **unbundling,** in which they disaggregate one procedure into more than one—as many as five—and then bill for each step separately. These practices are known as "overutilization" or "abuse." There is also a type of medical insurance fraud in which claims are made for services that were never performed (e.g., examinations, tests, X-rays without film; double-billing for a single service); this is a much more obvious type of fraud. Although fraud is much easier to prove legally than abuse, both kinds of insurance claiming are criminal. The *Washington Post* estimated in 1992 that health care fraud costs *$70 billion* each year.[84] However, during the first seventeen years of Medicaid and Medicare policing (1978–1995), the yearly successful prosecution of defrauders averaged only about 450 cases.[85]

One group of scholars—Paul Jesilow, Henry Pontell, and Gilbert Geis—have done extensive research on medical insurance fraud. In their *Prescription for Profit: How Doctors Defraud Medicaid,* they studied 147 physicians from New York, California, and Illinois, who were either suspended or excluded from the Medicaid and Medicare programs for fraud between 1977 and 1982.[86] About a third (36 percent) were foreign school graduates; among domestic schools, four colleges accounted for eighteen of the violators and fifteen schools each had two violators. California-trained doctors accounted for more than a quarter of all violators (28 percent) while those earning degrees in New York accounted for almost one in five of the violators (17 percent). The top five violating specialties were: general and family practitioners (27 percent), psychiatry (18 percent), general surgery (11 percent), internal medicine (8 percent), and obstetrics/gynecology (7 percent).[87]

Some medical specialties, by nature, facilitate apprehension for fraudulent insurance claims. Anesthesiologists, and particularly psychiatrists and psychologists, are easier targets for insurance fraud investigators because such specialists bill on the basis of time rather than on that of services such as examinations, injections, and treatments. There are several methods that can be used to document overcharging for time spent with patients. Practitioners who bill for more hours than are in a day's work are caught relatively easily by a computer, such as the following case involving a psychiatrist:

> [H]e billed [government insurance] for twenty-four to twenty-eight individual one-hour sessions on each of eight separate days. On one "twenty-six-hour day," he billed an additional ten hours for private patients, producing a thirty-six-hour billing day.[88]

One psychiatrist was apprehended after he billed for a time slot during which the "patient" was incarcerated.[89] Additionally, investigators have documented the hours spent with patients by photographing and timing traffic in and out of offices and waiting rooms, and then comparing the observed time of treatment with the hours billed. Undercover investigators have also sought treatment themselves and, using a contrived insurance identification card, determined whether the doctor billed the insurance company for the correct amount of time. Computers are also used to check both time-founded claims and claims for general medical procedures. However, in the Medicare program, for example, 90 percent of the claims flagged by the computer as suspicious are adjudicated by persons with no medical training, often only a high school education. These adjusters not only are inexperienced, but rushed—the average time spent on a questionable claim is seventy-two seconds according to a 1993 federal study.[90]

Because the illegality of overutilization is more nebulous than blatant fraud, definitions favorable to the practice of overutilization, and the specific techniques for it (such as unbundling), may be learned from colleagues through differential association. Sutherland would point here to a differential social organization in the medical profession around cheating insurance companies. Differential association into the practice of overutilization may be the product of learned neutralizations—say, a perceived necessity to practice defensive medicine (a denial of responsibility—"it is not my fault") or a belief that the rate of reimbursement falls below the going price for a service (a denial of injury—"I am not being overpaid"). Several of the Jesilow et al. case studies indicated this latter justification.

However, many cases in their study involving blatant fraud are most consistent with propensity-event theory rather than differential association. Note the *versatility* in both professional and personal deviances exhibited by the following medical offenders and the *stability* over time with which they occurred[91]:

> An internist was charged with 137 acts of insurance theft (involving office visits, injections, and electrocardiograms never performed) and 15 felony counts of narcotic distribution and sales.
>
> One woman physician billed for countless treatments that were never performed. She was also convicted of murdering her former partner in order to stop him from testifying against her (the murder conviction was later overturned on a technicality).
>
> A psychiatrist prescribed large amounts of drugs for his wife, took drugs himself, treated patients while he was on drugs, and billed the government for psychotherapy during the time he was having oral sex with a patient for whom he also prescribed excessive drugs.
>
> A doctor billed for expensive medical tests over several years when they were actually inexpensive tests performed by an outside laboratory. Earlier in his career he had been charged with medical negligence and excessively prescribing amphetamines. At the time he pleaded guilty to the insurance thefts, he was under indictment for meter-bypassing $4,000 worth of gas to heat his home.

Crime in the Legal Profession

Lawyers, as professionals, also have abundant opportunities to commit crime in the course of their occupation. Offenses can be carried out by attorneys for their own benefit, such as overbilling clients for their time or embezzling funds entrusted to them. Crimes can also be committed for the benefit of their clients, such as in the falsification of documents or promotion of perjury. Some crimes lawyers commit are particular to their profession, such as contempt of court by an officer of the court.

Fraud by Lawyers

There are several aspects of service delivery related to the practice of law that offer opportunity for fraud. As Abraham Blumberg explains:

> Legal service lends itself particularly well to confidence games. Usually, a plumber will be able to demonstrate . . . that he has performed a service by clearing up the stuffed drain, repairing the leaky faucet or pipe—and therefore merits his fee. He has rendered . . . a visible, tangible boon for his client in return for the requested fee. . . . In the practice of law there is a special problem in this regard, no matter what the level of the practitioner or his place in the hierarchy of prestige. Much legal work is intangible either because it is simply a few words of advice, some preventive action, a telephone call, negotiation of some kind, a form filled out and filed, a hurried conference with another attorney or an official of a government agency, a letter or opinion written, or a countless variety of seemingly innocuous and even prosaic procedures and actions.[92]

A question arises, then, about the worth or value of such activities. How much is a lawyer's service worth if he or she, through some simple advice over the telephone, saves a client several thousand dollars in taxes? The advice may only have taken a few minutes, but the resultant benefit to the client was substantial. The client would likely pay an hour's fee of three hundred dollars to that attorney for such advice. This fee-for-service system promotes overcharging clients because much of the work done by attorneys (except for court appearances and client conferences) takes place behind office doors outside the purview of the client. When an attorney informs a client that a negotiation with the opposing party has been completed, sending a bill for thirty or forty hours of work, the client is in no position to dispute the charges. Moreover, when the outcome of a case is uncertain, clients will not know initially how many hours will be required of the lawyer's time, permitting a huge potential for abuse. The fee-for-service legal system pits the financial interests of lawyers against those of their clients, and vice versa.

In a revealing study in the *University of Pennsylvania Law Review,* law professor Lisa Lerman asked twenty lawyers (and three law students) about the kinds of lies and fraud they saw in civil practice.[93] The vast majority of attorneys in her sample were in private practice. For billing procedures, the respondents discussed unnecessary work, padding bills, double-billing, and overestimating hours from noncontemporaneous records. Note that each time the mails or phones are used in fraudulent billing procedures, federal mail and wire fraud statutes are violated.

If Parkinson's law (noted earlier in this chapter) is correct, then the amount of work on a project will expand to fill the time allocated for its completion. Accordingly, when lawyers are given carte blanche discretion to spend time on a legal task, they are tempted to manufacture as many billable hours as the client is willing to pay, including work that is not done or is unnecessary. The amount of effort spent on legal research and other background materials are prime examples of how lawyers run their meters unnecessarily. Two of Lerman's respondents told of billing a wealthy corporate client for time spent accumulating materials that would enhance the firm's prestige but were not germane to the assignment by the client.[94]

Some of the respondents in Lerman's study openly admitted that their firms and others' padded bills or double-billed for a single service. Neutralizations were rampant, such as this "denial of injury": "[S]ome people in the firm feel like, 'well [if] they are a rich client [and] they can pay, we can put a couple more hours down than we worked. . . .' Certainly that's deception, to the tune of tens of thousands."[95] Similarly, a firm partner stated that it was acceptable to defraud a wealthy Asian client because "these people are so rich. . . . [T]hey've got so much money in these countries where there is nothing to buy, they might as well give it to me."[96]

This denial of injury neutralization is coupled with an appeal to higher loyalties when wealthy clients are billed for hours that actually involve work for poorer clients: "I generally bill as much as I can to the richest client [and underbill] clients who can't afford standard rates. . . . It's rough justice."[97] In a similar combination of the two neutralizations, two other respondent-lawyers stated that they billed a paying client for the time they spent on a *pro bono* (free legal service) case.[98] In a variation of the higher loyalty appeal, one attorney justified overbilling wealthy clients because the work done for them is eventually used for someone else.[99] This excuse: (1) assumes that the wealthy client was billed for work actually performed, in which case overbilling would not have occurred; and

(2) assumes that other clients will not be rebilled for the work already completed.

Lawyers in one firm were described to have billed twenty hours for a single day (even though they worked only ten); they also bragged about billing two clients for the same work and about manufacturing bogus billing hours.[100] Another told of a partner who embezzled a client's trust fund and fabricated hours to cover the theft.[101] One law student recounted that when he was a paralegal, he was instructed to bill two clients for the same time—one bill to client A for air travel time related to his case and another bill to client B for the time spent on his case during the travel time billed to client A.[102]

In another episode, an attorney immediately knew the answer to a client's question, wrote the answer in a letter, and then billed ten hours of research.[103] Another lawyer was said to have billed ten hours to clients for every two hours he worked. That particular attorney was under pressure to increase his billings, and the partners in his firm did not fault him for his fraudulent practices.[104]

The neutralization of denial of responsibility is also invoked as a justification for charging for undocumented time: one lawyer stated that an attorney does so much work for some clients that it is easy to lose track of the exact number of hours to bill.[105] While the lack of contemporaneous records may produce some underbilling, information from the Lerman respondents indicates it is much more likely to generate overbilling. One attorney stated that his margin of error for hourly billing is one-quarter to one-half[106]; this translates into a $50 to $100 mistake for each hour billed at $200. Another attorney said that if he cannot remember how many hours he has worked for a client, he bills at the higher number if he believes the client can afford it; another simply estimates that he spent "half this month on [a big client] . . . one hundred hours."[107] One attorney, in another variation of the appeal to higher loyalties, believed his billing errors to be fifteen minutes an hour, but justified the overcharging by reasoning that devoting more time to billing would reduce the quality of his other work.[108] One firm routinely took the hours billed on time sheets and artificially increased the billing rate by half—say, from $150 an hour to $225.[109] In this case, if the number of hours had been inflated in the first place, the client's bill would reflect additive and *then* multiplicative padding.

As Blumberg noted, clients are rarely in a position to question the amount of time spent on their case, and therefore there is an absence of perceived certainty of apprehension associated with padding bills. One lawyer observed that bills involving large amounts of work simply hide padding.[110] Lawyers also purposely send bills that are difficult to decipher.

Thus, although Rule 1.5 of the American Bar Association's (ABA) **Model Rules for Professional Conduct** (MRPC) mandates that each hourly based bill to a client should reflect the number of hours worked, the billing rates of those who performed the tasks, and details of any other charges, lawyers hide overbilling by purposely obscuring this information. Even if questioned by a client, one lawyer stated that she could easily lie:

> Oh yeah, on [such and such a date] I spent x amount of time, and . . . go through as if you had kept [contemporaneous and accurate] time records when in fact each week you've been fudging on them and padding them. . . . This is so common. . . . [I]t is the practice.[111]

Another lawyer noted that large clients are not concerned with the fact that their legal bills are grossly inflated because they can transfer the losses from those frauds to their customers.[112] In short, there is little perceived punishability associated with overbilling.

Professor Lerman's evidence is apparently only the tip of the iceberg of lawyer overbilling. She notes:

> Almost every time I talk with a practicing lawyer or a law student . . . the person tells me another story about lawyer deception. . . . [When] I look back over my notes from the interviews, [I] see many stories that I did not include because they were almost identical. . . . Most of the [interviewed] lawyers had done these things, sometimes often.[113]

Rule 1.5 of the *MRPC* states that lawyers should require only a "customary" fee commensurate with those charged locally. In 1986 after a new law allowed illegal immigrants to apply for American citizenship, the ABA found that some private attorneys exploited the illegals' ignorance by charging thirty times the going rate elsewhere for filling out the forms.[114] It also is not uncommon for lawyers to bill secretarial labor, such as typing and photocopying, at the same hourly rate as their own.

Professor Lerman's respondents also related how lawyers exaggerate their expertise and influence to dupe clients into hiring them. Depending on the extent of the exaggeration, this practice can go beyond puffery in advertising and constitute fraud since money is taken under false pretenses. Because lawyers believe that they can learn any part of the law readily, they see nothing wrong with misrepresenting the scope of their knowledge[115], even though doing so is a violation of *MRPC* Rule 7.4. Consumers undoubtedly would be outraged if members of other occupations—doctors, teachers, or auto mechanics—made similar self-aggrandizing and fraudulent claims. Not only do lawyers lie about how much experience they have and the number of cases they have won in a particular legal area, they often charge the client for the time they need to gain the expertise about which they originally lied.[116]

Jerome Carlin's study of the New York City Bar Association is also revealing about how lawyers defraud clients in a much more subtle way than padded billing, overcharging, and lying about expertise.[117] Carlin asked eight hundred lawyers their opinions regarding hypothetical ethical conflicts. The vast majority of attorney-respondents approved of subordinating clients' interests to their own financial considerations, a violation of *MRPC* Rule 1.3 (mandating diligence and zeal for the client) and fraudulent in the sense that the client believes that the attorney is acting as client-advocate.

The Criminality of Other Ethical Violations

Besides defrauding clients, lawyers commit other criminal ethical violations. There also are ethical violations that do not break the criminal law, but are nevertheless treated as criminal. For instance, it was just noted that Rule 1.3 of the *MRPC* states that a lawyer must be diligent and represent a client with zeal. Failure to do so can be viewed as a *de facto* criminal offense because it has been criminally punishable under contempt of court.[118]

Although paying kickbacks for attorney referrals (i.e., fee splitting) is legal in only four states (and is a violation of *MRPC* Rule 7.2), UCLA Professor Richard Abel determined from a national sample of six hundred attorneys that two-fifths of them did not believe the practice was a crime, and another fourth did not know whether it was legal. Of the remaining third who knew the practice to be an offense, almost half saw nothing wrong with it as long as the referral fee was not excessive.[119] In another example of criminal ethical violation, a study of Michigan lawyers concluded that more than two-fifths did not feel compelled to correct a "clearly false" sworn statement[120], an action that is a violation of *MRPC* Rule 3.3 and that may in some instances constitute the felony of "subornation of perjury."

According to *MRPC* Rule 8.3, lawyers are required to report to the authorities any attorneys who commit misconduct. This is a particularly important standard because lawyers are in a much better position than lay clients to know when professional misconduct has occurred. A 1985 West Virginia survey of one hundred attorneys in a continuing legal education class on ethics revealed that the vast majority had witnessed many violations of the disciplinary rules, but none had reported the offenders.[121] As the ABA's Committee on Professionalism concluded, very few lawyers are formally disciplined after it becomes known that they purposely ignored the violations of their cohorts.[122] The failure to report misbehaving colleagues would, in some instances, constitute misprision (hiding) of a felony, which is characteristically a misdemeanor punishable by incarceration.

Explaining Crime in the Legal Profession

Differential association was clearly supported by the foregoing evidence. Every one of Lerman's twenty-three respondents admitted to overbilling, working for a firm that overbills, or knowing about widespread overbilling practices. Most of her respondents also noted fraudulently misrepresenting expertise. There were obvious similarities among the justifications used by her attorneys for their illegal behavior, which means that they were probably learned from colleagues. Another consistent theme in the Lerman study was that medium- and large-sized law firms continually put pressure on employees to keep their billing hours as high as possible in order to produce more profit, and that the firms generally did not have any rules about the importance of proper billing procedures. This sort of atmosphere represents an occupational definition favorable to the violation of law.

Lerman's evidence also suggests that the *techniques* for criminal behavior are learned. Recall from chapter 4 Sutherland's assertions about a contagion effect in various industries, by which methods for illegal behaviors are transmitted from firm to firm. Identical diffusions have occurred in the legal profession, as evidenced by the following explanation of fraud committed through **premium billing** (by which lawyers arbitrarily charge unlimited amounts of extra money when they deem their work to be especially valuable): "It started in New York; [a large law firm] invented it, and it has caught on in a big way. . . . Our firm tries to do it to the extent that they can. . . . [I]nvestment bankers bill this way, why shouldn't we."[123] The Lerman study also indicated that the techniques for avoiding detection were learned from colleagues, such as the ways to hide overbilling and to handle the questions of clients.

The overwhelming evidence of occupational norms supporting criminal behavior in the legal profession seems contrary to propensity-event theory. Becoming a lawyer certainly requires a higher level of self-control—earning good grades in college and high scores on the law school entrance examination, late-night studies to graduate from law school and to pass the bar examination, and the meeting of mandatory deadlines. Propensity-event, then, cannot explain why the crime rate is so high in an occupation that should have so many higher self-control individuals.

It appears that under such extreme conditions as are found in the legal profession, people with high self-control can be corrupted through differential association. Perhaps it is only those who are able to maintain the loftiest professional ethics who can turn their heads away from such a crime-facilitative environment. These individuals may choose lawyer roles in which they are least likely to be tempted by criminality—governmental attorney such as prosecutor, public defender, or public agency lawyer; legal aid attorney for the poor; or a nonpracticing lawyer role such as an attorney for a corporation or nonprofit organization. Some lawyers who become frustrated with the conditions of the profession will leave it early, as forty thousand lawyers did annually in the beginning of the 1990s.[124]

Propensity-event would also emphasize the lack of deterrents to prevent lawyers' criminal professional behavior. Not only are attorneys likely to be successful at hiding their misdeeds from their clients and other lawyers, when their criminal behavior happens to be discovered by colleagues the probability of being reported is virtually nil. And if reported to the bar association by a client or a colleague, the probability of censure is also extremely remote. One study indicated that in the mid-1970s, thirteen of seventeen bar associations imposed sanctions in less than 8 percent of complaints filed; the highest sanctioning rate among the other four was 13 percent.[125] In 1987, the ABA found that the disciplinary agencies in thirty-five states employed six or fewer full-time attorneys for investigation and prosecution.[126] And, in 1986, the California Bar, which had more active members than any other state (almost 100,000), sanctioned only 185 lawyers, or about 2 percent of the complaints filed.[127]

Concluding Note: The Conflict between Profit and Profession

One factor that may help to explain occupational crimes by doctors and lawyers (and other professionals), at least those offenses that produce financial gain, is whether the offenders view their occupation as a business or as a profession. Professions have an almost quixotic public image, personified in the forms of the eloquent lawyer-statesman[128] and the gifted physician-healer.[129] Besides their romantic statuses, professions can be lucrative occupations, and many persons enter the professions in order to make a great deal of money. There then arises a conflict between profit and profession. This occupational role conflict causes a structural strain among professionals, and those who are more likely to see their profession as a business are more likely to violate ethical rules to generate more profit.[130] Those professionals who enter their field solely for the sake of the profession and are able to maintain that posture—even in the face of corrupting influences—are the least likely to prostitute the trust of their consumers for profit.

Key Terms

criminal unnecessary medical procedure
California Therapeutic Abortion Act
euthanasia
medical kickback
fee splitting
self-referral
pingponging
family gang
unbundling
ABA *Model Rules for Professional Conduct*
premium billing

Questions for Discussion

1. Why is professional occupational crime a distinct form of offending?
2. Explain how fee-for-service structures facilitate crime in the professions. How would prepaying professional services (e.g., a monthly fee) help to curb fraud in the professions? Would such a system reduce the quality of professional services rendered to clients and patients? Why or why not?
3. Explain how self-regulation in the professions can both encourage and discourage occupational crime.
4. Why are geographic variations in operation rates a poor measure of the extent of unnecessary surgery? What are the problems associated with using other methods to measure unnecessary surgery?
5. Discuss euthanasia as a criminal offense. If you do not consider it to be criminal behavior, which criterion would you use for committing euthanasia (physiological brain death or the social quality of life)? If you choose the social quality of life, should you be considering the patient or the patient's family? Why?
6. Discuss the deleterious effects of medical kickbacking in the areas of self-referrals and pharmaceutical gift-giving. What restrictions do you propose to regulate these two forms of medical kickbacking?
7. Discuss occupational anomie in medicine and law. Why is anomie criminogenic in those professions? How does occupational anomie reduce a profession's ability to regulate itself?
8. Discuss the ways in which lawyers lie to clients, including the various methods for overbilling.

Suggested Readings on Professional Occupational Crime

Stuart M. Berger, *What Your Doctor Didn't Learn in Medical School* (New York: William Morrow and Company, 1988).

Abraham S. Blumberg, "The Practice of Law as a Confidence Game: Organizational Cooptation of a Profession," *Law and Society Review* 1 (1967):15–39.

Diana Crane, *The Sanctity of Social Life: Physicians' Treatment of Critically Ill Patients* (New York: Russell Sage Foundation, 1975).

Elliot Freidson, *The Profession of Medicine* (New York: Dodd and Mead, 1970).

Paul Jesilow, Henry Pontell, and Gilbert Geis, *Prescription for Profit: How Doctors Defraud Medicaid* (Berkeley, CA: University of California Press, 1993).

Anthony Kronman, *The Lost Lawyer: Failing Ideals of the Legal Profession* (Cambridge, MA: Belknap/Harvard University Press, 1993).

Lisa G. Lerman, "Lying to Clients," *University of Pennsylvania Law Review* 138 (1990):659–760.

Sol M. Linowitz and Martin Mayer, *The Betrayed Profession: Lawyering at the End of the Twentieth Century* (New York: Charles Scribner's Sons, 1994).

Jack Olsen, *Doc: The Rape of the Town of Lovell* (New York: Atheneum, 1989).

United Way Chief William Aramony leaves U.S. District Court in 1995 after being sentenced to seven years in federal prison for looting the national charity to pay for illicit romances and exotic vacations.

7 *Individual Occupational Crime*

Occupational crime by individuals *as* individuals is a catchall category that includes all occupational crimes except those committed for organizations by their employees or by persons acting in their capacity as government authorities or professionals. This category includes the largest number of occupational crimes and criminals. Crimes against property—like theft, embezzlement, fraud, personal income tax evasion, and insider stock trading—constitute the bulk of individual occupational crime. But there are also many occupational crimes against persons committed by individuals, such as sexual molestation by teachers and babysitters and reckless endangerment of others by driving public transportation while intoxicated.

Employee Theft

It is difficult to estimate the amount of revenue lost through the varying forms of theft of cash, goods, and services by employees because so much of this activity remains undetected or unpublicized. The current estimate, provided by the U.S. Chamber of Commerce, is about $40 billion in losses to American businesses each year.[1] As much as three-quarters of losses attributable to employee theft goes undetected in some businesses.[2] Employee thefts can be relatively petty, such as the pilfering of pencils or the charging of personal long distance telephone calls to an employer. Computers have created sophisticated opportunities for employees to steal huge amounts of cash and property. Besides overt theft of cash, goods, and services, employee theft also encompasses fraudulently claimed paid sick leave, not working during working hours, abuses of discount privileges, claiming pay for unworked hours, excessive expense account reimbursements, and purposely damaging goods so that they may be purchased at a discount. Obtaining a job with faked credentials would also fall under defrauding employers. Theft of employers' trade secrets, such as industrial espionage and insider stock trading, involves crimes that promote unfair competition.

Employee theft of funds, property, and services is usually divided into three categories: larceny, embezzlement, and fraud. **Larceny** is the simple taking of something. **Embezzlement** is the misappropriation (theft or destruction) of something with which one has been entrusted. **Fraud** is the theft of something through the use of false pretenses. The theft of money from a cash drawer to which one has authorized access would be embezzlement, but theft from another's cash drawer (to which one does not have authorized access) would be larceny. The filing of a false report regarding reimbursable employee expenses or the number of hours worked is an example of theft under false pretenses.

As noted in chapter 2, the *Uniform Crime Reports* are virtually useless for determining occupationally related thefts. That chapter pointed out that law enforcement agency data do not usually reflect universes of offenders or offenses, and may not even reflect representative proportions of these categories. This is especially true in cases of employee theft because the victimized employer often seeks some sort of unofficial resolution to the problem, such as dismissal or restitution payment, rather than arrest.

Victim surveys also offer little help in determining the extent of employee theft. First, it is impossible in many cases to know the extent of inventory shrinkage in the retail sector that is due to employee theft rather than to shoplifting, although other sectors, such as service and manufacturing, would more easily equate missing materials with employee thievery. Second, while some victim organizations may be aware of the total losses due to employee theft, information about the persons who stole the property is limited only to those who are apprehended, and that sample may not be representative of the universe of employee thieves. Nonetheless, employer-apprehended offenders are more representative than law enforcement agency data on arrestees because so many apprehended employee thieves are not arrested.

Two of the earliest victim studies of employee theft, by Gerald

Robin[3] (involving 1,681 cases) and Alice Franklin[4] (involving 447 cases), were doctoral dissertations that examined apprehended department store workers who stole from or defrauded their employer. Sales personnel, as one would expect, were responsible for the greatest proportion of thefts—48 percent in Robin's study of three different companies, and 65 percent in Franklin's study of nine branches of a single company. In both studies, less than 2 percent of employees were apprehended for theft; the vast majority had been in their present positions for less than two years.

Whereas the victimization studies by Robin and Franklin based on retail employer-apprehended thieves indicated a 2 percent employee criminal rate, data from self-report employee surveys indicate thief rates up to five times higher for the same offenses. The most comprehensive of the self-report surveys was undertaken by Richard Hollinger and John Clark[5] (see box 2.3) and involved the three most labor-intensive American business sectors—retail, service (represented by hospital employees), and manufacturing. In all three sectors about a third of Hollinger and Clark's respondents admitted to the theft of cash or merchandise or to otherwise defrauding their employer: retail—35 percent; service—33 percent; manufacturing—28 percent. The most prevalent forms of theft involved misuse of discount privileges (retail), theft of supplies (service), and theft of raw materials (manufacturing). The majority of the respondents said that they stole only sporadically—a few times a year.

Hollinger and Clark also asked respondents about **production deviance**—taking long lunch or coffee breaks without approval, coming to work late or leaving early, using sick leave unnecessarily, doing slow or sloppy work, and working under the influence of alcohol or drugs. These behaviors can also be seen as theft (or defrauding) because workers are paid to do the best job possible for the entire time they are in the office or factory. The proportions of workers who admitted to at least one of these behaviors was about two-thirds for the retail and service sectors and four-fifths for the manufacturing sector.

The nonresponse rate in the Hollinger and Clark study was very close to half. As noted in chapter 2, nonrespondents in self-report surveys are known to have a higher offender rate than respondents, so the true thief rates may be even larger. Moreover, it was also noted in chapter 2 that respondents in self-report surveys are more likely to underreport their criminality than overreport it, so the thief (and theft) rates for respondents may also be underrepresentative in this respect. Given the information provided in this useful research, it is no surprise that many businesses are plagued by large volumes of relatively petty employee theft.

Not all employee theft is of the small potatoes variety documented by Hollinger and Clark. The following charges involving occupational embezzlement are cases in point from the first half of the 1990s: $29,000 (Frances Gordon—stole payroll funds by cashing unauthorized checks made payable to employees)[6]; $81,000 (William Cheek—embezzled rent and pension funds from a local federal housing program)[7]; $916,000 (M. L Vaughan—pension funds)[8]; $272,000 (Cona Meeks—bank funds)[9]; $1.5 million (William Aramony—United Way of America charity funds)[10]; $660,000 (Phyllis Isenberg—stole bank funds by pocketing customers' deposits and paying their withdrawals from others' accounts)[11]; $693,000 (U.S. Congressman Dan Rostenkowski—converted federal and campaign funds for personal use)[12]; $1.7 million (college president Lewis Nobles—siphoned donations to Mississippi College)[13]; $3 million (Becky Schafer—wrote checks on bank funds to pay personal debts)[14]; $10 million (Robert and Susanna Scaretta—took banks' cash held by their armored car firm).[15]

Academic researchers commit a unique type of fraud against their employers when they receive promotions or grant monies based on falsified research data. One of the earliest documented cases is that of biologist Paul Kammerer, who fabricated specimens of spotted salamanders in the early 1920s to prove Lamarckian evolution (i.e., that survival traits of species are acquired after birth and passed on). He was subsequently offered a prestigious position at the University of Moscow, but committed suicide after his fraud was exposed.[16] One of the most recent cases is that of Stephen Breuning, who falsified data on the benefits of a behavior modification drug he administered to mentally retarded children. He was sentenced to prison because his bogus research was supported by federal grant monies.[17]

Perhaps the best study to identify cheating in science was published in the *American Scientist* by Judith Swazey and her colleagues. They found that between 6 percent and 9 percent of students and faculty in chemistry, civil engineering, microbiology, and sociology reported that they have direct knowledge of faculty who have plagiarized or falsified data.[18] The "publish or perish" pressure in many American universities may motivate an individual to forge data or plagiarize the works of others. Scientists' conclusions are almost never audited in relation to their raw data. This lack of verification is primarily due to the fact that scientists trust in the honesty of their colleagues. Another reason for the lack of auditing, at least in the social sciences, is that it would often open a Pandora's box of ethical conflicts associated with the breach of confidentiality promised to subjects.

A particularly heinous area of academic fraud is that committed by medical researchers. As in cases of knowingly marketing an unsafe consumer product or performing unnecessary surgery, faking medical research is both a crime against property (it defrauds those who pay for the product) and a crime of violence (it promotes intrusive medical treatments that are incorrect and may allow disease to accelerate). Most medical research in the United States is funded by the National Institutes of Health (NIH), which spends about $6 billion annually. The NIH estimates that at any given time, its Office of Research Integrity is looking into approximately seventy cases in which research fraud has been alleged.[19]

One such case that surfaced in 1994 involved the forgery of breast cancer research data at eleven university hospitals. Investigations showed that the lying had been going on at some sites for almost fifteen years in the $9 million Surgical Adjuvant Breast and Bowel Project. Although the forgeries were known for at least three years, no action was taken by the supervisory institution, the University of Pittsburgh.[20] One major contributor to the research, Dr. Roger Poisson of the University of Montreal, faked the dates on which six women had received biopsies so that the women would be allowed into the study. He neutralized his fraud by invoking a denial of responsibility ("I [misunderstood] the rules to be guidelines") and an appeal to higher loyalties ("[I could not] tell a woman with breast cancer that she was ineligible to receive the best available treatment because she did not meet one criterion out of twenty-two, when I know this criterion has little or no intrinsic oncologic importance"). There is a question about the selflessness of Poisson's motives because the Montreal hospital was paid for each patient. Experts believe that the falsifications did not affect the validity of the study, which supported the use of lumpectomy (removing tumors) rather than mastectomy (removing the entire breast) in the early treatment of breast cancer.[21]

Explanations for Employee Theft

Perceived financial pressure, or "strain," may account for at least some of the motivation to steal from employers—what Donald Cressey termed an **unsharable financial problem** in his classic study of embezzlement.[22] This refers to a monetary bind about which the offender is ashamed (or afraid to share with others) and for which legitimate sources of money are unavailable. However, when Alice Franklin sought to ascertain the reason for employee thefts among 169 persons (mostly long-term employees), only a third of them were considered to have "needed money."[23] In contrast to actual need as a motivation, Don Gibbons has observed that some embezzlements develop as attempts to sustain standards of living for which legitimate income is insufficient.[24] Similarly, Gwynn Nettler's study of six major embezzlements in Canada revealed that "desire and opportunity generate theft more frequently in these instances than does a financial difficulty."[25] Only one of Nettler's embezzlers, an attorney, had stolen to meet current financial obligations. Dorothy Zeitz reached similar conclusions about the lack of offenders' pressing financial problems in her study of female embezzlers.[26] Kathleen Daly found the needs of self and family as well as greed to be among the motivations of both male and female embezzlers.[27] Cressey, too, later admitted that though an unsharable financial problem could be important to the process of embezzlement, it was "not critical."[28] In any case, a perceived need for money is not a explanation for employee theft because similarly strained individuals do not always turn to stealing.

Differential association would explain why, among those perceiving a financial strain, some would steal and others would not by pointing to the learning of "motives, drives, [justifications], and attitudes" favorable to employee pilfering. Such learning would involve intimate associates, including co-workers. Studies by Cressey, Donald Horning, Lawrence Zeitlin, Gerald Mars, and Michael Benson, presented in chapter 3, found that attitudes condoning employee theft were often given by offenders who in many cases learned them from cohorts on the job. Denial of injury ("the company can afford it"), denial of responsibility ("I was only 'borrowing' the money"), condemnation of condemners ("my employer doesn't pay me enough money for the work I do"), appeals to higher loyalties ("I distributed the stolen goods to deserving people"), and "metaphor of the ledger" ("I took the money, but I am otherwise a law-abiding person") were common. The "not paid enough" neutralization has been developed into an equity hypothesis by Gerald Mars—employees steal commensurate with their perceptions that they receive too little remuneration for their work.[29] Remember, however, that all of these justifications were documented by researchers after the offenses took place, and therefore they may simply reflect rationalizations to ease guilt feelings about knowingly wrongful behavior rather than attitudes developed before theft.

Although differential association would also point to learning the techniques of employee theft, persons who steal on the job need not "learn" the specific techniques for the taking of cash, merchandise, supplies, or other materials, as is hypothesized by differential association. Even in more sophisticated thefts, such as artful embezzlements, specific theft techniques and attitudes toward stealing are not necessarily learned from others.[30] Carl Klockars's study of a professional fence (a dealer in stolen goods), however, indicates that employee thieves sometimes are taught specific pilfering techniques. In the following passage, Klockars's fence explains how he told truck drivers the best ways to steal:

> See, I school my drivers, I mean, if they got an overload, that's a free thing, a gift. They can bring it to me just like it's legitimate. But stealin', I tell 'em, they just gotta use their heads. You pick a day when it's rainy an' cold an' the shipper's rushed. That's when you wanna throw on an extra carton. Or the same goes when you're deliverin'. If the guy's got five trucks waitin' he ain't gonna count what you got. It don't make sense to steal from your own truck either, if you can just as easy pick up a couple a cartons where somebody else unloaded 'em. Oh, I school my drivers; show 'em how to go about doin' things, you know.[31]

If the idea of propensity-event is going to be useful, it must explain employee thefts, since such thefts in many cases epitomize simplicity. In the case of embezzlement, for example, people merely have to retain property that is already in their possession. Propensity-event theory would be supported to the extent that employee offenders are more likely than nonoffenders to be involved in other forms of immediate self-gratification. Such self-gratification behaviors would include both those on the job (such as the production deviances documented by Hollinger and Clark) and away from employment (commission of other crimes involving both theft and violence, use of drugs and alcohol, gambling, and checkered marital and employment histories). The platitudinous cause of financial need to commit theft on the job has often been characterized as "wine, women, and wagering."[32] The fact that these behaviors (sex, adultery, gambling, and drug and alcohol abuse) are present among employee thieves (such as embezzlers) would, at least anecdotally, support propensity-event's postulates of stability and versatility of low self-control behavior patterns as the basis for crime at the jobsite. Something more reliable than anecdotal evidence is required, however.

Of much greater substance in support of propensity-event theory are consistent results from self-report studies. Hollinger and Clark's analysis clearly indicated that employees with higher levels of involvement in property theft are generally also more likely to participate in production deviance.[33] Second, William Terris measured the acceptability of theft among 470 applicants for jobs that involved the handling of cash and expensive goods. He then polygraphed the applicants about thefts from previous employers. Terris noted that the higher an applicant scored on the dishonesty scale, the more likely it was that he or she would make serious theft admissions in the polygraph examinations. Those who made theft admissions were also less punitive toward thieves and more accepting of common justifications for stealing.[34] In support of versatility, he found that the theft-prone were more likely to be proviolent and to use drugs.[35] Third, another self-report study in the food marketing industry found that, compared to those who did not admit to employee theft, those who did were more likely to have had more employers in the previous year and to endorse the attitudes that justified the legitimacy of employee theft.[36] The postulates of propensity-event theory seem to be well supported by observations about employee theft, at least among self-reports by lower-level employees.

Consumer Fraud

Consumer fraud committed by persons working for large organizations was discussed in chapter 4. Individuals can also commit consumer fraud as part of their dealings in a legitimate business. Consumer fraud is an individual occupational crime to the extent that its gains accrue directly and knowingly to employees, such as those working on a commission basis, or to owners of small businesses. The possibilities for fraud against consumers are virtually limitless; it can occur whenever goods or services are sold. In *The Popular Practice of Fraud*, T. Swann Harding documented fraud against consumers as early as the first century, when Pliny the Elder told of the adulterated honey on the market and of the fortification of wine with gypsum, lime, pitch, rosin, wood ashes, salt, sulphur, and artificial pigments. Pliny also denounced the fraudulent pharmacists of his day and provided tests for detecting food and drug adulteration.[37]

It has been estimated that consumer fraud accounts for about *one in every six dollars* of revenue derived from criminal activity in the United States.[38] Consumer fraud affects almost everyone. Legitimate businesses incur lost income when sales are diverted to consumer frauds, in many cases making it extremely difficult for them to compete effectively. Selling adulterated products or performing substandard building repair or construction exposes people to physical danger. Consumer fraud also undermines consumers' confidence in the marketplace and thwarts unredressed fraud victims' confidence in the criminal justice system.[39]

The axiom of *caveat emptor* ("let the buyer beware"), which insulates fraudsters from prosecution, is a relatively recent legal doctrine. In English law before about 1400, people who made bad business deals were forced to resolve their disputes informally because no legal precedent existed to protect them. It was not until the fifteenth and sixteenth centuries that consumer fraud was outlawed. English courts first ruled that consumer fraud was illegal only if the seller literally "warranted" untrue facts to be true, a situation known as "Trespass on the Case for Warranty." This concept was expanded around 1450 to include deceitful representations, even if they were not warranted, a situation known as "Trespass on the Case in the Nature of Deceit." Through the next three centuries, strict liability precedents developed that made the seller responsible for a misrepresentation even if it was unintentional. During the period from 1450 to 1750 courts enforced contracts only if they were approximately equitable and just; otherwise they were nullified.

Caveat emptor as a legal doctrine did not begin to develop until the latter part of the 1700s, when courts, siding with overall commercial interests rather than "the little guy," decided that business agreements were essentially sacred, even though this could mean a great bargain for one party and a terrible loss for another. In 1900, a person duped in a business deal could recover only if it could be shown that the seller purposely represented a fact upon which the buyer relied and thereby suffered damages.[40] As Gilbert Geis put it, *caveat emptor* was adopted "only when social conditions and power relations existed which allowed the pretense that there was such a sacred common-law doctrine."[41] *Caveat emptor* currently prevails, unless it can be shown that the goods were purposely sold under false pretenses. In such a case the seller is guilty of fraud. Under the notion of strict liability, laws also have developed under which the seller is liable for civil damages and a fine (but not incarceration) even if the goods were accidentally sold under false pretenses—such as when a product is marketed with unintentionally erroneous promotional materials.[42]

Fraudsters also prey on consumers' humanitarian, charitable, and spiritual instincts. In a nationwide telephone solicitation, one hundred thousand Americans were duped into buying inferior lightbulbs. The profits allegedly aided disabled workers. The bulbs, marketed under the brand name Torch, were overpriced by about 300 percent. An investigation by the State of New Jersey revealed that the bulb sellers' disabilities, which had been "certified" by licensed physicians, included obesity, acne, hay fever, and nervousness.[43] Tricksters sometimes take advantage of people when they are most vulnerable, such as during bereavement. In Cross Plains, Tennessee, for example, funeral director Bobby Wilks charged mourning families for expensive funerals and then buried their deceased without the coffins that had been purchased by the families.[44] Clergy fraud, too, has duped thousands. The most infamous case is probably that of "Praise the Lord" founder Reverend Jim Bakker and his confederates, who shocked the nation in 1988. Bakker sold shares in a theme park venture that never materialized, duping unsuspecting victims, many of whom were elderly, out of tens of millions of dollars. He was convicted on various federal charges, including mail and wire fraud, and received a whopping forty-five-year prison term and a half-million-dollar fine. The sentence was later found to be capricious, and was reduced to eight years with no fine. He served almost five years in prison and was released to five years on probation.[45]

Fraud is also common in service delivery. In the auto repair industry, mechanically inept customers must rely on the judgment of persons who are "experts," which puts them at the mercy of repair shops. In the late 1970s, American motorists were overcharged an average of at least one hundred fifty dollars per car per year for repairs. Of each dollar spent, fifty-three cents were wasted because of unnecessary repairs, overcharging, and services never performed or performed incompetently.[46] Even large, well-respected firms have been accused of automobile repair fraud—in 1992 Sears Roebuck was charged in California for pressuring employees to sell customers a wide variety of unnecessary services and repairs.

In perhaps the most colossal consumer fraud in modern history, Equity Funding Corporation of America (EFCA) duped its high-finance customers out of about $2 billion. EFCA made loans to customers for the purchase of its life insurance policies. The firm soon began to lose money. To generate cash, however, EFCA sold the policies to other insurers, receiving about $1.80 for each dollar in premiums sold in the first year. All subsequent life insurance premiums would go to the reinsurer rather than EFCA. Such transactions offered only a temporary solution to the company's cash flow problems. A further "solution" involved fraudulently inflating EFCA's assets in order to secure loans, which were used to acquire other companies with real assets. As this inflationary method of fraud came to an end, EFCA then began to falsify life insurance policies and sell the bogus policies to the reinsurer. EFCA even "killed off" nonexistent persons in order to obtain full beneficiary value on some of the fake policies. In all, some fifty-six thousand false policies were sold to reinsurers and at least $120 million in assets were fabricated. When EFCA fired one of its workers, he became disgruntled and told the story to an outsider, who in turn told the authorities. Eventually, twenty-two people pleaded guilty, and the crimes' mastermind, EFCA founder Stanley Goldblum, was sentenced to eight years in federal prison.[47]

Publicized case studies such as Equity Funding make interesting reading. Accurately determining the overall incidence of consumer fraud, however, is extremely difficult. Enforcement agency information on fraud, such as that found in the *Uniform Crime Reports,* does not distinguish between occupational and nonoccupational circumstances. Victim-generated information on consumer fraud is probably unreliable because, first, many victims may be unaware of a fraud and therefore underreport it. Second, consumers who claim fraud victimization may have merely made an unwise, but legal, transaction, and therefore overreport it. Philip Ennis's pioneering victim survey was noted in chapter 2 as an illustration of this—staff attorneys considered almost two-thirds (63 percent) of "victim"-respondent claims about consumer fraud to be "doubtful."

Three studies have used direct observation to determine the prevalence of consumer fraud in various aspects of the automobile industry. The methodologies of these studies were described in chapter 2, and their findings are presented here. In Paul Jesilow's auto repair fraud car battery study, about one shop in ten (34/313) was considered to be dishonest because the mechanic declared a chargeable battery to be unchargeable.[48] In the second study, Paul Tracy and James Alan Fox took several cars that had body damage to a representative sample of repair shops in Massachusetts to obtain repair estimates. The estimates were significantly higher when the repair shops were told that the car was insured than when they were told otherwise. This held true regardless of type of car, extent of damage, gender of driver, and location of repair shop.[49]

In the third study, John Braithwaite went to twelve used car lots in Queensland, Australia, noted the mileage on a sample of used cars, and then contacted the immediately previous owners to verify how much mileage was on the cars when they were sold to the dealer. Because people seem likely to remember their car's mileage at the time they trade it for a new one (it is a key factor in the trade-in value), Braithwaite considered former owners' responses to be valid. He concluded that over a third (thirteen of thirty-five, or 37 percent) of the cars appeared to have their odometer readings rolled back. The average discrepancy was about 10,000 miles and the greatest rollback was 53,000 miles. Based on the total number of used cars sold in Queensland, the rate translated into an estimate of over 70,000 odometer rollbacks each year.[50] In the United States it has been estimated that there is as high as a 50 percent chance in some areas of buying a used car that has had its odometer rolled back an average of 30,000 miles. Because for each 10,000 miles rolled back the consumer pays an extra $300 to $500, consumer loss on each illegal car averages as much as $1,500.[51]

As part of Braithwaite's study, twenty used car dealers were interviewed, excluding those who worked at the lots he used for direct observation. Braithwaite's subjects felt that in many significant ways car manufacturers use their market power to maximize their profits on new cars, while at the same time minimizing dealer profits.[52] Most dealers strongly supported the view that the intense competition in the cut-throat game of used car sales created pressure to violate the law. They continually pointed out that in the past, before consumer protection measures were instituted, rollbacks were common because of strong competitive market pressures. Besides rollbacks, respondents discussed other methods of fraud in their industry, such as refusing to honor warranties, telling the buyer the wrong year of car manufacture, and submitting untruthful loan applications to lenders.

Respondents gave answers that can be considered supportive of both differential association and propensity-event theory to explain the illegalities. For differential association, there was evidence supporting Sutherland's hypothesis about the diffusion of illegal practices. When one firm saw its competitor committing fraud and getting away with it, it believed it had to do the same in order to compete. Eventually, the industry became differentially socially organized around consumer fraud. Many respondents stated that honest people are weeded out of the business by dishonest people. This finding is consistent with the postulates of propensity-event theory for two reasons. First, stability of high self-control behavior would explain why honest dealers do not turn dishonest. Second, the theory implies that lower self-control individuals are naturally selected into jobs as one moves down the occupational hierarchy, and selling used cars is toward the low end of the job scale.

Most of the dishonest car dealers tended to justify what they did by denying any injury caused by their fraud. The following is illustrative:

> People pay too much attention to the mileage reading on a car. There might be a car with a low mileage reading but all sorts of faults and another perfect car with a high mileage reading. It doesn't matter what the mileage reading is, but how good the car is. . . . So if you turn the mileage reading back of a car in perfect order, you are encouraging the people to buy a good car.[53]

Condemnation of condemners was the most common justification in Braithwaite's study. Dealers unanimously believed that the public tries to cheat them at least as much as they cheat the public. One dealer stated, "They think because you are a used car dealer you are a liar. So they treat you like one and lie to you. Can you blame the dealer for lying back?"[54] Here, Braithwaite sees a self-fulfilling prophecy (something that is in fact false but becomes true because of a belief in it as being true). Because customers believe used car dealers are dishonest, they are dishonest in return. This phenomenon plays a role in creating illegal behavior by forcing the dealer into dishonesty. One could argue against Braithwaite's self-fulfilling prophesy hypothesis if it was true that the used car industry was dishonest before such a perception was created among consumers. Second, car dealers need not necessarily be dishonest because a citizen tries to be dishonest with them, especially when the car dealer is the expert and the citizen is the amateur at the used car game. In other words, dishonest used car dealers may simply be dishonest, regardless of market pressures and dishonest citizens.

Financial Institution Fraud

People defraud all types of financial institutions in the course of their occupation, including banks, savings and loans, and federal credit unions. However, it was the savings and loan (S&L or "thrift") frauds that rocked America in the 1980s. They are estimated to have cost the nation ultimately a half trillion dollars[55]—costs that stem from the government's insurance of S&L deposits that disappeared. Two prominent researchers of the S&L crisis, Kitty Calavita and Henry Pontell, note that thrift failures were in part spurred by a downturn in the economy:

> In the 1970s, economic conditions began to undermine the financial health of the savings and loan industry. Committed to low-interest mortgages from previous eras, prohibited by regulation from paying more than 5.5% interest on deposits, and with inflation at more than 13% by 1979, the [S&L] industry suffered steep losses.[56]

These economic setbacks forced the government to relax regulatory handcuffs on S&Ls, such as by allowing 100 percent real estate financing, eliminating restrictions on the amount of interest that could be paid, allowing S&Ls to be owned by a single individual, and increasing the maximum amount of their loans (to 30 percent of S&L assets on consumer loans and 40 percent of assets on nonresidential real estate, commercial, business, and corporate loans). The deregulation opened the door for speculative business ventures—some legal and some illegal—with depositors' money. The government estimates that criminal behavior was a factor in about three-quarters of S&L failures through the end of the 1980s.[57] Thus, some thrifts failed only because of criminal behavior, some only because of economic conditions, and some because of a combination of the two.

Five methods of fraud marked the S&L fiascos[58] (embezzlement by S&L employees was also common):

Misapplication of funds: Obtaining a loan for one purpose and using it for another purpose that had not been approved.

Nominee loans: Because of limitations on the proportion of an S&L's money that can be used for a single loan, person A borrows the maximum and then hires person B to do the same thing and give the money to person A. Nominee loans also were used by officers of S&Ls to loan themselves money through another person.

Check kiting: The defrauder with $25,000 in account A draws a check on A for $50,000 and deposits it in zero-balance account B. The crook then withdraws $25,000 from account B and deposits it back into account A. All goes well as long as both checks do not clear before another deposit is made.

Land flips: This method fraudulently inflates the value of a property. Mr. A buys a property for $50,000, then sells it to Ms. B for $250,000. Ms. B then sells it to Mr. C for $500,000. Mr. D then borrows $500,000 (the most recent value of the property) from an S&L, splits the profits with his accomplices, and defaults on the loan.

Kickbacks: Thrift officers receive kickbacks for approving loans that should not have been approved, then try to hide the kickback entirely or disguise it as a consulting or finder's fee.

During the two-year period ending on September 30, 1990, the Justice Department convicted 331 S&L felons for these five offenses and for embezzlement. Prison sentences averaged three and a half years.[59]

Two distinct types of fraud characterized the scandals. The first was **outsider fraud** committed by persons with no affiliation with a savings and loan institution—they simply defrauded the thrifts (e.g., by making false statements on loans, committing forgery, or check kiting). Outsider fraud of a financial institution involves occupational crime only when one's occupation was used to obtain money illegally, such as fraudulently obtaining a loan by using fabricated assets or inflated income from a legitimate business.

The second type of S&L fraud is **insider fraud** committed by persons working within the thrift institutions. Insider S&L frauds involved the use of a legitimate position within a thrift institution, so in all cases they were occupational crime. Inside defrauders may or may not collude with outsiders in their misdeeds. Pontell and Calavita describe collusive frauds involving insiders as **collective embezzlement.** Although fraud was used to procure the funds, Pontell and Calavita are correct in labeling these acts embezzlement because in all cases insiders took money that was entrusted to them. Insider frauds were by far the most expensive of the S&L crimes. Whereas organizational crime discussed in chapter 4 demonstrated how an organization uses employees to commit crimes for its benefit, Calavita and Pontell point to the opposite with many of the S&L crimes: employees used the organization to commit crimes for their benefit.

The case of Charles Keating, Jr. symbolizes insider fraud in the S&L debacle. Keating was convicted in California for fraudulently representing to investors, mostly the elderly, that the junk bonds sold by Lincoln Savings and Loan were as safe as certificates of deposit; that is, that they were insured by the federal government. Despite pleas for leniency by Mother Teresa, whose organizations received more than $1 million from Keating's companies, Keating was sentenced to the maximum of ten years by Los Angeles County Superior Court Judge Lance Ito in 1992. (Ito, of course, later became world famous as the judge in the 1994–1995 O. J. Simpson murder trial.) Keating was also sentenced to another twelve and a half years in prison after being convicted of more than seventy federal charges involving bank fraud, racketeering, and conspiracy. In addition, Keating used his position to plunder Lincoln Savings and its parent, American Continental Corporation of Phoenix, for millions of dollars that he spent on a lavish lifestyle, including trips to Switzerland, private jets, and a $2.2 million home in Florida. These thefts and other risky investment losses in the case cost American taxpayers a bailout of more than $2 billion.[60]

Individual Income Tax Evasion

Willful personal income tax evasion is an offense in which the taxpayer deliberately cheats the government and it is punishable by both civil and criminal penalties. It is included under the concept of occupational crime because, as noted in chapter 1, were it not for legally derived income, persons would not be able to evade income tax. Of course, income derived illegally is also taxable. Al Capone and other criminals, including drug traffickers, embezzlers, and extortionists, have been convicted for evading taxes. The present discussion, however, includes only offenders who evade tax payments on legally derived personal income.

Tax evasion encompasses failure to file a tax return and filing a false tax return (underreporting income or overstating deductions). Individuals who cheat on their federal taxes have the same cumulative criminal liabilities as organizations who cheat, as discussed in chapter 4: tax evasion (26 *USC* Section 7201), failure to pay taxes (26 *USC* 7202), mail and wire fraud if mails or wires are used (18 *USC* Sections 1341 and 1343, respectively), and making false statements to the federal government (18 *USC* Section 1001). Federal perjury provisions (18 *USC* 1621) have been used as a tax-cheating charge when the taxpayer knowingly signs incorrect tax returns "under penalty of perjury." As noted in the discussion of the U.S. Sentencing Guidelines in chapter 4, the federal government attempts to punish for "real offenses." Therefore, although a single instance of tax evasion may violate all of these statutes simultaneously, the offender will only be sentenced for a single act. Guidelines provide for a mandatory jail term if the tax loss is $1,700 or more. Sentences become longer as the amount of unpaid tax becomes higher. It was also noted that the U.S. Sentencing Commission has cited the increased punishment and deterrence of tax evaders as a manifest function of its sentencing ranges for this offense. Probation is not nearly as easy to procure since the guidelines went into effect. The recent cases of several celebrities are examples: professional baseball player Pete Rose (five months in prison)[61], hotel queen Leona Helmsley (thirty months in prison)[62], and former treasurer of the United States Catalina Villapando (four months in prison).[63]

The Extent of Income Tax Evasion

A 1990 government report cited twenty-one individual taxpayers who owed more than $50 million apiece—a total of more than $3.5 billion. Another 3,250 delinquent tax evaders were responsible for more than $11 billion in back taxes.[64] In 1990, the Internal Revenue Service (IRS) averaged almost a half million dollars in recovered back taxes for each investigator assigned to collection[65], but in 1992 the IRS failed to collect $127 billion that was owed.[66] Note that the recent advent of electronic filing of tax returns has been another source of cheating, accounting for an estimated $15 billion in tax fraud in a single year.[67] Three-quarters of the unpaid taxes are from noncomplying individuals, the remainder from noncomplying corporations.[68]

About one in forty thousand individual tax returns results in a conviction for tax evasion.[69] Self-report data tell us that a much greater proportion of taxed individuals willfully overstate deductions, underdeclare income, or fail to file. Mason and Calvin sampled eight hundred households in Oregon to ascertain levels of compliance with state and federal tax laws.[70] About one in four respondents (24%) admitted to practicing at least one form of evasion: 5.3 percent admitted overstating deductions; 14.5 percent admitted underreporting taxable income; and 8.5 percent admitted failure to file a tax return (these total more than 24 percent because violators could commit more than one form of evasion). This figure is about three times the 8 percent admitted evasion rate found for Oregonians in Charles Tittle's self-report study.[71] As high as the Mason and Calvin 24 percent figure might seem, however, it is not as high as in other countries. Joachim Vogel estimated a 34 percent willful tax noncompliance rate from self-reports in Sweden[72], and Marguerite Smith puts the rate at 40 to 50 percent for Italy and Argentina.[73] The IRS believes that Americans pay all but 17 percent of the taxes they owe.[74]

The government is very likely to collect much of the tax owed by persons whose tax payments are withheld by an employer, a practice that was started in the early 1940s. Workers paid in cash and those who are self-employed and not subject to withholding tax payments have the greatest opportunities to violate. According to the government, the following are the occupations whose members are most likely to underdeclare their taxable incomes by large proportions (reported in parentheses): auto dealers, restauranteurs, and clothing store operators (40%); telemarketers and traveling salespersons (30%); doctors, lawyers, barbers, and accountants (20%); farmers (18%); real estate and insurance agents (16%).[75] Men cheat on their taxes more often than women[76], and lower- and higher-income persons cheat more often than those in the middle class.[77]

Explaining Tax Evasion

Many of the persons who admit to cheating on their taxes do not perceive what they are doing to be morally wrong or consider it a serious offense. One evader's comment is typical of this genre of cheaters: "I don't think God gets pissed off for what you do on your income tax. Only the IRS does."[78] Persons are less inhibited about stealing from the government, the most diffuse of victims, than from other people, because it is impersonal and obviously will not suffer from the acts of one tax cheater. Justifications for tax cheating also include statements that the tax system is unfair, that the government is not representative of the people, that tax money is squandered by bureaucrats, and that everyone cheats on taxes anyway. The extent to which these attitudes favorable to the violation of tax laws are learned from significant others supports differential association as a theoretical explanation of tax evasion. Tax preparers may contribute to the ease with which taxpayers decide not to pay. Steven Klepper and Daniel Nagin have demonstrated that although tax preparers do not promote noncompliance in areas that are clearly defined by the IRS, they encourage tax cheating by helping taxpayers take advantage of legal ambiguities.[79]

Propensity-event would be supported only to the extent that tax cheaters are more likely to engage in other forms of crime and deviance than nonevaders, holding perceived punishment and opportunities for evasion constant. Tax cheating would also have to be a repetitive illegal behavior. As with embezzlement, tax cheating is an essential behavior for propensity-event to explain because of the minimal effort required to complete the crime (one simply does not give money to the government). Also present is an extremely low probability of punishment.

Persons who are not morally opposed to cheating on their taxes, regardless of whether it is because of differential association or low self-control, will refrain from cheating if they believe that they will be caught and severely penalized. The IRS realizes this, and uses deterrence as its major weapon against tax noncompliance. Somehow, the IRS has been relatively successful, given the true probability of apprehension, in convincing people that they will be caught if they cheat on their taxes. In 1990 and 1995, the IRS launched major media campaigns to increase taxpayer perceptions of apprehension. The 1990 campaign, epitomized in a November 7 cover story in *USA Today,* threatens that the "IRS Leaves No Stone Unturned"[80] to ascertain whether one's income declarations befit their lifestyle. The 1995 effort portrayed IRS auditors as private detectives instead of accountants.[81] Box 7.1 lists some of the ways that the IRS is allegedly checking up on Americans to catch them cheating on their taxes.

Most studies conclude that the IRS has been successful at deterring large scale tax cheating—people who believe they are least likely to get away with cheating are most likely to comply with the tax law.[82] More likely to violate are those who believe they can fool the IRS—such as by cheating a little across a large number of categories and by avoiding reporting items in one place that are inconsistent with items in other places.[83] In order for the IRS's campaigns to be most successful in scaring potential tax cheaters into compliance, then, the agency must convince people that their individualized methods of cheating on taxes are easily discoverable.

Securities Crime

The practice of **churning** refers to the buying and selling of stock in order to generate commissions for the stockbroker rather than maximize the client's profits. A client who has given the broker complete discretion to buy and sell is especially vulnerable to churning. The broker sells his or her services on the basis that they are in the best interests of the client, when, in fact, sometimes they are not. Brokers also have been known to underrepresent investment risks in order to induce a client to buy securities. Some brokers mix the "discretionary" accounts of customers with their own accounts, and assign winning trades to their personal ledgers and the losing transactions to the customers' accounts.

In her *Wayward Capitalists,* Susan Shapiro detailed various securities violations: clients order stock purchases, but the broker converts the payment for personal use without buying the stock; brokers use customers' stock for collateral on personal loans, or cash in a client's stock by forging the client's name. Shapiro's analysis of investigatory records of criminal stockbrokers reveals "the usual [financial strain as reasons for

BOX 7.1

The IRS Is Watching

Leona Hemsley at a 1991 press conference recounts her conviction for tax fraud. She was sentenced to thirty months in prison.

The Internal Revenue Service (IRS) is attempting to change their auditor-accountants into private detectives to catch more Americans who cheat on their income tax. If the IRS determines that the cost of your child's wedding, your furniture, or your address is too expensive to be commensurate with your declared income, you will be under scrutiny. One relatively easy way to check on potential cheaters is to peruse local government records, such as motor vehicle registrations (to see how much your car costs) and county tax rolls (to see if you own a boat or live in a house with a high assessed value). Your credit report is also fair game in determining whether your monthly obligations fit your monthly income. Court records are used to see if, say, arrested prostitutes are declaring all of their income.

(continued next page)

BOX 7.1

Continued

The IRS is trying to ferret out those who have the greatest opportunities to hide cash income by looking for: (1) handyman and babysitter ads in the newspaper to see if these incomes are reported; (2) barbers and hairdressers who do not report tips or pay social security tax; (3) firefighters who claim inflated on-the-job meal expenses; (4) owners of bed-and-breakfast inns who deduct normal living expenses; (5) yacht owners claiming illegal deductions for boat chartering; (6) private school records showing parents deducting tuition as child care; (7) flea market vendors who fail to report profits; (8) Little League umpires who do not report income; (9) golf and tennis pros who are paid in cash; and (10) building permits that list higher costs than contractors' declared income.

Critics of these IRS practices claim invasion of privacy. The IRS believes it is just clever.

Sources: Bill Montague, "Uncovering Tax Cheats," *USA Today* (November 7, 1990):1A+; Associated Press, "IRS Plans Detailed Investigations," *Albany Herald* (March 18, 1995):5A.

stealing]: expenses generated by divorce, alimony, and family illness; repaying loan sharks for gambling debts; extravagant living; liquor or cabaret bills; purchase of a new home . . . [and saving an] insolvent firm."[84]

Insider trading refers to any type of securities trading motivated by material nonpublic information that has been misappropriated. Material information is that which a prudent investor would consider important in making an investment decision, considering other available information. Nonpublic information is that which has not been made available to the general investing public. Misappropriated information is that which has been obtained wrongfully, such as by theft or by the breach of a fiduciary duty. Whether the information has been misappropriated may be the only question to be considered in a criminal trial.

"Insider trading" is somewhat of a misnomer for two reasons. First, many "insider trades" are actually made by outsiders—persons unconnected to the corporation to which the private trading information refers. Second, it is not illegal for persons inside corporations to trade that corporation's stock; indeed, trading of stock by insiders is often supported in order to reward past performance and to supply an incentive for future profitability.[85] Insider trading is illegal if it involves the buying or selling of securities while in possession of material nonpublic information that was wrongfully obtained or the use of which would be wrongful. It is based on Rule 10b-5 of the 1934 Securities Exchange Act[86], which forbids any person, in connection with the purchase or sale of any security

> (a) To employ any device, scheme or artifice to defraud, (b) To make any untrue statement of a material fact or omit to state a material fact necessary in order to make the statements made, in light of the circumstances under which they were made, not misleading, or (c) To engage in any act, practice, or course of business which operates or would operate as a fraud or deceit on any person.

Although Rule 10b-5 does not specifically mention insider trading[87], the courts and the Securities and Exchange Commission (SEC) have traditionally used it to require persons with material nonpublic information to refrain from trading on the information or to disclose it before trading in the company's securities.[88]

Obtaining such information wrongfully would include theft, bribery, misrepresentation, espionage through electronic or other means, or simply eavesdropping. Wrongful use includes a breach of duty to maintain information in confidence. Persons expected to retain securities information in confidence include issuers of stocks and commodities, securities holders, traders in securities, governmental entities, persons engaged in analyzing and disseminating information concerning securities, and persons who obtain confidential information from these sources. Insider trading is viewed as harmful behavior because it represents a form of unfair competition. Specifically, it undermines "the fair and honest operation of our securities market."[89]

Outsider trading is also illegal if the outsider, or "tippee," uses confidential information in a similar manner.[90] The first case expanding the insider trading law to outsiders was *In re Cady, Roberts Co.,* decided by the SEC in 1961.[91] The outsider's obligation to disclose the information or abstain from trading was based on the relationship providing "access to information intended only for a corporate purpose and not for personal benefit"[92] and the "inherent unfairness involved where a party takes advantage of such information knowing it is unavailable to those with whom he is dealing."[93] In the 1968 case of *SEC v. Texas Gulf Sulphur*[94], outsider trading law was extended to cover *anyone* possessing material nonpublic information. Such information must be disclosed because "[Rule 10b-5] is based in policy on the justifiable expectation of the securities marketplace that all investors trading on impersonal exchanges have relatively equal access to material information."[95]

Such a strict interpretation of the law forcing outsiders to disclose any information they possess that may be considered to be confidential and nonpublic was thought to inhibit legitimate market analysts from seeking useful and important information. Two cases from the early 1980s (*Chiarella v. United States* in 1980[96] and *Dirks v. SEC* in 1983[97]) narrowed outsider trading criminal liability to encompass only those instances in which the outsider knew or should have known that the information resulted from a breach of a fiduciary or trusted duty to keep the information secret. In *Chiarella,* an employee of a financial printing company caught a glimpse of to-be-printed takeover bids, and traded for a profit based on that information. In *Dirks,* an investment analyst received information from a former insider that a company's assets were inflated because of fraud. Dirks did not trade himself, but advised some of his investors to dump their stock in the overrated company. In both cases, the outsiders were deemed by the Supreme Court not to have a fiduciary duty with the sources of insider information, and therefore they could not be prosecuted under Rule 10b-5. The current general rule for outsider trading, taken from Justice Berger's dissent in *Chiarella,* is that it is illegal if the information was obtained illegally or otherwise through misappropriation. Under this interpretation, the printing company employee who glimpsed the takeover materials probably *would* be guilty because he stole the information.[98]

Outsider trading occupied the American spotlight during the late 1980s when several cases were featured in the media, including those of Ivan Boesky and Michael Milken (see box 7.2). Currently under U.S. Sentencing Guidelines, insider trading violations are treated the same as fraud, and are minimally punishable by probation for outsider traders (tippees) and six months in prison for insider traders (those who violated a fiduciary duty in disclosing or using the information). The fine is based on the amount of gain from the illegal activity. Insider trading enforcement is now being extended to other markets, including bonds and commodity futures.

Physically Harmful Individual Occupational Crimes

Chapter 4 discussed crimes involving physical harm or endangerment committed by individuals for the benefit of their employing organization—unsafe working conditions, environmental pollution, and the willful distribution of unsafe consumer products. Chapter 5 reviewed these offenses when committed by government officials—torture, genocide, and other assaultive behaviors. And chapter 6 considered them when the perpetrators were professionals—unnecessary surgery, sexual molestation by physicians, illegal abortion, and euthanasia.

Dangerous and overtly violent acts committed by individuals as in-

BOX 7.2

Ivan Boesky's Insider Trading Legacy to Wall Street

Probably the most infamous securities trading offender was Ivan Boesky, who bought stock in Fischbach Corporation in the mid-1980s based on confidential information. Boesky was implicated by Dennis Levine, whose insider trading case launched a host of probes into the industry. Boesky, once considered Wall Street's leading speculator in stocks of potential takeover targets, shocked the securities industry in November of 1986 when he pleaded *nolo contendre* to civil charges levied against him by the Securities and Exchange Commission (SEC). In November 1986, the SEC disclosed that Boesky had agreed to pay $100 million dollars in its civil case, the largest amount ever levied by the SEC. He was also banished from the industry. Boesky further pleaded guilty to one felony count of insider trading, for which he received a three-year prison sentence. He was charged with only one count even though he was known to have committed several other offenses (e.g., manipulating stock prices, unlawful takeover activity, and false record keeping), because he gave evidence to prosecutors about his confederates.[a]

One of those implicated by Boesky was Martin Siegel, a merger specialist with Kidder Peabody and Company, a subsidiary of General Electric. Siegel allegedly received $700,000 from Boesky in return for trading information.[b] The Kidder firm was charged with using Siegel's insider trading information in a civil suit by the SEC in 1987. The material information was allegedly passed on to Kidder by Siegel, who had learned it from an arbitrageur at an investment bank. Kidder pleaded *nolo contendre* and was fined $13.6 million (to disgorge profits) and $11.6 million (double penalty under the Insider Trading Sanctions Act).[c] The U.S. attorney in the case decided not to charge the firm criminally because it had cooperated in the investigation,[d] but Siegel pleaded guilty to criminal charges of illegal trading and paid $9 million in civil penalties.[e]

Boesky also implicated Michael Milken of the Drexel Burnham Lambert investment firm. The SEC charged the Drexel company, Milken, and five others in a 184-page indictment for offenses related to insider trading, rigged takeovers, falsified transactions, and the destruction of records. All told, more than sixty people were indicted on the basis of investigations launched after the Boesky affair. In addition to Siegel at Kidder and Milken at Drexel, top management from Wall Street giants such as Goldman-Sachs, Merrill Lynch, Paine Webber, and E. F. Hutton were also charged. Based on the pervasiveness of the insider trading scandals of the late 1980s, a differential social organization that favored that offense appears to have permeated Wall Street.

(continued next page)

BOX 7.2

Continued

The U.S. government has started to use the Racketeer Influenced and Corrupt Organizations Act (RICO), which was discussed in chapter 5, to target insider traders. Former U.S. Attorney Rudolph Giuliani (currently mayor of New York City) has effectively used RICO against insider traders such as Drexel Burnham Lambert and Princeton/Newport Partners. Giuliani employed RICO to force Princeton/Newport to liquidate and Drexel to plead guilty to six felonies (and pay a $650 million fine). While SEC convictions can include triple damages on insider-trading profits, RICO penalties are much more severe (recall that the law provides for forfeiture of the convicted person's total racketeering gains, triple victim damages, and incarceration for as long as twenty years). Giuliani gave Drexel a choice: settle or face indictment under RICO (which would have involved multiple civil suits with damages of hundreds of millions of dollars, freezing much of Drexel's assets, and federal prison terms). Drexel settled.[f] Six Princeton/Newport executives, however, chose differently, and they were convicted of a total of sixty-three counts of securities fraud, including RICO.[g]

a. Associated Press, "Boesky Handed 3 Years," *Albany Herald* (December 18, 1987):11A+.

b. Securities and Exchange Commission, *Fifty-third Annual Report* (Washington, DC: U.S. Government Printing Office, 1988), p. 11.

c. Ibid.

d. Associated Press, "Firm to Pay $25 Million Insider Penalty," *Evansville Courier* (June 4, 1987):12.

e. *U.S. News and World Report,* "Throwing the Book at Drexel," (September 19, 1988):41.

f. Associated Press, "Drexel Decided against the Risk," *Albany Herald* (December 25, 1988):4B.

g. Scot Paltrow, "6 Found Guilty of Racketeering and Securities Fraud," *Los Angeles Times* (August 1, 1989):IV–1+.

dividuals in the course of their occupation also occur. Examples often reflect immediate gratification tendencies, such as driving public transportation while intoxicated and sexual crimes committed by babysitters, schoolteachers, and hospital workers against persons in their charge.[99] Even the involvement of Tonya Harding in the knee clubbing of Olympic figure skater Nancy Kerrigan could fall within the conceptualization of individual occupational violent crime.[100] And box 7.3 discusses the abduction and deprogramming of citizens who lawfully practice religion. While some have seen such offenses as atypical occupational crimes compared to those that are usually emphasized by criminologists (such as corporate crime and embezzlement), the fact remains that all share the common characteristic of victimizing others through occupational opportunity. In many cases, were it not for the occupational opportunity to commit the offense, that offense (or one that would be similar) would not have been perpetrated.

BOX 7.3

Involuntary Deprogramming as Violent Occupational Crime

There have been many cases in which individuals have been forcibly taken from a location because a friend or relative does not agree with the person's involvement with a certain religious group or other organization. Attempts are then made to "deprogram" the individual's allegiance to the group. Although some consider their deprogramming a welcome rescue, others view it as a criminal victimization involving kidnapping and illegal imprisonment. Further, to the extent that religious practices are the reason for the kidnapping, violation of federal civil rights statutes (e.g., Title 18 *USC,* Section 241), discussed in chapter 5, would also be at issue. Such instances of abduction and deprogramming would be categorized as individual occupational crimes against persons.

One case in Boise, Idaho, is particularly interesting. It involved thirty-nine-year-old LaVerne Collins Macchio, a member of the Livingston, Montana based Church Universal and Triumphant. Ms. Macchio was reported missing by her boyfriend the night of November 21, 1991. Upon questioning Ms. Macchio's sister and mother, the Ada County sheriff's office was told that Ms. Macchio was safe and in good hands. In fact, she had been forcibly taken from her residence by four professional deprogrammers hired by her mother. She was held prisoner for seven days, during which her captives attempted an intense campaign to turn Ms. Macchio against her church. After her release Ms. Macchio cooperated with prosecutors and the deprogrammers were indicted for offenses that ranged from second-degree kidnapping to aiding and abetting kidnapping.[a]

The defendants pleaded not guilty by reason of *necessity.* The basic premise behind the necessity defense is that a person who is compelled to commit an illegal act in order to prevent a greater harm should not be punished.[b] The elements of necessity must include *all* of the following: (1) a specific threat or immediate harm; (2) the circumstances that necessitate the illegal act must not have been

(continued next page)

BOX 7.3

Continued

brought about by the defendant; (3) the same objective could not have been accomplished by a less offensive alternative available to the actor; and (4) the harm caused was not more serious than the harm avoided.[c] The trial judge allowed this defense to be heard by the jury.

Idaho Attorney General Alan Lance appealed the case to the Idaho Supreme Court in April of 1995. He argued that none, let alone all, of the specific elements of the necessity defense had been satisfied in the case and therefore the defense should not have been allowed as a matter of law. The Court agreed with Lance.

a. Karin Ronnow, "Defense Rests Its Case Friday in Boise Trial," *Livingston Enterprise* (April 9, 1993):1.

b. Alan G. Lance, J. Scott James, Roger Bourne, and Daniel Goldberg, "Brief of Appellant to the Supreme Court of Idaho, *State of Idaho v. Michael D. Howley, Charles Kelly, Joy DeSanctis, and Carmine DeSanctis,"* No. 20985, Supreme Court of the State of Idaho (April 21, 1995), p. 6.

c. Ibid.

We shall now turn to the final chapter of the book, which addresses ways to reduce occupational crime.

Key Terms

larceny
embezzlement
fraud
production deviance
unsharable financial problem
caveat emptor
misapplication of funds
nominee loans
check kiting
land flips
loan kickbacks
outsider fraud
insider fraud
collective embezzlement
tax evasion
churning
insider trading
outsider trading

Questions for Discussion

1. Distinguish among larceny, embezzlement, and fraud against an employer.
2. Explain the theoretical relevance of techniques of neutralization to

thefts against employers. Which techniques are most likely to be used? Why?

3. Because of their simplicity, it was noted in the text that embezzlement and failure to pay tax are essential behaviors to be explained by propensity-event theory. Aside from these two kinds of offenses, can you think of additional individual occupational crimes that also epitomize simplicity?
4. How would propensity-event theory hypothesize the effect of increased occupational opportunities for women on female rates of theft against employers and fraud against consumers? How might members of the women's movement respond to your answers?
5. Without giving names, do you personally know anybody who has willfully evaded income tax? Based on what you know about each case, explain the relevance of the theories discussed in chapter 3.
6. What would you suggest as a feasible plan for the Internal Revenue Service to increase taxpayer compliance? Be sure to consider the cost/benefit aspects of your suggestions. 6b. Which business activities facilitate the hiding of income? For each business you mention, discuss the ways you would use to catch income hiding (see box 7.2 for some hints).
7. It was noted that insider fraud in financial institutions (where an employee uses the organization to commit crime) is the opposite of organizational crime (where the organization uses the employee to commit crime). Besides insider fraud in financial institutions, discuss instances of employees using their organizational employer as a vehicle to commit crimes to benefit themselves.
8. In addition to overcharging for repairs and used car fraud, what other kinds of consumer frauds can be studied through direct observation? Be sure to include ethical and legal concerns about rights to privacy that may arise in the course of your study.
9. What might be some of the problems faced by prosecutors in their attempts to prove the crime of insider trading, given that it is defined as the "misappropriation of material nonpublic information"?
10. Look at box 7-3. Would you convict the defendants of their kidnapping charges? If not, which specific elements of the necessity defense do your believe were satisfied? If you agree that the necessity defense should not be allowed in this case, should the victim's mother and the deprogrammers also be charged under Title 18 *USC*, Section 241 (see chapter 5)—conspiracy to violate Ms. Macchio's First Amendment rights to freedom of religion? Why or why not? Would such prosecutions tend to deter this kind of behavior in the future?

Suggested Readings on Individual Occupational Crime

Donald Cressey, *Other People's Money: A Study in the Social Psychology of Embezzlement* (Glencoe, IL: Free Press, 1953).

Gary S. Green, "White-Collar Crime and the Study of Embezzlement," *Annals of the American Academy of Political and Social Science* 525 (1993):95–106.

Richard Hollinger and John Clark, *Theft by Employees* (Lexington, MA: Lexington Books, 1983).

Marcel LaFollette, "Research Misconduct," in Larry Salinger (ed.), *Deviant Behavior* (Guilford, CT: Dushkin Publishing Group, 1996).

Henry Pontell and Kitty Calavita, "Bilking Bankers and Bad Debts: White-Collar Crime and the Savings and Loan Crisis," in Kip Schlegel and David Weisburd (eds.), *White-Collar Crime Reconsidered* (Boston: Northeastern University Press, 1992), p. 196.

Lindsey Stellwagen, *Consumer Fraud* (Washington, DC: U.S. Government Printing Office, 1982).

David A. Wilson, "Outsider Trading: Morality and the Law of Securities Fraud," *The Georgetown Law Journal* 77 (1988):181–216.

Dorothy Zeitz, *Women Who Embezzle or Defraud: A Study of Convicted Felons* (New York: Praeger, 1981).

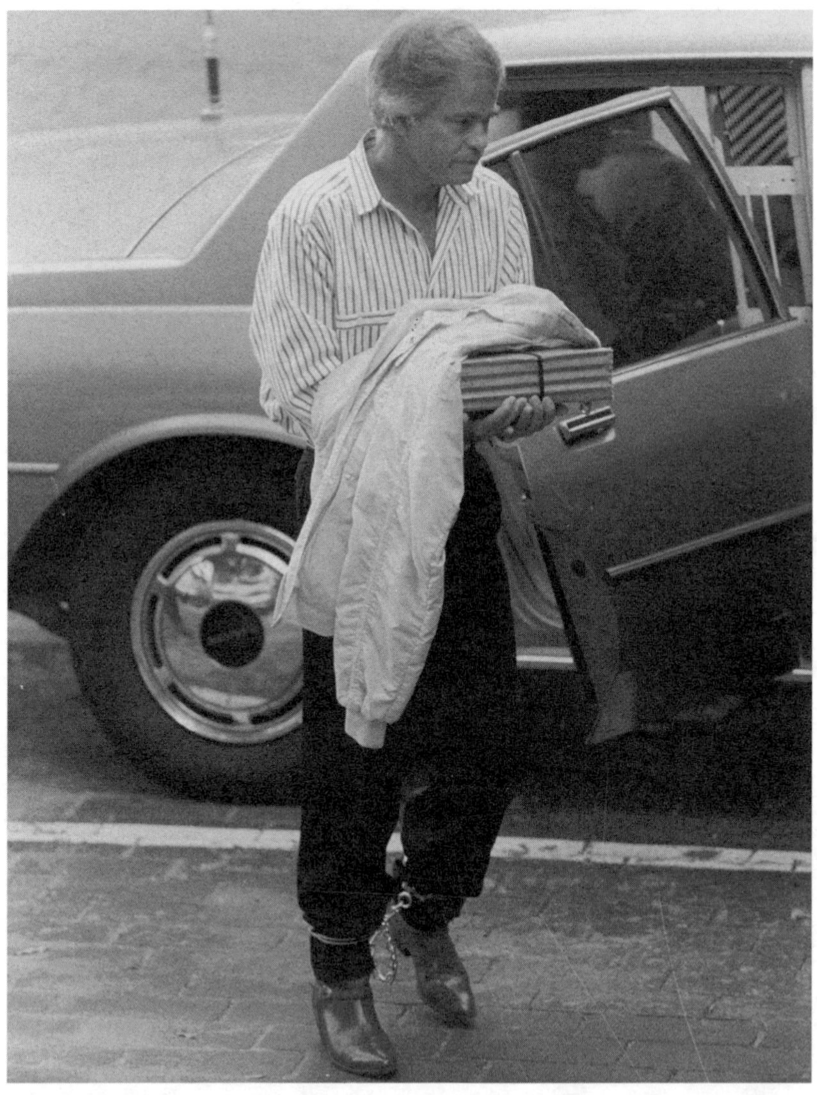

Jim Bakker arrives at the Charlotte, North Carolina, federal courthouse in 1991 for the resentencing hearing for his conviction on twenty-four counts of mail fraud, wire fraud, and conspiracy. Bakker's forty-five year sentence was reduced because it was considered to be too capricious and intemperate an attempt to deter future clergy fraud.

8 *Sanctioning, Social Control, and Occupational Crime*

Two internal personal forces that inhibit illegal behavior were discussed in chapter 3: (1) morality—the internalization of values that discourage violation of legal codes; and (2) deterrence—fear of the consequences or sanctions. Such sanctions can be imposed formally (conviction and punishment by the government) or without legal action (loss of respectability or loss of job). Sanctioning constitutes the heart of social control not only because threatened formal and nonformal sanctions can deter, but also because they infuse prolegal values through normative validation.

Incapacitation inhibits illegal behavior by restraining an individual from committing crime. The most common example of incapacitation is incarceration—prison inmates are, for the most part, blocked from committing crimes against society. But one need not incarcerate a person in order to incapacitate. Incapacitation of individuals (and organizations) can also occur through administrative mandates by courts, regulatory agencies, or professional organizations that prohibit occupational involvement (such as barring a bank embezzler from holding a position of financial trust or revoking the license of a physician or a hospital that defrauds insurance companies). Unlike deterrence and morality (which reflect personal choices about whether to commit crime), incapacitation is a sanction imposed on offenders by others.

Another sanction imposed on offenders by others is **rehabilitation,** which refers to changing offenders so that they refrain from committing future crimes. Unlike incapacitation, rehabilitation can be accomplished only if the offender is willing to change. Both individuals and organizations can be rehabilitated.

These four social control mechanisms will be discussed, where applicable, in terms of the U.S. Sentencing Guidelines[1] introduced in chapter 4, because the vast majority of the occupational crimes discussed in this book are punishable under the guidelines.

Morality

Teaching people that illegal occupational behaviors are morally inappropriate would be the most effective way to reduce occupational crime, but this is not easily accomplished. Differential association and propensity-event theories tell us that if young children are effectively taught to obey the law, they will not commit crimes later in life. Children who are taught to consider the feelings of others will be less likely to steal and to commit violence. The greater one's belief in the legitimacy of certain legal rules, the more likely one is to respect those rules. Moral teachings about the legitimacy of legal rules, then, should prevent many crimes, including occupational ones. Certainly, perceptions about what constitutes morally appropriate behavior (in an occupation and elsewhere) vary among individuals. Nevertheless, the *moral appropriateness of lawful behavior* can serve as the common focus of moral teachings.

Moral education discouraging illegal behavior must be continuous. It must start early in life and be reiterated constantly, because early moral socialization can be mitigated by subsequent procriminal associations. Previously we discussed the Harvard Business School professor who trained students to misrepresent their positions in negotiations and other business dealings. We also discussed Geis's price-fixing offenders who were socialized by their employers to believe that restraining trade was an acceptable way of life in the heavy electrical equipment industry. These kinds of teachings, though learned relatively late in life, can override weakly internalized anticriminal morality learned earlier in life.

Parents can teach their children to respect the property of others. Teachers in business schools can demonstrate to their students that it is legally wrong, and therefore morally inappropriate, to fix prices, misrepresent products, pollute the environment, manufacture unsafe products, and exploit labor. Teachers in medical schools can demonstrate that it is legally and professionally inappropriate to split fees, self-refer, double bill patients, and commit unnecessary surgery. Police and correctional officers can be taught that they have a duty to respect citizens' rights. Legal-moral education, then, should not stop in the home; it should continue throughout one's formal education and occupational socialization. Occupational legal morality must be constantly reinforced by educators, firms, industries, and immediate work groups.

Transgressions of criminal laws must be censured and sanctioned in order to promote normative validation. Persons must be informed of the demarcation between criminal and noncriminal behavior so that they can guide their personal behavior appropriately. If one is told that price-fixing is morally wrong but is not formally and informally punished for that behavior, then conflicting signals are being transmitted. The greater and more consistent the censure, the more likely a person is to learn which behaviors are acceptable and which are not. One of the major objectives of the U.S. Sentencing Guidelines is to reduce the proportion of offenders who avoid meaningful punishment, and in this regard the guidelines will promote normative validation.

It would be ideal if everybody practiced the Golden Rule: "Do as you would be done by." Unfortunately, as noted in our discussion about deterrence, persons are basically pain-avoiding and pleasure-pursuing beings. Convincing them that a behavior is the "right thing" may be insufficient to overcome their pursuit of pleasure. Punishing people formally and nonformally for their occupational crimes not only will invoke normative validation, it has the potential to create deterrents.

Deterrence

A great deal of discussion was devoted to deterrence in chapter 3. Those who are not morally opposed to committing occupational crime are generally believed to be rational about their illegal behavior.[2] If this is true, they should respond to effective punishment threats. But they also will ignore ineffective punishment threats. In other words, if either the apprehension rate or the severity of punishment is perceived by potential offenders to be insignificant, then they will not be deterred. Even if potential offenders believe they might be apprehended and indicted, they may also believe that they will have resources to hire quality defense attorneys with the skills to navigate through the labyrinth of options promoting discretionary reductions in state and federal penalties for their crimes.[3] The goal, then, is to create perceptions of apprehension and punishment that are sufficient to deter. Unfortunately, we can never know the proportion of potential offenders who are deterred by penalties; many noncriminals refrain from illegal behavior because they are morally opposed to it rather than deterred from it. And, we will only be able to identify some of those who are not deterred, because many undeterred criminals are never caught.

The three intimidations advocated as the most effective general deterrents for occupational crime are the threats of: (a) monetary penalties; (b) adverse publicity; and (c) incarceration. However, none of these threats will be able to deter unintentional occupational crimes (such as collective knowledge offenses and some strict liability crimes) because they happen by accident rather than by design.

Financial Deterrents

Many specific federal financial penalties in the U.S. Sentencing Guidelines for both individuals and organizations have been discussed throughout the book. Generally, the guidelines provide that some combination of the following be paid by convicted individual and organizational offenders: (1) victim restitution and any other costs that would be associated with righting the harm of the offense; (2) fine (based on the seriousness of the offense and the culpability of the offender); (3) disgorgement of any financial gain, including any social losses (such as harm to a marketplace in an antitrust crime); and (4) costs of prosecution.[4] The disgorgement of profits must be added to the fine, so the monetary penalty will always exceed the financial benefits of the offense.

The method for determining the fine for individuals and organizations is essentially the same, although organizational fines are much more substantial than fines for individuals (see box 8.1). First, the offense level is determined, including any mitigating and aggravating factors. The fine will fall somewhere within the amounts specified in box 8.1 for that offense level. The fine is primarily determined by (1) the need to demonstrate the seriousness of the offense and that the fine is punitive; (2) the need for deterrence and just punishment; (3) the role of the individual or organization in the crime; (4) consideration of any other financial obligations that have arisen as a result of the conviction (such as victim restitution and civil judgments); and (5) the effect of the fine on the financial well-being of the offender's dependents or the shareholders of the organization. For individuals, the fine is added to any incarceration associated with the offense level. For organizations, the fine is increased if the organization is large or the offense was condoned by higher executives. In no case can a fine be more than is allowed by statute. Organizations may also be sentenced to community service, which will entail at least some additional financial expenditure.

BOX 8.1

Fine Ranges under the U.S. Sentencing Guidelines

Individuals			*Organizations*	
Offense Level	**Minimum**	**Maximum**	**Offense Level**	**Base Fine**
1-3	$100	$ 5,000	6 or less	$ 5,000
4-5	$ 250	$ 5,000	7	$ 7,500
6-7	$ 500	$ 5,000	8	$ 10,000
8-9	$ 1,000	$ 10,000	9	$ 15,000
10-11	$ 2,000	$ 20,000	10	$ 20,000
12-13	$ 3,000	$ 30,000	11	$ 30,000
14-15	$ 4,000	$ 40,000	12	$ 40,000
16-17	$ 5,000	$ 50,000	13	$ 60,000
18-19	$ 6,000	$ 60,000	14	$ 85,000
20-22	$ 7,500	$ 75,000	15	$ 125,000
23-25	$10,000	$100,000	16	$ 175,000
26-28	$12,500	$125,000	17	$ 250,000
29-31	$15,000	$150,000	18	$ 350,000
32-34	$17,500	$175,000	19	$ 500,000
35-37	$20,000	$200,000	20	$ 650,000
38+	$25,000	$250,000	21	$ 910,000
			22	$ 1,200,000
			23	$ 1,600,000
			24	$ 2,100,000
			25	$ 2,800,000
			26	$ 3,700,000
			27	$ 4,800,000
			28	$ 6,300,000
			29	$ 8,100,000
			30	$10,500,000
			31	$13,500,000
			32	$17,500,000
			33	$22,000,000
			34	$28,500,000
			35	$36,000,000
			36	$45,500,000
			37	$57,500,000
			38+	$72,500,000

Source: United States Code Annotated, Title 18, Federal Sentencing Guidelines (St. Paul: West Publishing, 1995), pp. 996, 1193.

As powerful as some of the fine levels in box 8.1 might seem, in practice the monetary penalties in the guidelines probably invoke very little fear in defendants, particularly those who contemplate crimes within large organizations.[5] These are the reasons why:

First, the guidelines allow for a reduction in penalties when the individual or organizational offender cannot pay, making the higher fine amounts meaningless in such cases.[6] There also exists what John Coffee, Jr. has identified as a **deterrence trap,** whereby "[t]he maximum meaningful fine that can be levied against any [organization or individual] is necessarily bounded by its wealth."[7] Thus, it would be of no concern to a potential offender whether a threatened fine is $25,000 or $25 million if both sums are beyond the offender's ability to pay.

Second, organizations and individuals can pay fines, disgorgements, restitution, and prosecution costs over a period of time—a maximum of five years for organizations and one year (or the length of probation) for individuals.[8] This provision often makes payment too easy to have any jolting deterrent effect.[9] Third, a fine can be levied only to the extent that it does not adversely affect the future viability of an organization or the dependents of an individual.[10]

Fourth, and perhaps most important, are the reductions in fines allowed for organizations. If an organization brings its violation to the attention of the government before it is discovered by outsiders, it may pay only one twentieth of the fine.[11] If an organization demonstrates that it had a program in place to prevent and detect violations before the offense, even if that program is only of a cosmetic nature, the fine can be reduced substantially.[12] And, if an organization tells the government about the criminal activity of one of its competitors, it will also be given a fine reduction.[13] In short, there are many loopholes, mitigating factors, and other provisions that severely erode the guidelines' monetary deterrent value. Many of these loopholes and mitigations ignore the preoffense culpability of the individual or organizational offender, concentrating instead on how they behave after they have committed their offense and been caught.[14]

The imposition of fines and other monetary penalties for occupational offenders appears to be rather lax under the guidelines.[15] During fiscal year 1994, more than half of tax violators and a quarter of embezzlers paid no fine *and* no restitution.[16] The guidelines' monetary penalties also seem to be aimed primarily against smaller organizations. Of the first fifty cases sentenced under the organizational guidelines, 88 percent involved organizations with fifty or fewer employees.[17]

Civil cases brought by victims to recover any losses they suffered because of the offender's actions (known as **compensatory damages**) constitute another potential source of financial deterrence to occupational crime. In addition to compensatory damages, civil courts also allow juries to impose **punitive damages** (also known as "exemplary damages") to punish wrongdoers beyond compensatory damages.[18] Some members of the Supreme Court consider civil punitive damages to be so similar to criminal punishment that their imposition must be guided by due process safeguards.[19]

Civil judgments (generally imposed by juries) that include both compensatory and punitive damages have been made in a variety of cases that involve occupational crime, including unsafe consumer products and working conditions, environmental pollution, fraud, and medical incompetence. Juries are generally free to impose virtually any punitive damage award they choose, so organizations are subject to potentially devastating judgments. A $10 million punitive damage award by a West Virginia jury in a fraud case—more than 500 times the amount of the $19,000 compensatory damages it levied—was upheld by the Supreme Court in 1993.[20] One case in Dallas involved an initial $80 million in punitive damages.[21]

Such disproportionate punitive awards should cause potential offenders to consider at least the severity of such penalties. Whether they will perceive them to be certain or swift is another question. Evidence shows that plaintiffs win barely half of their cases in front of civil juries[22]; among those they win, punitive damages are awarded in only 6 percent of them.[23] Recent statistics indicate that punitive damages are extremely rare in unsafe product cases,[24] but in cases of medical incompetence, fraud, harms from pollution and toxic substances, and labor torts such as discrimination and harassment, punitive awards are more frequent and more expensive.[25]

Adverse Publicity Deterrents

Peter French refers to adverse publicity as the Hester Prynne Sanction, alluding to Hawthorne's character in *The Scarlet Letter* who was forced to wear the letter *A* because she was an adulteress.[26] The extent to which adverse publicity is perceived by potential occupational criminals to be painful is the extent to which they will avoid illegal behavior if adverse publicity is the probable sanction. It should be noted that stamina is going to affect the offender's perceptions of the potential consequences of an adverse publicity sanction. Larger organizations have the resources to launch counterpublicity campaigns and mount legal battles, and they can rely on diversified assets to take up any slack in revenue caused by adverse publicity. For them, any negative effects will be temporary. On the other hand, individuals and smaller organizations may not possess the resources to outlive or combat adverse publicity, in which case they may be more deterrable by publicity threats.

Adverse publicity can take two forms, formal and informal. The media is one major generator of informal adverse publicity. The appeal of an occupational crime story relative to other news of the day will determine whether media sources will generate adverse publicity about occupational offenses and offenders. Consumer and environmental groups, too, may produce adverse information. In localized occupational crime, such as by an attorney or small business owner, gossip constitutes a major form of informal adverse publicity. However, gossip and the news of the day cannot be regulated, so there is no way informal publicity can ensure sufficient and truthful coverage.

Formal publicity, on the other hand, involves a criminal or administrative sanction requiring an organization or individual to bear the expense of advertising the offense in various media sources that have been selected to reach particular audiences. The U.S. Sentencing Commission considers formal adverse publicity orders an appropriate sanction for organizations. Section 8D1.4.(a) of the U.S. Sentencing Guidelines states:

> The court may order the organization, at its expense and in the format and media specified by the court, to publicize the nature of the offense committed, the fact of conviction, the nature of the punishment imposed, and the steps that will be taken to prevent the occurrence of similar offenses.

As an example, a toy manufacturer convicted of false advertising could be sentenced to publicize this fact both in general media sources (such as weekly and monthly national news magazines) and those with a more specific market (such as magazines geared to children and parents).

A study by Brent Fisse and John Braithwaite looked at the effects of informal adverse publicity on organizations involved in scandals, including Allied Chemical, Ford, ITT, and General Electric. Overall, the authors found that the adverse publicity had little financial effect. Sales dropped in only a few cases, most of the organizations were sufficiently large and diversified so that the losses were relatively insignificant, and many were able to launch positive-image counterpublicity campaigns. However, the formal adverse publicity described in the guidelines may have a greater negative financial effect on convicted organizations because of its controlled imposition. This is especially true if the convicted company is not allowed to counteradvertise for a substantial period of time.

The more salient painful result of the guidelines' adverse publicity sanction seems to be embarrassment. Organizational executives want to avoid embarrassment of their firm because of its humiliating effect on themselves and their employees. Fisse and Braithwaite found that many executives cited low employee morale as perhaps the worst effect of their firms' scandals.[27] The humiliation of otherwise respectable individuals and organizations by a formal body (the government) and by others (peers, neighbors, competitors) is particularly painful. The shaming of a criminal organization at its own expense can be a poetically just punishment.

All told, formal adverse publicity sanctions have strong potential as a painful deterrent to those who make decisions within organizations. Perhaps adverse publicity should be extended to individuals. Braithwaite, in his *Crime, Shame, and Reintegration,* cautions that shaming should have as its ultimate goal the reintegration of the offender, not stigmatization.[28] Once the shaming process is over, organizational and individual offenders are to be restored to their former places.

Incarceration as a Deterrent

Threatening to incarcerate individuals who commit occupational crimes can be an extremely potent general deterrent because it should cause the potential offender to imagine all of the unpleasantries associated with modern human captivity, such as living with criminals and suffering the various pains of imprisonment (deprivations of liberty, security, autonomy, heterosexual relationships, and freeworld goods and services).[29] Beyond these pains, incarceration threatens a loss of respectability to an even greater extent than adverse publicity or other nonprison sanctions. Respectable persons usually care very much about their self-image and public evaluation, and there is no stronger criminal label than that imposed by incarceration. The threat of placing an "ex-con" label on a respectable person (and family) seems to be a salient enough deterrent above and beyond any imagined unpleasant incarceration experiences. Under the guidelines, all federal occupational criminals who commit moderately serious offenses are generally subject to incarceration.

Although imprisonment may be likely to generally deter potential offenders from committing an initial crime, it is probably less effective in specifically deterring offenders from recidivating. David Weisburd, Elin Waring, and Ellen Chayet[30], using a sample of more than seven hundred federal offenders (most of whom committed their offense in the course of their occupation), found that there was very little difference in rearrest rates between those who received a prison sentence and those who did not. One explanation for these findings is propensity-event theory—offending potential is relatively stable over time. Alternatively, the fact that these individuals had been convicted of a federal offense may have ruined their lives, and they then perceived few nonformal consequences for future offending. This would be especially true for the many who had a record before the federal offense that landed them in the study. Or their conviction record may have blocked future legitimate employment opportunities, making criminal means for survival more enticing. Whatever the reason(s), incarceration seems to be a minimal specific deterrent for occupational offenders.

Incarceration for occupational crime has three desirable aspects besides any specific and general deterrent effects. First, penalties that only punish organizations and do not incarcerate its employees tend to blur or eliminate individual accountability for deliberate offenses.[31] Second, it can be an appropriate punishment. As Gilbert Geis noted, "[occupational acts] committed in violation of the criminal law . . . are often of such a severe nature in terms of the physical and fiscal harm they cause others that they clearly deserve severe criminal penalties."[32]

Third, incarceration strongly promotes normative validation by sending the message that certain offenses are so serious that they must be punished by the severest penalty. A monetary penalty or an adverse publicity order are simply insufficient sanctions for offenses that cause serious human harm, because they imply that those harms can be excused on a financial basis. Brent Fisse believes nonprison sanctions "do not emphatically convey the message that serious offenses are unwanted. Rather, the impression fostered is that the commission of crime is permissible provided there is willingness to pay the going price."[33] One executive in the electrical equipment conspiracy, for instance, noted that his incarceration represented the major reason for a reevaluation of his actions. The stigma of a jail sentence, he said, had the effect of making people "start looking at the moral values a little bit."[34]

The incarceration patterns for occupational offenders under the guidelines are a mixed bag, however. For instance, a greater proportion of embezzlers and antitrust offenders, but fewer tax evaders, have been going to prison. By 1994, the lengths of incarceration imposed under the guidelines for some occupational offenses had markedly decreased from the first few years of the guidelines' implementation.[35]

Occupational Incapacitation

Incapacitation reduces crime by removing the physical opportunities to commit offenses. The criminal justice system incarcerates criminals, thereby incapacitating them from committing most offenses. Although prison inmates commit assault and theft against other inmates and guards and have been known to conduct forgery and tax-cheating schemes from their jail cells, for the most part, locking someone in prison physically restrains them from preying on society.

Unlike "common" crime, such as burglary, robbery, assault, and rape, occupational criminal activity is dependent on legitimate formalized roles in the economy. To incapacitate occupational criminals from opportunities for further occupational crimes, one need only administratively remove or disqualify offenders from their occupational role. Removing them from society and putting them in prison is not always necessary.

There is ample precedent in law supporting disqualification from both public and private sector occupations. Most states have laws providing that a felony conviction renders one either permanently or temporarily ineligible to pursue certain licensed vocations such as pharmacist, barber, and liquor store or pawnshop owner. Many states provide that convicted felons are barred from holding public employment or public office. The Federal Deposit Insurance Act of 1950 prohibits any person convicted of a criminal offense involving dishonesty or breach of trust from being employed by a federally insured bank, and the Security Exchange Act of 1934 bars stockbrokers from future securities licensing if they previously committed a securities crime.[37] Similar statutory provisions imposed as mandatory or discretionary aspects of sentences could be put into effect for doctors and lawyers, corporate executives, police officers, day care workers, or virtually any other occupational criminals convicted of certain crimes.

Section 5F1.5 of the U.S. Sentencing Guidelines speaks directly to occupational disqualification:

> (a) The court may impose a condition of probation or supervised release prohibiting the defendant from engaging in a specified occupation, business, or profession, or limiting the terms on which the defendant may do so, only if it determines that:
>
> > (1) a reasonably direct relationship existed between the defendant's occupation, business, or profession and the conduct relevant to the offense of conviction; and
> >
> > (2) imposition of such a restriction is reasonably necessary to protect the public because there is reason to believe that, absent such restriction, the defendant will continue to engage in unlawful conduct similar to that for which the defendant was convicted.

It is important that occupational disqualification under the guidelines does not exceed that which is sufficient to effect incapacitation from occupational crime. In one of the earliest cases testing such limits, *U.S. v.*

Mills, the defendant, who owned a used car lot, was convicted of turning back odometers. He was sentenced to probation, and as conditions of that probation he was ordered to seek employment outside the auto sales industry for the duration of his probation and to sell his used car business. The Fifth Circuit Court of Appeals found that the trial court's order to sell the business was beyond that which was necessary to cause occupational disqualification, given that it was possible to own, but not operate, the business.[38] The courts, then, have tried to limit overdisqualification by allowing only those conditions that are minimally necessary to incapacitate.

There remains another question about overdisqualification, however: Which persons should be subject to the incapacitative strategy? The guidelines attempt to incapacitate only those who are believed to commit a future crime if given the opportunity **(selective incapacitation).** Selective incapacitation is predicated on the idea that the court can accurately predict which persons need to be occupationally disqualified. But in fact such prediction is often incorrect, and the ramifications of an error are substantial. First, there can be a person who is predicted to be a nonrecidivist and is allowed to continue in the same occupational role, who then commits another occupational crime. This person is known as a **false negative** (the offender was predicted to be negative on the future criminality trait, but that prediction was false). An error on the other side would involve someone who is predicted to be an occupational recidivist and who is disqualified on that basis, but had that person not been disqualified no new crimes would have been committed. This situation represents a **false positive** (the person was predicted to be positive on the future criminality trait, but that prediction was false). The result of the false negative is an additional offense or several of them. The result of the false positive is the infliction of punishment on persons who need not have received that sanction.

There is another fundamental problem involved with selective incapacitation that goes beyond inaccurate prediction. Because incapacitation is rooted in crime control, there will be a tendency to concentrate on avoiding false negatives when predicting recidivism. This emphasis naturally increases the number of false positives because recidivism is likely to be overpredicted. Overprediction is especially likely in the area of selective occupational disqualification because, unlike overpredictions of street crime that necessitate huge imprisonment costs, there are no monetary considerations associated with occupational disqualification. In other words, when in doubt, believe the worst, because overestimating recidivism guarantees no future crime in that occupational capacity and costs the government nothing. Occupational false positives would be particularly likely to increase immediately after a false negative is discovered, just as parole boards are more cautious in granting paroles after one of their releasees has been involved in a serious crime.

It is easy to determine the number of false negatives: it is those who are not disqualified and commit another occupational crime. But it is impossible to determine the number of false positives, because the individuals who are predicted to reoffend become disqualified and do not have the opportunity to disprove the prediction. If the false positive rate associated with occupational disqualification is actually relatively high, then the punishment strategy becomes questionable since it inflicts unnecessary punishment. And, selective occupational disqualification would also add to disparities in sentences. Despite these inherent problems, John Braithwaite and Gilbert Geis believe that occupational incapacitation "can be a highly successful strategy in the control of [occupational] crime."[39]

Rehabilitation

Rehabilitation assumes that criminals are in need of correction and that they can be reshaped into productive and law-abiding citizens. Rehabilitation of criminals is founded upon a medical model—diagnosis of the problem, prescribed treatment, and ensuing recovery. While the penal system's attempt to rehabilitate human offenders has largely failed,[40] there remains the possibility of rehabilitating or correcting structures within organizations and occupational systems that facilitate legal violations.[41] Poor quality control may be the cause of violations of pure food laws, inadequate monitoring of promotional materials may be the cause of warranty fraud, and fee-for-service systems in medicine and law may be conducive to overbilling. Organizations and occupational systems may be quite amenable to correctional treatment if their constituents are supportive of change.

The U.S. Sentencing Commission has made organizational rehabilitation an integral part of its sentencing structure. To effect organizational rehabilitation, the commission created **federal organizational probation,** which can be imposed for as long as five years.[42] Federal organizational probation *must* occur if: (1) it is necessary to secure payments (e.g., restitution, fines, or other penalties) or the completion of community service; (2) *organizations employing more than 50 people do not, at the time of sentencing, have an internal policing program to effectively prevent and detect law violations;* (3) the organization or an offender who is a higher-level manager committed a similar crime less than five years before sentencing; (4) *the sentence is necessary to effect changes in the organization to* *reduce the chance of future violations;* (5) the organization was not sentenced to a fine; or (6) probation is necessary to ensure reduction in future offending by the organization or to punish it sufficiently (emphasis added).[43]

The U.S. Sentencing Commission believes that the court should have a strong hand in the care of an organization after its conviction. The guidelines recommend the following rehabilitative conditions of probation if either (2) or (4) above apply:

1. The organization develops and submits to the court a program to prevent and detect violations of law, including a schedule for implementation.
2. Upon approval by the court of the program, the organization shall notify its employees and shareholders of its criminal behavior and its program. Such notice shall be in a form prescribed by the court.
3. In order to monitor whether the organization is following the program, the organization shall submit to a reasonable number of regular audits of books and records by the probation officer or experts hired by the court (the costs of the experts will be paid by the organization). The organization shall also submit to interrogations of knowledgeable individuals within the organization.[44]

Any failure to comply with these or other conditions of probation will result in the revocation of probation and resentencing to more punitive sanctions. Because organizational rehabilitation under the guidelines has been in effect for such a short time, systematic information on the success of the approach is not yet available. It would seem, however, that when such stringent mandates to change the way an organization operates are accompanied by such intense court scrutiny, positive and long-lasting results are promising—assuming that an organization will take its rehabilitation process seriously. After all, there are many ways an organization can withhold or falsify information about its past and current violations and dupe both outside experts and employees acting as internal monitors.

Increasing the Criminalization of Occupational Crime

None of the crime control methods we have discussed—normative validation, deterrence, occupational incapacitation, or organizational rehabilitation—will work unless offenders are sanctioned. Even if formal and nonformal sanctions are meted out to occupational offenders, a sufficient number of criminals must be caught in order for the strategies to have any hope of reducing crime in significant proportions. At this time, no matter which area of occupational crime is being considered—organizational, state authority, professional, or individual—enforcement levels are very low.

Increasing the Criminal Justice Response

It was noted earlier that the application of sanctions to lawbreakers by prosecution and conviction is known as "criminalization." Turk emphasized that the most salient factor in the criminalization process is the extent to which enforcers consider the behavior in question to be harmful. He considered the harm-perceptions of "lower-level enforcers" (police and regulatory inspectors) to be of prime importance, because they make many of the initial decisions about whether to charge persons. This is especially true of regulatory inspectors whose discretion forms the sole basis for administrative legal enforcement. One can add the victims of occupational crime to the list of lower-level enforcers because victims must decide whether to bring an occupational offender to the attention of the authorities and to press the authorities to pursue the matter criminally.

To increase "lower-level" enforcement against occupational crime, consideration should be given to: (1) increasing the staffs of federal and local enforcement agencies and limiting their discretion (or at least socializing them away from discretionary behavior); and (2) educating citizens about identifying the harms associated with victimization by occupational crime, and encouraging them to report possible violations to the local or federal authorities. Increasing victim reporting and raising enforcement budgets are the most obvious ways to enhance lower-level enforcement against occupational criminals.

Perceptions of prosecutors and judges ("higher-level" enforcers) about the harmfulness of an illegal behavior are also important if occupational crime is to be penalized more severely. Prosecutors are the most important actors in the criminalization of occupational crimes because they decide whether to pursue sanctioning and to be zealous about this pursuit once the offense has been brought to their attention by lower-level enforcers.

Michael Benson, Francis Cullen, and William Maakestad[45] found through a national survey of local prosecutors that the most important factors in the promotion of prosecution of corporate occupational crime, in conjunction with the culpability of the offender, are: (1) whether the offense causes substantial physical harm (such as injury or environmental pollution) or substantial financial harm (such as widespread consumer fraud); (2) whether the jurisdiction is an urban area; and (3) whether the prosecutor's office has a special unit that focuses on economic and corporate crime. This last finding is consistent with Diane Vaughan's[46] call for prosecutors to establish in-house units that specialize in pursuing harmful organizational and other occupational offending. Overall, local prosecutors did not perceive corporate crime to be a very serious criminal problem, and they subordinated its prosecution to that of street crime.

A study by Stanton Wheeler, Kenneth Mann, and Austin Sarat[47] concluded that it was judges' perceptions of the harm of an offense, the culpability of an offender, and considerations for general and specific deterrence that primarily dictated sentencing of federal offenders who violated laws such as those concerned with occupational crime. However, the time frame for that study was fiscal years 1976–1978, before the U.S. Sentencing Guidelines, and at that time considerable judicial discretion prevailed in the imposition of sentences. Since 1987, U.S. Sentencing Guidelines have curtailed that discretion. As of 1994, legislatures in sixteen states also had passed mandatory sentencing guidelines, each with more or less discretion allowed. Other states have enacted determinate sentencing laws that bind a judge to specific legislatively determined statutory penalties with little discretion. Although sentences under guidelines and determinate statutes are meted out by judges, in essence these cases reflect legislative action to increase criminalization and support normative validation, deterrence, and incapacitation.

One must not forget that formal sanctions encourage nonformal sanctions, which also help to control occupational crime. If formal criminalization fosters public embarrassment, then normative validation and deterrence should be enhanced. If formal criminalization fosters the inability to procure future employment, then deterrence will be enhanced.

Increasing the Regulatory System Response

Our system of regulating organizational occupational crime currently is rooted in administrative law—regulatory agencies such as the EPA, FDA, USDA, CPSC, OSHA, FTC, SEC, and the IRS establish regulations and interpret statutes affecting organizational behavior. The current model for regulating organizational occupational offending simulates that of the criminal justice system—investigation, indictment, conviction, and punishment of violators.

Laureen Snider has identified several major problems within this traditional regulatory model.[48] First, regulatory agencies tend to encourage compliance by employing persuasion and education rather than criminal charges. Agency workers will weigh the benefits and pitfalls of prosecution, often concluding that criminal charges are not the path to take. They may believe that their jobs will be lost or a political upheaval will result if official action is taken. Second, there is the tendency to pick on the "little guy"—the largest conglomerates generally receive the least agency attention and the smallest organizations the most, both in terms of the number of citations and the proportion of criminal, rather than civil, charges. Larger organizations also receive the most petty sanctions—fines that are minuscule relative to profits and resources. Incarceration is extremely rare for regulatory violations. It was mentioned in chapter 4, for instance, that a negligent death must occur before a person faces incarceration under OSHA law. Almost all other violations are punishable by relatively insignificant monetary penalties. Third, Snider believes that strict liability laws punish wrongly since offending may be through ignorance, mistake, or incompetence. And fourth, the adversary process in some cases is criminogenic because it allows the offender the opportunity to continue wrongdoing until the case is adjudicated, which can be a long time given the legal resources of large organizations compared to those of the agency.

These obvious difficulties in the adversarial enforcement model have prompted scholars to search for cooperative model alternatives. In particular, John Braithwaite has proposed two alternatives to the strict criminalization model. The first, and most novel, is **enforced self-regulation:**

> Under enforced self-regulation, the government would compel each company to write a set of rules tailored to the unique set of contingencies facing that firm. A regulatory agency would either approve these rules or send them back for revision if they were insufficiently stringent. At this stage in the process, citizens' groups and other interested parties would be encouraged to comment on the proposed rules. Rather than having governmental inspectors enforce the rules, most enforcement duties and costs would be internalized by the company, which would be required to establish its own independent inspectorial group. The primary function of governmental inspectors would be to ensure the independence of this internal compliance group and to audit its efficiency and toughness. Such audits would pay particular attention to the number of violators who had been disciplined by each company. Naturally, old-style direct government monitoring would still be necessary for firms too small to afford their own compliance group.[49]

According to Braithwaite's plan, the government would formally sanction violators of the privately written and publicly ratified rules. Regulatory agencies would not accept any set of private rules that was not consistent with minimum requirements set by the legislature. If the internal compliance team does not report discovered violations, then the individual members of that team would be subject to severe sanctioning, including incarceration. The plan is intuitively appealing because it puts in place a monitoring system without the governmental expenditure needed to achieve that level of enforcement. The approach has other advantages: (1) complex rules that attempt to apply to all organizations would not be necessary, since its own rules would be tailored by each organization; (2) rules could be rapidly adjusted in the face of changing business environments; (3) rules likely would be more comprehensive, usually going beyond the minimum standards; and (4) organizations would probably be more committed to rules they wrote themselves. And of importance to crime control, more offenders probably would be caught.

Those caught could be subject to severe informal and formal sanctions. Formal sanctions would be easier for courts to mete out under self-regulation because it would be easier for government prosecutors to prove their case and obtain convictions. More certain and severe informal sanctions would also be forthcoming, because the organizational punishment system for violation of internal rules could be farther-reaching than its punishment system for violation of governmental regulations. And according to Braithwaite, "Compliance would become the path of least [organizational] resistance."[50]

Braithwaite presents several current examples of enforced self-regulation or variants of it. The Federal Aviation Administration has for a long time monitored airline companies' compliance with their personal sets of rules that are within the mandates of governmental standards. Braithwaite also points to the Toxic Substance Control Act of 1976, which authorizes the EPA to order manufacturers to test suspect chemical substances, to monitor internally compliance with act procedures, and to indicate proposed quality control protocols. The FTC has long had the authority to institute new internal organizational policies and establish internal monitoring systems for firms convicted of misrepresentation in advertising. Note also the similarity between the guidelines' mandates (for organizational responsibility to create internal environments that prevent and detect legal violations) and Braithwaite's enforced self-regulation model.

Braithwaite is aware of problems inherent in policies of enforced self-regulation, such as the increased cost to regulatory agencies because of the need to approve procedures for a vast number of rules. Moreover, there would be a danger of cooptation of the regulatory process by business, because there would be a tendency to overparticularize government-business relationships. It also is doubtful that Western jurisprudence will easily accommodate private rules that are publicly enforced. Further, government bureaucracies being what they are, organizations might have to bear increased costs because of delays and red tape associated with getting new company rules approved. Companies also might write their rules in ways that would assist them to evade the spirit of the law. And to what extent can we expect the internal compliance monitoring group to be completely honest, given that to do its job properly it must bite the hand that feeds it? A case in point is the Consumer Product Safety Commission rule, discussed in chapter 4, mandating that organizations who become aware of a danger in their product must notify the commission about the hazard. Many companies did not voluntarily comply because the financial costs of product recall were enormous. It is somewhat naive to believe that organizations are going to regulate themselves honestly, especially when large chunks of profit are at stake. Nevertheless, in spite of its potential problems, Braithwaite's ideas about enforced self-regulation might go far to increase enforcement against both criminal organizations and employees, while at the same time increasing thresholds of voluntary compliance.

Braithwaite's second alternative to a strict criminalization model takes the following steps[51] that begin with a cooperative mentality and escalate into a punishment mentality: (1) the regulatory agency tries to convince the offending organization to comply; (2) official, legally binding warnings are issued; (3) mandatory fines are assessed; and, finally (4) mandatory criminal sanctions are imposed, including incarceration for executives and delicensure of the organization. This escalation model employs the best features of the cooperation model. It provides the organization with the chance to rectify what is perhaps unintentional wrongdoing without a protracted battle that ties up agency resources and allows the violation to continue. And ultimately, if all else fails, it invokes the criminalization model, providing normative validation, deterrence, and incapacitation.

Some have been leery of a turn from adversarial criminalization strategies to cooperative ones. Snider cautions that: (1) Braithwaite's second model described above (moving from cooperation to civil penalties to criminal sanctioning) is nothing new—it is exactly what a good agency should do under a criminalization strategy; (2) the power of larger organizations is far greater in many cases than that of regulators, so the latter will be unable to negotiate evenly; and (3) the importance of various economic interests and effects on economic policies are ignored in cooperative models.[52] Nevertheless, it is clear that the current strategy of adversarial criminalization often is ineffective, counterproductive, and unfair, and perhaps these innovative alternatives, or variants of them, will improve the efficacy of regulatory enforcement against organizational occupational crime.

Fairness in Sanctioning

Before closing this chapter, it is important to consider the fairness aspect of sanctions. Because occupational criminals constitute a diverse lot and because the circumstances surrounding occupational offending are wide-ranging, certain formal and nonformal sanctions will be more effective than others in reducing certain crimes and in affecting certain criminals. One must be careful not to invoke formal or informal punishments that are more severe than the offense and offender warrant. When formal and informal sanctions are imposed only on the basis of hoped-for crime reduction, they often are too harsh. Recall from chapter 7 the example of Jim Bakker, the evangelist who defrauded his congregation out of millions of dollars in the early 1980s. He was sentenced to prison for forty-five years as a general deterrent to future clergy fraud. On appeal, that sentence was later reduced dramatically because it was considered capricious and intemperate; in the effort to deter, an unfair example had been made of Bakker.

Punishment for occupational crime should be handed out under the principle of **desert.**[53] This means that the punishment should coincide with the harmfulness of the offense and the culpability of the offender. The punishment should be **equitable** (like offenders receive like punishments) and **proportional** (more serious punishments are reserved for the more serious offending). Most sentencing guidelines in the name of greater deterrence and incapacitation, give greater punishments to offenders with past criminal histories. According to the principle of desert, this is unacceptable because the basis for increased punishment is some unknown future event rather than past behavior. However, based on desert, one could punish offenders who repeat their occupational crimes more harshly than first-time offenders on the grounds that they *deserve* a harsher sanction because they have been previously censured.[54] To a great extent, the U.S. Sentencing Commission has tried to uphold these requirements for fair punishment, at least on paper. Whether the punishments imposed under the U.S. Sentencing Guidelines actually meet these criteria for fair punishment is a matter of opinion.

Some have argued that it is virtually impossible to determine the exact punishment that is appropriate for a crime or the precise offenders to be sanctioned, especially in cases of organizational occupational crime.[55] The "seriousness" of an offense is an evaluation that is relative to the definer. In practice, the concrete meanings of such abstractions as "desert," "equitable," "proportional," "harm," and "culpability" are determined by clashes among parties with differing interests and understandings and differing power to influence the creation and application of laws.

A Concluding Comment

The purpose of this book has been to highlight the opportunities for crime that are associated with various occupational roles. The book has tried to familiarize the student with a wide perspective on theoretical, legal, and empirical issues in the study of occupational crime.

The reduction and control of occupational crime are formidable tasks, but they can be accomplished. Iconoclastic approaches to enforcing occupational crime laws—such as enforced self-regulation, adverse publicity, occupational disqualification, and organizational rehabilitation—are sorely needed. We cannot lose sight of the fact that the powerful and respectable positions of many occupational offenders often protect them against formal and informal censures. This cannot be allowed to continue if we expect to control their illegal behavior. Punishing these elite would also make our society more equitable, for their criminal behaviors deserve the same response as that of others.

Key Terms

incapacitation
rehabilitation
deterrence trap
compensatory damages
punitive damages
Hester Prynne sanction
occupational incapacitation
selective incapacitation
false negative
false positive
federal organizational probation
enforced self-regulation
desert
equitable punishment
proportional punishment

Questions for Discussion

1. It was stated that it is impossible to ascertain the proportion of potential criminals who are deterred, only some of those who are not deterred. Why?
2. Explain the "deterrence trap" in relation to punishing occupational criminals.
3. How can crime control rationales lead to punishments that are greater than the offender deserves?
4. Explain and critique Braithwaite's enforced self-regulation model in terms of practicality and potential effectiveness.
5. How accurate do you believe federal judges will be in assigning occupational disqualification as a condition of probation? In other words, will there be high false positive and high false negative rates? Why?
6. Under the U.S. Sentencing Guidelines, it was declared that organizations will receive substantial reductions in their fines if they can demonstrate that before the offense they had a program to prevent

and detect violations. Do you believe that organizations will put such programs in place as a cosmetic gesture and then commit crimes anyway? Explain.

7. How heavily do you believe an individual's post-conviction demeanor should weigh on sentencing? An organization's post-conviction demeanor?
8. Why does rehabilitation have a better potential to help organizations than individuals?
9. Should adverse publicity also be used as a sanction against individuals? Why or why not?
10. Explain some of the inherent problems associated with the concept of deserved punishment.

Suggested Readings on Reducing Occupational Crime

John Braithwaite, "Enforced Self-Regulation: A New Strategy for Corporate Crime Control" *Michigan Law Review* 80 (1982):1466–1507.

John Braithwaite, *Crime, Shame, and Reintegration* (New York: Cambridge University Press, 1989).

John Braithwaite and Gilbert Geis, "On Theory and Action for Corporate Crime Control," *Crime and Delinquency* 28 (1982):292–314.

John Coffee, Jr., "'No Soul to Damn; No Body to Kick': An Unscandalised Inquiry into the Problem of Corporate Punishment," *Michigan Law Review* 79 (1981):386–459.

Brent Fisse, "Sanctions against Corporations: Economic Efficiency or Legal Efficacy?" in W. Byron Groves and Graeme Newman (eds.), *Punishment and Privilege* (Albany, NY: Harrow and Heston, 1986).

Kenneth Mann, "Punitive Civil Sanctions: The Middle Ground between Criminal and Civil Law," *Yale Law Review* 101 (1992):1795–1874.

Martin McDermott, "Occupational Disqualification of Corporate Executives: An Innovative Condition of Probation," *Journal of Criminal Law and Criminology* 73 (1982):604–41.

Diane Vaughan, *Controlling Unlawful Organizational Behavior: Social Structure and Corporate Misconduct* (Chicago: University of Chicago Press, 1983).

Notes

Chapter One: The Concept of Occupational Crime

1. John Noonan, *Bribes* (New York: MacMillan, 1984), p. 11.
2. Gilbert Geis, "Introduction," in Gilbert Geis (ed.), *White-Collar Criminal* (New York: Atherton Press, 1968), p. 11.
3. Charles Schafer and Violet Schafer, *Breadcraft* (San Francisco, CA: Yerba Buena Press, 1974), p. 8.
4. Jerome Hall, *Theft, Law, and Society* (Indianapolis, IN: Bobbs-Merrill, 1952), p. 36.
5. Gilbert Geis, "From Deuteronomy to Deniability: A Historical Perlustration on White-Collar Crime," *Justice Quarterly* 5:7–32 (March, 1988).
6. Franz Schmidt, *A Hangman's Diary* (Montclair, NJ: Patterson-Smith, 1973), p. 111.
7. *The New American Desk Encyclopedia* (New York: Signet Books, 1984), p. 801. For an interesting discussion of the muckrakers, see Gilbert Geis, "The Evolution of the Study of Corporate Crime," in Michael Blankenship (ed.), *Understanding Corporate Criminality* (New York: Garland Publishing, 1993).
8. Matthew Josephson, *The Robber Barons* (New York: Harcourt Brace, 1934).
9. Edwin H. Sutherland, *White Collar Crime* (New York: Dryden Press, 1949), p. 9.

10. Edwin H. Sutherland, "The White Collar Criminal," in V. C. Branham and S. B. Kutlash (eds.), *Encyclopedia of Criminology* (New York: Philosophical Library, 1949), p. 511; Geis, "White-Collar Crime: What Is It?" in Kip Schlegel and David Weisburd (eds.) *White-Collar Crime Reconsidered* (Boston: Northeastern University Press, 1992), p. 34.
11. Gilbert Geis and Colin Goff, "Introduction" in Edwin H. Sutherland, *White-Collar Crime: The Uncut Version* (New Haven, CT: Yale University Press, 1983), p. xxiv.
12. Charles R. Henderson, *Introduction to the Study of the Dependent, Defective, and Delinquent* (2d ed.) (Boston: D.C. Heath, 1901), p. 250; Geis and Goff, "Introduction," p. xxiv.
13. Edward Alsworth Ross, "The Criminaloid," in Gilbert Geis (ed.), *White-Collar Criminal* (New York: Atherton Press, 1968), pp. 26–32.
14. Albert Morris "Criminals of the Upperworld," in Gilbert Geis (ed.), *White-Collar Criminal* (New York: Atherton Press, 1968), p. 35.
15. Ibid., pp. 37–38.
16. Edwin H. Sutherland "White-Collar Criminality," in Gilbert Geis (ed.), *White-Collar Criminal* (New York: Atherton Press, 1968), p. 51. [Originally published in *American Sociological Review* 5:1–12 (February, 1940).
17. Ibid., p. 47.
18. Ibid., p. 51.
19. Ibid.
20. Gilbert Geis and Colin Goff, "Edwin H. Sutherland: A Biographical and Analytical Commentary," in Gilbert Geis (ed.), *On White-Collar Crime* (Lexington, MA: Lexington Books, 1982), p. 180.
21. "Poverty Belittled as Crime Factor," *Philadelphia Inquirer* (December 12, 1939), p. 17; Geis and Goff, "Edwin H. Sutherland," p. 187.
22. "Hits Criminality in White Collars," *New York Times* (December 28, 1939), p. 12; Geis and Goff, "Edwin H. Sutherland," p.187.
23. Ibid., p. 180.
24. Sutherland, "White-Collar Criminality," p. 40.
25. Geis, "White-Collar Crime: What Is It?," p. 33.
26. Hermann Mannheim, *Comparative Criminology* (London: Routledge & Kegan Paul, 1965), p. 470; Geis and Goff, "Introduction," p. xxxiii.
27. Sutherland, *White Collar Crime.*
28. Marvin Wolfgang, Robert Figlio, and Terrence Thornberry, *Evaluating Criminology* (New York: Elsevier, 1978), pp. 95–96.

29. Edwin H. Sutherland, "Is 'White-Collar Crime' Crime?," *American Sociological Review* 10 (1945): 132–39.
30. Wolfgang et al., *Evaluating Criminology,* pp. 95–96.
31. Paul W. Tappan, "Who Is the Criminal?" *American Sociological Review* 12 (February 1947):96–102.
32. Sutherland, "White-Collar Criminality."
33. Ibid.
34. Thorsten Sellin, "The Significance of Records of Crime," *Law Quarterly Review* 67 (1951):489–504, p. 490.
35. Ernest W. Burgess, "Comment to Hartung," *American Journal of Sociology* 56 (1950):25–34.
36. Jack Douglas and John Johnson (eds.), *Official Deviance: Readings in Malfeasance, Misfeasance, and Other Forms of Corruption* (Philadelphia: J.B. Lippencott, 1977).
37. Earl R. Quinney, "The Study of White-Collar Crime: Toward a Reorientation in Theory and Research," *Journal of Criminal Law, Criminology, and Police Science* 55 (1964):208–14.
38. John P. Clark and Richard Hollinger, "On the Feasibility of Empirical Studies of 'White-Collar Crime'" in Robert F. Meier (ed.), *Theory in Criminology* (Beverly Hills, CA: Sage Publications, 1977).
39. David R. Simon and D. Stanley Eitzen, *Elite Deviance* (Boston: Allyn and Bacon, 1982).
40. M. David Ermann and Richard Lundman (eds.), *Corporate and Governmental Deviance* (New York: Oxford University Press, 1978).
41. Ray Michalowski, *Order, Law and Crime* (New York: Random House, 1985).
42. Hal Pepinsky, "From White Collar Crime to Exploitation: Redefinition of a Field," *Journal of Criminal Law and Criminology* 65 (1974):225–33.
43. Stephen E. Brown and Chau-Pu Chiang, "Defining Corporate Crime: A Critique of Traditional Parameters" in Michael Blankenship (ed.), *Understanding Corporate Criminality* (New York: Garland Publishing, 1993).
44. James William Coleman, "Toward an Integrated Theory of White-Collar Crime," *American Journal of Sociology* 93 (1987):406–39, p. 407.
45. Sutherland, *White Collar Crime,* p. 9n. Gilbert Geis has pointed out that Sutherland erred here, for the actual title of the book to which Sutherland was referring was *Adventures of a White Collar Man* by A. P. Sloan, Jr. and B. Sparkes (New York: Doubleday, 1941). See Geis, "White-Collar Crime: What Is It?," p. 34.

46. Sutherland, *White Collar Crime*, Chapter 13.
47. Ibid., p. 220.
48. Edwin H. Sutherland, "Crime of Corporations," in Albert Cohen, Alfred Lindesmith, and Karl Schuessler (eds.), *The Sutherland Papers* (Bloomington, IN: Indiana University Press, 1956), p. 79; Geis, "White-Collar Crime: What Is It?," p. 35.
49. See, in particular, James William Coleman, *The Criminal Elite* (3d ed.) (New York: St. Martin's Press, 1994), p. 5.
50. See, e.g., Stanton Wheeler, Kenneth Mann, and Austin Sarat, *Sitting in Judgement: The Sentencing of White-Collar Criminals* (New Haven, CT: Yale University Press, 1988); and David Weisburd, Stanton Wheeler, Elin Waring, and Nancy Bode, *Crimes of the Middle Classes* (New Haven, CT: Yale University Press, 1991). Both monographs, using essentially the same data set on federal offenders, include in their definition of "white-collar criminal" those persons whose "business" role was constructed solely for illegal purposes. These include, for instance, offenders who: operate completely bogus mail order schemes (Ibid., p. 29), submit tax returns under false names (Ibid., p. 33), and submit utterly fraudulent loan applications (Ibid., p.31). See also David O. Friedrichs, *Trusted Criminals: White-Collar Crime in Contemporary Society* (Belmont, CA: Wadsworth, 1996), p. 193, who includes "contrepreneurs" (those who carry out a swindle while only appearing to be engaged in a legitimate business) as white-collar criminals.
51. Herbert Edelhertz, *The Nature, Impact and Prosecution of White-Collar Crime* (Washington, DC: U.S. Government Printing Office, 1970), p. 3. For a critique of this and other definitions of white-collar crime, see David O. Friedrichs, "White Collar Crime and the Definitional Quagmire: A Provisional Solution," *Journal of Human Justice* 3 (Spring 1992):5–21.
52. Bureau of Justice Statistics, *Dictionary of Criminal Justice Data Terminology* (Washington, DC: U.S. Government Printing Office, 1981), p. 215.
53. Albert Biderman and Albert Reiss, Jr., *Data Sources on White-Collar Law-Breaking* (Washington, DC: U.S. Government Printing Office, 1980), p. xxviii.
54. Coleman, *Criminal Elite*, p. 5.
55. Biderman and Reiss, *Data Sources on White-Collar Law Breaking*, p. xxvii.
56. Susan Shapiro, "Collaring the Crime, Not the Criminal: Reconsidering the Concept of White Collar Crime," *American Sociological Review* 55 (1990):346–65.

57. Sutherland, "White-Collar Criminality," p. 42.
58. Sutherland is supposed to have stated this to Edwin Lemert, a fellow sociologist. See Richard F. Sparks, " 'Crime as Business' and the Female Offender," in Freda Adler and Rita Simon (eds.), *The Criminology of Deviant Women* (Boston: Houghton Mifflin, 1979); Geis, "White-Collar Crime: What Is It?," p. 35.
59. Friedrichs, "White-Collar Crime and the Definitional Quagmire."
60. Gilbert Geis and Robert Meier (eds.), *White-Collar Crime: Offenses in Business, Politics, and the Professions* (New York: Free Press, 1977), p. 25.
61. Travis Hirschi and Michael Gottfredson, "The Significance of White-Collar Crime for a General Theory of Crime," *Criminology* 27 (1989):359–71.
62. Gilbert Geis, "Avocational Crime," in Daniel Glaser (ed.), *Handbook of Criminology* (New York: Rand McNally, 1974), p. 283.
63. Friedrichs, *Trusted Criminals,* pp. 10, 111.
64. *Jacobellis v. Ohio* 378 US 184 (1964), p. 197.
65. Hirschi and Gottfredson, "Significance of White-Collar Crime."
66. Marshall Clinard and Richard Quinney, *Criminal Behavior Systems: A Typology* (New York: Holt, Rinehart and Winston, 1967), p. 131.
67. Gerald Robin, "White-Collar Crime and Employee Theft," *Crime and Delinquency* (July 1974):251–62, p. 262.
68. Robert Dubin, *The World of Work* (Englewood Cliffs, NJ: Prentice-Hall, 1958), p. 4.
69. See, e.g., Charles Tittle, *Sanctions and Social Deviance: The Question of Deterrence* (New York: Praeger, 1980).
70. Michalowski, *Order, Law and Crime,* p. 317, in Friedrichs, "Definitional Quagmire," p. 8.
71. See, e.g., Marshall Clinard and Peter Yeager, *Corporate Crime* (New York: Free Press, 1980); Ronald C. Kramer, "Corporate Criminality: The Development of an Idea," in Ellen Hochstedler (ed.), *Corporations as Criminals* (Beverly Hills, CA: Sage, 1984); John Braithwaite and Brent Fisse, "On the Plausibiality of Corporate Crime Theory," in William Laufer and Freda Adler (eds.), *Advances in Criminological Theory* (Volume 2) (New Brunswick, NJ: Transaction Books, 1990); Michael Blankenship, "Understanding Corporate Criminality: Challenges and Issues," in Michael Blankenship (ed.), *Understanding Corporate Criminality* (New York: Garland, 1993); See also Laura Schrager and James Short, "Toward a Sociology of Organizational Crime," *Social Problems* 25 (1977):407–19.
72. Ross, "The Criminaloid," p. 26.
73. Ibid.

74. Sutherland, "White-Collar Criminality," p. 50.
75. President's Commission on Law Enforcement and Administration of Justice, *Challenge of Crime in a Free Society* (New York: Avon Books, 1968), p. 158.
76. Francis Cullen, Richard Mathers, Gregory Clark, and John Cullen, "Public Support for Punishing White-Collar Crime: Blaming the Victim Revisited?" *Journal of Criminal Justice* 11 (1983):481–93, p. 482. See also T. David Evans, Francis Cullen, and Paula Dubeck, "Public Perceptions of Corporate Crime," in Michael Blankenship (ed.), *Understanding Corporate Criminality* (New York: Garland Publishing, 1993).
77. Donald J. Newman, "Public Attitudes Toward a Form of White-Collar Crime," in Gilbert Geis (ed.), *White-Collar Criminal* (New York: Atherton, 1968).
78. Donald C. Gibbons, "Crime and Punishment: A Study of Social Attitudes," *Social Forces* 47 (1969):391–97.
79. Louis Harris, "Changing Morality: The Two Americas," *Time* (June 6, 1969):26–7.
80. John Braithwaite, "Challenging Just Deserts: Punishing White-Collar Criminals," *Journal of Criminal Law and Criminology* 73 (1982):723–64, pp. 732–33.
81. John E. Conklin, *Illegal but Not Criminal: Business Crime in America* (Englewood Cliffs, NJ: Prentice-Hall, 1977), p. 27.
82. Donald Black, "Common Sense in the Sociology of Law," *American Sociological Review* 44 (1979):18–27, p. 20.
83. Marvin Wolfgang, Robert Figlio, Paul Tracy, and Simon Singer, *The National Survey of Crime Severity* (Washington, DC: U.S. Government Printing Office, 1985); Peter Rossi, Emily Waite, Christine Bose, and Richard Berk, "The Seriousness of Crimes: Normative Structure and Individual Differences," *American Sociological Review* 39 (1974):224–37.
84. Wolfgang et al., *The National Survey of Crime Severity.*

Chapter 2: Counting and Recording Occupational Crimes and Criminals

1. Thorsten Sellin, "The Significance of Records of Crime," *Law Quarterly Review* 67 (1951):489–504, p. 490.
2. 377 F.2nd 667 (1967).
3. Peggy Giordano, Sandra Kerbel, and Sandra Dudley, "The Economics of Female Criminality: An Analysis of Police Blotters," in Lee Bowker (ed.), *Women and Crime in America* (New York:

Macmillan, 1981); Darryl Steffensmeier, "On the Causes of 'White-Collar Crime': An Assessment of Hirschi and Gottfredson's Claims," *Criminology* 27 (1989):345–58.

4. Ibid.
5. For a discussion about the problems in interpreting embezzlement arrests as occupationally related offenses, see Gary S. Green, "White-Collar Crime and the Study of Embezzlement," *Annals of the American Academy of Political and Social Science* 525 (1993):95–106.
6. See, e.g., Freda Adler, *Sisters in Crime* (New York: McGraw-Hill, 1975), pp. 16, 156, 252; Travis Hirschi and Michael Gottfredson, "Causes of White-Collar Crime," *Criminology* 27 (1987):949–74; Michael Gottfredson and Travis Hirschi, *A General Theory of Crime* (Palo Alto, CA: Stanford University Press, 1990), Chapter 9.
7. Albert Biderman and Albert J. Reiss, Jr., *Data Sources on White-Collar Law-Breaking* (Washington, DC: U.S. Government Printing Office, 1980); See also Charles F. Wellford and Barton L. Ingraham, "White-Collar Crime: Prevalence, Trends, and Costs," in Albert R. Roberts (ed.), *Critical Issues in Crime and Justice* (Thousand Oaks, CA: Sage, 1994), pp. 85–88.
8. Biderman and Reiss, *Data Sources on White-Collar Law Breaking,* pp. xxxii–xxxiii.
9. Edwin H. Sutherland, "Is 'White-Collar Crime' Crime?" *American Sociological Review* 10 (1945):132–39.
10. Sally S. Simpson, Anthony R. Harris, and Brian A. Mattson, "Measuring Corporate Crime," in Michael Blankenship (ed.), *Understanding Corporate Criminality* (New York: Garland Publishing, 1993).
11. Philip Ennis, *Criminal Victimization in the United States: A Report of a National Survey* (Washington, DC: U.S. Government Printing Office, 1967).
12. Biderman and Reiss, *Data Sources on White-Collar Law-Breaking,* p. xlii.
13. See, e.g., Michael Hindelang, *Criminal Victimization in Eight American Cities* (Cambridge, MA: Ballinger, 1976).
14. Ennis, *Criminal Victimization in the United States,* p. 108.
15. Gary S. Green, *Citizen Reporting of Crime to the Police: An Analysis of Common Theft and Assault* (Unpublished Ph.D. dissertation. Philadelphia: University of Pennsylvania, 1981), p. 33.
16. James S. Wallerstein and Clement J. Wyle, "Our Law-Abiding Law-Breakers," *Probation* 25 (1947):107–12.
17. See, e.g., James F. Short, Jr. and F. Ivan Nye, "Exent of Unrecorded

Juvenile Delinquency: Tentative Conclusions," *Journal of Criminal Law, Criminology, and Police Science* 49 (1957):296–302; Michael Hindelang, Travis Hirschi, and Joseph Weis, *Measuring Delinquency* (Beverly Hills, CA: Sage, 1981).

18. See, e.g., Charles Tittle, *Sanctions and Social Deviance: The Question of Deterrence* (New York: Praeger, 1980); Herald Grasmick and Donald Green, "Legal Punishment, Social Disapproval, and Internalization as Inhibitors of Illegal Behavior," *Journal of Criminal Law and Criminology* 71 (1980):325–35.
19. Hindelang, Hirschi, and Weis, *Measuring Delinquency.*
20. Delbert S. Elliott, "Review Essay: *Measuring Delinquency*," *Criminology* 20 (1982):527–37, p. 528.
21. Biderman and Reiss, *Data Sources on White-Collar Law-Breaking,* p. xli.
22. Robert M. O'Brien, *Crime and Victimization Data* (Beverly Hills, CA: Sage, 1985).
23. Martin Gold, "Undetected Delinquent Behavior," *Journal of Research in Crime and Delinquency* 3 (1966):37–46.
24. John P. Clark and Larry L. Tifft, "Polygraph Interview Validation of Self-Reported Delinquent Behavior," *American Sociological Review* 31 (1966):516–23; Gary S. Green, "Resurrecting Polygraph Validation of Self-Reported Crime Data: A Note on Research Method and Ethics Using the Deer Poacher," *Deviant Behavior* 11 (1990): 131–37.
25. Tittle, *Sanctions and Social Deviance.*
26. Robert Mason and Lyle Calvin, "A Study of Admitted Tax Evasion," *Law and Society Review* 12 (1978):73–89.
27. Joachim Vogel, "Taxation and Public Opinion in Sweden: An Interpretation of Recent Survey Data," *National Tax Journal* 27 (1974):499–510.
28. R. Folsom, "A Randomized Response Validation Study: Comparison of Direct and Randomized Reporting in DUI Arrests" (Unpublished manuscript. Research Triangle Park, NC: Research Triangle Institute, 1974).
29. Vernon L. Wright, "Use of Randomized Response Technique to Estimate Deer Poaching," in K. Beattie (ed.), *Environmental Law Enforcement Theory and Principles: A Sourcebook* (Volume 2) (Stevens Point, WI: College of Natural Resources, University of Wisconsin, 1980).
30. Paul E. Tracy and James Alan Fox, "The Validity of Randomized Response for Sensitive Measurements," *American Sociological Review* 46 (1981):187–200.

31. Paul E. Tracy and James Alan Fox, "The Randomized Response Approach to Criminological Surveys," in James Alan Fox (ed.), *Methods in Quantitative Criminology* (New York: Academic Press, 1981), p. 43.
32. See, e.g., J. Moors, "Optimization of the Unrelated Question Randomized Response Model," *Journal of the American Statistical Association* 66 (1971):627–29; B. Greenberg, R. Kuebler, J. Abernathy, and D. Horvitz, "Application of the Randomized Response Technique in Obtaining Quantitative Data," *Journal of the American Statistical Association* 66 (1971):243–50; R. Folsom, B. Greenberg, D. Horvitz, and J. Abernathy "The Two Alternative Questions Randomized Response Model for Human Surveys," *Journal of the American Statistical Association* 68 (1973):525–30.
33. Tracy and Fox, "The Validity of Randomized Response for Sensitive Measurements."
34. Gary S. Green, "General Deterrence and Television 'Cable Crime': A Field Experiment in Social Control," *Criminology* 23 (1985): 629–45.
35. Carol K. Sigelman and Lee Sigelman, "Authority and Conformity: Violation of Traffic Regulations," *Journal of Social Psychology* 100 (1976):35–43.
36. Richard Schwartz and Sonia Orleans, "On Legal Sanctions," *University of Chicago Law Review* 34 (1967):274–90.
37. Herald M. Groves, "An Empirical Study of Tax Compliance," *National Tax Journal* 11 (1958):241–301.
38. See, e.g., John Noonan, *Bribes* (New York: Macmillan, 1984), pp. 604–19.
39. John Braithwaite, "An Exploratory Study of Used Car Fraud," in Paul R. Wilson and John Braithwaite (eds.) *Two Faces of Deviance* (Queensland, Australia: University of Queensland Press, 1979).
40. Paul E. Tracy and James Alan Fox, "A Field Experiment on Insurance Fraud in Auto Body Repair," *Criminology* 27 (1989):589–603.
41. Paul Jesilow, *Deterring Automobile Repair Fraud: A Field Experiment* (Unpublished Ph.D. dissertation. Irvine, CA: University of California, 1982).
42. Ibid., p. 124.
43. See discussion in Green, "General Deterrence and Television 'Cable Crime'" about his problems in determining exactly who was stealing cable signals.
44. Jesilow, *Deterring Automobile Repair Fraud,* p. 80.
45. See, e.g., Gilbert Geis, "The Heavy Electrical Equipment Antitrust Case of 1961," in Gilbert Geis (ed.), *White-Collar Criminal* (New

York: Atherton, 1968); Diane Vaughan, *Controlling Unlawful Organizational Behavior* (Chicago: University of Chicago Press, 1983); Andrew Hopkins, "Controlling Corporate Deviance," *Criminology* 18 (1980):198–214.

46. Howard Becker, B. Greer, Everett Hughes, and Anslem Strauss, *Boys in White: Student Culture in Medical School* (Chicago: University of Chicago Press, 1961).
47. Marshall Clinard and Peter Yeager, *Corporate Crime* (New York: Free Press, 1980), pp. 67–68.
48. John Gaubatz, "Law Students Given Bad Role Models," *Palm Beach Review* (July 6, 1987):9–10.

Chapter Three: Explanation of Occupational Criminality

1. See, e.g., Jack P. Gibbs, "The Methodology of Theory Construction in Criminology," in Robert F. Meier (ed.), *Theoretical Methods in Criminology* (Beverly Hills: Sage, 1985); Jack P. Gibbs, "The State of Criminological Theory," *Criminology* 25 (1987):821–40.
2. Thorsten Sellin, *Culture Conflict and Crime* (New York: Social Science Research Council, 1938).
3. Edwin H. Sutherland, *White Collar Crime* (New York: Dryden Press, 1949), p. 220.
4. For a discussion, see, e.g., Pat O'Malley, "Marxist Theory and Marxist Criminology," *Crime and Social Justice* 29 (1986):70–87.
5. Paul Hirst, "Marx and Engels on Law, Crime, and Morality," in Ian Taylor, Paul Walton, and Jock Young (eds.), *Critical Criminology* (London: Routledge and Kegan Paul, 1975).
6. George B. Vold and Thomas J. Bernard, *Theoretical Criminology* (3d ed.) (New York: Oxford University Press, 1986), pp. 310–11.
7. Ibid., Chapter 16.
8. This historical example is addressed in chapter 4.
9. See, e.g., Richard Quinney, *The Social Reality of Crime* (Boston: Little Brown, 1970); Jeffery Reiman, *The Rich Get Richer and the Poor Get Prison* (New York: John Wiley & Sons, 1979); Frank Pearce, *Crimes of the Powerful: Marxism, Crime, and Deviance* (London: Pluto, 1976).
10. Reiman, *The Rich Get Richer and the Poor Get Prison.*
11. George B. Vold, *Theoretical Criminology* (New York: Oxford University Press, 1958), pp. 204–07.
12. Sutherland, *White Collar Crime,* p. 220.
13. Austin Turk, *Criminality and Legal Order* (New York: Rand McNally, 1969).

14. Sutherland, *White Collar Crime,* p. 257.
15. James Bovard, *Lost Rights* (New York: St. Martin's Press, 1994), p. 67.
16. Ibid., pp. 169–70.
17. See Donald R. Cressey, "The Poverty of Theory in Corporate Crime Research," in William Laufer and Freda Adler (eds.), *Advances in Criminological Theory* (Volume 1) (New Brunswick, NJ: Transaction Press, 1989).
18. See, e.g., Elio Monachesi, "Cesare Beccaria," in Hermann Mannheim (ed.), *Pioneers in Criminology* (2d ed.) (Montclair, NJ: Patterson Smith, 1972).
19. See, e.g., Gilbert Geis, "Jeremy Bentham," in Hermann Mannheim (ed.), *Pioneers in Criminology* (2d ed.) (Montclair, NJ: Patterson Smith, 1972).
20. Gary S. Green, "Citizen Gun Ownership and Criminal Deterrence: Theory, Research, and Policy," *Criminology* 25 (1987):63–81.
21. Mary Owen Cameron, *The Booster and the Snitch* (New York: Free Press, 1964).
22. Gilbert Geis, "The Heavy Electrical Equipment Antitrust Cases of 1961," in Gilbert Geis (ed.), *White-Collar Criminal* (New York: Atherton, 1968), p. 114.
23. See, e.g., Derek Cornish and Ronald Clarke (eds.), *The Reasoning Criminal: Rational Choice Perspectives on Offending* (New York: Springer Verlag, 1986).
24. For a detailed discussion of these three groups, see Ernest van den Haag, "The Neoclassical Theory of Crime Control," in Robert F. Meier (ed.), *Theoretical Methods in Criminology* (Beverly Hills, CA: Sage, 1985); Green, "Citizen Gun Ownership and Criminal Deterrence."
25. Mark Dowie, "Pinto Madness," in Stuart L. Hills (ed.), *Corporate Violence: Injury and Death For Profit* (Totowa, NJ: Rowman and Littlefield, 1988), p. 14; Francis Cullen, William Maakestad, and Gray Cavender, *Corporate Crime under Attack* (Cincinnati, OH: Anderson, 1987), p. 162.
26. van den Haag, "The Neoclassical Theory of Crime Control."
27. See, e.g., Jack P. Gibbs, *Crime, Punishment and Deterrence* (New York: Elsevier, 1975), pp. 79–82; Johannes Andenaes, *Punishment and Deterrence* (Ann Arbor, MI: University of Michigan Press, 1974), Chapter 2.
28. Franklin Zimring and Gordon Hawkins, *Deterrence: The Legal Threat in Crime Control* (Chicago: University of Chicago Press, 1973), pp. 30–32.

29. Edwin H. Sutherland, "White-Collar Criminality," in Gilbert Geis (ed.), *White-Collar Criminal* (New York: Atherton, 1968), p. 51.
30. See, e.g., Walter Miller, "Lower-Class Culture as a Generating Milieu of Gang Delinquency," *Journal of Social Issues* 14 (1958):5–19; Marvin Wolfgang and Franco Ferracuti, *The Subculture of Violence* (London: Tavistock, 1967); Richard Cloward and Lloyd Ohlin, *Delinquency and Opportunity* (New York: Free Press).
31. Edwin H. Sutherland and Donald R. Cressey, *Criminology* (9th ed.) (Philadelphia: Lippencott, 1974), pp. 75–76.
32. Sutherland, *White Collar Crime,* p. 255–56.
33. Ibid., p. 256.
34. Ibid., p. 255.
35. Geis, "The Heavy Electrical Equipment Antitrust Cases of 1961."
36. Ibid., p. 109.
37. Ibid., p. 112.
38. Ibid., p. 108.
39. Sutherland, *White Collar Crime,* p. 221.
40. Donald Cressey, *Other People's Money* (Glencoe, IL: Free Press, 1953).
41. Marshall Clinard, "Criminological Theories of Violations of Wartime Regulations," *American Sociological Review* 11 (1946): 258–70.
42. See, e.g., Gibbs, "The Methodology of Theory Construction in Criminology"; Gibbs, "The State of Criminological Theory."
43. See, e.g., Robert L. Burgess and Ronald L. Akers, "A Differential Association-Reinforcement Theory of Criminal Behavior," *Social Problems* 14 (1968):128–47; Ronald Akers, Marvin Krohn, Lonn Lanza-Kaduce, and Marcia Radosevich, "Social Learning and Deviant Behavior: A Specific Test of a General Theory," *American Sociological Review* 44 (1979):636–55.
44. Gibbs, *Crime, Punishment and Deterrence,* pp. 79–82; Johannes Andenaes, *Punishment and Deterrence,* Chapter 2.
45. Robert K. Merton, "Social Structure and Anomie," *American Sociological Review* 3 (1938):672–82.
46. Ibid., p. 675.
47. For a general discussion, see Steven F. Messner and Richard Rosenfeld, *Crime and the American Dream* (Belmont, CA: Wadsworth, 1994).
48. Merton, "Social Structure and Anomie," p. 676.
49. Diane Vaughan, "Toward Understanding Unlawful Organizational Behavior," *Michigan Law Review* 80 (1982):1377–1402, p. 1380.
50. Ibid., p. 1381.

51. Robert Agnew, "Foundation for a General Strain Theory of Crime and Delinquency," *Criminology* 30 (1992):47–87.
52. Sutherland and Cressey, *Criminology*, p. 76.
53. Gresham Sykes and David Matza, "Techniques of Neutralization," *American Sociological Review* 22 (1957):667–70.
54. Carl Klockars, *The Professional Fence* (New York: Free Press, 1974), pp. 151–61.
55. See, e.g., James William Coleman *The Criminal Elite* (2d ed.) (New York: St. Martin's Press, 1989), pp. 211–17; Arnold Binder, Gilbert Geis, and Dickson Bruce, *Juvenile Delinquency* (New York: MacMillan, 1988), p. 168.
56. Donald M. Horning, "Blue Collar Theft: Conceptions of Property Attitudes toward Pilfering and Work Group Norms in a Modern Industrial Plant," in Erwin Smigel and H. Lawrence Ross (eds.), *Crimes against Bureaucracy* (New York: Van Nostrand Reinhold, 1970).
57. Lawrence R. Zeitlin, "A Little Larceny Can Do a Lot for Company Morale," *Psychology Today* 14 (June, 1971):22–26, 64.
58. Erwin Smigel, "Public Attitudes toward Stealing as Related to the Size of the Victim Organization," in Erwin Smigel and H. Lawrence Ross (eds.), *Crimes against Bureaucracy* (New York: Van Nostrand Reinhold, 1970).
59. Thorsten Sellin and Marvin Wolfgang, *The Measurement of Delinquency* (New York: John Wiley & Sons, 1964).
60. Marshall Clinard and Peter Yeager, *Corporate Crime* (New York: Free Press, 1980), p. 72.
61. Gilbert Geis, "Deterring Corporate Crime," in Ralph Nader and Mark J. Green (eds.), *Corporate Power in America* (New York: Grossman, 1973), p. 183; Clinard and Yeager, *Corporate Crime*, p. 72.
62. Zeitlin, "A Little Larceny Can Do a Lot for Company Morale."
63. Gerald Mars, "Dock Pilferage: A Case Study in Occupational Theft," in Paul Rock and Mary McIntosh (eds.), *Deviance and Social Control* (London: Tavistock, 1974).
64. Cressey, *Other People's Money*, pp. 102–36.
65. Ibid.
66. Michael Benson, "Denying the Guilty Mind: Accounting for Involvement in White Collar Crime," *Criminology* 23 (1985): 585–607, p. 594.
67. Clinard and Yeager, *Corporate Crime*, p. 70.
68. Benson, "Denying the Guilty Mind," p. 594.
69. Associated Press, "'Robin HUD' Says Others Took Money Too," *Albany Herald* (June 17, 1989):6a.

70. Benson, "Denying the Guilty Mind," p. 595.
71. Clinard and Yeager, *Corporate Crime,* p. 69.
72. Vold and Bernard, *Theoretical Criminology,* p. 241.
73. Sutherland and Cressey, *Criminology,* p. 75.
74. Geis, "The Heavy Electrical Equipment Antitrust Cases of 1961."
75. Cf., James William Coleman, *The Criminal Elite* (3d ed.) (St. Martin's Press, 1994), p. 204, who treats these excuses as neutralizations rather than as internalized values learned through occupational differential association.
76. The antecedent of propensity-event is Travis Hirschi's social control theory. See, Travis Hirschi, *Causes of Delinquency* (Berkeley, CA: University of California Press, 1969).
77. Michael Gottfredson and Travis Hirschi, *A General Theory of Crime* (Palo Alto, CA: Stanford University Press, 1990).
78. Travis Hirschi and Michael Gottfredson, "Causes of White-Collar Crime," *Criminology* 25 (1987):949–74, p. 949.
79. Ibid., p. 959.
80. Ibid.
81. Some scholars have misinterpreted this aspect of propensity-event theory by assuming that persons have either high or low self-control. See, e.g., Michael Benson and Elizabeth Moore, "Are White-Collar and Common Offenders the Same? An Empirical and Theoretical Critique of a Recently Proposed General Theory of Crime," *Journal of Research in Crime and Delinquency* 29 (1985): 251–72.
82. Hirschi and Gottfredson, "Causes of White Collar Crime," pp. 959–60.
83. Gottfredson and Hirschi, *A General Theory of Crime,* p. 89.
84. Ibid.
85. The phrase Gottfredson and Hirschi use is, "revenge without court delays," ibid.
86. See, e.g., David Weisburd, Stanton Wheeler, Elin Waring, and Nancy Bode, *Crimes of the Middle Classes* (New Haven, CT: Yale University Press, 1991), p. 67; Benson and Moore, "Are White-Collar and Common Criminals the Same?"
87. Robert Sampson and John Laub, *Criminology in the Making: Pathways and Turning Points through Life* (Cambridge, MA: Harvard University Press, 1993).
88. Gibbs, "The Methodology of Theory Construction in Criminology"; Gibbs, "The State of Criminological Theory."
89. See, e.g., Terrence Thornberry, "Toward an Interactional Theory of Delinquency," *Criminology* 25 (1987):863–92.

Chapter Four: Organizational Occupational Crime

1. See, e.g., Marshall Clinard and Peter Yeager, *Corporate Crime* (New York: Free Press, 1980); Ronald C. Kramer, "Corporate Criminality: The Development of an Idea," in Ellen Hochstedler (ed.), *Corporations as Criminals* (Beverly Hills, CA: Sage, 1984); John Braithwaite and Brent Fisse, "On the Plausibility of Corporate Crime Theory," in William Laufer and Freda Adler (eds.), *Advances in Criminological Theory* (Volume 2) (New Brunswick, NJ: Transaction, 1990); Michael Blankenship, "Understanding Corporate Criminality: Challenges and Issues," in Michael Blankenship (ed.), *Understanding Corporate Criminality* (New York: Garland, 1993); See also Laura Schrager and James Short, "Toward a Sociology of Organizational Crime," *Social Problems* 25 (1977):407–19.
2. See note 1.
3. Peter Blau and W. Richard Scott, *Formal Organizations* (San Francisco: Chandler, 1962), p. 1.
4. This definition is taken from the 1982 Resource Conservation and Recovery Act, Title 42 *United States Code*, Section 6928 (f) (5).
5. For a discussion of issues related to criminality and close corporations, see Kathleen F. Brickey, "Close Corporations and the Criminal Law: On 'Mom and Pop' and a Curious Rule," *Washington University Law Quarterly* 71 (1993):189–204.
6. See, e.g., Kitty Calavita and Henry Pontell, " 'Other People's Money' Revisited: Collective Embezzlement in the Savings and Loan and Insurance Industries," *Social Problems* 38 (1990):94–112. For the concept of "organization as weapon," see Stanton Wheeler and Mitchell Lewis Rothman, "The Organization as a Weapon in White-Collar Crime," *Michigan Law Review* 80 (1982):1403–26.
7. See, e.g., Nicolette Parisi, "Theories of Corporate Criminal Liability," in Ellen Hochstedler (ed.), *Corporations as Criminals* (Beverly Hills, CA: Sage, 1984); Barbara Belbot, "Corporate Criminal Liability," in Michael Blankenship (ed.), *Understanding Corporate Criminality* (New York: Garland, 1993); Brent Fisse, "The Duality of Corporate and Individual Criminal Liability," in Ellen Hochstedler (ed.), *Corporations as Criminals* (Beverly Hills, CA: Sage, 1984).
8. Donald R. Cressey, "The Poverty of Theory in Corporate Crime Research," in William Laufer and Freda Adler (eds.), *Advances in Criminological Theory* (Volume 1) (New Brunswick, NJ: Transaction, 1989).
9. Parisi, "Theories of Corporate Criminal Liability," p. 41.

10. Ibid.
11. Braithwaite and Fisse, "On the Plausibility of Corporate Crime Theory."
12. Gilbert Geis, "A Review, Rebuttal, and Reconciliation of Cressey and Braithwaite & Fisse on Criminological Theory and Corporate Crime," in Freda Adler and William Laufer (eds.), *Advances in Criminological Theory* (Volume 6) (New Brunswick, NJ: Transaction, 1995).
13. All defendants were eventually acquitted. For discussions of legal issues, see, e.g., Alana L. Helverson, "Can a Corporation Commit Murder?" *Washington University Law Quarterly* 64 (1986):967–84; Ken Polk, Fiona Haines, and Santina Perrone, "Homicide, Negligence and Work Death: The Need for Legal Change," in Michael Quinlan (ed.), *Work and Health* (Melbourne, Australia: Macmillan Education, 1993); Michael Bixby, "Was It Accident or Murder? New Thrusts in Corporate Criminal Liability for Workplace Deaths," *Labor Law Journal* (July 1990):417–23.
14. *Indiana Code,* Section 35-42-1-5.
15. Francis Cullen, William Maakestad, and Gray Cavender, *Corporate Crime under Attack* (Cincinnati: Anderson, 1987), pp. 209–12.
16. Associated Press, "Cracking Down on Express Mail" *Albany Herald* (December 13, 1993):1A+.
17. Edwin H. Sutherland, "Is 'White-Collar Crime' Crime?" *American Sociological Review* 10 (1945):132–39, pp. 135–36.
18. Ibid., p. 136.
19. This plea arose in the case of *Alford v. North Carolina,* 400 U.S. 25 (1971).
20. See, e.g., Pamela H. Bucy, *White-Collar Crime: Cases and Materials* (St. Paul, MN: West Publishing, 1992):197–98. For an excellent review of American organizational criminal liability, see William Laufer's "Corporate Bodies and Guilty Minds," *Emory Law Journal* 43 (1994):647–730 and "Culpability and the Sentencing of Corporations," *Nebraska Law Review* 71 (1992):1049–94. For a review of European corporate criminal liability, see L. H. Leigh, "The Criminal Liability of Corporations and Other Groups," *Michigan Law Review* 80 (1982):1508–28.
21. See, generally, Parisi, "Theories of Corporate Criminal Liability"; Belbot, "Corporate Criminal Liability"; Busy, *White-Collar Crime,* Chapter 6.
22. Belbot, "Corporate Criminal Liability," p. 220.
23. Ibid.
24. Ibid., p. 221.

25. American Law Institute, *Model Penal Code,* Section 2.07 (1) (c) (Philadelphia: American Law Institute, 1962).
26. Ibid.
27. See discussion in Bucy, *White-Collar Crime,* pp. 193–203.
28. Ibid., p. 201.
29. 421 U.S. 658 (1975). For discussions of legal issues associated with strict liability, see, generally, Tracey C. Spiegelhoff, "Limits on Individual Accountability for Corporate Crimes," *Marquette Law Review* 67 (1984):604–40; John C. Coffee, Jr., " 'No Soul to Damn; No Body to Kick': An Unscandalised Inquiry into the Problem of Corporate Punishment," *Michigan Law Review* 79 (1981):386–459.
30. *U.S. v. Dotterweich,* 320 U.S. 280 (1943).
31. H. L. A. Hart, "The Aims of the Criminal Law," *Law and Contemporary Problems* 23 (1968):422–25.
32. See, generally, Parisi, "Theories of Corporate Criminal Liability," pp. 50–51; Bucy, *White-Collar Crime,* pp. 203–05.
33. 821 F.2nd 844 (1st Cir., 1987).
34. Title 31 *United States Code,* Section 5313.
35. Bucy, *White-Collar Crime,* pp. 204–05.
36. The following discussion is taken from various sections of *Federal Sentencing Guidelines, Title 18 United States Code Annotated* (St. Paul, MN: West Publishing, 1995).
37. Individuals are required in all cases to pay a trivial "assessment" that ranges from fifty dollars for nonserious misdemeanors to two hundred for felonies. The U.S. Sentencing Guidelines also mandate a financial penalty for a "criminal purpose" organization equal to the amount necessary to dissolve all of its net assets (i.e., assets after creditors have been paid), up to the statutory maximum. "Criminal purpose" organizations are those that operate primarily for a criminal purpose or by criminal means, such as those that set up fronts to commit fraud or distribute drugs. See ibid., pp. 1189–90. Such offenses do not fall within our definition of occupational crime because they are not committed in the course of an occupation that is legal.
38. Edward Gross, "Organizations as Criminal Actors," in Paul Wilson and John Braithwaite (eds.), *Two Faces of Deviance* (Queensland, Australia: University of Queensland Press, 1979), p. 199.
39. Edward Gross, "Organization Structure and Organizational Crime," in Gilbert Geis and Ezra Stotland (eds.), *White-Collar Crime: Theory and Research* (Beverly Hills, CA: Sage, 1980), p. 63.
40. Charles Perrow, "The Analysis of Goals in Complex Organizations," *American Sociological Review* 26 (1961):854–65, p. 855.

41. Gross, "Organizations as Criminal Actors," p. 200.
42. Oliver Williamson, *Corporate Control of Business Behavior: An Inquiry into the Effects of Organization Form on Enterprise Behavior* (Englewood Cliffs, NJ: Prentice-Hall, 1970), p. 143.
43. Sally Simpson, "Strategy, Structure, and Corporate Crime: The Historical Context of Anticompetitive Behavior," in Freda Adler and William Laufer (eds.), *Advances in Criminological Theory* (Volume 4) (New Brunswick, NJ: Transaction, 1993), p. 84.
44. Gordon Tullock, *The Politics of Bureaucracy* (Washington, DC: Public Affairs Press, 1965).
45. Anthony Downs, *Inside Bureaucracy* (Boston: Little Brown, 1967), p. 147.
46. Some scholars control for the size of the organization (e.g., according to sales volume) in these comparisons and others do not. Works that support the idea of accounting for size of organization are Marshall Clinard and Peter Yeager, *Corporate Crime;* and Sally Simpson, Anthony Harris, and Brian Mattson, "Measuring Corporate Crime," in Michael Blankenship (ed.), *Understanding Corporate Criminality* (New York: Garland, 1993) (see the discussion on opportunity-sensitive rates in chapter 2 of the present work). Works that do not consider size include Sally Simpson, "The Decomposition of Antitrust: Testing a Multi-Level, Longitudinal Model of Profit Squeeze," *American Sociological Review* 51 (1986):859–75; and Dan Dalton and Idalene Kesner, "On the Dynamics of Corporate Size and Illegal Activity: An Empirical Assessment," *Journal of Business Ethics* 7 (1988):861–70. Dalton and Kesner argue against controlling for organizational size in indexing violations because to do so is like indexing a "person's crimes per/inch or per/pound" (p. 863). On the contrary, it seems more intuitively appealing to argue that not controlling for size is much more like comparing the criminality of ten persons to that of one person, which of course would not be sensible.
47. Peter Asch and Joseph Seneca, "Characteristics of Collusive Firms," *Journal of Industrial Economics* 23 (1975):223–47; George Hay and Daniel Kelley, "An Empirical Survey of Price-Fixing Conspiracies," *Journal of Law and Economics* 13 (1974):13–38; Simpson, "The Decomposition of Antitrust," p. 868.
48. Clinard and Yeager, *Corporate Crime,* pp. 127–32, who equalized for firm size by figuring the violation rate per $100 million in annual sales. Simpson, although not presented in "The Decomposition of Antitrust," also found relative size was not a strong predictor of violation (telephone conversation, Sally Simpson and Gary Green,

February 13, 1995). See also H. C. Finney and H. R. Lesieur, "A Contingency Theory of Organizational Crime," in S. B. Bacharach (ed.), *Research in the Sociology of Organizations* (Volume 1) (Greenwich, CT: JAI Press, 1982), p. 272: "[B]ig does not necessarily mean 'bad' when it comes to [organizational] crime." Other studies of large organizations that do not control for size have shown that size is directly related to the number of violations, which we would expect because larger organizations have greater opportunity to commit offenses (see note 46 above). See, e.g., Simpson, "The Decomposition of Antitrust"; Dalton and Kesner, "On the Dynamics of Corporate Size and Illegal Activity."

49. Robert Lane studied labor violations among smaller firms. He determined size of organization by the number of employees (from four to one hundred). See Robert Lane, "Why Businessmen Violate the Law," *Journal of Criminal Law, Criminology, and Police Science* 44 (1953):151–65.
50. Lane found, for labor violations at least, that either: (1) there is no relationship between violation rate and organizational size (leather and textile industries); or (2) as an organization becomes larger, it is *less* likely to violate regulations (metal industry). Ibid.
51. See, e.g., Gilbert Geis, "The Heavy Electrical Equipment Antitrust Cases of 1961," in Gilbert Geis (ed.), *White-Collar Criminal* (New York: Atherton, 1968); Victor Bart and John B. Cullen, "The Organizational Bases of Ethical Work Environments," *Administrative Law Quarterly* 33 (1988):101–25; Lane, "Why Businessmen Violate the Law"; Marshall Clinard, "Criminological Theories of Violations of Wartime Regulations," *American Sociological Review* 11 (1946): 258–70; Marshall Clinard, *Corporate Ethics and Crime: The Role of the Middle Manager* (Beverly Hills, CA: Sage, 1983).
52. Diane Vaughan, "Toward an Understanding of Unlawful Organizational Behavior," *Michigan Law Review* 80 (1982):1377–1402.
53. Ibid., p. 1390.
54. Ibid., p. 1391.
55. Christopher Stone, *Where the Law Ends: The Social Control of Corporate Behavior* (New York: Harper & Row, 1975), p. 236.
56. See, e.g., Barry Staw and Jerry Ross, "Behavior in Escalating Situations," *Research in Organizational Behavior* 9 (1987):39–78.
57. Diane Vaughan, *The Challenger Launch Decision: Risky Technology, Culture, and Deviance at NASA* (Chicago: University of Chicago Press, 1996).
58. Gary Rabe and M. David Ermann, "Corporate Concealment of Tobacco Hazards: Changing Motives and Historical Contexts," *De-*

viant Behavior 16 (1995):223–44; Dennis A. Gioia, "Pinto Fires and Personal Ethics: A Script Analysis of Missed Opportunities," *Journal of Business Ethics* 11 (1992):379–89.

59. S. E. Brenner and E. A. Molander, "Is the Ethics of Business Changing?" *Harvard Business Review* 55 (1977):59–70.
60. Clinard, *Corporate Ethics and Crime,* Chapter 5; Sally Simpson, "Corporate Crime and Corporate Crime Deterrence: Views from the Inside," in Kip Schlegel and David Weisburd (eds.), *White-Collar Crime Reconsidered* (Boston: Northeastern University Press, 1992).
61. Amitai Etzioni, "The U.S. Sentencing Commission on Corporate Crime: A Critique," *Annals of the American Academy of Political and Social Science* 525 (1993):147–56, p. 156.
62. Clinard, *Corporate Ethics and Crime,* p. 136.
63. See, e.g., Edwin H. Sutherland, *White Collar Crime* (New York: Dryden Press, 1949); Clinard and Yeager, *Corporate Crime;* Geis, "The Heavy Electrical Equipment Antitrust Cases of 1961,"; Harold C. Barnett, "Industry Culture and Industry Economy: Correlates of Tax Noncompliance in Sweden," *Criminology* 24 (1986):553–74.
64. Clinard and Yeager, *Corporate Crime,* p. 62; See also Geis, "The Heavy Electrical Equipment Antitrust Cases of 1961," p.109.
65. Lane, "Why Businessmen Violate the Law."
66. Victor and Cullen, "The Organizational Basis of Ethical Work Environments."
67. Sutherland, *White Collar Crime,* p. 246.
68. Barnett, "Industry Culture and Industry Economy," p. 565.
69. Sutherland, *White Collar Crime,* p. 266; Simpson, "The Decomposition of Antitrust," p. 862, and "Strategy, Structure, and Corporate Crime," p. 85, uses the same example independent of Sutherland (telephone conversation, Sally Simpson and Gary Green, February 13, 1995); See also on mimicry, Michael Hannan and John Freeman, "The Population Ecology of Organizations," *American Journal of Sociology* 82 (1977):929–64; Paul DiMaggio and Walter Powell, "Institutional Isomorphism," *American Sociological Review* 42 (1983):147–60.
70. Sutherland, *White Collar Crime,* pp. 246–47.
71. Ibid.
72. Ibid., p. 221.
73. For research indicating that females have more business ethics than males, see, e.g., Richard Beltramini, Robert Peterson, and George Kozmetsky, "Concerns of College Students Regarding Business Ethics," *Journal of Business Ethics* 3 (1984):195–200; Paul Miesing

and John Preble, "A Comparison of Five Business Philosophies," *Journal of Business Ethics* 4 (1985):465–76; Michael Betz, Lenehan O'Connell, and Jon Shepard, "Gender Differences in Proclivity for Unethical Behavior," *Journal of Business Ethics* 8 (1989):321–24; John Tsalikis and Marta Ortiz-Buonafina, "Ethical Beliefs' Differences of Males and Females," *Journal of Business Ethics* 9 (1990):509–17; Peter Arlow, "Personal Characteristics in College Students' Evaluations of Business Ethics and Corporate Social Responsibility," *Journal of Business Ethics* 10 (1991):63–69; Durwood Ruegger and Ernest King, "A Study of the Effect of Age and Gender upon Student Business Ethics," *Journal of Business Ethics* 11 (1992):179–86. For research indicating that older persons have more business ethics than younger ones, see, e.g., Arlow, "Personal Characteristics in College Students' Evaluations of Business Ethics and Corporate Social Responsibility"; Miesing and Preble, "A Comparison of Five Business Philosophies"; Ruegger and King, "A Study of the Effect of Age and Gender upon Student Business Ethics"; Justin Longnecker, Joseph McKinney, and Carlos Moore, "The Generation Gap in Business," *Business Horizons* (September/October, 1989); John Barnett and Marvin Karson, "Managers, Values, and Executive Decisions: An Exploration of the Role of Gender, Career Stage, Organizational Level, Function, and the Importance of Ethics, Relationships, and Results in Managerial Decision Making," *Journal of Business Ethics* 8 (1989):747–71; James R. Harris, "Ethical Values of Individuals at Different Levels in the Organizational Hierarchy of a Single Firm," *Journal of Business Ethics* 9 (1990): 741–50.

74. One model that considers the saliency of rational choice and moral factors in organizational crime was proposed by Raymond Paternoster and Sally Simpson, "A Rational Choice Theory of Corporate Crime," in Ronald V. Clarke and Marcus Felson (eds.), *Advances in Criminological Theory* (Volume 5) (New Brunswick, NJ: Transaction, 1995). However, apart from morality and deterrence are unintentional acts that constitute strict liability offenses, including the unavoidable accidents associated with inherently dangerous sectors such as the nuclear, petrochemical, mining, space exploration, and some manufacturing industries. See Charles Perrow, *Natural Accidents—Living with High-Risk Technologies* (New York: Basic Books, 1984). The point of Perrow's work in the present context is that no matter how much morality and rational choice organizational workers employ, they may nevertheless fall victim to the inevitable failures associated with high-risk industries. These failures should be viewed

as part of an organizational process that cannot be manipulated by changes in morality or fear of punishment.

75. For examples of these practices and an examination of attitudes behind them, see Francis Cullen, Edward Latessa, and Joseph Byrne, "Scandal and Reform in Collegiate Athletics: Implications from a National Survey of Head Football Coaches," *Journal of Higher Education* 61 (1990):50–64.
76. Associated Press, "AAA: Motorist Getting 'Pot Luck' on Octane Ratings," *Albany Herald* (April 27, 1990):10A.
77. Sutherland, *White Collar Crime,* p. 116.
78. *Federal Trade Commission v. General Motors Corporation and Libby-Owens Ford Glass,* Docket #7643, 1959; Simpson, "The Decomposition of Antitrust," p. 867.
79. *American Brands, Inc. v. R. J. Reynolds Co.,* 413 F.Supp. 1352 (S.D.N.Y. 1976), p. 1357; Shari Seidman Diamond, "Using Psychology to Control Law: From Deceptive Advertising to Criminal Sentencing," *Law and Human Behavior* 13 (1989):239–52, p. 241.
80. Ibid.; *American Home Products Corporation v. Johnson and Johnson,* 577 F.2nd 160 (2d Cir. 1978), p. 167.
81. See, e.g., Ivan Preston, *The Great American Blow-up* (Madison, WI: University of Wisconsin Press, 1975); Clinard and Yeager, *Corporate Crime,* pp. 219–20; James William Coleman, *The Criminal Elite* (3d ed.) (New York: St. Martin's Press, 1994), pp. 23–24. For a discussion of FTC crackdown on mock-up advertising, see Bruce E. Fritch, "Illusion or Deception: The Use of 'Props' and 'Mock-ups' in Television Advertising," *Yale Law Journal* 72 (1962):145–61.
82. Associated Press, "Meat Inspectors Find Wendy's Short of Beef," Albany Herald (October 28, 1994):1A+.
83. Associated Press, "Michigan, Wal-Mart Settle Dispute over Ads," *Albany Herald* (March 19, 1994):5B.
84. Associated Press, "Paper Plate Claim Questionable," *Albany Herald* (September 19, 1993):6D.
85. Associated Press, "FDA Seizes Citrus Hill OJ, Challenges 'Fresh' on Label" *Albany Herald* (April 25, 1991):2C; Associated Press, "P&G Dropping 'Fresh' Label," *Albany Herald* (April 28, 1991):2B; Associated Press, "Company Drops 'Fresh' Label, *Albany Herald* (May 4, 1991):10A; Associated Press, " 'Fresh' Idea: FDA Cracks Down on Product Label Claims, Substantial Changes Eyed in '93," *Albany Herald* (May 9, 1991):3C.
86. Ken Foskett, "Mattress Chain to Pay $60,000 to Settle False Advertising Charges," *Atlanta Constitution* (July 18, 1990):E1.

87. Kurt Eichenwald, "Prudential and Texas Set Accord," *New York Times* (January 19, 1994):C1.
88. For a general discussion of the history of the federal legislation against defrauding the government, see W. Bruce Shirk, Bennett D. Greenberg, and William S. Dawson III, "Truth or Consequences: Expanding Civil and Criminal Liability for the Defective Pricing of Government Contracts," *Catholic University Law Review* 37 (1988): 935–91.
89. Reuter News Service, "Aerospace Firm to Settle Case Initiated by Whistleblowers," *Atlanta Constitution* (May 13, 1990):H2.
90. Shirk et al., "Truth or Consequences," p. 939.
91. Associated Press, "Federal Government Suing State of Ohio," *Albany Herald* (May 26, 1990):6B. Note that governments are not organizations according to the definition set out at the beginning of this chapter (see text accompanying note 4), so one could argue that, technically, this is not an organizational occupational crime. According to the definition by Blau and Scott (see text accompanying note 3), however, governments are organizations.
92. Associated Press, "Colleges Misuse Research Funds," *Albany Herald* (May 9, 1991):3C.
93. Associated Press, "Foreign Tax-Dodgers Targeted," *Albany Herald* (July 13, 1990):10A; "IRS: Foreign Firms Dodge Taxes" *Atlanta Constitution* (July 11, 1990):A1+.
94. Associated Press, "GAO: Corporations Underreport Income," *Albany Herald* (April 17, 1991):3B.
95. Associated Press, "Georgia Pacific Guilty of Tax Evasion," *Albany Herald* (October 3, 1991):3A.
96. Associated Press, "Senior-Citizen Group Settles with IRS" *Albany Herald* (August 31, 1994):5A.
97. William Huth and Don MacDonald, "The Impact of Antitrust Litigation on Shareholder Return," *Journal of Industrial Economics* 37 (1989):411–26. The 90 percent figure is approximate, and is taken from Kathleen Maguire and Ann L. Pastore (eds.), *Sourcebook of Criminal Justice Statistics, 1994,* U.S. Department of Justice, Bureau of Justice Statistics (Washington, DC: U.S. Government Printing Office, 1995), p. 477 (Table 5.42).
98. "Natural" monopolies are excluded under Section 2 of the Sherman Act. A natural monopoly is one in a popular sense, such as owning the only theater in town, or owning a patent on a unique invention. These are not illegal because anyone is free to enter such markets.
99. Public Law 101–588, Section 4(a).

100. Edward A. Snyder, "New Insights into the Decline of Antitrust Enforcement," *Contemporary Policy Issues* 7 (1989):1–18.
101. Mark A. Cohen, "The Role of Criminal Sanctions in Antitrust Enforcement," *Contemporary Policy Issues* 7 (1989):36–46.
102. *Nash v. United States,* 229 U.S. 373 (1913).
103. U.S. Attorney General, *Report of the Attorney General's National Committee to Study Antitrust Laws* (Washington, DC: U.S. Government Printing Office, 1955), pp. 349–50.
104. David Eckert, "Sherman Act Sentencing: An Empirical Study," *Journal of Criminal Law and Criminology* 71 (1980):244–54, pp. 244–45.
105. Ibid.
106. Kathleen Maguire and Ann L. Pastore (eds), *Sourcebook of Criminal Justice Statistics, 1993,* U.S. Department of Justice, Bureau of Justice Statistics (Washington, DC: U.S. Government Printing Office, 1994), p. 494 (Table 5.22).
107. See *United States Sentencing Guidelines, Title 18, United States Code Annotated,* Section 2R1.1 (St. Paul, MN: West Publishing, 1995).
108. Maguire and Pastore, *Sourcebook of Criminal Justice Statistics, 1994,* p. 466 (Table 5.29).
109. John Braithwaite, *Corporate Crime in the Pharmaceutical Industry* (London: Routledge and Kegan Paul, 1984), p. 177.
110. Ibid., p. 187.
111. Clinard and Yeager, *Corporate Crime,* p. 140.
112. See, e.g., Sally Simpson, "The Decomposition of Antitrust"; Sally Simpson, "Cycles of Illegality: Antitrust Violations in Corporate America," *Social Forces* 65 (1987):943–63; Barry Staw and Eugene Szwajkowski, "The Scarcity-Munificence Component of Organizational Acts," *Administrative Science Quarterly* 20 (1975):345–54.
113. Simpson, "The Decomposition of Antitrust"; Simpson, "Cycles of Illegalities."
114. Associated Press, "Baby Formula Makers Probed for Price Fixing," *Albany Herald* (December 31, 1990):1A.
115. Associated Press, "Cox to Pay Settlement," *Albany Herald* (August 11, 1991):3C.
116. Associated Press, "Justice Conducting Antitrust Probe on Auto Pricing," *Albany Herald* (October 11, 1994):9A.
117. Associated Press, "Six Airlines Agree to Rules that Prevent Price-Fixing," *Albany Herald* (March 18, 1994):1A.
118. Associated Press, "Phone Company Admits Violations, Fined $10 Million," *El Paso Times* (February 16, 1991):10D.

119. Associated Press, "Nintendo Settles Price-Fix Charges," *Albany Herald* (April 10, 1991):3B.
120. Associated Press, "Borden Pleads Guilty to Price-Rigging," *Albany Herald* (September 15, 1993):2B.
121. Associated Press, "Unisys Pleads Guilty in Defense Fraud Case," *Albany Herald* (September 6, 1991):1A+.
122. Associated Press, "AIA Settles Anti-Competition Suit," *Albany Herald* (July 6, 1990):2B.
123. Associated Press, "Door Company Fined $6 Million for Price-Fixing," *Albany Herald* (June 15, 1994):5D.
124. Upton Sinclair, *The Jungle* (New York: Vanguard Press, 1906).
125. Robert B. Downs, "Afterword," in Upton Sinclair, *The Jungle* (New York: New American Library of World Literature, 1964), p. 345.
126. Ibid., 348.
127. Ibid., 349.
128. Ibid.
129. James William Coleman, *The Criminal Elite* (2d ed.) (New York: St. Martin's Press: 1989), pp. 139–40.
130. Stuart Chase and F. J. Schlink, *Your Money's Worth* (New York: Macmillan, 1927); Arthur Kallett and F. J. Schlink, *100,000 Guinea Pigs* (New York: Vanguard Press, 1933).
131. Braithwaite, *Corporate Crime in the Pharmaceutical Industry,* pp. 113–14.
132. Ralph Nader, *Unsafe at Any Speed: The Designed-in Dangers of the American Automobiles* (New York: Grossman, 1965).
133. Clinard and Yeager, *Corporate Crime,* p. 80.
134. Paul Weaver, "The Hazards of Trying to Make Consumer Products Safer," *Fortune* (July 1975):133–40.
135. U.S. Consumer Product Safety Commission, 1991 *Annual Report to Congress* (Washington, DC: U.S. Government Printing Office, 1992), pp. G6–G8.
136. Braithwaite, *Corporate Crime in the Pharmaceutical Industry,* pp. 65–75.
137. See, e.g., Morton Mintz, "At Any Cost: Corporate Greed, Women, and the Dalkon Shield," in Stuart L. Hills (ed.), *Corporate Violence: Injury and Death for Profit* (Totowa, NJ: Rowman and Littlefield, 1988).
138. Gilbert Geis, "Avocational Crime," in Daniel Glaser (ed.), *Handbook of Criminology* (Chicago: Rand McNally, 1974).
139. Braithwaite, *Corporate Crime in the Pharmaceutical Industry,* pp. 60–65.

140. Cullen et al., *Corporate Crime under Attack.*
141. Associated Press, "Airline Pleads Guilty," *Albany Herald* (March 21, 1991):4B.
142. Associated Press, "Delta Faces Possible Fines for Violations," *Albany Herald* (June 19, 1991):4B.
143. Associated Press, "Toy Distributors Sued Over Imports," *New York Times* (August 21, 1990):A12.
144. Associated Press, "Government Says Firm Sold Dangerous Rattles, Pacifiers," *Albany Herald* (August 16, 1994):4A.
145. Associated Press, "Military Contractor Must Pay $2 Million Fine," *Albany Herald* (January 9, 1993):7A.
146. Associated Press, "Four Former Executives of Drug Firm Indicted," *Albany Herald* (October 12, 1991):5A.
147. Associated Press, "FDA to Probe Whether Grocer Selling Expired Baby Formula," *Albany Herald* (February 4, 1994):5B.
148. U.S. Department of Labor, *Annual Report, Fiscal Year 1993* (Washington, DC: U.S. Government Printing Office, 1994), p. 14.
149. James Bovard, *Lost Rights* (New York: St. Martin's Press, 1994), pp. 97–98.
150. Associated Press, "Burger King Pays $500,000 to Settle Child Labor Lawsuit," *Albany Herald* (November 22, 1992):2B.
151. U.S. Department of Labor Press Releases: #93-304, "A & P to Pay $490,000 Child Labor Penalty" (July 28, 1993); #93-312, "Department of Labor and Food Lion Enter into Wage-Hour Agreement" (August 3, 1993); #93-178, "U.S. Labor Department Settles Child Labor Case with Publix Super Markets" (August 16, 1993).
152. U.S. Department of Labor Press Release, #94-230, "Labor Department Finds More Than $400,000 in Back Wages Due Southeastern Garment Workers" (December 15, 1994).
153. U.S. Department of Labor, *Annual Report,* p. 15.
154. Gray Boyden and Evan Kemp, "Flunking Testing: Is Too Much Fairness Unfair to School Kids?" *Washington Post* (September 19, 1993); Bovard, *Lost Rights,* p. 180.
155. See, e.g., Harry M. Caudill, "Manslaughter in a Coal Mine," in Stuart Hills (ed.), *Corporate Violence: Injury and Death for Profit* (Totowa, NJ: Rowman and Littlefield, 1988).
156. See, e.g., Mark J. Green, "The Corporation and the Community," in Ralph Nader and Mark J. Green (eds.), *Corporate Power in America* (New York: Grossman, 1973).
157. See, e.g., Richard Guarasci, "Death by Cotton Dust," in Stuart L. Hills (ed.), *Corporate Violence: Injury and Death for Profit* (Totowa, NJ: Rowman and Littlefield, 1988).

158. See, e.g., John Braithwaite, *To Punish or Persuade* (Albany, NY: State University of New York Press, 1985).
159. See, e.g., Nancy Frank, "Murder in the Workplace," in Stuart L. Hills (ed.), *Corporate Violence: Injury and Death for Profit* (Totowa, NJ: Rowman and Littlefield, 1988).
160. U.S. Department of Labor, *Annual Report,* p. 16.
161. Warren Farrell, *The Myth of Male Power* (New York: Simon and Schuster, 1993): pp. 106, 382.
162. U.S. Department of Labor, *Annual Report,* p. 16.
163. Ibid., p. 17.
164. Ibid.
165. Ibid., p. 18.
166. Ibid.; See also Braithwaite, *To Punish or Persuade.*
167. U.S. Department of Labor, *Annual Report,* p. 19.
168. Associated Press, "Wrecks, Homicides Top Causes of On-the-Job Deaths," *Albany Herald* (August 11, 1994):3A.
169. Ibid.
170. Ann Lebowitz, "Overview: The Health of Working Women," in Diana Chapman Walsh and Richard Egdahl (eds.), *Women, Work, and Health: Challenges to Corporate Policy* (New York: Springer-Verlag, 1980), p. 47; Jurg Gerber and Susan Weeks, "Women as Victims of Corporate Crime: A Call for Research on a Neglected Topic," *Deviant Behavior* 13 (1992):325–47, p. 335.
171. Gerber and Weeks, "Women as Victims of Corporate Crime."
172. Ibid.
173. Farrell, *The Myth of Male Power,* Chapter 4.
174. Ibid., p. 106. Farrell cites five of the most dangerous professions and their proportionate male employment: firefighting (99%); logging (98%); heavy trucking (98%); construction (98%); and coal mining (97%).
175. Associated Press, "Fatal Fire Sparks Workplace Safety Debate," *Albany Herald* (September 8, 1991):4B; Associated Press, "Imperial Foods Owner Surrenders," *Albany Herald* (March 12, 1992):2A; John P. Wright, Francis T. Cullen, and Michael Blankenship, "The Social Construction of Corporate Violence: Media Coverage of the Imperial Food Products Fire," *Crime and Delinquency* 41 (1995): 20–36.
176. Ibid.
177. Robert G. Schwartz, Jr., "Criminalizing Occupational Safety Violations: The Use of 'Knowing Endangerment' Statutes to Punish Employers Who Maintain Toxic Working Conditions," *Harvard Environmental Law Review* 14 (1990):487–509, p. 491.

178. Title 42 *United States Code,* Section 6928 (Supp. V 1987).
179. See Schwartz, "Criminalizing Occupational Safety Violations" for a detailed legal and historical discussion.
180. Ralph Nader, "Foreword," in John Esposito, *Vanishing Air* (New York: Grossman, 1970), p. viii.
181. R. Mendelsohn and G. Orcutt, "An Empirical Analysis of Air Pollution Dose Response Curves," *Journal of Environmental Economics and Management* 6 (1979):85–106; Ronald C. Kramer, "Corporate Criminality," p. 20.
182. Chapter 425, Sec. 13, 30 Stat. 1121, 1152 (1899).
183. Title 33 *United States Code,* Section 407.
184. Robert A. Milne, "The *Mens Rea* Requirement of the Federal Environmental Statutes: Strict Criminal Liability in Substance but Not Form," *Buffalo Law Review* 37 (1988/89):307–36, p. 310.
185. Ibid., pp. 310–11.
186. Chapter 758, 62 Stat. 1155.
187. Milne, "The *Mens Rea* Requirement of the Federal Environmental Statutes," p. 312.
188. Michael J. Lynch, Mahesh K. Nalla, and Keith W. Miller, "Cross-Cultural Perceptions of Deviance: The Case of Bhopal," *Journal of Research in Crime and Delinquency* 26 (1989):7–35, p. 27.
189. Milne, "The *Mens Rea* Requirement of the Federal Environmental Statutes," p. 317.
190. Ibid.
191. Environmental Protection Agency, *Summary of Enforcement Accomplishments, Fiscal Year 1987* (Washington, DC: U.S. Government Printing Office, 1988), p. 2.
192. Bovard, *Lost Rights,* p. 69.
193. Ibid., p. 72.
194. Harold C. Barnett, "Crimes against the Environment: Superfund Enforcement at Last," *Annals of the American Academy of Political and Social Science* 525 (January 1995): 119–133, p. 121.
195. Ibid., p. 133. For a discussion of Superfund, see Harold C. Barnett, *Toxic Debts and the Superfund Dilemma* (Chapel Hill, NC: University of North Carolina Press, 1994).
196. Bovard, *Lost Rights,* p. 71.
197. Ibid.
198. Ibid.
199. Ibid.
200. Ibid.
201. Ibid.
202. Ibid., p. 72.

203. Barnett, "Crimes against the Environment," pp. 131–32.
204. Ibid., p. 132.
205. Joseph F. Dimento, "Can Social Science Explain Organizational Noncompliance with Environmental Law?" *Journal of Social Issues* 45 (1989):109–32, pp. 121–22.
206. Ibid., p. 124
207. Ibid.
208. Michael Johnston, *Political Corruption and Public Policy in America* (Belmont, CA: Brooks/Cole, 1982), p. 20.
209. Clinard and Yeager, *Corporate Crime,* p. 157.
210. Sutherland, *White Collar Crime,* p. 220.
211. Clinard and Yeager, *Corporate Crime,* p.155.
212. Irwin Ross, "How Lawless Are Big Companies?" *Fortune* (December 1, 1980):55–61.
213. James William Coleman, *The Criminal Elite* (2d ed.), pp. 132–36.
214. Clinard and Yeager, *Corporate Crime,* p. 158.
215. Ross, "How Lawless Are Big Companies?" pp. 58–61.
216. Clinard and Yeager, *Corporate Crime,* chapter 7.
217. Ibid.
218. Associated Press, "Officials at Lockheed Knew of Payoffs, Newspaper Says," *Albany Herald* (December 10, 1995):1B; Associated Press, "Lockheed Pleads Guilty to Bribery Plot," *Albany Herald* (January 28, 1995):15A.

Chapter Five: State Authority Occupational Crime

1. David R. Simon and D. Stanley Eitzen, *Elite Deviance* (Boston: Allyn and Bacon, 1981), p. 197.
2. Associated Press, "Postal Workers Charged in Fraud," *Albany Herald* (April 20, 1988):1A.
3. Albert J. Reiss, Jr., "Police Brutality: Answers to Key Questions," *Society* 5 (8) (1968):10–19.
4. This example was given in David L. Carter, "Theoretical Dimensions in the Abuse of Authority by Police Officers," in Thomas Barker and David L. Carter (eds.), *Police Deviance* (2d ed.) (Cincinnati: Anderson, 1991), p. 198.
5. Reiss, "Police Brutality."
6. Associated Press, "Rodney King 'Upset' at 2½-Year Sentence," *Albany Herald* (August 5, 1993):1A.
7. Associated Press, "LA to Pay Rodney King $3.8 Million," *Albany Herald* (August 4, 1994):5A.
8. Associated Press, "Four Officers Charged in Beating," *Albany Her-*

ald (November 17, 1992):5A; "Milestones," *Time,* (October 25, 1993):25.

9. 105 S.Ct. 1694 (1985).
10. Carter, "Theoretical Dimensions in the Abuse of Authority by Police Officers"; Mark Blumburg, "Police Use of Deadly Force: Exploring Some Key Issues," in Thomas Barker and David L. Carter (eds.), *Police Deviance* (Cincinnati: Anderson, 1991). See also Victor E. Kappeler, Richard D. Sluder, and Geoffrey P. Alpert, *Forces of Deviance: Understanding the Dark Side of Policing* (Prospect Heights, IL: Waveland Press, 1994) for materials on police brutality and other police criminality.
11. Jerome Skolnick, *Justice without Trial: Law Enforcement in a Democratic Society* (New York: John Wiley & Sons, 1966).
12. Ibid.
13. Ibid.
14. Phillip Zimbardo, "Pathology of Imprisonment," Society 9 (1972): 4–8.
15. Carl Klockars, "The Dirty Harry Problem," *Annals of the American Academy of Political and Social Science* 452 (November 1980): 33–47.
16. Thomas Barker, "An Empirical Study of Police Deviance Other Than Corruption," *Journal of Police Science and Administration* 6 (1978):264–72.
17. Jaxon van Derbeken, "LAPD Finds 1st Officer Guilty in King Beating," *Los Angeles Daily News* (December 12, 1992):1–NEWS.
18. Michael Gottfredson and Travis Hirschi, *A General Theory of Crime* (Palo Alto, CA: Stanford University Press, 1990), p. 89.
19. Many local police departments require only a high school education for employment; thus, with law enforcement, one can have a "career" that is respectable and secure without having to attend college.
20. Klockars, "The Dirty Harry Problem," pp. 46–47.
21. 91 S.Ct. 1999 (1971)
22. M. David Ermann and Richard Lundman, *Corporate and Governmental Deviance* (4th ed.) (New York: Oxford University Press, 1992), pp. 12–16.
23. Associated Press, "Cops Convicted of Abusing Homeless," *Albany Herald* (December 18, 1992):15A.
24. *U.S. v. Lynch* 189 F2d 476 (1950).
25. *U.S. v. Ramsey* 336 F2d 512 (1964).
26. *Irvine v. California* 347 U.S. 128 (1954).
27. Julian Roebuck and Stanley C. Weeber, *Political Crime in the*

United States: Analyzing Crime by and against the Government (New York: Praeger, 1978), p. 111.
28. David B. Kopel and Paul H. Blackman, "The God Who Answers by Fire: The Waco Disaster and the Necessity of Criminal Justice Reform." Paper presented at the American Society of Criminology Annual Meeting, Miami, FL (November 1994); revised December 23, 1994: p. 95.
29. Ibid.
30. *U.S. v. Jackson* 235 F2d 925 (1956).
31. *Catlette v. U.S.* 132 F2d 746 (1943).
32. *U.S. v. Georvassilis* 498 F2d 883 (1974).
33. *Imbler v. Pachtman* 424 U.S. 409 (1976).
34. *U.S. v. Senak* 527 F2d 129 (1975).
35. *U.S. v. Hoffman* 498 F2d 879 (1974).
36. *Williams v. U.S.* 341 U.S. 97 (1951).
37. *U.S. v. Wiseman* 445 F2d 129 (1971).
38. Associated Press, "Judge Gets 1½ Years for Exchanging Sex for Favorable Rulings," *Albany Herald* (April 20, 1994):5A.
39. Associated Press, "Women Inmates Contend Coerced Sex with Guards," *Albany Herald* (March 11, 1992):8A; *Day 1*, American Broadcasting Company, March 14, 1995.
40. Ibid.
41. Associated Press, "Women Inmates Contend Coerced Sex with Guards."
42. Los Angeles Daily News Service, "Sex Assault Charge against L.A. Deputy," *Orlando Sentinel* (October 26, 1991):A4.
43. Allen D. Sapp, "Sexual Misconduct by Police Officers," in Thomas Barker and David L. Carter (eds.), *Police Deviance* (2d ed.) (Cincinnati: Anderson, 1991), pp. 144–47. (Reprinted by permission of Anderson Publishing; copyright 1991 by Anderson Publishing.)
44. Gottfredson and Hirschi, *A General Theory of Crime*, p. 89.
45. Associated Press, "Fire Inspector Charged in Theft from Purse," *Albany Herald* (May 4, 1991):2A.
46. Associated Press, "Ex-Deputy, Wife Await Sentencing," Albany Herald (February 25, 1991):3A.
47. Stephen Masters, "Sylvester Policeman Arrested," *Albany Herald* (December 11, 1990):3A.
48. Associated Press, "Ex-drug Agent Convicted on Drugs, Gun Charges," *Albany Herald* (July 24, 1992):3A.
49. Associated Press, "Former DEA Agent Faces Drug Sentence," *Albany Herald* (April 17, 1991):3B.

50. Whitman Knapp, *The Knapp Commission Report on Police Corruption* (New York: George Brazziler, 1973), p. 184.
51. Ibid., p. 186.
52. Ibid.
53. James Inciardi, *Criminal Justice* (2d ed.) (San Diego, CA: Harcourt, Brace, Jovanovich, 1987), pp. 273–75.
54. Knapp, *The Knapp Commission Report on Police Corruption.*
55. U.S. Attorney General, *Annual Report of the Attorney General of the United States, 1986* (Washington, DC: U.S. Government Printing Office, 1987), p. 75.
56. Ibid., pp. 74–75.
57. Gottfredson and Hirschi, *A General Theory of Crime,* p. 89.
58. John Noonan, *Bribes* (New York: Macmillan, 1984), Chapter 18.
59. Ibid.
60. See Title 18 USC Section 1346. This legislation was in direct response to the Supreme Court ruling in *McNally v. U.S.* 107 S.Ct. 2875 (1987). See, generally, Craig Bradley, "Mail Fraud after *McNally* and *Carpenter*: The Essence of Fraud," *Journal of Criminal Law and Criminology* 79 (1988):573–622. *McNally* removed prosecution for mail and wire fraud in cases of political bribes unless a tangible financial victimization was involved or potentially involved. Section 1346 restored the pre-*McNally* ability of federal prosecutors to pursue mail and wire fraud prosecution in political bribe cases. In essence, by passing Section 1346, Congress overrode the Supreme Court's decision in *McNally.*
61. See Ellen S. Podgor, "Tax Fraud-Mail Fraud: Synonymous, Cumulative or Diverse?" *Cincinnati Law Review* 57 (1989):909.
62. David M. Jones, "Organization or Individual Corruption? An Examination of Operation Greylord," *Justice Professional* 7 (1992):35–52; G. J. Bensinger, "Operation Greylord and Its Aftermath," *International Journal of Comparative and Applied Criminal Justice* 12 (1988):111–18.
63. Associated Press, "Federal Judge Sentenced," *Albany Herald* (September 6, 1991):1A+.
64. Associated Press, "From Assemblyman to Convict," *Albany Herald* (February 19, 1994):9A.
65. Associated Press, "Former Sheriff Pleads Guilty," *Albany Herald* (December 5, 1993):6B.
66. Associated Press, "Former Tift Deputy Gets 10-Year Term," *Albany Herald* (December 12, 1990):3A.
67. Associated Press, "Judge Pleads Guilty," *Albany Herald* (August 8, 1991):1A.

68. Lee May, "5 Legislators in S. Carolina Face Bribery Charges," *Los Angeles Times* (August 25, 1990):A–27; John Monk and Henry Eichel, "Federal Grand Jury Indicts 5 S. Carolina Legislators," *Los Angeles Daily News* (August 25, 1990):11; Associated Press, "Officials Accused of Selling Votes," *Albany Herald* (August 25, 1990):1A.
69. Associated Press, "U.S. Congressmen Indicted on Sex, Extortion Charges," *Albany Herald* (August 23, 1994):6A.
70. Gottfredson and Hirschi, *A General Theory of Crime*, p. 89.

Chapter Six: Professional Occupational Crime

1. *Oxford American Dictionary* (New York: Avon Books, 1980), p. 533.
2. Elliot Freidson, *The Profession of Medicine* (New York: Dodd and Mead, 1970), pp. 71–72.
3. Paul Jesilow, Henry Pontell, and Gilbert Geis, *Prescription for Profit: How Doctors Defraud Medicaid* (Berkeley, CA: University of California Press, 1993), p. 71.
4. Ibid., p. 73.
5. Paul Jesilow, Henry Pontell, and Gilbert Geis, "Medical Criminals: Physician and White-Collar Offenses," *Justice Quarterly* 2 (1985):151–65, p. 161.
6. Francis Cullen, Gregory Clark, Bruce Link, Richard Mathers, Jennifer Niedospial, and Michael Sheahan, "Dissecting White-Collar Crime: Offense Type and Punitiveness," *International Journal of Comparative and Applied Criminal Justice* 9 (1985):16–27.
7. Jesilow et al., "Medical Criminals," p. 153.
8. Henry Pontell, Paul Jesilow, Gilbert Geis, and Mary Jane O'Brien, "A Demographic Portrait of Physicians Sanctioned by the Federal Government for Fraud and Abuse against Medicare and Medicaid," *Medical Care* 23 (1985):1028–31, p. 1029.
9. John Jones, *Plain Concise Practical Remarks on the Treatment of Wounds and Fractures* (New York: John Holt, 1775). (The author is indebted to Ira Rutgow for providing references found in notes 9–12.)
10. Ibid.
11. See Ernest Amory Codman, "The Product of a Hospital," *Surgical Gynecology and Obstetrics* 18 (1914):491–97.
12. John Bowman, "Hospital Standardization," *Bulletin of the American College of Surgeons* (1920).
13. See, e.g., J. Wennberg and A. Gittelsohn, "Health Care Delivery in

Maine 1: Patterns of Use of Common Surgical Procedures," *Journal of the Maine Medical Association* 66 (1975):123–49; J. Wennberg and A. Gittelsohn, "Small Area Variations in Health Care Delivery," Science 142 (1973):1102–08; C. E. Lewis, "Variations in the Incidence of Surgery," *New England Journal of Medicine* 281 (1969): 880–84; N. Roos and L. Roos, "High and Low Surgical Rates: Risk Factors for Area Residents," *American Journal of Public Health* 71 (1981):591–600. For a review, see Lucian L. Leape, "Unnecessary Surgery," *Health Services Research* 24 (1989):351–407.

14. Wennberg and Gittelsohn, "Small Area Variations."
15. A. D. Baldwin, "Tonsillectomy and Adenoidectomy in Massachusetts," *New England Journal of Medicine* 285 (1971):1537.
16. Wennberg and Gittelsohn, "Health Care Delivery in Maine 1."
17. D. E. Detmer and T. Tyson, "Regional Differences in Surgical Care Based upon Uniform Physician and Hospital Discharge Abstract Data," *Annals of Surgery* 187 (1978):187.
18. Stuart M. Berger, *What Your Doctor Didn't Learn in Medical School* (New York: William Morrow and Company, 1988), pp. 43–45.
19. E. Vayda and Ira Rutgow, "A Decade of Surgery in Canada, England and Wales and the United States," *Archives of Surgery* 117 (1982):146.
20. See, e.g., Berger, *What Your Doctor Didn't Learn;* Lewis, "Variations in the Incidence of Surgery"; Wennberg and Gittelsohn, "Small Area Variations."
21. Leape, "Unnecessary Surgery," pp. 359–65.
22. J. Wennberg, "Dealing with Medical Practice Variations: A Proposal for Action," *Health Affairs* 3 (1984):6–31.
23. For a list of these studies, see Leape, "Unnecessary Surgery," p. 370.
24. U. S. Department of Health, Education, and Welfare, *The Federal Employees Health Benefits Program—Enrollment and Utilization of Health Services 1961–1968* (Washington, DC: U.S. Government Printing Office, 1971).
25. G. R. Perkoff, W. Ballinger et al., "Lack of Effect of an Experimental Prepaid Group Practice on Utilization of Surgical Care," *Surgery* 77 (1975):619–23. This study sample was extremely small and may not be valid.
26. J. LoGerfo, R. Efird et al., "Rates of Surgical Care in Prepaid Group Practices and the Independent Setting," *Medical Care* 17 (1979): 1–10.
27. Berger, *What Your Doctor Didn't Learn,* p. 43.
28. A. Greenspan, H. Kay et al., "Incidence of Unwarranted Implanta-

tion of Permanent Cardiac Pacemakers in a Large Medical Population," *New England Journal of Medicine* 318 (1988):158–63.

29. C. Winslow, J. Kosecoff et al., "The Appropriateness of Performing Coronary Artery Bypass Surgery," *Journal of the American Medical Association* 260 (1988):505–09.
30. N. Roos, L. Roos, and P. Henteleff, "Elective Surgical Rates—Do High Rates Mean Low Standards?" *New England Journal of Medicine* 297 (1977):360–65.
31. C. Winslow, J. Kosecoff et al., "The Appropriateness of Carotid Endarterectomy," *New England Journal of Medicine* 318 (1988): 721–77; N. Merrick, R. Brook et al., "Use of Carotid Endarterectomy in Five California Veterans Administration Medical Centers," *Journal of the American Medical Association* 256 (1986):2531–35; M. Chassin, J. Kosecoff et al., "Does Inappropriate Use Explain Geographic Variations in the Use of Health Care Services?" *Journal of the American Medical Association* 258 (1987):2533–37.
32. Pontell et al., "A Demographic Portrait," p. 1030.
33. P. Keisling, "Radical Surgery: Let's Draft the Doctors," *The Washington Monthly* 14 (1983):26–34; Jesilow et al. "Medical Criminals," pp. 159–60.
34. Henry Pontell, Paul Jesilow, and Gilbert Geis, "Practitioner Fraud and Abuse in Government Medical Benefit Programs: Government Regulation and Professional White-Collar Crime," *Law and Policy* 6 (1984):405–24, p. 411.
35. Wennberg and Gittelsohn, "Small Area Variations."
36. Elliot Freidson, *Professional Dominance* (New York: Atherton Press, 1970).
37. Pontell et al., "Practitioner Fraud and Abuse," p. 411.
38. Ibid., p. 413.
39. Michael Gottfredson and Travis Hirschi, *A General Theory of Crime* (Palo Alto, CA: Stanford University Press, 1990), p. 89.
40. S. Kardner, M. Fuller, and I. Mensh, "A Survey of Physicians' Attitudes and Practices Regarding Erotic and Nonerotic Contact with Patients," *American Journal of Psychiatry* 130 (1973):1077–81.
41. Nannette Gartrell et al., "Psychiatrist-Patient Sexual Contact: Results of a National Survey, I: Prevalence," *American Journal of Psychiatry* 143 (1986):1126–31.
42. Sidney Wolfe, Phyllis McCarthy, Alana Bame, and Durrie McKnew, *Questionable Doctors (New York State Listing)* (Washington, DC: Public Citizen's Health Research Group, 1993), p. 20.

43. Associated Press, "Therapist Arrested on Assault Charges," *Albany Herald* (November 14, 1992):A2.
44. Associated Press, "Doctor May Lose License for Misconduct," *Albany Herald* (April 25, 1991):1C.
45. Associated Press, "Optometrist Disciplined," *Albany Herald* (November 1, 1989):3B.
46. Jesilow et al., *Prescription for Profit,* p. 141.
47. Kardner et al., "A Survey of Physicians' Attitudes."
48. Gottfredson and Hirschi, *A General Theory of Crime,* p. 89.
49. Jack Olsen, *Doc: The Rape of the Town of Lovell* (New York: Atheneum, 1989).
50. Ibid., p. 433.
51. Richard Perez-Pena, "Doctor Arrested in a Second Sex Case," *New York Times* (May 6, 1993):B8.
52. Dean Poling, "Sellek Changes Plea to Guilty," *Valdosta Daily Times* (January 30, 1992):1A.
53. Ann Burgess, "Physician Sexual Misconduct and Patients' Responses," *American Journal of Psychiatry* 13:1335–42.
54. Cesare Lombroso, *Crime: Its Causes and Remedies* (Boston: Little Brown, 1911); Jesilow et al., "Medical Criminals," p. 155.
55. 410 U.S. 113, 1973.
56. See, e.g., Herbert Packer and Ralph Gampell, "Therapeutic Abortion: A Problem in Law and Medicine," *Stanford Law Review* 11 (1959):417–37.
57. L. Lader, "The Scandal of Abortion Laws," *New York Times Magazine* (April 25, 1965):30–35.
58. Jesilow et al., "Medical Criminals," p. 157.
59. Joseph Sanders, "Euthanasia: None Dare Call It Murder," *Journal of Criminal Law, Criminology, and Police Science* 60 (1969): 351–59.
60. Associated Press, "Kevorkian Charged Again," *Albany Herald* (January 5, 1994):7A; Associated Press, "Murder Charges Against Kevorkian Dropped, Assisted Suicide Added," *Minot Daily News* (August 31, 1995):A2.
61. Diana Crane, *The Sanctity of Social Life: Physicians' Treatment of Critically Ill Patients* (New York: Russel Sage Foundation, 1975).
62. Ibid., p. 2.
63. R. Morrison, "Death: Process or Event?" *Science* 173 (August 20, 1971):694–98, p. 696.
64. D. A. Karnofsky, "Why Prolong the Life of a Patient with Advanced Cancer?" *California Bulletin of Cancer Progress* 10 (1960):9–11, p. 9.
65. Crane, *The Sanctity of Social Life,* p. 204.

66. Henry Pontell, *A Capacity to Punish* (Bloomington, IN: Indiana University Press, 1984).
67. Edwin H. Sutherland, *White Collar Crime* (New York: Dryden Press, 1949), p. 12.
68. *United States Sentencing Guidelines, Title 18 United States Code* (St. Paul, MN: West Publishing, 1995), pp. 225, 1234.
69. Title 42 *United States Code,* Sections 1320a–7a(b).
70. *United States Sentencing Guidelines,* pp. 225, 1234.
71. American Medical Association Council on Ethical and Judicial Affairs, "Conflicts of Interest: Physician Ownership of Medical Facilities," *Journal of the American Medical Association* 267 (May 6, 1992):2366–69, p. 2367.
72. State of Florida Health Care Cost Containment Board, *Joint Ventures among Health Care Providers in Florida* (Draft report) (Tallahassee, FL: State of Florida, 1991); see also Jack Anderson, "Physicians' Kickbacks Insult," *Albany Sunday Herald* (June 9, 1991):4A.
73. Office of Inspector General, *Financial Arrangements between Physicians and Health Care Businesses* (Department of Health and Human Services (Washington, DC: U.S. Government Printing Office, 1989).
74. B. J. Hillman, C. A. Joseph, M. R. Mabry, J. H. Sunshine, S. D. Kennedy, and M. Noether, "Frequency and Costs of Diagnostic Imaging in Office Practice: A Comparison of Self- Referring and Radiologist-Referring Physicians," *New England Journal of Medicine* 323 (1990):1604–08.
75. American Medical Association, *Current Opinions of the Judicial Council* (Section 4.04, 1984).
76. American Medical Association Council on Ethical and Judicial Affairs, "Conflicts of Interest: Physician Ownership of Medical Facilities," p. 2368.
77. Ibid., pp. 2368–69.
78. Ibid., p. 2369.
79. Joe Graedon and Teresa Graedon, "Are Drug Makers 'Bribing' Doctors?" *Albany Herald* (January 14, 1990):5B.
80. Ibid.
81. Ibid.
82. Ibid.
83. Pontell et al. "Practitioner Fraud and Abuse," p. 406.
84. Albert B. Crenshaw, "Health Care Fraud Costs $70 Billion," *Washington Post* (May 12, 1992):7.
85. L. J. Davis, "Medscam," in Lawrence M. Salinger (ed.), *Deviant Behavior* (Guilford, CT: Dushkin Publishing Group, 1996), pp. 93–97.

86. Jesilow et al., *Prescription for Profit.*
87. Ibid., pp. 103–05.
88. Ibid., p. 135.
89. Ibid., p. 136.
90. Associated Press, "Congressional Report: Medicare Examiners Inexperienced, Rushed," *Albany Herald* (August 19, 1993):5A.
91. Jesilow et al., *Prescription for Profit,* Chapter 4.
92. Abraham S. Blumberg, "The Practice of Law as a Confidence Game: Organizational Cooptation of a Profession," in George Cole (ed.), *Criminal Justice: Law and Politics* (4th ed.) (Monterey, CA: Brooks/Cole, 1984), p. 196.
93. Lisa G. Lerman, "Lying to Clients," *University of Pennsylvania Law Review* 138 (1990):659–760.
94. Ibid., pp. 706–09.
95. Ibid., p. 709.
96. Ibid., p. 712.
97. Ibid., p. 709
98. Ibid., pp. 709, 712.
99. Ibid., p. 712.
100. Ibid., pp. 709–10.
101. Ibid., p. 710.
102. Ibid.
103. Ibid., p. 711.
104. Ibid., pp. 710–11.
105. Ibid., p. 712.
106. Ibid., p. 717.
107. Ibid.
108. Ibid.
109. Ibid., pp. 715–16.
110. Ibid., p. 712.
111. Ibid., p. 717.
112. Ibid., p. 716.
113. Ibid., p. 758.
114. Sol M. Linowitz and Martin Mayer, *The Betrayed Profession: Lawyering at the End of the Twentieth Century* (New York: Charles Scribner's Sons, 1994), p. 144.
115. Lerner, "Lying to Clients," p. 721.
116. Ibid.
117. Jerome Carlin, *Lawyers' Ethics: A Survey of the New York City Bar* (New York: Russell Sage Foundation, 1966).
118. *People v. Buster* 77 Ill. App. 2d 224, 222 N.E. 2d 31 (1966). For a general discussion of ethical violations in the legal profession as oc-

cupational crime, see Ellen S. Podgor, "Criminal Misconduct: Ethical Rule Usage Leads to Regulation of the Legal Profession," *Temple Law Review* 61 (1988):1323–50.

119. Richard A. Abel, *American Lawyers* (New York: Oxford University Press, 1989), p. 143.
120. Linowitz and Mayer, *Betrayed Profession,* pp. 141–42.
121. Lerner, "Lying to Clients," p. 757.
122. Linowitz and Mayer, *Betrayed Profession,* p. 142.
123. Lerner, "Lying to Clients," p. 714.
124. Ibid., p. 760. These forty thousand who quit the profession are replaced by an approximately equal number of new lawyers.
125. Ibid., p. 747.
126. Ibid.
127. Ibid., p. 748.
128. See, e.g., Anthony Kronman, *The Lost Lawyer: Failing Ideals of the Legal Profession* (Cambridge, MA: Belknap/Harvard University Press, 1993), Chapter 1.
129. See, e.g., Elliot Freidson, *Professional Dominance.*
130. Richard Quinney, "Occupational Structure and Criminal Behavior: Prescription Violations by Retail Pharmacists," *Social Problems* 11 (1963):179–85.

Chapter Seven: Individual Occupational Crime

1. Jane Applegate, "Employee Theft Saps Many Firms," *Los Angeles Times* (September 9, 1990):D3.
2. Ibid.
3. Gerald Robin, "Employees as Offenders," *Journal of Research in Crime and Delinquency* 6 (1969):17–33.
4. Alice P. Franklin, *Internal Theft in a Retail Organization* (Unpublished Ph.D. dissertation. Columbus, OH: The Ohio State University, 1976).
5. Richard Hollinger and John Clark, *Theft by Employees* (Lexington, MA: Lexington Books, 1983).
6. Luthene Bush, "Former Tara Clerk Sentenced to Prison," *Albany Herald* (December 21, 1990):5A.
7. Associated Press, "Housing Director Pleads Guilty," *Albany Herald* (October 4, 1994):12A.
8. Associated Press, "Man Accused of Embezzling Pension Funds," *Albany Herald* (December 10, 1994):1B+.
9. Associated Press, "Bank Employee Pleads Guilty," *Albany Herald* (October 26, 1993):5B.

10. Associated Press, "Former United Way Leader Convicted of Fraud," *Albany Herald* (April 4, 1995):5A.
11. Los Angeles Times News Service, "Former Bank Worker Charged with Embezzling $600,000," *Los Angeles Times* (August 8, 1990):B5.
12. Associated Press, "Prosecutor: Rostenkowski Seeks 'License to Steal,'" *Albany Herald* (September 4, 1994):14A.
13. Associated Press, "FBI Captures Former College President," *Albany Herald* (January 28, 1995):11A.
14. Associated Press, "They Buy the American Dream," *Albany Herald* (October 13, 1990):1A+.
15. Fred Bleakley, "Suspicions by Rivals Open up a Scandal at Armored-Car Firm," *New York Times* (February 17, 1993):A1.
16. Robert Merton, *The Sociology of Science* (Chicago: University of Chicago Press, 1973), p. 310.
17. David O. Friedrichs, *Trusted Criminals* (Belmont, CA: Wadsworth, 1996), pp. 110–11.
18. Marcel LaFollette, "Reseach Misconduct," in Lawrence M. Salinger (ed.), *Deviant Behavior* (Guilford, CT: Dushkin Publishing Group, 1996).
19. Jack Anderson, "Con Artists Wear Lab Coats," *Albany Herald* (September 8, 1990):4a.
20. Associated Press, "Investigation Reveals Falsified Cancer Research Data," *Albany Herald* (June 16, 1994):8A.
21. Associated Press, "Doctor Changed Data to Help Patients," *Albany Herald* (May 19, 1994):2a.
22. Donald Cressey, *Other People's Money: A Study in the Social Psychology of Embezzlement* (Glencoe, IL: Free Press, 1953).
23. Franklin, *Internal Theft in a Retail Organization,* p. 113.
24. Don Gibbons, *Society, Crime, and Criminal Careers* (Englewood Cliffs, NJ: Prentice Hall, 1973).
25. Gwynn Nettler, "Embezzlement without Problems," *British Journal of Criminology* 14 (1974):70–77, p.74.
26. Dorothy Zeitz, *Women Who Embezzle or Defraud: A Study of Convicted Felons* (New York: Praeger, 1981).
27. Kathleen Daly, "Gender and Varieties of White-Collar Crime," Criminology 27 (1989):769–93.
28. John Laub, "Interview with Donald Cressey," in John Laub (ed.), *Criminology in the Making* (Boston: Northeastern University Press, 1983), p. 138.
29. Gerald Mars, "Dock Pilferage: A Case Study in Occupational Theft," in Paul Rock and Mary McIntosh (eds.), *Deviance and Social Control* (London: Tavistock, 1974). See also Edward Sieh,

"Employee Theft: An Examination of Gerald Mars and an Explanation Based on Equity Theory," in Freda Adler and William Laufer (eds.), *Advances in Criminological Theory,* Volume 4 (New Brunswick, NJ: Transaction, 1993). Hollinger and Clark, in *Theft by Employees,* also employ equity theory as an explanation for employee theft.

30. See, e.g., Cressey, *Other People's Money.*
31. Carl Klockars, *The Professional Fence* (New York: Free Press, 1974), p. 125.
32. Cressey used this term in *Other People's Money,* p. 154. James William Coleman describes it as "slow horses and fast women" in *The Criminal Elite* (New York: St. Martin's Press, 1985), p. 81. See also "bookies, babes, and booze," in Herbert Bloch and Gilbert Geis, *Man, Crime, and Society* (New York: Random House, 1962), p. 336. In today's world, one would hope that these authors would be aware that these are sexist comments. Of course it is not the women who are responsible for the employee theft; it is the men who chase them.
33. Hollinger and Clark, *Theft by Employees,* p. 46.
34. William Terris, "Attitudinal Correlates of Employee Integrity: Theft-Related Admissions Made in Pre-employment Polygraph Examinations," *Journal of Security Administration* 1 & 2 (1979): 30–39.
35. William Terris, "Attitudinal Correlates of Employee Integrity," *Journal of Police and Criminal Psychology* 1 (1985): 60–68.
36. Food Marketing Institute, "Picking out the Bad Tomatoes: The Second Annual Report on Employee Theft in the Supermarket Industry," *Security Management* 36 (1992): 6–7.
37. T. Swann Harding, *The Popular Practice of Fraud* (New York: Longmans, Green, and Co., 1935), p. 25.
38. Frank Hagan, *Introduction to Criminology* (Chicago: Nelson-Hall, 1986), p. 16.
39. Lindsey Stellwagen, *Consumer Fraud* (Washington, DC: U.S. Government Printing Office, 1982).
40. Information for this summary of the history of *caveat emptor* is taken from Jonathan Sheldon and George Zweibel, "Historical Development of Consumer Law," in Egon Bittner and Sheldon Messinger (eds.), *Criminology Review Yearbook (Volume 2)* (Beverly Hills, CA: Sage Publications, 1980).
41. Gilbert Geis, "From Deuteronomy to Deniability: A Historical Perlustration on White-Collar Crime," *Justice Quarterly* 5 (1988): 7–32, p. 14.

42. See, e.g., Andrew Hopkins, "Controlling Corporate Deviance," *Criminology* 18 (1980):198–214.
43. Robert Flaherty and Tedd Cohen, "Rascality Springs Eternal," *Forbes* (April 20, 1979):87–88.
44. Associated Press, "Funeral Director Charged," *Albany Herald* (October 15, 1988):1A+.
45. Associated Press, "Bakker Sentence Reduced," *Albany Herald* (August 23, 1991):1A+; Associated Press, "Bakker Moved to Georgia Camp," *Albany Herald* (July 17, 1993):2B; Associated Press, "Jim Bakker is Free after Five Years," *Albany Herald* (December 1, 1994):8A.
46. Ralph Blumenthal, "Automobile Repair is Due for a Major Overhaul Soon," *New York Times* (June 4, 1979):E4.
47. Lee Seidler, Frederick Andrews, and Marc Epstein, *The Equity Funding Papers* (New York: John Wiley and Sons, 1977).
48. Paul Jesilow, *Deterring Automobile Repair Fraud: A Field Experiment* (Unpublished Ph.D. dissertation. Irvine, CA: University of California, 1982).
49. Paul E. Tracy and James Alan Fox, "A Field Experiment on Insurance Fraud in Auto Body Repair," *Criminology* 27 (1989):589–603.
50. John Braithwaite, "An Exploratory Study of Used Car Fraud," in Paul R. Wilson and John Braithwaite (eds.), *Two Faces of Deviance* (Queensland, Australia: University of Queensland Press, 1979).
51. Danny Carter, "Warning: Odometer Tampering Said 'Cottage Industry' in Georgia," *Albany Herald* (May 25, 1988):3A.
52. Braithwaite, "An Exploratory Study of Used Car Fraud." This perception has also been reported in William Leonard and Marvin Weber, "Automakers and Dealers: A Study of Criminogenic Market Forces," *Law and Society Review* 4 (1970):407–24.
53. Braithwaite, "An Exploratory Study of Used Car Fraud," p. 119.
54. Ibid.
55. Associated Press, "Victims of Keating Say Sentence Too Lenient," *Albany Herald* (July 10, 1993):5B.
56. Kitty Calavita and Henry Pontell, "Savings and Loan Fraud as Organized Crime: Toward a Conceptual Typology of Corporate Illegality," *Criminology* 31 (1993):519–48, p. 529.
57. Henry Pontell and Kitty Calavita, "Bilking Bankers and Bad Debts: White-Collar Crime and the Savings and Loan Crisis," in Kip Schlegel and David Weisburd (eds.), *White-Collar Crime Reconsidered* (Boston: Northeastern University Press, 1992), p. 196.
58. Alan Farnham, "The S&L Felons," *Fortune* (November 5, 1990): 90–108.

59. Ibid., p. 90.
60. Karen Nikos, "Keating Says He Spent Millions of Firm's Cash," *Los Angeles Daily News* (December 10, 1992):8–NEWS; Associated Press, "Keating Taken to Prison," *Albany Herald* (April 11, 1992):1A+; Associated Press, "Former Savings Boss Sentenced," *Albany Herald* (July 9, 1993):5A; Associated Press, "Victims of Keating Say Sentence Too Lenient."
61. Joe Strauss, "A Contrite Pete Rose Sentenced to 5 Months," *Atlanta Journal and Constitution* (July 20, 1990):A1.
62. Associated Press, "Helmsley to Get Early Release," *Albany Herald* (June 11, 1993):7A.
63. Associated Press, "Former U.S. Treasurer Gets 4 Months in Prison," *Albany Herald* (September 14, 1994):7A.
64. Associated Press, "Drug Dealer among Top Tax Scofflaws," *Albany Herald* (August 2, 1990):11A.
65. Ibid.
66. Associated Press, "IRS Audit 'Enforcement' Decreases, Losing $127 Billion in Tax Collections," *Albany Herald* (May 19, 1994):11A.
67. Cable News Network, July 19, 1993.
68. Marguerite Smith, "Who Cheats on Their Income Taxes," *Money* (April 1991):100–08, p.102.
69. This figure is from two independently derived estimates. See Smith, "Who Cheats on their Income Taxes," p. 107 (based on 1990) and Gary S. Green, *Occupational Crime* (Chicago: Nelson Hall, 1990), p. 217 (based on 1986).
70. Robert Mason and Lyle Calvin, "A Study of Admitted Tax Evasion," *Law and Society Review* 12 (1978):73–89.
71. Charles Tittle, *Sanctions and Social Deviance: The Question of Deterrence* (New York: Praeger, 1980).
72. Joachim Vogel, "Taxation and Public Opinion in Sweden: An Interpretation of Recent Survey Data," *National Tax Journal* 27 (1974):499–510.
73. Smith, "Who Cheats on Their Income Taxes," p. 102.
74. Associated Press, "IRS Plans Detailed Investigations," *Albany Herald* (March 18, 1995):5A.
75. Smith, "Who Cheats on Their Income Taxes," p. 104.
76. Charles Tittle, *Sanctions and Social Deviance;* Mason and Calvin, "A Study of Admitted Tax Evasion."
77. Smith, "Who Cheats on their Taxes."
78. Ibid., pp. 103–04.
79. Steven Klepper and Daniel Nagin, "The Role of Tax Preparers in Tax Noncompliance," *Policy Sciences* 22 (1989):167–94.

80. Bill Montague, "Uncovering Tax Cheats," *USA Today* (November 7, 1990):1B+, p. 2B.
81. Associated Press, "IRS Plans Detailed Investigations."
82. See, e.g., Mason and Calvin, "A Study of Admitted Tax Evasion"; Charles Clotfelter, "Tax Evasion and Tax Rates: An Analysis of Individual Returns," *Review of Economics and Statistics* 65 (1983):363–73; Joel Slemrod, "An Empirical Test for Tax Evasion," *Review of Economics and Statistics* 67 (1985):232–38; Robert Kagan, "On the Visibility of Income Tax Violations," in J. Scholz, J. Roth, and A. Witte (eds.), *Paying Taxes: An Agenda for Compliance Research* (Philadelphia: University of Pennsylvania Press, 1989); Steven Klepper and Daniel Nagin, "The Anatomy of Tax Evasion," *Journal of Law, Economics, and Organization* 5 (1989):1–24.
83. Klepper and Nagin, "The Anatomy of Tax Evasion."
84. Susan Shapiro, *Wayward Capitalists* (New Haven, CT: Yale University Press, 1984).
85. Elizabeth Szockyj, "Insider Trading: The SEC Meets Carl Karcher," *Annals of the American Academy of Political and Social Science* 525 (1993):46–58.
86. Title 15 *United States Code,* Section 78(j) (1982).
87. However, see Section 16 of the act.
88. For an excellent discussion of insider trading, see, e.g., David A. Wilson, "Outsider Trading: Morality and the Law of Securities Fraud," *The Georgetown Law Journal* 77 (1988):181–216.
89. Szockyj, "Insider Trading: The SEC Meets Carl Karcher," p. 47.
90. Others have called it "outsider-insider trading." See Kimberly Kempf, Nasser Arshadi, and Thomas Eyssell, "It is Insider Trading, but the Offenders Are Really Outsiders," *Journal of Crime and Justice* 15 (1992):111–37.
91. *In re Cady Roberts Co.,* 40 SEC 907 (1961).
92. Wilson, "Outsider Trading," p. 186.
93. Ibid.; *Cady Roberts,* p. 912.
94. *SEC v. Texas Gulf Sulphur,* 401 F. 2nd 833 (2nd Circuit, 1968).
95. Ibid., p. 848.
96. *Chiarella v. United States,* 445 U.S. 222 (1980).
97. *Dirks v. SEC,* 463 U.S. 646 (1983).
98. Wilson, "Outsider Trading," pp. 188–93.
99. See, e.g., Associated Press, "AIDS-Infected Baby Sitter Sentenced [After Assaulting Child]," *Albany Herald* (April 16, 1993):6B; Associated Press, "Engineer Pleads Guilty to Manslaughter in Accident [Because of Intoxication]," *Albany Herald* (February 16,

1988):1A+; Associated Press, "Judge: Pilots Showed Impaired Judgement (sic) [Because of Intoxication]," *Albany Herald* (August 21, 1990); Associated Press, "Priest Sentenced [For Molestation]," *Albany Herald* (May 25, 1990):5A; Associated Press, "Nursing Home Aide Gets Life [For 5 Homicides]," *Albany Herald* (November 2, 1989):6A; Associated Press, "Male Nurse Pleads Guilty to Raping 7 in Recovery," *Albany Herald* (February 4,1995):3A.

100. Associated Press, "Harding Pleads Guilty to Hindering Prosecution," *Albany Herald* (March 17, 1994):1A.

Chapter Eight: Sanctioning, Social Control, and Occupational Crime

1. *Federal Sentencing Guidelines, Title 18 United States Code Annotated,* (St Paul: West Publishing, 1995) (hereinafter, *Guidelines*).
2. See, e.g., John Braithwaite and Gilbert Geis, "On Theory and Action for Corporate Crime Control," *Crime and Delinquency* 28 (1982):292–314.
3. For an excellent discussion of the role of the defense attorney in convincing the government to reduce charges against occupational criminals, see Kenneth Mann, *Defending White-Collar Crime* (New Haven, CT: Yale University Press, 1985).
4. *Guidelines,* Sections 5E, 8B, 8C. There are also special assessments for individuals ranging from $50 to $200; the court has no discretion in these assessments (see *Guidelines,* Sections 5E1.3). The court must also impose any assessments on organizations that are defined by statute (*Guidelines,* Section 8E1.1).
5. For a general discussion of this point, see Amitai Etzioni, "The U.S. Sentencing Commission on Corporate Crime: A Critique," *Annals of the American Academy of Political and Social Science* 525 (1993):147–156.
6. *Guidelines,* Sections 5E1.2(a), 8C3.3.
7. John Coffee, Jr., " 'No Soul to Damn; No Body to Kick': An Unscandalised Inquiry into the Problem of Corporate Punishment," *Michigan Law Review* 79 (1981):386–459, p. 390.
8. *Guidelines,* Sections 5E1.2(g), 8C3.2 Application Note 1.
9. See Brent Fisse, "Sanctions against Corporations: Economic Efficiency or Legal Efficacy?" in W. Byron Groves and Graeme Newman (eds.), *Punishment and Privilege* (Albany, NY: Harrow and Heston, 1986).
10. *Guidelines,* Sections 8C3.3(b), 5E1.2(f).
11. This calculation is based on a reduction in the organizational culpa-

bility score from five (starting point) to zero (deducting five points for bringing the violation to the attention of the government—Sections 8C2.5(a), 8C2.5(g)(1)). According to Section 8C2.6, an organization with a culpability score of zero or less pays between .05 (one twentieth) and .2 of the base fine.

12. *Guidelines,* Section 8C2.5(f).
13. *Guidelines,* Section 8C4.1(a).
14. For an analysis of pre- and post-conviction considerations in punishing organizations and their employees, see William Laufer, "Culpability and Sentencing of Corporations," *Nebraska Law Review* 71 (1992):1049–94.
15. See, e.g., Kathleen Maguire and Ann L. Pastore (eds.), *Sourcebook of Criminal Justice Statistics, 1994,* U.S. Department of Justice, Bureau of Justice Statistics (Washington, DC: U.S. Government Printing Office, 1995), "Table 5.34: Fines and Restitution Ordered in U.S. Sentencing Guideline Cases, 1994."
16. Ibid. Because of missing cases, these figures may not be exact.
17. Saul M. Pilchen, "When Corporations Commit Crimes: Sentencing under the Federal 'Organizational Guidelines,'" *Judicature* 78 (1995):202–06, p. 206; U.S. Sentencing Commission, *1993 Annual Report* (Washington, DC: U.S. Government Printing Office, 1994), p. 169.
18. For a general discussion of punitive damages, see Kenneth Mann, "Punitive Civil Sanctions: The Middle Ground between Criminal and Civil Law," *Yale Law Review* 101 (1992):1795–1874.
19. See Justice O'Connor's dissent in *Browning Ferris v. Kelco Disposal* 492 U.S. 257 (1989).
20. *TXO Production Corporation v. Alliance Resources* 113 S.Ct. 2711 (1993); see also *BMW of North America, Inc. v. Gore* (U.S. Supreme Court #94-896), Decided May 20, 1996.
21. Bureau of Justice Statistics, *Civil Jury Cases and Verdicts in Large Counties* (NCJ-154246) (Washington, DC: U.S. Government Printing Office, 1995), p. 14.
22. Ibid., p. 7.
23. Ibid.
24. Ibid., p. 9.
25. Ibid., p. 8.
26. Peter French, "Publicity and the Control of Corporate Conduct," in Brent Fisse and Peter French (eds.), *Corrigible Corporations and Unruly Law* (San Antonio, TX: Trinity University Press, 1985).
27. Brent Fisse and John Braithwaite, *The Impact of Publicity on Corpo-*

rate Offenders (Albany, NY: State University of New York Press, 1985).

28. John Braithwaite, *Crime, Shame, and Reintegration* (New York: Cambridge University Press, 1989).
29. Gresham Sykes, *The Society of Captives* (Princeton, NJ: Princeton University Press, 1958), Chapter 4.
30. David Weisburd, Elin Waring, and Ellen Chayet, "Specific Deterrence in a Sample of Offenders Convicted of White-Collar Crimes," *Criminology* 33 (1995):587–607.
31. Fisse, "Sanctions against Corporations."
32. Gilbert Geis, "Corporate Penalties for Corporate Criminals," *Criminal Law Bulletin* 8 (1972):377–92, p. 377.
33. Fisse, "Sanctions against Corporations," p. 29.
34. Gilbert Geis, "The Heavy Electrical Equipment Antitrust Cases of 1961," in Gilbert Geis (ed.), *White-Collar Criminal* (New York: Atherton Press, 1968), p. 114.
35. See, e.g., Maguire and Pastore, *Sourcebook of Criminal Justice Statistics, 1994,* "Table 5.23: Offenders Sentenced to Prison, U.S. District Courts, 1982, 1986–92," "Table 5.32: Sentences Imposed under the U.S. Sentencing Commission Guidelines, 1994."
36. For a review of occupational disqualification in law, see Martin McDermott, "Occupational Disqualification of Corporate Executives: An Innovative Condition of Probation," *Journal of Criminal Law and Criminology* 73 (1982):604–41.
37. See Title 12 *United States Code,* Section 1829 and Title 15 *United States Code,* Section 780 (b)(4)(B).
38. *United States v. Mills* 51 CrL 1146 ([5th Cir.], 1992); Dean J. Champion, *Probation, Parole, and Community Corrections* (Upper Saddle River, NJ: Prentice-Hall, 1996), p. 40.
39. Braithwaite and Geis, "On Theory and Action for Corporate Crime Control," p. 197.
40. See, e.g., Robert Martinson, "What Works—Questions and Answers about Penal Reform," *Public Interest* 35 (1974):22–54.
41. See Braithwaite and Geis, "On Theory and Action for Corporate Crime Control"; Andrew Hopkins, "Controlling Corporate Deviance," *Criminology* 18 (1980):198–214.
42. *Guidelines,* Section 8D1.2; For a general discussion of federal organizational probation under the *Guidelines,* see William Lofquist, "Organizational Probation and the U.S. Sentencing Commission," *Annals of the American Academy of Political and Social Science* 525 (1993):157–69.
43. *Guidelines,* Section 8D1.1.

44. *Guidelines,* Section 8D1.4.
45. Michael Benson, Frances Cullen, and William Maakestad, "Community Context and the Prosecution of Corporate Crime," in Kip Schlegel and David Weisburd (eds.), *White-Collar Crime Reconsidered* (Boston: Northeastern University Press, 1992); "Local Prosecutors and Corporate Crime," *Crime and Delinquency* 36 (1990): 356–72.
46. Diane Vaughan, *Controlling Unlawful Organizational Behavior: Social Structure and Corporate Misconduct* (Chicago: University of Chicago Press, 1983).
47. Stanton Wheeler, Kenneth Mann, and Austin Sarat, *Sitting in Judgment: The Sentencing of White-Collar Criminals* (New Haven, CT: Yale University Press, 1988).
48. Laureen Snider, "Cooperative Models and Corporate Crime: Panacea or Cop-Out?" *Crime and Delinquency* 36 (1990):373–90.
49. John Braithwaite, "Enforced Self-Regulation: A New Strategy for Corporate Crime Control," *Michigan Law Review* 80 (1982): 1466–1507, pp. 1470–71.
50. Ibid., 1482.
51. John Braithwaite, *To Punish or Persuade* (Albany, NY: State University of New York Press, 1985).
52. Snider, "Cooperative Models and Corporate Crime."
53. See, e.g., Andrew von Hirsch, *Doing Justice* (New York: Hill and Wang, 1976).
54. See, e.g., Andrew von Hirsch, "Giving Criminals Their Just Deserts," *Civil Liberties Review* 3 (1976): 23–35.
55. See, e.g., John Braithwaite, "Challenging Just Deserts: Punishing White-Collar Criminals," *Journal of Criminal Law and Criminology* 73 (1982):723–64.

Index

Photo Credits

p. 2: AP/Wide World Photos
p. 28: AP/Wide World Photos
p. 56: The Bettmann Archive
p. 92: The Bettmann Archive
p. 115: UPI/Bettmann Newsphotos
p. 124: UPI/Corbis-Bettmann
p. 128: UPI/Bettmann
p. 137: Reuters/Bettmann
p. 150: *clockwise*: Reuters/Corbis-Bettmann, AP/Wide World Photos, AP/Wide World Photos, Reuters/Bettmann
p. 154: UPI/Bettmann Newsphotos
p. 173: AP/Wide World Photos, AP/Wide World Photos
p. 182: AP/Wide World Photos
p. 216: Wide World Photos, Inc.
p. 235: Reuters/Bettmann
p. 246: AP/Wide World Photos